LET'S
TALK!

PETER DOSECK

ISBN:0-9793192-6-9
978-0-9793192-6-6

Published by

LIFEBRIDGE
BOOKS
P.O. BOX 49428
CHARLOTTE, NC 28277

Printed in the United States of America.

DEDICATION

I dedicate this book to my faithful and loving family.
You have believed in me, stood with me and supported me.
A simple "Thank you" will never be enough for the confidence
and love you have given me. To my wife Phyllis with all my love.
To my daughter Nicole with great pride. To Randy my son-in-law
with many thanks. And to my three cherished grandchildren,
Alexis, Lincoln and Quinten with anticipation of all you
will become in Jesus. I love you all with all my heart.

CONTENTS

(CONTINUED)

FOREWORD

I am absolutely delighted to write a few words about Peter Doseck's new book, "Let's Talk." It addresses a subject which is dear to my heart. Many years ago God launched me into the healing ministry and challenged me to build a healing university by speaking inside my spirit. It was a directive from Heaven that changed my life forever.

As I look back over the journey the Lord has allowed me to experience, there have been many decisions I have been asked to make which would have been impossible on my own. At these critical junctures I have only one place to turn. I get alone with God and enter into fellowship and communion with Him. As a result, my heavenly Father and I have become such good friends I never take a step without Him.

God is waiting to speak to you, but are you ready to hear?

When I was a young boy, my mother asked me again and again, "Are you listening?"

I knew what she was saying: "Are you really *hearing* me?"

As you open the pages of this book, shut out what is happening around you. Block everything else out of your mind and listen closely to what the Lord wants to drop into your spirit. Have a listening heart.

I know that I know that I know "Let's Talk" will open the windows of Heaven for you in a way that perhaps you've never experienced in your lifetime. Read every word with faith because it's going to touch your life.

– Oral Roberts

PREFACE

"**H**ello! Is anybody home?"

"Who's there?"

"It's Me!"

"Me who?"

"It's a still, small voice. Who else would it be?"

"Oh, it's you, Lord."

Is this how you feel when God speaks—a little out of touch and confused? This is how far too many people feel today. Some wonder if the Lord decided to close up Heaven and rest for awhile, it's been so long since they heard His voice. Others wonder if God really does speak to us anymore, or if He's gone silent to test us somehow.

If you are unsure whether Heaven is open and if God still speaks to His people, you are not alone. In reality, these are very interesting questions: "Is Heaven open to all?" and "Does God really speak to people on earth today?"

Maybe you wonder if God speaks audibly, like He did to Abraham and Moses. Does God speak in dreams and visions, like He did to Daniel and Peter—or does He send angelic messengers, as He did to Paul?

We all want to believe Heaven is open and that God's ways of speaking to us are the same as they were in the Bible, but how do we really know? How can you be sure if it's okay for *you* to approach the throne of God, expecting Him to speak to you personally?

I believe Heaven is wide open, and that God is trying to speak to you much more often than you think. The Bible tells us the Lord never leaves us nor forsakes us, so it seems logical to me that because He is with us, He would be trying to communicate.

I am absolutely certain that God wants you to feel comfortable in His presence so He can tell how much He loves you. I am equally sure He longs to teach, warn and tell you of things to come. He also desires to give you messages to help others—messages that will draw them closer to Him.

9

For me, the questions are not, "Is Heaven open? or "Does God speak?", but "Do we know how to experience the open Heaven and hear when God does speak?"

In my years of study, I have found eight primary ways God speaks to His children. First, He communicates to us through His Word, the Bible. God speaks by way of dreams and visions, through signs and wonders, and angels. God also speaks audibly, through the five-fold ministry gifts, through the gifts of the Spirit and through the fruit that you and others bear. Each of these eight ways can be broken down into sub-categories that reveal so many more ways God can speak to us individually; ways we can personally understand.

NEW BEGINNINGS

Eight is the number of new beginnings, and since we are in a dimension of newness in Christ, I believe God has opened Heaven and chosen to speak to us using these eight primary ways because we are His sons and daughters. I am also convinced He speaks to us because He loves us so much, He just can't help Himself.

When we hear God's voice, we grow. 1 Peter 2:2 says: *"As newborn babes, desire the sincere milk of the word, that ye may grow thereby."* We develop in the things of God as children do—by intake and by use.

As children grow and exercise their muscles they become more confident, more coordinated, and more proficient in life skills. In the same way, when we as believers exercise our faith in experiencing the open Heaven and hearing God's voice, we will grow in these areas, too.

Applying your faith in the things of God will enable you to mature and rise to higher levels and greater success in and for the Kingdom. Using what you know will keep you moving forward, while failing to do so will cause you to lose what you have, just like failing to use a muscle will cause it to shrink and atrophy.

So, first you must learn Heaven is truly open to you, and that you can hear the voice of God personally. Then you must exercise yourself in this knowledge and grow more confident, more skilled, and more sure of your ability to experience all God has for you.

It's important to understand that when the Lord speaks to you, it is because He desires to deliver you from your own carnal purposes, from your own ineffective ways and from the snare of the adversary. This is why accessing the open Heaven and hearing God when He speaks is so vital for every believer.

And this is why I wrote this book, to help you discover how to experience the open Heaven in your life. God is speaking, of this I am sure. Now it's time for you to hear His voice and receive all He has for you.

Is Heaven open? You better believe it! Is God speaking to you? Yes, He is! Can you hear His voice? Absolutely!

He is saying, "Let's talk!"

– Peter Doseck

PART ONE

MESSAGES FROM HEAVEN

Chapter 1

An Open Heaven

As I stood on the worn tan carpet, staring at the picture of my daughter hanging on the north wall, I heard the voice of God. I immediately closed my eyes and froze, unable to move a muscle. Could it really be Him? Could it be the answer, the voice that I had been seeking for weeks on end?

I dared not talk back, but I finally got up the courage to open my eyes and look carefully behind me. When I discovered that no one was there, I quietly whispered, "Yes, Lord?" in more of a question than an answer.

I had been saved for about six months, and not one soul had ever mentioned hearing the audible voice of God, so it was with great trepidation that I launched out and believed the Lord was speaking to me. I don't know what I expected next, but the conversation which followed changed my life forever.

How I came to this point was really very simple. I had read a story in the Bible where a man named Eli told a young boy named Samuel that the voice he had heard during the night was the voice of God. Eli told Samuel to answer the Lord by saying, *"Speak Lord, for thy servant heareth"* (1 Samuel 3:9). When I read that story, it jumped in my spirit. So, the baby Christian that I was, I decided I would ask God to speak to me. I didn't know any better than to mimic what I saw in the Bible.

Every day I would come home from work and spend about two hours with my family. I'd do my chores, and afterward I'd go into my bedroom and pray until about 9:00 P.M. when my daughter Nicole went to bed. Then I'd go into the living room and pray there until approximately 3:00 A.M. I'd sleep around two hours, and then get up and go to work. I did this day after day after day for weeks on end.

Hour after hour and day after day my prayer went something like this, "Here I am, Lord. If you want to talk to me, I'm waiting." I told you I did not know any better than to do what I read in the Word. So, I followed what Eli told Samuel to do; I prayed, and then I waited to hear from God. Then, on this wonderful appointed day, God talked back. Once I got over the initial shock, I spoke with my heavenly Father like I'd known Him for a thousand years.

During this conversation, God called me to preach. I told Him I didn't think I was smart enough to preach, but He reassured me He would teach me. I told God I didn't *want* to preach, but He told He was calling me, so what was I to do? I said, "Okay Lord, I'll do it!"

After my encounter with God, I excitedly asked my pastor to come over to my house, and I shared with him what had happened. Much to my surprise he told me that God did not speak to people anymore. I thought to myself, "I may be dumb, but I'm not deaf. Somebody was in this room."

I immediately left that church determining I did not need to be with a pastor who thought God was a deaf mute. I decided I did not want to stay where they did not believe the whole Bible.

So you can see that from the beginning of my walk with the Lord, hearing His voice has been an important part of my life. My baby Christian experience is not the norm, I assure you, but God met me where I was and called me to a place I would never have dreamed of going, all because I believed God was still in the business of speaking to His children.

God spoke to me from the realm of Heaven because I boldly and innocently approached Him expecting to hear. With childlike faith, I entered the throne room and heard the voice of the Lord.

HEAVEN IS OPEN

Luke 12:32 says: *"Fear not, little flock; for it is your Father's good pleasure to give you the kingdom."*

The Kingdom of God consists of everything Heaven has to offer. Is there healing there? Oh, yes. Is there blessing there? Of course. These are great, but Heaven encompasses so much more.

Heaven is full of angels, full of God's presence, full of answers, visitations and declarations. There are revelations, destinies and purposes, direction, callings and giftings there.

Everything you have ever wondered about has an answer waiting for you in Heaven. There are no unsolved mysteries and no lack of wisdom there. Heaven is open with everything you need, and the throne of God is waiting for you to approach boldly. God is waiting with arms open wide, and He eagerly desires to invade earth in and through your life. What are you waiting for?

I have had many personal experiences with the blessings of an open Heaven. One recent event is still very fresh in my mind.

Not long before finishing this book, I was ministering in Boston, MA, in a beautiful Portuguese speaking church. One evening before the service began I was in a hotel room praying and putting the final touches on my message. As I was in prayer, the angel of the Lord appeared in the room.

His appearance was sudden, and I could hardly stay on my feet as he stood before me. I continued to stagger even after he left because it was such a powerful experience. He showed me a crown, and then he placed it on my head. It was gorgeous with green, red and blue gemstones. As he placed it upon me, I thought of the first crown God had delivered to me when I entered into the dimension of miracles for crusades around the world.

I thought about how amazing it was that God had chosen to send an angel to visit me again. I felt so blessed that once more, a heavenly being had been sent from the throne to deliver a special gift. I also marveled at the sudden entrance of the visitor. Although you can never prepare for an angelic visit, the feeling this unexpected appearance gave me was more intense than anything I had ever experienced before.

As I dwelt on these things, the angel placed a ring on my finger. It was so beautiful with a very deep, dark red stone in the center. I noticed it resembled the ring that Brother Oral Roberts wears. I had seen the ring in several personal visits with him in recent years, so I immediately recognized the similarity, and I wondered why they appeared to be the same.

Then, as suddenly as he had appeared, the angel was gone, and that was the end of the vision. Although its purpose was not fully revealed to me at the time, the vision was infused into my mind and soul, and I knew something very special had happened that night. Though not a word had been spoken, God had clearly sent me a message from Heaven.

When the visitation was over, I wrote it down in the front of my Bible. You might say, "Well, anyone could make that up and write it down, but who could prove it ever happened?" God could!

Later that evening, after the service was over, the pastor of the church was with me. He spoke softly and apologized through his interpreter for being disobedient to God earlier, and then he revealed to me that God had told him about my angelic visitation.

He shared how when he had arrived at church that evening, he had come into the presence of several angels he had never met nor seen before. When he asked who they were, he had been told they were the company of angels who travel with me in my miracle crusades. (I had known of their existence since a break-through crusade in Russia several years earlier when I had fasted and prayed during a particularly difficult crusade until one night, an angel came into our midst, the leader of a company of healing angels, and that evening an entire deaf school, some 25–30 people, received their hearing.)

This dear pastor explained that this company of angels had told him about my visitation. When I heard this, I asked my assistant to run and get my Bible so I could show my friend what I had written. Not only did God speak to me through this visitation, but He also spoke to this pastor, and both of us were blessed by this one event.

Hearing from God is a great blessing, one that should not be missed by any believer. What the Lord did for me and for this dear man of God in Boston, He wants to do for you. Whether you have been aware of it or not, Heaven is wide open and waiting for you to access it in a far greater dimension than you have ever known. It's time to walk through the door and enter in.

PARTICIPATING IN THE KINGDOM

As a pastor, I have discovered there is one thing which separates Christians who hear from God from those who don't. Those who hear are active participants in the Kingdom of God, while those who do not are usually only experiencing the Kingdom without really participating.

Here's what I mean. There are people who diligently seek the Kingdom of God, and then there are those who only inhabit the Kingdom of God. When people seek the Kingdom of God, the fullness of that Kingdom comes upon them and overtakes them. For those who do not seek, the blessings of the Kingdom will always be just out of reach.

There are some who say, "Well, it's just all up to God. If He wants me to have something, He will get it to me." While I understand it is all God, you have to realize what He has made available to you, and you are the one who has to seek in order to find, to knock in order for it to be opened, and to ask in order for it to be given (see Matthew 7:7).

Now, let me explain a term here. The Kingdom of God, the Kingdom of Heaven and the Kingdom of Christ are all descriptions of basically the same thing. They can be broken down and dissected, that is true, but they are so interwoven in the scripture, I have chosen for the purpose of this book to simply refer to the Kingdom of God in general.

The Kingdom of God is the realm of God, the realm of Heaven, and the realm into which we as believers have been born through the blood of Jesus. It is very real, and it is active all around us. This Kingdom is where God operates, and it is the avenue through which He will speak to you, so it is very important to understand how it works.

The Kingdom of God is a realm which is beyond human reason. It cannot be experienced by mere intellect or by the senses of man. If you try to rationalize what God desires for you to have there, you will miss out because the Kingdom is not a mental, rational or sense-driven kingdom, but a spiritual domain revealed by the Word of God.

In modern times the Body of Christ has tried to reach God by reason, and too many Christians have attempted to intellectualize Him without success. Most of the time the Kingdom of God does not make sense to the human mind, but it is not any less real just because we cannot touch, see, hear, or encounter it with our natural senses.

Let's be honest, we only have limited understanding of how things work in the natural, let alone the supernatural. Just try to explain how a baby is formed in the womb, for instance. You'll get so far, and then you'll have to admit it is beyond human reason. Do we discount the development of a child just because we do not understand it all? No. We have to learn to accept certain things by faith.

Do you really know how electricity works? Probably not, but you still use the light switch, don't you? Do you fully understand gravity? I doubt it, but that does not stop you from depending on it every morning when you step out of bed.

We take things by faith and trust natural laws every day, so it should not be surprising to discover that in the Kingdom of God there are certain laws we will simply have to accept by faith, even though we cannot explain them with our natural intellect. To participate in the Kingdom, it is not important for us to dissect every detail to see how things work, but we do need to make sure our reasoning does not interfere with what God has for us through faith in Him.

OUR RESPONSIBILITY

In the Kingdom, man is not without responsibility when it comes to experiencing God in His fullness. There are things required of us before we can experience all God has for us in this life, including entering an open Heaven and hearing His voice. Things such as sacrifice, paying the price, putting time aside and dealing with faults so we can meet God in the way He desires for us to know Him (see James 4:8).

Colossians 3:1 says: *"If ye then be risen with Christ, seek those things which are above, where Christ sitteth on the right hand of God."*

Here we see that our first responsibility is to seek, and if we are commanded to seek something, we can be sure God wants us to find it. The Lord is not trying to keep you from enjoying an open Heaven, but the Holy Spirit is working to help you enter into, experience, and to hear the voice of God there.

Some will focus on the materialistic rewards promised when we seek the things which are above, but more so than physical blessings, the visitation and the experience of Heaven connecting with us on earth is a much greater reward. As you seek today, your reward will be a pre-determined place and a moment in time where you will experience the reality of the Kingdom of God in a way that you have never known it before. This is God's will for you.

Too many of us believe God is waiting to meet with us in the sweet by and by, but I beg to differ. We have hundreds of accounts in the Bible of natural men who experienced hearing the voice of God from an open Heaven. Why then do so many Christians today believe they have to wait until death to visit, hear from or experience Heaven? It's because they do not understand how the Kingdom of God works. You can hear from God in the here and now if you will make a determined effort to seek, because the ability to hear Him is an inherited trait possessed by every born again person (see John 10:3-5).

God's voice is available to those who seek the Kingdom. He tells us in Isaiah 55:8-11: *"For my thoughts are not your thoughts, neither are your ways my ways, saith the Lord. For as the heavens are higher than the earth, so are my ways higher than your ways, and my thoughts than your thoughts. For as the rain cometh down, and the snow from heaven, and returneth not thither, but watereth the earth, and maketh it bring forth and bud, that it may give seed to the sower, and bread to the eater: So shall my word be that goeth forth out of my mouth: it shall not return unto me void, but it shall accomplish that which I please, and it shall prosper in the thing whereto I sent it."*

This scripture reveals that our second responsibility is to recognize God's Word is His voice, and we have to respond to the Word before it will prosper. The Word of God is a seed, and the potential of the seed is a revelation of Him, His will and His salvation, but our response must be one of faith in Him.

Sinners in hell today who heard the gospel on earth cannot say that God's Word did not work for them. It did, but sadly, they failed to respond. When this happens, we reap the consequences, but if we respond in faith, we reap the blessings and the benefits.

Our third responsibility is to obey the Word. Whatever we read in the Bible, we are responsible to obey and do. "Love thy neighbor as thyself." "Love the Lord your God with all your mind, soul and strength." "Do good to them that hate you." These are just a few of the commands we must respect and obey in order to enter the open Heaven and hear God's voice.

We don't earn the right to hear by our obedience, because nothing in the Kingdom of God comes by works alone, but we close the door to hearing if we do not obey. Disobedience is like wearing earplugs. God will still send His Word, but you will not be able to hear it.

In 1 Corinthians 16:13 we read: *"Watch ye, stand fast in the faith, quit you like men, be strong."* This brings us to responsibility number four which is to disconnect ourselves from human reasoning and natural thinking, and reconnect ourselves to thoughts of faith. We will only live as those in covenant relationship when we disconnect ourselves from the influence of our intellect, natural senses, mental rationale and human reasoning. When we seek the Kingdom, we must walk by faith and not by sight (see 2 Corinthians 5:7).

So, we are responsible to seek, to respond to the Word as God's voice, to obey, and to disconnect from human reasoning. If we will be diligent to do these four things, we will enter the open Heaven, and we will hear God speak.

IN THE KINGDOM OF GOD

If we're going to truly seek to hear God's voice, we need to make sure we are in a position to respond to the openness of Heaven, which means we need to make certain we are in the Kingdom of God in the first place. Jesus told us how to enter when He spoke to Nicodemus in John 3:2-5: *"The same came to Jesus by night, and said unto him, Rabbi, we know that thou art a teacher come from God: for no man can do these miracles that thou doest, except God be with him.*

"Jesus answered and said unto him, Verily, verily, I say unto thee, Except a man be born again, he cannot see the kingdom of God.

"Nicodemus saith unto him, How can a man be born when he is old? Can he enter the second time into his mother's womb, and be born? Jesus answered, Verily, verily, I say unto thee, Except a man be born of water and of the Spirit, he cannot enter into the kingdom of God."

Here we see that through the new birth, by grace through faith in Christ Jesus, we are born into the Kingdom of God, and we are given the right to experience an open Heaven from that moment on. If you are a Christian, one born of God, you are in a position to hear from Him right now.

Just as you were born into this earth and do not think it is strange to make connections with the world around you, so you were born into the Kingdom of God through the new birth and should not find it unusual to make connections with Heaven. Because you were born on this planet, you have rights here on earth. When you were born into the Kingdom of God, you were given certain rights there, too.

You don't think it is abnormal to experience this world while you are alive, so why would you think it is abnormal to experience the Kingdom of God while you are alive in Him? The problem is we have all been taught, "When I get to Heaven..." thus and so.

Thank God for "When I get to Heaven..." This is what I am living and waiting for. I am watching night and day for the return of the Lord, keeping myself filled with God, working with a hammer in one hand and a Bible in the other, anticipating that His return may come at any moment. I am looking forward to Heaven, but I am not discounting experiencing Heaven while I am still here on earth.

We have been born again to live with God eternally, and we should look forward to the fullness of that promise with joy, but we also have to realize eternal life starts when we are born again, not when we die (see 1 John 5:11). This being true, while I live on earth I am determined to stay connected to Heaven and to hear the voice of God here and now. I don't want to just be mindful of Heaven and talk about it, I want to experience Heaven on a daily basis.

We also notice in John 3:2-5 how Nicodemus realized that Jesus had a connection with God which enabled Him to live differently than any other man he had ever known. Nicodemus understood Jesus lived in a dimension where He walked with God, and God walked with Him.

Jesus operated in a heavenly connection and demonstrated the Kingdom of God everywhere He went. Paul spoke of this in 1 Thessalonians 1:5: *"For our gospel came not unto you in word only, but also in power, and in the Holy Ghost, and in much assurance..."* Jesus lived this verse in all of its fullness, and He showed us God's will for our lives. We should be operating in the same heavenly connection Jesus operated in, and we should hear God's voice just as He did (see John 14:12).

In Ephesians 2:6 we read: *"And hath raised us up together, and made us sit together in heavenly places in Christ Jesus."* Notice this verse is in the past tense, not in future tense. When you were born into the Kingdom, you were given a seating in Heaven that is equal to Christ Jesus, a seating granted because of His substitution for you on the cross.

Because of this, it should not be unusual for you to tell another believer that an angel came with a message from Heaven, or that God spoke in a dream, or that He communicated with you in an audible voice. These things are normal for Heaven, so as one seated in heavenly places in Christ Jesus, they should be normal for you on earth.

I constantly hear people tell each other what the devil said to them. "The devil told me this" or "The devil told me that. Oh that devil!" When I hear this, I always wonder if they ever hear from God. The reason individuals are so in tune with the voice of the devil is because the world system and the kingdom of darkness are far more real to them than their seating in heavenly places.

If you are a Christian, you are already seated in Heaven. God did not place you there without expecting you to receive the benefits of that seating. God does this so you might experience Heaven, not just after you die, but while you live.

As we read in Colossians 1:13: *"Who hath delivered us from the power of darkness, and hath translated us into the kingdom of his dear Son."* Notice again, this translation is in the past tense. It is already done, not something waiting to be accomplished.

You are in the Kingdom of God now, seated in heavenly places in Christ

Jesus, and you have been translated into the Kingdom of His dear Son. Now it's time to live like it.

CITIZENS AND AMBASSADORS

Because you have been born again, seated in heavenly places and translated into the Kingdom, you are a citizen of Heaven already. Did you know this? Your translation into the Kingdom of God empowers you with the benefits of heavenly citizenship here and now, not just in the sweet by and by.

Most of us know we have a heavenly home waiting for us, but we live as if we are separated from the Kingdom of God on a daily basis. It's not that we don't experience little breakthroughs in our giving, or in the area of healing and so forth, but there is far more to the Kingdom of God than just materialistic blessing and health.

Don't get me wrong, these blessings are good things, and we should not belittle them, but God is waiting for us to seek Him and His Kingdom in a much greater dimension so we can enjoy Heaven to it fullest potential right now. We should live as Heaven's citizens though we reside on earth.

Let me give you an example to help you better understand. Let's suppose you visited Ireland and you loved it so much you applied for citizenship there. You would retain the benefits of your homeland citizenship, plus you would gain the benefits of becoming an Irish citizen. With dual citizenship, you could move freely from one country to the other without any hindrance, and you could receive the benefits of each nation simultaneously.

You would feel completely free to move about in your country of birth, and you would feel equally free to move about in your adopted land. You would not question your right to experience anything either country had to offer.

Now, suppose they gave you citizenship, but refused to allow you to enter the country. Would that be fair? No way. If they tried to keep you out, you would demand your rights until they allowed you entrance. You would be upset and forceful in your demands.

You should be just as bold to access the rights of your citizenship as a Christian. You are a part of the kingdom of the earth and a part of the Kingdom of God at this moment. You have dual citizenship in a sense, and you have been given equal rights and privileges in each realm. You have the authority to move freely on earth and in heavenly places.

I do not think Jesus is hindered in the Kingdom of God today. I think He is experiencing that realm to it fullest potential right now. If you also believe this, then it's time to believe the words of Jesus in John 17:16: *"They are not of the world, even as I am not of the world."* This is talking about you. You are no longer only of this world. You are of Heaven, too, just like Jesus is.

Truthfully, you should be more familiar with Heaven than you are with earth because you are an ambassador for Heaven (see 2 Corinthians 5:20). This means that this world is not your primary abode; Heaven is. On earth, you represent another realm so that Jesus can be seen in and through you.

Ambassadors are representatives of a land in every respect. They understand and operate in every right of citizenship in their native country, and also in the land in which they are called to live. They have been given the right of representation and enjoy all of the privileges of those who sent them.

Ambassadors personally experience every benefit their home country has to offer so they can represent it knowing full well what that country is all about. An effective, good ambassador is a blessed man or woman who has tasted and experienced the fullness of life in his native land, one who has had eye to eye contact with its citizens and hands on experience with what it's like to live there.

You too can have this close, intimate relationship with Heaven so you can properly represent it and tell others what it is like there. This is what accessing Heaven means; it's not just about you anymore, now it concerns those who can be touched by God through you.

You should not only know about and hear from God for the purpose of personal experience, but you should know Him and hear from Him daily so you can report to others the goodness of the Father which will lead them to repentance (see Romans 2:4).

So many Christians want to hear from God, but they do not know how. They have needs that go unmet, desires which go unfulfilled and futures that are cloudy at best, all because they have no idea how to hear the voice of their Heavenly Father. I pray this is not you! You already have a right to the gateway of Heaven, but perhaps you are unaware of this amazing fact. The key is to find the gateway, access it and enter in.

COME BOLDLY

The Bible tells us in Hebrews 4:16: *"Let us therefore come boldly unto the throne of grace, that we may obtain mercy, and find grace to help in time of need."*

This is the gateway to Heaven, opened by grace, and it is the key to accessing the benefits of the Kingdom and hearing God's voice. We come boldly to the throne of grace just as an ambassador for a nation comes confidently to the governmental seat of that nation. We arrive with assurance because we have been given the right of access.

Interestingly, this verse shows us whose responsibility it is to decide to enter the realm of Heaven. It is yours. *"Come boldly"* means *"You* come boldly. You decide, and then you come."

Let me ask this question. Where is the throne of grace located? It's in Heaven of course. It is God's throne. He abides in Heaven, so therefore, His throne is also there. When you approach the throne of grace, you approach it in Heaven. The physical you remains on earth, but the inner you, your spirit, comes before God in Heaven.

Do you think this means you can approach just one dimension of God, or do you believe you can draw near to His fullness? I believe we can experience the fullness of all God has and all He is.

When Jesus told us to pray: *"Our Father which art in Heaven"*, He was not just revealing a God that answered prayer, He was showing us a God of accessibility in every area (see Matthew 6:9). I wonder if you've ever considered how many times you can pray in a day. One hundred? One thousand? One million? I asked this question in church one time and a lady replied, "A zillion." I don't know how many a zillion is, but I know it would take constant prayer to reach it!

We can make a connection with the throne of grace a zillion times a day if we want to, because there is no limit to how often we can approach. This tells me we have as much access to Heaven and to the voice of God that flows from there as we decide to have.

"Let us therefore…" It is our decision to enter the realm of Heaven. God does not decide for us, but we make the choice for ourselves.

The best news is that God always responds when we come boldly. He has an open door for us to not only live in the Spirit, but to walk in and hear from the Spirit at our discretion. Heaven is open, and now is the time to enter in.

THE SPIRIT WALK

Paul said: *"Walk in the Spirit, and ye shall not fulfil the lust of the flesh"* (Galatians 5:16). In other words, since you are in the Spirit, why don't you decide to walk and stay there?

Here's the problem: Most Christians do not truly want to walk in the Spirit, they just think they do. They really want to live any old way, as if the benefits of the Kingdom will just fall on them, but that's not how it works.

Look at what Isaiah 64:4-5 says: *"For since the beginning of the world men have not heard, nor perceived by the ear, neither hath the eye seen, O God, beside thee, what he hath prepared for him that waiteth for him.*

"Thou meetest him that rejoiceth and worketh righteousness, those that remember thee in thy ways: behold, thou art wroth; for we have sinned: in those is continuance, and we shall be saved."

God reveals Himself to those who seek after Him, to those who work righteousness and live holy. I didn't write this; God did, and it's so simple. If you live right, you will experience the Lord, but if you ignore His Word, you will not see and hear what He desires for your life.

You must be willing to pay the price to live according to His principles and walk in the Spirit to enter an open Heaven and hear God's voice. You must come boldly to the throne of grace and expect to receive. It's not complicated; just seek Him and live right, that's all. Those who do what is expected and required will experience the Kingdom, and those who don't, won't!

You live this way in the natural and don't even realize it. If you have children, especially older children, I can guarantee at times you are closer to some of them than you are to others. This closeness is not a result of you treating them any differently, but it is the result of their response to you. When a child responds to your love and care, you are able to give them more, but if they keep you at arm's length, you cannot reach them no matter how much you desire to.

This is why those who do as the Bible says and come boldly will receive and hear His voice, but those who disobey, will not. God meets you at your discretion, not His; therefore, you can experience as much of God as you desire.

The Father gave His Son to bring you into the Kingdom, so it's a given that He's not trying to keep you out, but you may keep yourself outside because you've become too busy to come confidently, or because you have not chosen to live right and walk in the Spirit as you have been commanded to do. Whether or not you walk in the Spirit is not God's choice. It is your decision to connect with Heaven, or to walk in the flesh and stay disconnected.

God does not just show up with grace to help in time of need because He feels like it. He does so when you walk in the Spirit and approach His throne of grace with boldness. If you live right and come, He provides, but if you do not, God's hands are essentially tied. Here's my advice: Don't ever tie God's hands or fall prey to the plans of the enemy and shut the door on His voice.

"Let us come boldly to the throne of grace..." also implies that we can enter into and move in and out of the Kingdom of God at will. Some may say, "Oh, I couldn't do that! You don't know me. That won't happen to me."

I disagree. I don't believe it is a strange thing for a Father to visit His children, or for children to visit their Father. It's not unusual, but it does take faith—not faith in yourself, but faith in Him.

Heaven is open, and God is saying, "Let's talk." He is waiting to visit you whenever you are ready to boldly approach Him. He will speak to you there and tell you secret things about your life. He will show you what is to come and guide you in the way you should go. He will impart wisdom for raising your children, discernment for living with your spouse, healing for your body, dreams for your future, purpose for your calling and anointing for your tomorrows. It's all waiting for those who will come boldly, for those willing to live holy and right, for those unafraid to approach and prepared to hear.

God is ready to speak, but the question is, are you ready to hear from Heaven?

CHAPTER 2

GOD'S LOVE LETTER TO YOU

Mrs. Blackburn had spent months agonizing over whether she should retire from her job. For twenty years it had been the source of many friendships, some good times and some not so good, but always it was a comfort to know that each morning she had a place to go and a task to complete.

Friends and family tried to lend their support as she struggled to make up her mind, and some even offered advice, but nothing anyone said seemed to make a difference. She just could not decide whether it was time to go, or time to take a breath and continue on.

One day, as she sat praying for the umpteenth time over the decision, a gentle leading drew her to pick up the Bible and turn to the book of Jeremiah. Not really sure what to read, she leafed through the first few pages, until her eyes landed upon these words: *"...retire, stay not"* (Jeremiah 4:6).

Astounded at what she saw, Mrs. Blackburn blinked her eyes in disbelief and read it again. It had not changed. It still said: *"...retire, stay not."* Elated and finally at peace in her mind, my long-time congregation member did retire, and she has never looked back.

How amazing that God cared enough to speak so plainly to this dear saint and give her assurance concerning a life-changing decision. God is no respecter of persons. What He did for one, He desires to do for all. Just ask Him, as Mrs. Blackburn did, and He will answer you, too.

THE WAY OF LIFE

Proverbs 6:23 tells us: *"For the commandment is a lamp; and the law is light; and reproofs of instruction are the way of life."*

The words God speaks provide revelation, reproof, instruction and direction. They give us insight, understanding and inspiration, and His words are a light in a dark world and hope for generations to come.

It should come as no surprise, then, to discover that the number one way God speaks to His children is through His Holy Word, the Bible. Unfortunately, for many believers this is the least pursued and the least liked way to hear from the Lord. That said, it is the surest way to hear from God, and it is also the primary source for verifying the other ways He communicates.

Seeking God's voice in His Word is kind of like studying a good road map before you go on vacation. When you travel to a new place, the success of your trip is entirely dependent upon understanding the map. Likewise, your success in life relies upon reading, understanding and hearing God through His Word.

The problem is, too many Christians have access to the greatest map of all time, the Bible, yet they fail to read, understand and use it, preferring instead to stumble through life on their own. Just as it's not wise to take a road trip without a map, it's equally ignorant to travel through life without the direction of God's Word.

The wise man and woman will go to the Bible first, expecting to find the answer there rather than attempting to find their own way. The wise man will study to show himself approved and discover the answer in God's Word. The wise woman will meditate on the Word until revelation comes that will guide her to her destination.

The truth of the matter is, the Word of God is the only reliable and unchangeable thing in this world. Everything else around you, including you, is in a constant state of change. Your perceptions are changing. Your family is growing and changing. Thanks to gravity, your body is changing. Your job is changing. Your neighborhood is changing. Everything around and about you is in transition, and yet, God's Word never changes.

This makes the Bible the single most reliable source of information in the world. When God speaks to you from His Word, you will be able to solidly stand on what He says for all eternity. You'll never have to wonder about it again, and that Word will be an established, sure Word that will become a way of life.

Though some consider the Bible a common thing, truth be told the Word of God is the most supernatural treasure on earth. It is full of healing and deliverance, wisdom and might, promises, provision, blessing and victory. It is eternal and unchanging, everlasting and unshakeable. It is always right, always on time, always at your fingertips. Everything you will ever need is in God's Word because the Word is God (see John 1:14).

Hear and Obey

God is more than willing to speak through His Word to help you in every situation you face because there is no problem too big or too small for the Word. The key is to obey what you read.

Jeremiah 11:3-4 says: *"And say thou unto them, Thus saith the Lord God of Israel; Cursed be the man that obeyeth not the words of this covenant, which I commanded your fathers in the day that I brought them forth out of the land of Egypt, from the iron furnace, saying, Obey my voice, and do them, according to all which I command you: So shall ye be my people, and I will be your God."*

Notice the underlined phrase where God called the words of His covenant His voice. The voice of the Lord is the covenant of God, and the covenant of God is the commandment of God, the Word of God. These are all one and the same. God's Word is His voice.

God holds us accountable to obey His Word just as if He spoke it audibly every day. If you will honor this principle and accept it as His voice, you will establish your life on the solid rock that cannot be moved when the storms of life blow against you.

In Jeremiah 7:28 we read: *"But thou shalt say unto them, This is a nation that obeyeth not the voice of the Lord their God, nor receiveth correction: truth is perished, and is cut off from their mouth."* Here we see that when Israel failed and became separated from God, it was because they did not obey His voice.

We must never allow ourselves to disrespect the Word of God in this manner. We should honor the fact we have such free access to its leather-bound pages. Let's keep our focus on the Source of the words written for our benefit, and remember that these printed pages are actually a love letter from

God written for each of us personally.

A More Sure Word

The apostle Peter writes: *"And this voice which came from heaven we heard, when we were with him in the holy mount. We have also a more sure word of prophecy; whereunto ye do well that ye take heed, as unto a light that shineth in a dark place, until the day dawn, and the day star arise in your hearts"* (2 Peter 1:18-19).

Here Peter tells us the Word of God is more reliable than any prophetic utterance, even more so than the things he heard on the mount of transfiguration. Though Peter was shaken to the core when he saw Jesus transfigured before him and heard the voice of God come down from Heaven, yet he trusted the written Word of God more than this amazing experience.

He goes on to say: *"Knowing this first, that no prophecy of the scripture is of any private interpretation. For the prophecy came not in old time by the will of man: but holy men of God spake as they were moved by the Holy Ghost"* (2 Peter 1:20-21).

Peter understood that, as great as his experience had been and as wonderful as the memory of it was, he could never depend on an audible voice as much as he could on the prophetic Word written by God through inspired, holy men.

In 2 Corinthians 6:16 we learn: *"And what agreement hath the temple of God with idols? For ye are the temple of the living God; as God hath said, I will dwell in them, and walk in them; and I will be their God, and they shall be my people."*

Notice the words I have underlined, *"as God hath said."* When did God say, *"I will dwell in them, and walk in them; and I will be their God, and they shall be my people?"* He said this in Ezekiel 11:19-20, 36:27-28 and 37:26-28.

What God said through His written Word became the basis upon which the apostle Paul built the Corinthian church. Paul was so confident in the written Word of God that he based the guidance of his life and the order of the church upon the words of a prophet.

Paul did not look for a new word, but rather based the doctrine of the church on a declared word. He did not wait for a new revelation, but relied upon the already established word of the Lord. He went back to the firm foundation we all build upon, the writings of the prophets, and used it to orchestrate the order of holiness and separation from a lost and dying world. Paul gave the Corinthian church a personal guideline for their lives written by Ezekiel hundreds of years earlier, yet it was still as fresh and powerful the day Paul was inspired to write it in the New Testament. What's even more amazing is that the Bible is just as relevant and powerful for your life today. You can be sure that God is still speaking to you from the pages of His Holy Word.

I encourage you to handle scripture carefully, just as if it was a personal love letter written especially for you. In reality, this is what it is. Every time you read "God hath said…" you can't get any more personal, more prophetic, more right on time or any more "fresh for today" than that.

When you curl up in the easy chair with the Bible tonight, you will be praying as I said so many years ago, "God, speak to me. Speak into my life. Give me a sure word that I may live."

His precious Word is living water poured out of God's Spirit, as if He is speaking it just to you. He may speak it to a thousand other people, but when you sit down and turn the pages of the Bible, breaking the bread of life, God is speaking in a supernatural way and breathing faith into your spirit personally.

One of my church members wrote this testimony: "When I am reading the Word, sometimes a verse will just pop out at me. Then I know I can stand on that verse for myself, for my family, or for whomever the Lord Jesus has brought to my mind."

God's Word is very personal, giving you direction for your life, and it should be the primary way you hear from God each and every day. Drink in its pages as a thirsty man drinks in cool waters. Consume it as manna sent from Heaven. Treasure it above all else, and the Holy Spirit will make it as real to you as it was to the "holy men of God" who were inspired to write it so long ago.

You can be sure that God's Word never changes because it is a living, breathing, ever-present word of the Lord, and it is God's voice in the world today.

SEEK TO HEAR GOD'S VOICE IN HIS WORD

Every method God uses to speak to us will ultimately bring us back to His Word, because God never speaks anything which is contrary to His written

Word. Never. So going to the Bible first when you need to hear His voice is the wisest thing you could ever choose to do.

How do you discover the voice of God in the Word of God? You find it by seeking. Matthew 7:7-8 says: *"Ask, and it shall be given you; seek, and ye shall find; knock, and it shall be opened unto you: For every one that asketh receiveth; and he that seeketh findeth; and to him that knocketh it shall be opened."*

We discover one way to seek in Proverbs 6:20-22, which states: *"My son, keep thy father's commandment, and forsake not the law of thy mother: Bind them continually upon thine heart, and tie them about thy neck. When thou goest, it shall lead thee; when thou sleepest, it shall keep thee; and when thou awakest, it shall talk with thee."*

God's Word can talk to you, and according to this verse it will speak to you if you will be diligent to "bind it upon your heart" and "tie it around your neck." In other words, you should seek, find and keep what you find before your eyes.

Here's my practical advice: If you want to hear from God, go to the Word and begin a search on the subject you need to hear about. Do you need a word for healing? Find all the scriptures you can find on healing and let God speak to you. Do you need a word for your life's direction? Look up all of the verses on being led of God and let Him speak to you there also.

If had a financial problem, I wouldn't waste time wringing my hands with worry; I'd go to the Word and research every scripture I could locate on finances and read until I heard from Heaven. I would find out how God met the needs of every person from Genesis to Revelation. I would locate those scriptures and make certain they were bound in my heart. I'd keep them before my eyes and make them my primary focus during the day and into the night. I would keep them with me continually.

I would think on those scriptures and mull them over all day long, speaking them to myself and praying them out loud. I would meditate, going over and over them until the light of God's voice broke through. I would not quit until I heard God speak. I would seek and keep on seeking, knock and keep on knocking until I had what I needed.

STUDY TO HEAR GOD'S VOICE IN HIS WORD

Paul writes to young Timothy: *"Study to shew thyself approved unto God, a workman that needeth not to be ashamed, rightly dividing the word of truth"* (2 Timothy 2:15).

In essence, this verse could say, "So, you want to hear from God? Prove it!" We prove our desire by the study of God's Word.

Reading scripture is a vital part of hearing from the Lord because it will give you an overall understanding of who God is and how He does things, but the study of God's Word will take you deeper. Search the scriptures. Dig into them. Run the references and discover how connected and in order God's Word truly is.

When you study, you will lay line upon line, precept upon precept, here a little and there a little, until you find the treasure you are looking for (see Isaiah 28:10). The Holy Spirit will lead you from scripture to scripture, from revelation to revelation and from glory to glory.

God declares: *"For this is the covenant that I will make with the house of Israel after those days, saith the Lord; I will put my laws into their mind, and write them in their hearts: and I will be to them a God, and they shall be to me a people"* (Hebrews 8:10).

We are living in the days this scripture is talking about. When God speaks to you during a time of study, there is a supernatural engraving which takes place in your heart, an inscribing of His Word that will see you through and bring you to a place of victory.

As you continue in God's Word, you will also likely notice something Jesus told us about in Matthew 12:34. Here Jesus said: *"O generation of vipers, how can ye, being evil, speak good things? For out of the abundance of the heart the mouth speaketh."*

This is a great secret to Kingdom living and the key to hearing God's voice when you study His Word: What you put in your heart will be what comes out of your mouth in crisis. If you study regularly, you will find that God will make your heart a reservoir from which to draw in future situations. If you put the Word in, when the troubles of life arise, the Word will speak to you, flow out of you and see you through.

When you search the Word, study it and seek God's voice diligently by "binding it upon your heart" and "tying it about your neck," you are planting it deep down inside, and it's the only way you will be able to hear God's voice when you need it. You don't always have time to do a word search in the

Bible when trouble strikes, but if the Word abides in you because you've been obedient to put it in your heart by daily study, you will never be far from the voice of God.

You will have a pool of revelation waiting to be released just when you need it, if and only if you have been responsible to put the Word in. It's like a computer. What goes in, is what comes out. Put the Word in, and it will naturally come out at just the right moment.

FASTING TO HEAR GOD'S VOICE IN HIS WORD

In the ninth chapter of Daniel we find an amazing story. Daniel had set himself to understand the writings of the prophet Jeremiah concerning the future of Israel. He prayed earnestly for understanding, but he also did something else. Daniel fasted. The result of his fast was an angelic visitation. The angel Gabriel came and gave Daniel the understanding of the Word of God that he sought so diligently.

This was an extraordinary outcome, one which was repeated in Daniel's life in the very next chapter. While God still does use angels to deliver messages today, as I and many others have experienced, in this section I want to focus on Daniel's fasting rather than on his results.

Fasting is a separation from food and pleasure for a set time in order to focus your attention on the Kingdom of God, allowing Him to do what He desires to do. Fasting pulls us aside from the normal, daily routines of life and centers our attention on the things of the Kingdom and on hearing from God. In doing this, we close off our fleshly cravings and open ourselves to be more attentive to our spiritual desires. Fasting allows us to see more clearly and hear God's voice more readily.

In Daniel's case, what he needed to hear was an interpretation of scripture. Knowing that God is not a respecter of persons, you can do what Daniel did and expect to hear the voice of the Lord explain a portion of scripture that you cannot understand.

This is so important when you find a verse you believe is your answer, but you can't quite hear the voice of God in it. Maybe you've already sought and studied, but you still don't know what to do. The answer is, don't give up, keep pressing in. Press in with a time of fasting and see what God will do.

Daniel 9:23 tells us: *"At the beginning of thy supplications the commandment came forth, and I am come to shew thee; for thou art greatly beloved: therefore understand the matter, and consider the vision."*

Here we see here how God desired to give Daniel the information he asked for from the beginning. Daniel did not extract something God did not want to give, but simply put himself in a position to hear and receive by his fasting.

Jesus says: *"But thou, when thou fastest, anoint thine head, and wash thy face; that thou appear not unto men to fast, but unto thy Father which is in secret: and thy Father, which seeth in secret, shall reward thee openly"* (Matthew 6:17-18). God is ready to openly reward you with understanding of His Word and to speak a word in due season. If you are ready and willing to fast while you seek Him, you will find He is always ready and willing to answer.

MEDITATE FOR REVELATION
TO HEAR GOD'S VOICE IN HIS WORD

Paul writes: *"For this cause also thank we God without ceasing, because, when ye received the word of God which ye heard of us, ye received it not as the word of men, but as it is in truth, the word of God, which effectually worketh also in you that believe"* (1 Thessalonians 2:13).

Yes, God does speak through preachers, which we will learn about in Part Two. He speaks through the Word that is preached and delivers His message corporately as well as individually.

We can read scripture, seek our answer, study the Word diligently, fast for understanding and also listen to the Word preached to hear God's voice, but there is something even deeper that can be gleaned when we meditate God's Word.

Proverbs 6:20-22, Genesis 12:7 and Joshua 1:7-9 all talk about meditating the Word of God, but how do we do this? We meditate the Word by thinking about what we've read and studied, by writing it down and reminding ourselves of it all day long, and by speaking it out of our mouths over and over.

Proverbs 4:20-22 describes meditation this way: *"My son, attend to my words; incline thine ear unto my sayings. Let them not depart from thine eyes;*

keep them in the midst of thine heart. For they are life unto those that find them, and health to all their flesh."

This scripture reveals the three main seed receptors which allow entrance of God's Word into your heart. They are your ears, your eyes and your mind, and they are all connected to your heart. You hear, but you can forget. You see, but you can lose sight. To really benefit from the Word, you have to get what you hear and see to a place of permanency in your heart by meditation.

Meditation of God's Word has nothing to do with what our modern society calls meditation. We don't cross our legs and hum to get a revelation of God's Word, because that's a form of humanism.

When we meditate on the Word, we think on it. We mull it over, like a cow chews its cud, all day long. We go over and over it until we extract every last ounce of flavor. We also meditate by speaking God's Word, muttering it to ourselves so that our ears hear it again and again. We meditate God's Word by writing it down and reading it repeatedly.

By doing so, we allow the three seed receptors continual access to the Word of God. Eventually, if you stick with it, revelation will come, and you will hear God's voice in His Word clearer than you have ever heard it before.

Revelation is the voice of God that is hidden in the Word of God. It will speak to you and open up your eyes to see what He needs you to see in order to bring the promise to pass in your life.

Revelation is like putting a spot light on a certain portion of the Word. You may have read it a thousand times before, but when revelation comes, it will be as if you've never seen it before. It will speak to you, and deliver you in your time of trouble.

In Ephesians 1:17-18 we find: *"That the God of our Lord Jesus Christ, the Father of glory, may give unto you the spirit of wisdom and revelation in the knowledge of him: The eyes of your understanding being enlightened; that ye may know what is the hope of his calling, and what the riches of the glory of his inheritance in the saints."*

The word "know" in this scripture means to hear, correctly perceive and rightly divide God's course. The "hope of His calling" means God's will for your life. As the spirit of wisdom and revelation is given unto you, God's voice in His Word will rise up and unveil the direction you need to fulfill His will in your life.

Before I read, study and meditate God's Word, I always pray, "Oh, Lord, please help me hear what You are saying to me today. I pray that the faith which is in these pages will come to my spirit. Anoint my ears, my mind and my heart. Let the faith that is in every miracle, and every word, be infused in my spirit that I may walk worthy of You unto all pleasing, being fruitful unto every good work."

Without the light of revelation, I will walk hopelessly unholy, unpleasing, bearing no fruit and without the faith of God's Word being active and effective in my life. This kind of failure is not an option for me. I pray it is not for you either.

Revelation of God's Word is like discovering another facet on a diamond ring. Every lady who has ever received an engagement ring knows what I mean by this. I've heard that the diamond sparkles like nothing else in the world for the first few days it is on her finger, and every time she looks at it she sees another color, another beautiful facet she never saw before.

It's the same with revelation of God's Word. Every time you look at a verse, you may see the light of revelation reflected just a bit differently than the time you looked before. God's Word is like the most precious diamond ever made. Every verse has endless facets just waiting to be discovered, and revelation is the light that brings them to your attention and reveals another level of glory you did not know existed before.

Every scripture unfolds who God is, and since He is never-ending, so is the revelation of His Word. You could study for a thousand years and never reach the fullness of all the Lord has to say to you. It's an amazing concept to wrap your mind around. The Word is God, and He is infinite, beyond our understanding; therefore, we know revelation of His Word will never run dry.

Don't ever let yourself think, "Oh, I've heard that before" or "I've read that hundreds of times." When you give in to this kind of mentality, you risk missing the most spectacular revelation you have ever encountered.

As scripture states: *"But we all, with open face beholding as in a glass the glory of the Lord, are changed into the same image from glory to glory, even as by the Spirit of the Lord"* (2 Corinthians 3:18). This is revelation. It shows you one degree of glory, and reserves another for a time when it is needed. God's Word is so rich and deep, it will always show you something new even when you think you have discovered it all.

In Romans 10:17 we learn, *"So then faith cometh by hearing, and hearing by the word of God."* Faith does not come by hearing one time, but by hearing and hearing and hearing; by seeking, studying and meditating. We need to keep our nose in the Book and allow God to speak something new every time we read.

Revelation is worth the effort and the wait. Don't ever be in a hurry to leave a verse when God speaks revelation to you. Take your time to meditate the Word and let it soak in. Allow it to penetrate your mind and engrave itself upon your heart. Revelation is sent for your benefit, so always take as long as you need to drink in the depths of its fullness. If you do, you will find that the light of revelation is the most beautiful light on earth.

STAY FAITHFUL TO HEAR HIS VOICE IN HIS WORD

You can also discover God's voice in His Word through faithfulness. When you desire to hear the Father speak, you need to stay faithful to that which you are already committed. Keep doing what you've been doing all along, and God will be able to direct you to something different if need be. It's possible to redirect a moving ship, but it's hard to steer something that's standing still.

There's a great example of this in Acts 16:9. Paul was on his way to a certain city when God spoke to him in a dream and told him to go to Macedonia instead. Could God have directed Paul if he was standing still? Perhaps. But because Paul was busy doing what he knew to do in the Kingdom, it was easy for God to get his attention and send him somewhere else.

So here's the point: If you find direction for your life in God's Word, don't drop everything you've been doing for Jesus and wait in a corner until you are sent to some spectacular place. Just keep doing what you've been doing, and let God lead you.

For instance, has the Lord called you to preach and you're busy babysitting in the nursery? Keep on babysitting until God moves you to your first pulpit or another opportunity opens up. Stay busy with what you've been doing for Jesus and don't get ahead of God. Times and seasons often have to pass before fulfillment of a word manifests. Stay faithful to your commitments, and God will reward you in due time.

1 Corinthians 7:2-5 gives us a marvelous key to Kingdom living. Here Paul told the Corinthian church there would be occasions when they would

draw away and fast, but when those times were over, they needed to get back to the consistencies of life.

If you really want to hear from God, you've got to discipline yourself to stay faithful to everyday Christian living. It is not practical to run off to a motel and be alone for six months while you hear from God. That would be great, but if you're a wife and mom, the kids will starve, and your husband will run out of socks in just a few days! You have to learn to listen right in the midst of everyday life.

If you will be diligent to do what you have been doing, right down to going to work every day or folding the clothes when they come out of the dryer, God will find you wherever you are, and He will get His message across to you. Your heavenly Father knows where you live, and knows the ins and outs of your everyday life. This is simple, but so very important: You need not exit the world altogether to hear God's voice.

Having said that, I need to qualify this point a little. Even though you do not need to be physically separated to hear the voice of God, you do need to be spiritually and mentally separated because you cannot do two things at once, at least not effectively.

Imagine a water skier holding the rope behind a speeding boat. That rope is his lifeline. As long as he grips onto it, he will go wherever the boat goes, but if he lets go, he will fall and be left stranded in the lake.

The skier is having a good time, doing tricks, jumping the wake and waving at people passing by. He's having a ball when suddenly, along comes another boat, and a friend holds out an apple pie for the skier. It's his mama's apple pie, and he absolutely loves it. So, what's the skier to do?

If he lets go of the rope, he knows the boat will go on without him, and the fun will be over. He'll sink, and the apple pie will get a good soaking right along with him. He's in a tight spot, but he has a brilliant idea, or so he thinks. He will simply hold onto the rope with one hand and balance the pie with the other. It might be brilliant, if it wasn't so impossible to accomplish!

If you've ever water skied, you know how this story will end. The man and the apple pie will both be under water very soon, because his attention will be divided. He won't be able to ski and eat pie at the same time, at least not for very long. The first unexpected wave will knock him down, and poof! There goes mama's pie!

Likewise, you cannot focus your attention on the Word of God and listen to the local news at the same time. You can't look at God's words of faith and listen to the enemy's words of doubt simultaneously. You can't be immersed in the world system and be diligently seeking God's voice at the same time.

When the opportunity arises to seek, study and meditate the Word, it's time to shut the TV off, lay the evening newspaper aside, or let the dishes soak for 15 more minutes. It's time to concentrate on seeking God's voice.

Though you live in the world, Jesus said you need not be of it (see John 15:19;17:14-16). You need to give God your undivided attention at some point in your hectic day in order to hear His voice in the Word. You can live your everyday life, but you need to search your heart and make sure your attention is not divided between God and the world system.

I'm not talking about carving out huge chunks of time. Just 15 to 30 minutes will do. As long as you are faithful in little, God will reward you with much. Give the Lord your complete attention for some portion of every day, and I guarantee you will hear God's voice in His Word, and you will be changed.

REFOCUS

There will be times when you discover things about yourself which may surprise you when you seek God's voice in His Word. You may find you are living less holy than you thought you were.

When you make this discovery, you can know for sure something has distracted you. You've let the world or circumstances draw you away, and you have allowed your attention to wander. If not corrected, soon you will become blind to the things God once inscribed upon your heart.

I'm sure you've heard of cataracts. A cataract is a clouding of the lens, which is the part of the eye that allows us to see clear, sharp images. Over time, dead cells accumulate inside the lens, causing it to cloud, and this makes everything appear blurred and unclear.

You can develop spiritual cataracts which are just as debilitating. Spiritual cataracts can come because they allow your attention to be divided between the Word and the world. They can also surface because of involvement in sin. The deadness of sin can accumulate over time and cause cloudy spiritual vision. Left unchecked, the deadness of iniquity will cause you to see blurry images, and you will begin to think wrong is right and right is wrong. You will become confused and lose track of where you are, because the clarity you once enjoyed is now gone, and cloudiness is all you have left.

You cannot afford spiritual blindness! You have to keep your spiritual eyesight intact by making the Word top priority in your life. Taking out spiritual cataracts will require careful removal of all of the distractions and all of the deadness of sin, making sure that you are faithful to obey the commandment to: *"Come out from among them and be ye separate"* (2 Corithians 6:17).

Again, I'm not talking about living life physically separated from the world, but I am referring to living spiritually separated and sanctified. Sanctification is simply a decision, a cutting away of the deadness of sin and a determination to live in the newness of life in Christ Jesus. You don't have to change addresses to come out from among them, but you do need to change your priorities and your attitudes.

You need to refocus and allow the voice of God to rise up out of the Word to remove the spiritual cataracts which have built up over time. When you do, the Word will penetrate your heart again, and it will act as a protective shield, warding off all attempts of the enemy to distract you from your future course. Your heart will become impenetrable and molded for a life of victory. The grace and love of God you rediscover in God's Word will make you live right, and sin will be an option no more. Once again, you will have a heart that is clean and devoted to the Lord; all because you obeyed and set yourself apart unto Him.

STAY CLEAN AND REFRESHED

Of course, this leads us to something else to think about. There's only so much space in your heart, so once you've cleaned the slate, you need to keep it that way.

Here's what I mean. You wouldn't leave a love note to your spouse on some old scrap of paper that's filled with other writing, would you? No. You'd find a clean, empty piece of paper and write in big letters so your spouse wouldn't miss it. There's nothing easier to miss than an important note in the middle of a laundry list of other junk. In the same way, God's not going to write over the top of other things or write in between the world's lines and leave your heart in such a mess that you can't read it, because that would be wasting His time.

You need to erase the world's writings from your heart so God will have a clean, prepared place to write His Word. Then, the things that are spoken and written by God will give you focus. They will act like blinders on a race horse. You won't be able to see what's going on to the right or to the left, so they won't be a distraction or a hindrance to you anymore.

The words written on your heart by God will form the guidelines by which you live. They will order your steps of integrity and cause you to walk blamelessly before the Lord. You will never desire to go back to the world again, and your only focus will be to hear, *"Well done, thou good and faithful servant"* (Matthew 25:21).

When a word of the Lord is inscribed on your pure heart, you won't have to work to make a lifeless confession of faith, because what God inscribes will be life-filled, and it will flow from your mouth like air from your lungs. You don't have to think when you breathe; neither will you have to think to speak words of faith. They will bubble up from inside and become a normal part of your vocabulary. No longer will they be words of faith that require your focused attention; they'll just be words of faith which come easily and naturally.

God told Habakkuk: *"Write the vision, and make it plain upon tables, that he may run that readeth it"* (Habakkuk 2:2). When God speaks to you, there is not only a word spoken for a moment in time, but there is an engraving of that word upon your heart which empowers you to run the race that is set before you for all time.

Life is a race, a series of sprints, and then long, long marathons. Sometimes you will seem to be moving full steam ahead, but then will come days when you have to back down to a slow, steady pace. During each season of your walk with God, you will need the stamina and strength of the engraving of God's Word upon your heart to sustain you.

As time goes by, you will need to put more and more of the Word in so you can be refreshed, just as the marathon runner is revitalized by a bottle of water or a piece of fruit. No man can make it to the end of a long race on the fuel he puts in his body at the beginning; he must continue to refuel all along the way. You will, too.

It is necessary to seek God daily, and allow Him to speak to you through the Word as often as you need it. In the long race called life, you will never be able to sustain yourself from infrequent refueling, or be infused with enough strength to get by from just one engraving, but you will need a lifetime of this to keep you going to the finish line.

I challenge you to do as the marathon runner does. He never stops, and he never slows down, but as he travels the path set before him he will regularly reach out and grab for refreshment, even as he continues going forward. Reach for your own daily refreshment in the Word, so that you can finish your course and win your race in due season.

TIME WILL TELL

It may surprise you, but you can actually discover God's voice in His Word through the passage of time. Let me prove it.

Jesus says in Mark 4:26-29: *"So is the kingdom of God, as if a man should cast seed into the ground; And should sleep, and rise night and day, and the seed should spring and grow up, he knoweth not how. For the earth bringeth forth fruit of herself; first the blade, then the ear, after that the full corn in the ear. But when the fruit is brought forth, immediately he putteth in the sickle, because the harvest is come."*

The Kingdom of God is all about seedtime and harvest. It's all about sleeping and rising, day after day, and waiting for a manifestation of that which you desire. It's no different when you want to hear the voice of God.

When God speaks to you, He may speak in part and expect you to be wise enough to wait for the fullness of what He has to say. You have to be patient while God is speaking. If He gives you only a small portion of the revelation at a time, be still and recognize you're not ready for the whole thing yet. If you get the first part right, then God will give you phase two.

The problem is, too many Christians don't realize God is giving them direction in part, so they take off with only a portion of what they need to succeed. What they end up with is a half-baked idea that nobody wants to hear about. You wouldn't operate this way in the kitchen, trying to bake a pie with only half of a recipe, for instance, would you?

Hardly. If you did, the final result would most likely taste like cardboard, because the first ingredients listed in a recipe are usually the staple ones such as flour and salt, not the items that make it taste delicious, like sugar and berries. If you're smart you will wait until God gives you the whole recipe, including all the mixing and baking instructions, before you run off to bake

45

your life-purpose pie.

I had to face my own impatience as a young man called to the ministry. My church was very small in the first stages, and I begged God to use me more. The trouble was, I wasn't ready for more. My wife Phyllis told me so one day. She said, "Honey, God will give you what you can handle." This did not sit well with me at first because I only had a few people in my church, and I thought I was ready for many more. But, much to my dismay, she was exactly right.

In due season, when I was finally ready, God opened the doors and filled our little church, then a bigger one, then another and another and another until today, we have more people in our church than reside in our town. Was it worth the patience and the waiting? Absolutely! What God did for me, He will do for you as He equips and prepares you.

The Lord loves you more than He loves your call or ministry, so if He gives you "here a little and there a little" when it comes to your life's call, He is doing it because of His great concern for your well-being. God spoke to me years ago and said, "Son, I will never jeopardize your salvation to win the world." This was life-changing for me because at that time I was praying, "Send me! Send me! Send me!" God knew I wasn't ready to go yet, so He made me see that He would rather wait until I was, than send me too soon and watch me fail.

We see a perfect example of this concept in the life of the apostle Paul. We read Paul's own words in Galatians 1:15-16, which says: *"But when it pleased God, who separated me from my mother's womb, and called me by his grace, to reveal his Son in me, that I might preach him among the heathen; immediately I conferred not with flesh and blood."*

Paul was called from the day he was confronted by Jesus on the road to Damascus, but it wasn't until much later he received his marching orders and was sent forth with Barnabas to preach to the Gentiles. Paul had a portion of his call revealed early in his Christian walk, but he had to wait for the fullness of it to manifest before he could actually do what God had called and equipped him to do (see Acts 9:10-19).

When God speaks to you in part, hold onto it as Paul did, and watch over it like a precious gift. Protect, pray over, and nurture it, but don't be in a hurry to launch out. Wait for God's completing direction. Remember, the Lord is not in the process of just speaking to you; He is in the process of developing and changing you unto the fullness of the measure of the stature of Christ (see Ephesians 4:8-16). Your personal salvation and well-being are more important to Him than anything else in your life.

When you are searching God's Word for His voice, especially regarding life-changing decisions, do not become impatient, because this will draw you into a pit where you will fulfill your own purpose, and you will ultimately perish by the sword of the enemy. I'd much rather wait than die. I would much rather spend a lifetime getting the first line and the first precept right, than spend my life wishing and waiting for the second line and precept while doing nothing for Jesus.

Allow God to reveal His voice through His Word and then lead you to fulfill all He has called you to be—one step at a time. Every race is won just that way—one step at a time. Every mountain is conquered, you guessed it—one step at a time.

Be patient, diligent and faithful. In His perfect timing, God will speak through His Word and give you a completing word that will direct you to a lifetime of victory.

CHAPTER 3

DREAMS AND VISIONS

"I had a dream once that my sister and I were on the side of a hill looking at a pond. The sun was out, but there were little mounds of snow all around. (This was exactly what the weather had been like just the day before.)

"As we watched, we saw three children swimming in the pond, and we also saw several alligators in the water nearby. My sister and I rushed to warn the children of the danger they were in.

"While we stood at the edge of the pond, my sister touched the water to feel the temperature. Suddenly, an alligator tore through the surface of the water and bit down on her little finger. He clamped his jaw and dragged her under the water.

"I could hear her cries, but I stood frozen, feeling totally helpless, not knowing what to do. That's when I woke up in an awful panic."

What would you do if you had this dream? Would you check for alligators in your bathtub? Would you swear you'd never swim in a pond again? Would you call your sister and warn her, or would you just let it go and assume it didn't really mean anything?

The answer is crucial, because while you don't know it yet, the life of someone very dear to you hangs in the balance. God is trying to warn her by speaking to you in a dream, but will His message get through to its intended destination, or will you drop the ball and let your loved one die?

Thankfully, the woman who related this dream to me did exactly what she should have done. She prayed about what she had seen in the dream, and then did what she believed God wanted her to do. She called her sister and warned her that an attack of Satan was coming. She also told her that God said if she would submerge herself in the living water, the Word of God, although the attack would come, she would be okay.

Her sister humbly admitted she had not been in the Word much lately and

49

promised she would get back into it, and it was a good thing she did. Not long after that call, she discovered she had breast cancer. In her case it was more than just a diagnosis, it was a death sentence because the cancer was so advanced, the doctors weren't giving her much hope.

Thank God she had listened to the warning in her sister's dream and had restored her faith by getting back in the Word before it was too late. Soon after the diagnosis she came to church with her sister, and I was privileged to pray for her. Praise God, I am happy to say that after the touch of Jesus, this woman no longer has cancer!

Can you see the great mercy of the Lord here? Though the dream was a warning, it was based on God's love and mercy. This God-given dream unveiled the plan of the enemy, but it did not stop there. It also gave direction for a way of escape through faith born of the Word. Because this woman gave heed to the voice of God heard in the dream, she was delivered from the snare of the enemy and withdrawn from his purpose, just as the Lord said she would be in Job 33:14-18: *"For God speaketh once, yea twice, yet man perceiveth it not. In a dream, in a vision of the night, when deep sleep falleth upon men, in slumberings upon the bed; Then he openeth the ears of men, and sealeth their instruction, that he may withdraw man from his purpose, and hide pride from man. He keepeth back his soul from the pit, and his life from perishing by the sword."*

There will be times when God will attempt to speak to you, but you will not be able to hear. It may be because of the busyness of the day, or as a result of imbedded unbelief in a particular area, or even because of the intensity of the battles you are facing. Whatever the case, there will be occasions when God will have to abandon His attempts to reach you in your waking hours and will resort to speaking to you in a dream.

A dream is simply a night vision, and a vision is a day dream, or an open-eyed dream, so the concepts we will discover in this chapter pertain to both dreams and visions.

These are supernatural languages through which God delivers important messages. As a Christian, God wants you to understand these messages, so it is imperative for you to learn to interpret the language of the Spirit on your own.

Here's what I mean. When I travel to a foreign country, it's normal for me to find an interpreter to help me in my crusade, but if I decided to move to that country permanently, I would learn the language myself so I could move about freely without an interpreter tagging along everywhere I went. I would become fluent in the language so that I could operate in the nation without being dependent on someone else to tell me what everyone around me was saying. I would want to understand what people said to me personally.

It is just as necessary for you to learn the language of the Spirit, the language of dreams and visions, so you can hear and understand from Heaven for yourself. You don't want to have to rely on another person to tell you what God says all of the time, so you've got to learn to hear and interpret His language on your own.

In Acts 9:10, we find this account: *"And there was a certain disciple at Damascus, named Ananias; and to him said the Lord in a vision, Ananias. And he said, Behold, I am here, Lord."*

Notice that God spoke to Ananias in a vision—through what this man saw. Dreams and visions are just as much the voice of God as His written Word. They are equally of His Spirit, and in these last days, they are for all believers (see Acts 2:16-18). This is why discerning your dreams is so important.

WAS THAT GOD?

Dreams and visions are very personal things. They can be life-changing, or even life-saving, as we saw in our opening story, so it's vital for you to first learn to recognize the source of every dream.

In general, you will find three basic sources for all dreams and visions. They can come from God, from your own imagination, or from the influence of the devil. Those sent by God are essential messages which are delivered to help you succeed and overcome obstacles in life. Those which come from your own imagination will likely be misleading and send you off in the wrong direction, and those from the devil will surely bring trouble if you give them any recognition.

To discern the difference between these three types of dreams, you have to weigh out the purposes and the benefits. A dream sent by the devil has only one purpose, and that is to deceive you. It may appear as a nightmare which produces fear, or it may come in some less recognizable form, but in the end, there will be no good purpose and no benefit at all.

God-given dreams have a definite purpose and clearly defined benefits. They show you something very significant about your life or your future, and they provide a solution for problems you may be facing. The trouble is, sometimes dreams that come from your imagination can mimic God-given dreams, so you have to learn to tell the difference.

We've all had a "pizza dream" or two. You know the kind I'm talking about. For whatever reason you ate supper late, and then you spent the night tossing, turning and dreaming wild and crazy things. That's what I call a pizza dream. It probably has nothing to do with God and everything to do with your eating habits.

Others of us have vivid imaginations that may not be satisfied during the day, and we will find ourselves dreaming strange dreams all night long. These may seem like they carry a message, but after careful discernment you will find they are simply your mind's way of letting off steam. These should be tossed aside and ignored.

But then there are the dreams which come from Heaven, the voice of God sent to intervene when you do not hear during the day. These can be very vivid and long lasting, or they can be nothing more than a few moments, a single picture in time. Whatever form a Heaven-sent dream may take, it is designed to deliver a message God feels so strongly about, He is willing to interrupt your sleep to get His point across.

One of the easiest ways to tell the difference between a God-given dream and one that is birthed by your own imagination is to ask yourself what you remember about the dream. When you woke up, did you immediately recall every detail, or did the dream begin to fade as your brain awoke to a new day? God-given dreams tend to stick with you, right down to the last detail, while dreams born of your own mind tend to quickly disappear from memory.

God-given dreams will be defined by a distinctive purpose, and there will always be a directive you should heed. God-sent dreams may warn, lead and guide, provide wisdom, reveal the future, give a life-changing idea, or even show you something that will help someone else.

Remember, according to Job 33:17-18, a God-sent dream is designed to protect you from your own humanistic purpose and to keep you from destruction. It has been sent with a divine purpose, and it is your responsibility to discover that purpose. By first discerning the source of every dream, you eliminate the influence of the two kinds that are *not* from God so you can focus on the dreams that *are* Heaven-sent.

You will probably make some mistakes when you are first trying to discern the source of your dreams. Don't panic, but simply ask for help from someone who knows more than you do. We all have to start somewhere, so there is no shame in the learning process. As you grow, you will begin to distinguish God-given dreams from all others quickly, which can be crucial when you are dealing with a warning dream.

In my opinion, a warning dream is probably the most important kind of dream, simply because action must be taken to avoid the reason for the warning. When a God-given dream contains a caution about something, be careful to avoid the fear that will surely accompany it.

You have to remember that the purpose of a warning dream is to help you deliver yourself from the hand of the enemy, so when God gives you such a dream, He will also provide you with a way of escape. I encourage you to listen to His warning and do whatever it takes to protect yourself and prepare for the things that lie ahead.

Warning dreams are sent to give you a heads-up about the future, not to make you fearful. They are God's way of saying, "Look out!" If you will discover the reason for the danger sign and act accordingly, you will be saved from whatever the devil meant for evil and find yourself in the middle of what God means for your good.

LED BY A VISION

Dreams and visions are often used by God to lead, guide and direct us. We see a great example in the tenth chapter of Acts. Here, Peter had a supernatural encounter with God while he was praying on the roof of his house and anticipating a good meal. While he prayed, Peter found himself in a trance where God gave him an open vision of all the creatures of the world. Then God spoke to him and said: *"Rise, Peter; kill and eat"* (Acts 10:13).

Peter responded by saying something like this: "No way! I have never eaten that unclean stuff, and I never will!" Peter rejected what God was trying to say at first because for a moment, he did not remember that visions can be the voice of God.

Not long before this experience, Peter had preached about dreams and visions in Acts 2:17, where he said: *"And it shall come to pass in the last days, saith God, I will pour out of my Spirit upon all flesh: and your sons and your daughters shall prophesy, and your young men shall see visions, and your old men shall dream dreams."*

Although Peter preached this, he evidently did not fully understand it. Thankfully, God persisted in giving Peter the same vision three times until it finally sunk in. Peter did as he was told, and he was changed forever because of his obedience. In fact, you and I have directly benefitted from Peter's vision, because the preaching of the gospel to the gentile world began as a result of this very vision.

When God gives you a dream or a vision, He is trying to say something you need to hear, just as He did to Peter. You may not recognize the message immediately, just as Peter was confused initially, and it may not be unveiled to your senses or your mind right away, but you can stand fast knowing there is a message in it which will lead, guide, direct or warn you of things to come.

Dreams and visions are signs of the last days outpouring of the Holy Spirit. I believe you and I have been born into this generation for a purpose. We have been designated to live in this time frame by God's choice, and I believe the Lord will speak to us now more than ever before in dreams and visions which will empower us to live supernaturally, no matter what the world and those around us may face.

Christians should not have to wait for things to happen to them, rather they should be fully aware of what lies ahead because they are listening intently for God's voice in every situation. The open Heaven is not just for messages of love and grace, but it is also for messages which sometimes shake us to the core and make us wake up to see the danger we're in. Don't despise correction if it comes in a dream, but praise God for it, and for the fact that He loves you enough to find a way to make you hear Him.

I encourage you to receive God-given dreams and visions as the Father's loving voice, and allow Him to transform you, even as you allow the Word of God to change you. Let them redirect your steps when necessary and stir you to action when the time demands it. Above all else, allow God's voice to do what He sent it to do.

INTERPRETATION PLEASE

Once God has given you a dream or a vision with a defined purpose, it's up to you to take the next step of faith, which is to believe and press in for the interpretation. An interpretation is simply an unveiling of what has been said through the dream or the vision. It is an untwisting of the many symbolic things you saw and heard.

God-given dreams are often full of symbolism, so hearing His voice will only come when the interpretation is received and the symbolic message is revealed. These symbol-filled dreams cannot be taken at face value, but must be interpreted according to the Word of God.

For instance, you might dream you were racing down a roadway, and you ran into a rushing stream that you could not cross. Suddenly, out of nowhere an eagle drops out of the sky and carries you across the violent waters to safety. This would be a neat dream, but I wouldn't advise you to begin watching the sky for an eagle every time you take a road trip!

God is not telling you you're supposed to start an eagle transport business either, but He may be letting you know some rough waters are ahead, and that the only way over them is to wait upon the Lord so He can renew your strength and empower you to mount up with the wings of eagles to soar over your problem (Isaiah 40:31). You won't know for sure what the dream means until God tells you.

In Acts 2:1-4, you can read how the Holy Spirit came upon men and women on the Day of Pentecost and gave them a supernatural utterance that required interpretation to understand. Dreams and visions are similar in nature. They are God-given, supernatural utterances which take picture form, and they also need to be interpreted.

God said something on the Day of Pentecost. In like manner He is saying something every time He gives you a dream or a vision. There is a message to be received and an interpretation to be discovered. Until you interpret the dream or vision, it will be a supernatural event, but it will not change your life. Only with the interpretation of the Lord can you take what you saw and run with it.

WAITING FOR THE INTERPRETATION

It takes time to learn how to interpret the dreams that come to you, because dreams can be funny things. No two are exactly alike. Some may be long and drawn out, and filled with symbolism. Others will be short, a single picture in time, as it were, but both will need to be interpreted according to the Bible.

There are many ways to seek God's interpretation for your dream or vision. The first is found in I Corinthians 14:13 which says: *"Wherefore let him that speaketh in an unknown tongue pray that he may interpret."*

When a dream comes that you believe is from God, the first thing you should do is pray and ask Him to show you what He meant. Ask the Lord to reveal the hidden direction and unveil the enlightenment you need to move ahead.

Simply ask God to give you the interpretation just as He gave you the dream. Ask Him to speak to you, and then be very careful to listen and weigh what you hear according to God's Word. The Bible will always be your final answer. If your dream is from the Lord, it will direct you to the Word, and it will agree with the Word.

Someone may ask, "Why does God speak in symbols? Why doesn't He just say what He means?" I don't know, honestly. Why did God make birds with wings and dogs with paws?

I don't know why, but what I do know is that when God speaks to us in a language we cannot understand, He is not attempting to confuse us, but He is trying to bring us to a place which will cause us to turn, trust and have faith in Him. Don't try to figure it out with your mind, just draw near to God, and He will draw near to you with the answer (see James 4:8).

Interpretation of your dream or vision may arrive immediately, or it may come over time through a season of prayer and fasting. When we fast, we take ourselves away from the world and shut our senses down so that we can hear God more clearly. Just as when we take time to fast and meditate the Word to hear His voice in a particular scripture, we can also fast and meditate on a dream or vision to hear what the Lord has to say.

God told Joshua to meditate on His Word by day and by night that he may prosper and have good success (see Joshua 1:8). It's no different with a dream or a vision. If God speaks to you in a dream, then you can spend time meditating on it just as you do the written Word, and God will prosper you with the interpretation so that you will have good success.

Don't just think about the dream for a moment and then toss it away, but keep it before you until the interpretation is made clear and you understand it. Do not give up quickly, but take as much time as you need to consider the interpretation before you run off and make major changes in your life.

Remember, God's Word is a seed. If the farmer who planted the apple seeds had been impatient, he would have left the orchard before it was fully grown and missed his blessing. Give God time to show you the fullness of what He's trying to say to you, and don't be in a hurry.

God does not intend to hide anything from you, but He is trying to break down the barriers between the two of you so that He can speak to you face to face. In time, you will understand the fullness of His message, and you will live victoriously as a result.

A MESSAGE MISUNDERSTOOD

There are moments when things do not turn out quite the way God intended for them to. When this happens, it is not the time for placing blame, but for learning from mistakes and resolving to do better next time. I relate the following story, as told by a member of our church, to underscore this point.

"I was pregnant, after years of trying, and my husband and I were elated. In fact, we were beyond elated and nearing ecstatic. We were pricing all of the baby items we would need, and planning the nursery. We play-argued over baby names, and talked endlessly about what the future would hold. Our dream was finally coming to pass.

"One night, I had a very vivid dream. In it, I was driving a car down a highway near my parent's home. I was driving fast, and as I approached the intersection where I would need to turn, I had to slow down for a big red truck that was stopped ahead of me.

"I was anxious to get going, so I inched up as close to the back of the truck as I could to see why it was stopped in such an odd place. I got too close and accidentally tapped the rear bumper of the truck. I immediately backed up, making sure I had not caused any damage.

"As I looked toward the front of the truck, I saw the driver in the rearview mirror. He was obviously angry with me for bumping into his vehicle, and I could see him cursing. He slammed the truck into reverse and acted as if he was going to back right into me.

"Realizing I was in danger, I sped around him, turned the corner, and started high-tailing it to my mom and dad's house. Fear gripped my heart when I looked in the mirror and saw that the truck was barreling after me on the road. I floored it, and raced to what I believed would be safety.

"When I reached my parent's home, I ran into the house, but no one was there. It was just me and my little Pomeranian dog, who had suddenly appeared in my left arm. I held her close and ran to look out the window to see if the truck was still coming. Sure enough, the truck and its angry driver were on the way.

"When the truck pulled alongside the house, the driver slammed on the

57

brakes and jumped out of the truck, still cursing as he came toward the front door. I hid and listened, completely overwhelmed with fear. He pounded on the door, yelling at the top of his lungs, and tried to kick in the door.

"I ran to the back of the house and locked myself in the bathroom, hoping against hope that he would simply go away. But he didn't. He came around to the back door and smashed his way into the house.

"Now, I was in a full-out panic. I held the dog tighter and tighter under my arm and tried to think of what to do. I could hear him roaming the house, trying to find me, and I felt totally helpless.

"After what seemed like eternity, I heard him pause outside the bathroom door, and I knew my cover had been blown. I looked around the room for a weapon, and finding none, I took a deep breath, kicked the door open, hoping for the element of surprise, and grabbed a pair of scissors lying on a shelf outside the bathroom door.

"My surprise tactic worked. I held the scissors to his face, yelling and screaming at the top of my lungs, and I pushed him out the back door. I quickly locked the house down, grabbed a cordless phone just in case, and prepared to wait for him to leave.

"I heard the truck start up, and I thought it was all over. I crept to the window to see, but what I saw sent shivers of terror up and down my spine. Instead of leaving, he was backing the truck up for another approach. He was going to ram the house, with me in it!

"I squeezed the dog tightly and ran out the back door. I ran as fast as I could away from the house and the crazed truck driver, and then I saw something I did not expect. I saw a lady from our church standing in the field behind the house. She was on a prayer team with me, but she was extremely skinny, not at all like herself.

"I called out to her as I ran past, dialing 911 as I went. I asked her to stay with me, but I did not stop to chat. I just kept running at full speed right on past her.

"I looked back just in time to see the truck slam into the house. The impact was so great, the truck came straight through and was headed right for me. The house blew up, and my childhood home was immediately engulfed in flames.

"I looked into the driver's eyes for one split second, and I saw that he realized I was calling the police. Much to my relief, he stopped the truck and reversed his course. As he drove off, still cursing loudly, I suddenly realized that my little dog was gone. I had lost track of her in the chaos, and I had no idea what had happened to her. That was when I woke up."

What a dream! What do you think God was trying to say? The lady who shared this story with me thought she knew exactly what the dream was about. In fact, she confidently rebuked what she thought was a storm about to come upon her. She was convinced it was going to be an emotional battle which was a result of something in her past and relating to her childhood home, but instead something much more tragic was on the way. Having thought she had dealt with the dream, unfortunately she simply moved on and tried to put it out of her mind.

A different kind of trouble came very unexpectedly, and this woman had a miscarriage a short time later. Still, she did not immediately associate what had happened to her with the dream. Later, as time passed and the healing began, she realized how many mistakes she had made in the interpretation process.

She had shared the dream with a friend early on, but did not fully comprehend what her friend had suggested the dream might mean. With the wisdom of her friend in hindsight, and the careful consideration the passage of time brings, she came to understand the real meaning, and what it was that God had been trying to tell her.

She learned that the truck driver represented the devil, and the red truck represented his anger. She had bumped into him by using her faith to get pregnant, and he was not happy about it. The house represented her life, and the dog represented her baby. This may seem strange until you understand that she had a habit of calling the family dog, "baby girl."

The lady in the field represented her prayer life, which was extremely "skinny," if you remember from the dream. In fact, that was what the whole dream was trying to warn her about, that she needed to "fatten up" her prayer time because the devil was coming after her to steal, kill and destroy.

Now, this story is not about placing blame, but I do tell it as a warning. We must never, ever take a dream which depicts destruction lightly. Even if you think you know what it means, as this woman did, ask someone to help you verify what you believe. It may be that you are too close to the situation to see clearly, or you are too busy to take enough time to get the correct interpretation, as this woman freely admitted once all was said and done.

Don't let tragedy come to your house after God tries to warn you in a dream, but take it very seriously, and make sure you know what you are dealing with before you put it to rest.

JOSEPH AND THE DREAMS

If ever there was a man who understood enduring tragedy, it was Joseph. Let me tell you his story, an account of great loss and of greater redemption, all because of the correct interpretation of a dream.

Joseph found himself living in a strange land even while he was a citizen of another. In a sense, he was an ambassador for the Kingdom of God. Joseph had gone ahead of his brethren into a nation which would one day provide life-sustaining food for them, and where they would live until it was time for God to bring them out. Joseph did not go ahead of his brothers willingly, but was sold into slavery and forced to go where he did not want to. Thankfully, God was protecting him in his time of trouble.

The Lord's hand of favor first took Joseph to Potiphar's house where he ruled over all Potiphar had. Joseph's unplanned journey into the land of Egypt seemed to be bearing fruit.

But then came trouble, a test of Joseph's commitment. Potiphar's wife made a lying accusation against him, and he landed in prison for something he had not done. For a time, things looked pretty bleak for God's man.

One day, in the midst of the darkness of his prison, Joseph noticed two of his cellmates, Pharaoh's butler and baker, looking very distressed. He asked them what the trouble was, and they explained how they both had dreams on the very same night and were upset because they did not understand their meaning.

Look what Joseph said to these men: *"...Do not interpretations belong to God? Tell me them, I pray you"* (Genesis 40:8).

The men eagerly told Joseph what they had witnessed in their dreams. Their stories were vivid and full of symbolism, but Joseph easily interpreted the dreams for each man, and he specifically asked the butler to remember him for his kindness.

Well, just as Joseph said in his interpretations, three days later the butler was reinstated to his prior position, but the baker was executed for his crime. Much time passed, two years in fact, until one day a guard came to Joseph and told him he was being called before Pharaoh. At last, Joseph had been remembered.

Pharaoh had dreamed a dream that no one could interpret; not the magicians or the wisest men in Egypt. In the midst of this crisis, the butler remembered Joseph's ability to interpret, and he told Pharaoh that there was a man who could help him discover the meaning of his puzzling dream.

Pharaoh sent for Joseph, who came before him, interpreted the dream and told him exactly what it meant. Pharaoh was so grateful, he immediately released Joseph from prison, and then to everyone's amazement, he elevated him to second in command in the whole nation (Genesis chapters 40 and 41).

Because Joseph sought God's interpretation, he prospered and had good success, just as the Bible said. You can find this too if you will diligently seek God's interpretation for every God-given dream in your life.

I encourage you to study the story of Joseph, especially his interpretation of these three dreams. It will be a great lesson for you, showing how God uses certain symbols to get His message across.

EVERYTHING IN BALANCE

A dream or a vision is God speaking first, that you may speak later. Habakkuk 2:2 says: *"And the Lord answered me, and said, Write the vision, and make it plain upon tables, that he may run that readeth it."* You cannot declare or write a vision until you have first seen and understood it.

When God gives you a dream or a vision, you have to decide whether to hold it or release it. The dream or vision comes from God, but it is your responsibility to do with it what you will. Will you wait for God's interpretation and prosper, or will you lay it aside and miss the meaning?

You've got to pray and ask God to give you the interpretation, and then be patient and look to the Word for answers. It's very important to use common sense and godly wisdom when handling dreams and visions.

Once you believe you have the interpretation, especially if it is a warning dream, check it with someone who has more experience than you do. And then let time tell the tale. Sometimes waiting a day or two before you jump in a lake, just because you saw it in a dream, will give you time to consider and judge it before you act. Remember, dreams and visions will never override God's written Word. They may direct you or warn of things to come, but they will never lead you outside the confines of God's established order in the Word.

Once you have the interpretation and have checked it thoroughly, now it's time to act upon it. If you don't like what you saw, do something about it. Rebuke the storm, if you saw one coming. Prepare yourself and get into the Word so that your faith will be ready to overcome whatever the enemy tries to send your way.

If you think the dream was a warning, stop doing whatever made God caution you. If you're in sin, ask for forgiveness and get out! If you're going the wrong way, turn around! Don't just let a dream or vision lie dormant. God sent you the message for a reason, so act on what He showed you and do something by faith.

The worst thing you could do is let a dream or vision slip away without acting on it. The Bible tells us that he who is faithful in little will be faithful in much. You must take action on even the smallest dreams so you will be found faithful for more when the time comes for more. Don't ever despise the day of small beginnings (see Zechariah 4:10).

Handling dreams and visions will be a lifetime responsibility. With experience, however, you will become better able to tell when a dream is from God, and what it is that He is trying to say. While you are learning, do what the Bible says and try the spirits to see if they are of God (see 1 John 4:1). Practice makes perfect, even in spiritual matters.

A dream or a vision may be just the beginning of a message from the Lord. Isaiah 28:10 says: *"For precept must be upon precept, precept upon precept; line upon line, line upon line; here a little, and there a little."*

We are not always ready to hear an entire message from God, so He may have to give us a small portion at a time so we can digest it slowly and understand. Sometimes we can handle the prime rib, while at other times all we can do is sip a little milk. God knows exactly how much to give us at any given moment.

He will only lead you as far as He knows you are ready to go. If that's five minutes from now, then He'll show you five minutes from now. If that's one month from now, then He'll show you one month from now. Sometimes, a God-given dream may give you direction for a moment in time, but not necessarily for a lifetime. A dream may warn you of things to come in the near future, but not reveal your entire future.

If the Lord gives you a message in part, the first portion of what He has to say to you, take time to ask for the interpretation, and then act upon it. Once you have been faithful with the first part, God will give you the remainder of the message, so that together, you will have the whole.

And remember this: God never speaks to you unless He has change in mind. When He communicates through a dream or a vision, He is sowing seeds in you for fruitfulness in life. Everything in the Kingdom of God works by the seed principle. God sows, time passes, the seed grows into a plant, then blossoms and bears fruit. It's the same with dreams and visions.

A God-given dream may empower you with a seed of illumination so that over time, as the seed matures, you will come to know what to do in a given situation. God's words, whether written or in dreams and visions, always bear fruit and always produce light to show you the way (see Psalm 119:105).

Don't ever let the passage of time deter you from seeking the interpretation of a dream, or from waiting for the rest of a message. With God, a thousand years is as a day and a day is as a thousand years. God's time is not necessarily your time, so exercise patience and let Him give you what you need, when you need it.

KEEPING A RECORD

When God gives you a dream, the details are significant, so be sure to write them down, including everything you saw and heard. This will give you a place to record a written version of the interpretation when you discover it, and this documentation will help you when you encounter future dreams and visions.

My wife Phyllis has been given many, many dreams by God, and she has developed her ability to receive the interpretation of her dreams over the years. She always tells people to write down everything they saw and heard in a dream right away. Don't let the day pass, but grab a piece of paper as soon as you wake up and jot down every detail you can remember.

What did you see? Who was in the dream? Who was the main player in the dream, you, or someone else? Where were you? What colors did you see? What words or sounds did you hear? You never know what tiny detail may be the key to unlocking the mystery of a dream.

Once you write it all down, pray and ask God for the interpretation. Let it soak in over time, and then write the interpretation down too. This way, you'll begin to accumulate a written record of your dreams, and you will soon be able to recognize patterns and what certain symbols, colors and numbers mean.

God is very orderly. He does not just throw out a bunch of symbolic pictures without purpose, but He lays before you an intricate puzzle, that when unraveled will reveal a message from His heart to yours. God counts the hairs on your head, friend, so keeping detailed records is a very godly thing to do.

So many Christians live by every wind that blows and fail to keep track of anything in the Kingdom. This is not God's way. I encourage you to keep track of what God says to you in your dreams and visions, so you will not only be better able to interpret the next dream or vision, but so you can check on yourself and make sure you are living up to the message God gave you as time goes by.

The Lord has prepared a path for your future good. If the signposts which direct you down that path take the form of dreams and visions, they ought to drive you closer to the Word, closer to God's divine presence, and closer to your destiny by faith. This is how you will know a dream or a vision is from Heaven.

CHAPTER 4

SIGNS AND WONDERS

Moses stood very still, looking down at the rod in his hand. The God of all creation had just asked him a question, and he was not at all sure what to make of it. "What is that in your hand?" asked God. It seemed simple enough, and he should have had no trouble answering, but the problem was, the voice that had asked the question was coming out of a bush which was on fire, but was not burning up. The whole thing was a little unnerving.

Moses quietly answered, "A rod." In other words, "It's a stick, God. Can't you see that for yourself?" Of course God could see the stick, but He wanted to know if Moses could see the piece of wood for what it was about to become, a sign that would convince Pharaoh to let the children of Israel go.

He looked back at the bush after he had answered, not quite sure what to expect next. "Cast it on the ground!" was the Lord's booming response. And so, Moses tossed the rod on the ground, and right before his very eyes it became a serpent.

Moses reacted just like I would have and bailed as fast as he could. I don't need a word of the Lord to tell me what to do when a snake comes around. I know it's time to go, and so did Moses.

Then God did something even stranger. He told Moses to pick up the snake by the tail. This is where Moses proved what he was made of because he actually did what God commanded. In spite of his fear, he came back to the snake, reached down obediently and grabbed that thing by the tail. Lo and behold, it turned right back into a stick! Now, God had Moses' attention!

The Lord told Moses this was to be the sign that he would use to prove to Pharaoh that He had sent him. Just to make sure Moses was well equipped, God told him to put his hand in his robe at chest level. Moses did, and when he removed his hand it was leprous. I don't know what Moses was thinking at this moment, but my guess is that he was not as impressed by this sign. But then God told Him to put it back in again, and when he withdrew his hand this time, it was back to normal. So, Moses had two signs in his arsenal for his appointment with Pharaoh.

We all know this story, but I want you to consider how the signs God used to speak to Moses impacted him. First, a bush spontaneously combusted, but it did not burn up. That's pretty good for starters. It definitely got Moses looking in the right direction.

Then Moses saw an image in the bush, the angel of the Lord to be precise. As he looked on this great sight and wondered, God spoke to him out of the bush. I'd have been pretty impressed by now, but God did not stop there. He went on to give Moses two more unmistakable signs, things that he could recreate in his future meeting with Pharaoh. Only then did God send Moses on his way (see Exodus chapters 3 and 4).

Why do you think God did all this? Was He just bored, or was He trying to make a point which was larger than mere words could convey?

There are times when simply hearing a still, small voice will not do. Suppose God had just spoken to Moses in his own heart while he tended sheep on the back side of the desert. Do you think Moses would have actually done what God told him to do? Would he have ventured to go and make demands on Pharaoh based on an inner feeling or a thought? Probably not. This situation called for unmistakable evidence, and so that is what God delivered.

THE PURPOSE OF SIGNS AND WONDERS

Signs and wonders do what mere words cannot. They convince the unconvincible. Sometimes people are hard-headed, and a dramatic sign is the only way to get their attention. At other times, the situation is so urgent, as in the case of Moses and the deliverance of Israel, that God will choose to use signs and wonders to bolster faith.

God has spoken through signs and wonders from the very beginning of creation, and when He speaks this way, He always has something crucial to say.

When God formed the heavens and the earth through signs and wonders brought forth by His Word, He declared that He is the Creator of all things, the Master and Lord of the universe. When He later brought the great flood and destroyed all but eight people and two of each creature on earth, He declared He is the Rewarder of righteousness and a destroyer of sin.

When God gave a son to Abraham and Sarah after Sarah's time had passed, He declared that He is the Provider, the One who resurrects deadness and keeps His covenant promises. When God opened the Rea Sea and allowed the children of Israel to pass through, He declared He is the Deliverer, the One who sets captives free.

When God delivered David from the hand of Saul, He declared He is the One who puts men upon thrones and the One who brings them down. When God sent judgment upon Israel and allowed them to be taken into captivity, but then delivered them from their enemies after a season, He declared that He is the God who rewards obedience and keeps His covenant to a thousand generations.

When God delivered Daniel from the mouth of the lion, He revealed He is the Protector of the innocent, and the One who serves justice upon unrighteous men. When He saved Shadrach, Meshach and Adebnego from the fiery furnace without so much as the scent of smoke, God declared that He is the Sanctifier, the One who sets us apart from the world.

When God brought forth Jesus, born of a virgin in the city of David, He declared that He is the Redeemer and Savior of all who call upon His name. And when God reached down from Heaven and raised Jesus from the dead, He declared He is the Resurrection and the Life for all who believe.

The greatest sign and wonder of all will be when God sends Jesus back to earth in great power and glory to rule and reign forever. In so doing, God will declare once and for all that Jesus is Lord! God has been speaking to us through signs and wonders from day one, and He will continue to speak through them until the end of time.

SIGNS AND WONDERS TODAY

God uses signs and wonders to speak to us today, just as He uses dreams and visions. These are supernatural occurrences that change the atmosphere, and abnormal activities through which God speaks and in which a message is hidden. Because they are supernatural in nature, most often they require interpretation to understand what God is saying.

Acts 2:18-19, speaking of the last days in which we live, says: "*And on my servants and on my handmaidens I will pour out in those days of my Spirit;*

and they shall prophesy: And I will shew wonders in heaven above, and signs in the earth beneath; blood, and fire, and vapour of smoke."

In every sign and wonder, there is an important message. When God does something unusual in the heavens or on the earth, He's not just showing off; He is trying to say something. When He speaks through signs and wonders, He is most often speaking to the church, but there will be times when He will speak to the world, too.

God is in relationship with us, and He desires more than anything that we hear His voice. When He sends a sign or a wonder to give us a message, He intends for us to understand the message so that we can benefit from it.

In 1 Corinthians 14:6-11 we read: *"Now, brethren, if I come unto you speaking with tongues, what shall I profit you, except I shall speak to you either by revelation, or by knowledge, or by prophesying, or by doctrine? And even things without life giving sound, whether pipe or harp, except they give a distinction in the sounds, how shall it be known what is piped or harped? For if the trumpet give an uncertain sound, who shall prepare himself to the battle? So likewise ye, except ye utter by the tongue words easy to be understood, how shall it be known what is spoken? For ye shall speak into the air. There are, it may be, so many kinds of voices in the world, and none of them is without signification. Therefore if I know not the meaning of the voice, I shall be unto him that speaketh a barbarian, and he that speaketh shall be a barbarian unto me. "*

God is not a barbarian to us nor are we to Him. We are to understand one another completely; therefore, when the Father speaks in an unusual way, He fully intends for us to receive the understanding of the sign or the wonder so that we can go forward with the message and prosper in that which has been said.

INTERPRETING SIGNS AND WONDERS

Signs and wonders are like dreams and visions in many ways. They contain spiritual messages which need to be interpreted according to God's Word, just as dreams and visions do. The same methods of seeking God's interpretation we learned about in chapter three will apply to interpreting signs and wonders.

As with dreams and visions, you should take time to consider each sign and wonder to discern first of all where it came from. If it is determined to have been sent by God, you should immediately ask Him for the interpretation, and for understanding of what He is trying to say to you.

You should begin to seek the interpretation from the written Word of God first because, as always, a Heaven-sent message will lead you to the Word, and it will agree with scripture. It is essential to remember that signs and wonders will never add to God's Word. They will confirm the Word and draw you to it, but they will never establish anything new.

Paul says it this way: *"But though we, or an angel from heaven, preach any other gospel unto you than that which we have preached unto you, let him be accursed"* (Galatians 1:8). Don't ever fall into the trap of believing a lying sign or wonder that goes against established, sound doctrine.

You can meditate on what you saw and heard, as you learned to do with dreams and visions. You can also spend time in prayer and fasting to find the answer. Again, make sure you write down what you saw or heard, and make a note of the interpretation so you will have a written record for the future.

Always check the interpretation you think you heard with someone more experienced than you. Use common sense and move slowly when responding to a supernatural occurrence. As we saw with Peter in the last chapter, God won't be upset if you question things at first; He'll just keep sending the message until you get it right.

And don't be surprised if the sign or wonder is only a part of what God wants you to know. There may be times when the Lord will reveal a portion of a message in a sign or a wonder, and then He will give you the remainder in due season.

Remember what we read in Isaiah 28:10 from the previous chapter: *"For precept must be upon precept, precept upon precept; line upon line, line upon line; here a little, and there a little."*

A sign or a wonder may be just the beginning of a message, and the interpretation may be only a glimpse of what God needs you to see. With patience, seeking, fasting and prayer, you can rest assured you will receive the remainder of the message in full, and you will be blessed. God truly desires for you to hear and understand His voice completely so that every message can bring His intended purpose to pass. This is why He speaks in so many amazing ways.

SIGNS, WONDERS AND JESUS

In Luke 7:18-23, Jesus verified who He was to the disciples of John the Baptist by declaring the signs and wonders He had done in His ministry. John had seen the Spirit of God descend upon Jesus like a dove, and he had heard the audible voice of God announce who Jesus was, yet in a pinch, he struggled with what he knew.

Jesus could have pointed to the many things He had preached, or to the many times God had spoken about Him in prophecy, but instead He chose to encourage John by pointing to the signs and wonders of His ministry to confirm His identity. To John, they had a voice like no other. They declared in resounding tones who Jesus was, the Christ, the Son of the living God.

The healings did not just say, "God is good." To John they said, "The Lord has come!" To John, the miracles Jesus did were the verification of what had been declared at His baptism at the river Jordan. They confirmed the word God had spoken, and they gave John great comfort in knowing that Jesus was who He said He was. John could rest assured that he had not spent his life in vain. The Messiah had come, and he had been His witness.

In John 12:37-41, we see how Jesus used signs and wonders to declare God's will and His identity to the multitudes: *"But though he had done so many miracles before them, yet they believed not on him: That the saying of Esaias the prophet might be fulfilled, which he spake, Lord, who hath believed our report? And to whom hath the arm of the Lord been revealed? Therefore they could not believe, because that Esaias said again, He hath blinded their eyes, and hardened their heart; that they should not see with their eyes, nor understand with their heart, and be converted, and I should heal them. These things said Esaias, when he saw his glory, and spake of him."*

When we read this passage, we realize the miracles Jesus did were meant to reveal who He was, yet the people could not see this. God was speaking to them with amazing signs and glorious wonders, but because their hearts were hardened, they could not understand.

In Matthew 16:2-4, Jesus said: *"…When it is evening, ye say, It will be fair weather: for the sky is red. And in the morning, It will be foul weather to day: for the sky is red and lowring. O ye hypocrites, ye can discern the face of the sky; but can ye not discern the signs of the times? A wicked and adulterous generation seeketh after a sign; and there shall no sign be given unto it, but the sign of the prophet Jonas. And he left them, and departed."*

What was the sign of Jonah? Just as Jonah had been in the belly of the whale for three days, Jesus prophesied His destiny would be to remain in the belly of the earth for three days. The sign of Jonah was a prophetic proclamation of the work of the cross.

God spoke to the world through this sign and wonder of Jesus' death, burial and resurrection to declare that redemption had come, sin had been defeated, Satan had been overthrown, and the gateway of Heaven had been opened so that everyone could come to God by faith in Jesus.

This was a sign meant for the entire world, a clear indication of God's intent for mankind, and it spoke volumes to lost humanity. No longer was man at his own mercy, but he could now embrace the mercy of God. No longer was man condemned to live by the works of the law, but because of the resurrection of Jesus he could live by the faith of his Father in Heaven. Most important, this sign brought closure and fulfillment to every Old Testament sign which had pointed to the coming Savior. Jesus had come with a New Covenant, and the time of the old was no more.

THE SIGN OF HEALING

There are some things God will unveil through signs and wonders that are more subtle, but will still draw the attention of men back to God. He uses these to speak to us and to the world today in order to declare who Jesus is.

For instance, have you ever been healed? Then God spoke to you through a sign and a wonder to reveal that He is the Healer. The sign of healing spoke something to you no words ever could. Your personal healing is a sign and a testimony of who God is to you, Jehovah Rapha, the God who heals you. And now, being convinced by the sign of healing, you can proclaim the love of God to a lost and dying world through your testimony, and the sign given to you will become a light to those around you.

Both now and forever you will proclaim that God is a healing God. You will never be convinced otherwise because you heard in a way no man can deny that He is the Healer. Verified by His Word, you are convinced that the Lord heals today just as He did so long ago. This is what signs and wonders do—they confirm the Word of God (see Mark 16:20).

I saw this truth in action in 2007 as I ministered in a church in Brazil. A young man of about 30 stood before me one evening, and he had a problem

71

that was not visible, but which had impacted his life in a devastating way. This young man's right leg was shorter than his left leg. The reason you could not tell was because he wore special shoes with a lift in them that enabled him to walk fairly normally. The young man told the interpreter that the leg was short as the result of a birth defect.

As he stood there in front of thousands of people, many of them pastors and other ministers from all over Europe and South America, I had no idea that he had come that night at the request of a friend, but in his heart he did not believe in miracles. In fact, he thought what we were doing was some sort of side show or a hoax. He had no idea what was about to encompass him on this great, appointed night.

When I learned what his problem was, I told him to sit down on a chair on the front row. A television camera hovered over us and zoomed in so that the entire crowd could see what God was going to do. My assistant removed the man's shoes, and I heard a few gasps as it became obvious just what it was going to take to solve the problem. This young man's right leg was at least four inches shorter than his left leg.

I'm sure there were some in the room who thought this was going to be an impossible task because they did not know my God. They did not know the God of signs and wonders yet, but they were about to meet Him. What men thought was impossible, God knew was clearly possible.

I began to pray in the name of Jesus. The interpreter repeated every word I said, and the crowd leaned forward in anticipation. I rebuked the devil and commanded the leg to grow out, and guess what happened. Nothing. I prayed again, and I laid hands on him from hip to toe, and still nothing. To the skeptic, I'm sure it looked like we were defeated. I only thank God that I did not know about this young man's doubt at the time.

Not one to back down from a fight, I decided right then and there I was going to stick with this until his leg grew out, one way or another. And so I prayed louder, and louder. Soon the crowd began to pray with me. And then, the leg moved about a half an inch. A shout went up, and the battle was on! No one in the room was going to give up now that they had seen a glimpse of the miraculous. I kept on praying, using the name of Jesus, and the crowd got louder and louder, praying in their native tongue. We just kept going, while the young man sat there with his head bowed, weeping.

Finally, after three of the longest minutes of my life, the right leg stretched out to the exact length of the left leg. A shout of victory went up! This sign broke through the door of the miraculous, and the miracle conference was wide open. From that moment on, the miracles flowed freely. Deaf ears were opened. More and more legs grew out. People jumped out of wheelchairs, and canes went flying! All because of one sign that revealed the open Heaven to the people.

As the crowd was praising with a loud voice for the sign they had just witnessed, and the glory of the Lord filled the room, I took the young man on stage with me and asked him to walk the length of the platform so that the entire audience could see what a wonderful job the Lord had done. This young man walked normally for the first time since birth without the aid of his special shoes. He was weeping uncontrollably now, hands raised in gratitude and worship.

It did not seem it could get any better, but it did, because the Lord began to speak to the people through me. I prophesied and told them that this miracle was a prophetic sign that was a symbol of what God had in store for them. They were going to begin to walk in newness of life, with a steadfast assurance like never before. They would walk as this young man was walking, in the realm of the miraculous.

In that moment, sheer pandemonium broke loose. Every person in that packed auditorium was leaping, praising and shouting unto God with the voice of triumph. This sign and wonder spoke words that my preaching could not convey. They needed no translator, for the Lord Himself shouted from the platform, "I am the Lord that Healeth thee! I am the Alpha and the Omega, the First and the Last! I was the Creator in the beginning, and I shall be the Creator for all time! I Am that I Am! Whatever you need, I Am!"

THE SIGN OF BLESSING

Maybe the sign you experienced was a blessing which came as the result of an offering sown into the Kingdom. Your miracle harvest speaks loudly that God is Jehovah Jireh, your provider, the One who blesses and makes a way when there seems to be no way.

Others may scoff and say, "God does not care", but you know He loves you and cares for your every need because you saw the sign of divine provision come to pass in your life.

Now, you are a voice of witness, declaring who God is and how much He cares. You have experienced a sign and a wonder, and you can never be shaken when it comes to believing in God's willingness to provide. You know what you know because the Lord confirmed His Word with a sign following.

A lady in our church told me this story that will show you just what I mean:

"My husband and I lost the first home we ever bought together to foreclosure due to a job loss a few years ago. It was devastating and impacted us on many levels. It was toughest on my husband because it made him feel as if he was somehow failing our family and was not the man God had called him to be. Although none of that was true, this is what he felt.

"One night in church, a man was preaching in Pastor Doseck's stead while he was in another country. As this person took up the offering he said, 'God told me to tell you to pray and ask Him what He would like you to give, so that's what we're going to do. Just bow your heads and pray. I'm not going to say anymore.'

"I bowed my head and asked God what I should give, knowing full well I did not have a dime on me. Immediately I heard God tell me to give $150.00. I said a silent, 'Okay, Lord', and lifted my head back up, not having a clue where it was going to come from. I knew we did not have that much money on hand because we were still in the recovery mode from some financial challenges that had come along after we lost the house. Money in our home was still an elusive thing!

"On the way home I prayed and asked God where the $150.00 would come from. Instantly I knew that I should sell some coins my dad had given me years earlier, and that I would receive the $150.00 from that sale. I also knew this offering was special, and that God intended to multiply it back so that we could buy another house. It was a lot for me to swallow because our credit score was very low, but I thanked God for being faithful and went on home.

"The next night I told my husband, and I could see the skepticism written all over his face, but he helped me list the coins on an online auction anyway, and we proceeded to wait for the auction to end in one week.

"I had a ball coming home every night and asking how many bids we had received that day, which of course was always zero. I would just smile and say, 'It's going to happen. You just wait and see. They're going to sell for $150.00, and we're going to sow it, and then God is going to get us in a house of our own again.' My husband would look at me like I was crazy, but I was not moved.

"Finally, the end of the auction came, and the total profit from all of the coins amounted to $152.26. We actually made an extra $2.26! We wrote out the check and joyfully placed it in the offering bucket on Sunday.

"Within two weeks, our credit score jumped up out of the gutter and back into normal territory, all by itself. What was impossible with men was very possible with God! The look on my husband's face as he came out of our office and told me what he had just discovered was priceless.

"To make a long story short, we got pre-approved for a loan, found our dream home and bought it. Though we paid less than the value of the home, another miracle in itself, by God's grace we achieved something we never could have on our own. Only the Lord could do something so wonderful!"

I think you can see what the sign of the sold coins was all about. It was about restoring the faith of a man who had been beaten down by circumstances. When God took something of no value and miraculously assigned value to it, right down to the last dollar, this man heard God say, "I've got your back, son. Don't worry about it. This one's on Me."

This is what we all want to hear, that God is on our side. Of course we know He is, but a wonder coming to pass right before our eyes is always a nice way to hear the truth one more time. Faith can be strengthened this way, and the purposes of God restored.

Signs and wonders are amazing things, glimpses of the majesty and glory of our Heavenly Father. They can move us to walk in a level of faith we never thought possible, knowing that the God who did one sign or wonder, is surely capable and willing to do more.

No matter what you have been delivered from, whether it be sickness, lack, depression or addiction, you have been on the receiving end of God's declaration that He is the Deliverer, the One who sets captives free. Your testimony can now bear witness to the Word of God which will set others free, too.

You will be a sign. Think of that. Think of the impact your testimony will have on all those who have watched you struggle. Your new-found freedom will shout louder than any words you could speak, and will hopefully lead them to seek their own freedom.

In reality, every promise fulfilled in your life is a sign and a wonder to the world, a proclamation that Jesus is alive and well, that He loves them and is waiting to hear them call upon His name so they, too, may be saved. This is exactly why we should never be afraid to tell our stories whenever we can, because we never know who God may want to speak to through the sign He did for us.

SIGNS ARE WITNESSES

"Jesus loves you!" is a message every Christian is eager to deliver to the world, but when the world is in such a mess, how can we assure them what we say is true? This is where signs and wonders are most helpful.

If you say, "Jesus loves you" to a sick man, what better way to confirm that word than with a sign of healing following. When you lay hands on someone and God confirms His Word with the sign of healing, you have just proven your words beyond any doubt. Words are only philosophy until they are backed up with power.

Jesus always preached and healed, and so did His disciples. Shouldn't we, today's disciples, preach and heal, too? God's Son sent us into all the world to preach the gospel just as He did, with signs and wonders following, confirming His Word.

The same is true of every promise in scripture. It is one thing for you to preach and share it with others, but until that Word is fulfilled by signs and wonders, it will remain lifeless and bear no fruit. If God is willing to confirm His Word when we preach it just as He did when Jesus preached, we should expect signs and wonders to follow us just as they followed Him.

One of my long-time staff members, a man named Craig, related this testimony to me years ago, and I have been waiting for the right place and time to share it. That place and time is now. Here's the sign that became a great witness in Craig's life, as he related it to me in his own words:

"Several years ago I was driving down the road, going about 50 mph, when I suddenly lost control of the vehicle, slid off the road and down an embankment, and slammed into a tree. While sliding down the five foot drop-off, I thought to myself that I should probably jump out of the van. I opened the door and tried to get out, but because I had my seat belt on, I could not get unfastened in time to jump clear.

"When the van hit the tree I was still hanging out the door, so there was nothing between me and the tree at impact. I was thrown back into the steering wheel, which broke instantly along with the steering column, and my head slammed into the windshield.

"As I bounced back with an incredible force, my seat broke off, and the top of the van came crashing down on top of me, slicing my head open. I was knocked unconscious, and to any passerby, I probably looked dead.

"When I woke up, (and I have no idea how much later), I could not move any part of my body. Blood was running down my face and into my eyes. I squinted to see, and saw only broken glass surrounding me.

"I immediately thought about my family, and I asked God if I was going to die. To my surprise, He answered, "It's up to you." To this day I do not know if His voice was audible or not, but I do know that it calmed me down right away. His answer assured me that He would love me just as much if I chose to let go right then and move on into glory, as He would if I chose to fight to live. I also knew that if I decided to live, I absolutely could.

"I had spent the last several months praying fervently, anywhere from two to three hours every morning, so when God said it was up to me whether to live or die, I knew if I was going to live, I would have to use His Word to birth a miracle in my body. I was confident that I was full of the Word because of the intensity of my prayer times, and so after I made my decision to live, I let the Word begin to bubble out of me. I felt as if there was no room for fear in me, only faith.

"The first verse that came to mind was, 'I shall live and not die, and declare the works of the Lord' (Psalm 118:17). I began to prophesy to my body that the life of God was in me, and that I was healed by the stripes of Jesus, along with a bunch of other scriptures (see 1 Peter 2:24). It wasn't long before I could move my fingers, and then my hands. Soon, I was able to pull myself out of the van, and I began to limp around a little.

"Of all the places in the world, I had landed in a grave yard. I looked from end to end, and realizing no one there could help me, I raised my hands and began to praise God as I limped back and forth between the grave stones. My head continued to bleed, and I felt I had several broken bones in my body, but I was determined to keep going until somebody found me. My left hip was really messed up; it seemed to be out of place.

"Suddenly, I saw headlights coming my way, and I knew help would not be far behind. Though I probably looked like some sort of monster, bleeding and stumbling between the grave stones, I calmly asked the guy who stopped his car a few feet away from me to please call an ambulance.

"When the emergency crew arrived, one of the EMTs commented on what a miracle it was that I was alive. She said they had just come from an accident in which there was much less damage to the car, but the driver was already dead by the time they arrived.

"They strapped me to a board and placed me in the ambulance. I closed my eyes for a moment, relieved that I had made it this far, when suddenly somebody jerked my left leg up in the air without warning, and snapped my hip back into place. I struggled to lean forward, and I yelled at the EMT for handling my leg without giving me a heads-up. She assured me that no one had touched me, and that I should just calm down and lie still.

"Later that evening, two friends of mine came to the hospital to tell me that as they had approached the accident scene that night, they saw my leg go up in the air with no one touching me, and that it had twisted, and then gone back down. They were convinced it was an angel. I had to say I was too, because my hip did not have any problem by the time I reached the hospital.

"Thirty-five x-rays later, the doctors were still puzzled that they could not find any serious damage anywhere, although this did not stop a nurse from announcing to me that I would never walk out of the hospital.

"Upon hearing her gloomy prediction, some believers in the room began to pray for me, and the head surgeon finished the prayer for them on his way in the room. He proceeded to stitch up my head, and then he told me to rise up and walk in the name of Jesus.

"They sent me home banged up and barely able to move, but alive. I continued to pray with my prayer partners every morning. They would bring a ladder along, hoist me into their truck, and carry me out for prayer time.

"Recovery was slow and painful, but as the days went on I began to walk steadily, jog, and even run, much to the amazement of most of the doctors who knew of my case. I can truly say that God is good, and He watches over His Word to perform it!" (see Jeremiah 1:12).

Do you see how this miracle sign became a witness of God's goodness to so many people? Everyone from the guy who came on the accident scene, to the ambulance crew, to the hospital staff, to Craig's family and friends—they all heard God say loud and clear, "I am God your healer!" (see Exodus 15:26).

This testimony, beyond any reason, proved the Lord could do anything. No longer could anyone convince Craig, or anyone who knew him, that God was not a healing God. His sign and wonder were markers of His glory, showing the world He is alive, and that He still cares for us today.

Mark 16:19-20 tells us: *"So then after the Lord had spoken unto them, he was received up into heaven, and sat on the right hand of God. And they went forth, and preached every where, the Lord working with them, and confirming the word with signs following. Amen."*

These signs and wonders, just like the one Craig received, were God's confirmation of His love to a lost and dying world. He said to them, as He said to Craig, "I love you. I am aware of you, and I am working for you. Now, you choose. Will you live, or will you die?" The choice is always ours to make.

We can even choose what to do with what God says. We can hear His voice in a sign or a wonder and proclaim what we hear to those around us as a witness, or we can keep it hidden and never tell anyone, allowing God's voice to simply fade away. I think we should all earnestly seek to be used by the Lord to speak words of encouragement to saints and sinners alike through signs, wonders and miracles. I don't ever think we should be silent when God touches our lives this way.

God desires to speak through signs and wonders every day of our lives, if we will allow Him access to our faith and boldly walk through when a door of opportunity presents itself. Let's give Him free access to speak as He chooses to those around us from now on.

SIGNS ARE SEEDS

Signs and wonders are an essential part of God's supernatural vocabulary. They are voices which can be seen and heard, and that make us dependent upon Him. Remember, Jesus taught us the Kingdom of God is like a man sowing a seed. The man plants the seed, then he sleeps and rises, day after day, and the plant grows up and bears fruit. The man has no idea how the process works, he just knows that it does (see Mark 4:26-28).

So it is with signs and wonders. We see and hear about them, but we do not understand completely how they operate. We only know they deliver a message that speaks to us like no other. They are wonderful, supernatural events that draw us closer to God and bring us revelation for our tomorrows.

Just as the seed planter has to exercise faith and trust the process, we also need to have the same trust when God speaks to us in signs and wonders, especially if He chooses to give us just a portion of a message. We cannot short circuit the Kingdom. We see, we hear, we ask God for the interpretation, we understand in part, and we believe God will finish the message in due season.

Signs and wonders are seeds of witness, proclaiming God's great and awesome ability, His wonderful love and mercy, His glorious power and might. They are promises of a new tomorrow, and the first-fruits of our inheritance in Christ.

May it be said of us as it was of the disciples when Jesus returned to Heaven: *"And they went forth, and preached every where, the Lord working with them, and confirming the word with signs following. Amen"* (Mark 16:20).

CHAPTER 5

HEAVEN'S MESSENGERS

Was pacing the room and praying fervently, as I had been doing for the last hour. When I reached the end of my path and turned to head the other direction, I suddenly found myself stopped dead in my tracks. I had a strange sensation that someone was in the room with me, but I could not see who, or what. I had been fasting for several days, and I had been praying in a hotel room for the last three days, so I should not have been surprised to discover I had a visitor, but I was a little unnerved by the sense of someone watching me. I paused for a moment, very interested to see who it was.

When I did not see or hear anything, I began to pace again, and I resumed praying in the Spirit. Just when I reached my turn-around point at the west end of the room, a glow appeared in the upper part of the northwest corner. It was more than a glow, to be honest. It was like a beam of light that was blazing into being. It was full of beautiful shafts of color-filled light, and it was more powerful than anything I had ever seen. Ever so slowly, a shape began to be distinguishable in the midst of the vision.

I actually squinted against the brightness of it all, and then I saw him, the most interesting angel I had ever seen. He looked like brilliant mercury, a kind of highly polished silver that was both liquid and solid at the same time. He was staring right at me, his eyes boring into mine, and I dared not say a word.

I knew enough to keep my mouth shut until the angel chose to open his. While angels are not to be worshiped, they are to be respected, for they have just come from the throne of God. They have come to help you or to deliver a very important message, so the last thing you want to do is babble on in front of them. It's best to be still and wait.

And so I waited. Finally, he spoke. I cannot tell you the message he gave me because it was too personal and very holy to me, but I can say that his words set me on a course which changed my life and ministry. Once the message was delivered, the work of the angel was done, and he left me without a word of goodbye. Angels are like that—to the point and without fanfare. They come, they speak, and then they go.

ANGELS AND THE REDEEMED

The Bible says in Hebrews 12:22: *"But ye are come unto mount Sion, and unto the city of the living God, the heavenly Jerusalem, and to an innumerable company of angels."* This verse shows us there are so many angels at God's disposal, it would be hard for us to count them all.

Angels are a very active part of the life of the redeemed. In fact, Hebrews 1:14 says of them: *"Are they not all ministering spirits, sent forth to minister for them who shall be heirs of salvation?"* Angels are sent as servants who attend to the needs of believers and who do God's will in the Kingdom.

The word angel is mentioned over 300 times in the Bible, and there are nearly 100 recorded appearances of them to human beings in scripture. Many of the references have a common phrase associated with them, and that is, "Fear not." Evidently, fear can shut down the activity of the angelic host in the life of a believer. We should not be fearful of angels, but we do need to learn and discern, just as with dreams and visions, and signs and wonders.

Scripture declares: *"For the word of God is quick, and powerful, and sharper than any twoedged sword, piercing even to the dividing asunder of soul and spirit, and of the joints and marrow, and is a discerner of the thoughts and intents of the heart. Neither is there any creature that is not manifest in his sight: but all things are naked and opened unto the eyes of him with whom we have to do"* (Hebrews 4:12-13).

I can assure you that everything we discuss in this book will be taken from the Word of God and interpreted by the Word, because it is scripture that determines what is right and wrong in any doctrine or teaching. This is especially important when it comes to understanding the work of angels. In today's spirit-hungry world, there are many false teachings concerning angels floating around, some even in the Body of Christ, so it is vital that you know the source of every teaching before you believe it.

Don't ever let a theory determine what you will believe about something in the Bible. Let God's Word interpret itself and show you what is true and what is false. If you allow yourself to look at a theory which is taught outside the confines of the Word of God, you will fall into error.

And don't rely on any other man's stories or experiences more than you rely on God's Word, either. If all I had was a story, I would not have much to offer, but because I can judge my stories by the light of the Word of God, I feel confident sharing them with you for the purpose of illustration.

Here is a rule of thumb that will help you decide what and who to trust. When you are learning something new and you hear someone relate a personal experience concerning it, ask yourself one question. Does the experience direct you to the Word of God? If so, good, but if it draws you away from the Bible and directs you to the doctrine of a mere man, you need to flee, lest you find yourself on the brink of destruction. Be very careful what you listen to and what you read about angels. Make sure you are learning from a person who stays "line upon line, precept upon precept", within the confines of God's Word.

ANGELS CLASSIFIED

It is essential to note there are two basic classifications of angels—those that are good and holy, and those that are evil and unholy.

The Bible says: *"I charge thee before God, and the Lord Jesus Christ, and the elect angels, that thou observe these things without preferring one before another, doing nothing by partiality"* (1 Timothy 5:21). This verse is referring to the elect angels, to those who are good and holy, those that do the bidding of God for you and me. These angels belong to, worship and serve God.

On the other hand, there are fallen angels who belong to, worship and serve the devil. They are those who fell with Satan in his rebellion (see Isaiah 14; Ezekiel 28).

We find the fallen angels described in Revelation 12:1-4: *"And there appeared a great wonder in heaven; a woman clothed with the sun, and the moon under her feet, and upon her head a crown of twelve stars: And she being with child cried, travailing in birth, and pained to be delivered. And there appeared another wonder in heaven; and behold a great red dragon, having seven heads and ten horns, and seven crowns upon his heads. And his tail drew the third part of the stars of heaven, and did cast them to the earth: and the dragon stood before the woman which was ready to be delivered, for to devour her child as soon as it was born."*

The red dragon is the devil, and the stars refer to the fallen angels. When the devil rebelled against God and fell, he took one-third of the created angelic host with him. This percentage sounds high, but when we look back at Hebrews 12:22, we see that even with the one-third fallen, God still has so many angels at His disposal, they cannot be numbered by man.

Jesus said: *"Thinkest thou that I cannot now pray to my Father, and he shall presently give me more than twelve legions of angels?"* (Matthew 26:53). A legion is a great multitude, so Jesus confirmed He had a large company of angels at His disposal.

The Bible never tells us God has created any new angels. Evidently, He does not need any more than He has right now. So, we can trust the fact there are plenty of good and holy angels available for any mission God needs accomplished. There is no lack in the heavenlies!

SERVANTS FOR THE SAINTS

Let's go back to Hebrews 1:14 which tells us: *"Are they not all ministering spirits, sent forth to minister for them who shall be heirs of salvation?"*

We see here that all angels do not stay in Heaven. While some are designated to remain there for specific purposes, most are sent to earth to help believers when needed. We have our citizenship in Heaven, but we are not residents yet. When we get to Heaven we won't need angelic help anymore, but right now we do.

As Christians, you and I make sacrifices and daily take up our cross. We live a crucified life, which is a life of the supernatural, so it takes a touch of Heaven to live by faith as we do. Angels are one way God delivers His supernatural touch and His strength.

Do you remember reading when Jesus was in the garden of Gethsemane? The intensity of His battle was beyond description, and His sweat became as drops of blood. When Jesus was at His weakest moment and His need was the greatest, God sent an angel to strengthen Him and see Him through to the cross (see Luke 22:43). The angel that was sent ministered to Jesus in a way no man could.

As the psalmist writes: *"The angel of the Lord encampeth round about them that fear him, and delivereth them"* (Psalm 34:7). If you are one who fears and honors God, then you, too, are eligible for angelic service when needed and directed by God, just as Jesus was. This angelic help will come when you need it, just as it did for Jesus, not necessarily when you desire it.

In Psalm 91:11 we read: *"For he shall give his angels charge over thee, to keep thee in all thy ways."* The angels are ready to heed God's call and intervene to help you in your time of trouble. They are sent from Heaven to minister, attend to and serve you as you carry out Kingdom purposes.

God's good and holy angels are here for your benefit. If you will learn about them from the only trust-worthy source, the Bible, you will have a fuller understanding, and you may open the door for your own visitation.

MESSENGERS FROM HEAVEN

We see that angels can strengthen and help, but can they still speak? The word angel in the Hebrew language, the original language of the Old Testament, comes from a root word that means "messenger." In Greek, the original language of the New Testament, angel also comes from a root word that means "messenger".

God never changes, and neither have angels. What angels were in the Old Covenant, they remain in the New. They are messengers of God sent from Heaven to do His bidding, those who have been dispatched by God and given the opportunity to be agents between Heaven and earth. Angels spoke in the Old Testament, in the New Testament, and they still speak today.

Now there were a few times in the Bible when God called a man an angel. When He did, He was simply referring to the man's calling as one designated to deliver His message, one called to speak to a certain group of people for Him. We see this in Revelation 2:1 where Jesus said: *"Unto the angel of the church of Ephesus write; These things saith he that holdeth the seven stars in his right hand, who walketh in the midst of the seven golden candlesticks."*

In this case, the word angel refers to the pastor at the church at Ephesus, because he was the one designated to deliver God's Word to that particular church. There was not an angel ruling over the church at Ephesus. We know this because angels are never given governmental rule or control over man, but are only sent to help man.

Angels are messengers, plain and simple. God gives them a word to deliver, and they are obedient to do it. Angels must *speak* to deliver their messages, so when they do, what they say will be a direct quote from God. Angels cannot add to or take away from the message given them lest they be found disobedient.

85

You can rest assured that God's holy angels are obedient all the time, because they fear God and do not regard man. They act as loyal servants. Would that we would all obey so well.

THE GOVERNMENT OF ANGELS

In Matthew 28:18, we read: *"And Jesus came and spake unto them, saying, All power is given unto me in heaven and in earth."* All power would include power over angels, both good and evil. So we see the order, rule and structure of angels is subject to Jesus (see Colossians 1:16; Ephesians 1:21-22). Angels are attendants sent to help us, but we do not rule them at our discretion. The eternal God-head governs the angels of Heaven and also maintains authority over the fallen angels.

Angels are servants of God, not our personal slaves. We should not request or demand anything of an angel directly, and we should never ask God for an encounter with one of them. Even more, we definitely should never, ever worship angels. Paul made this perfectly clear when he said: *"Let no man beguile you of your reward in a voluntary humility and worshipping of angels, intruding into those things which he hath not seen, vainly puffed up by his fleshly mind, And not holding the Head, from which all the body by joints and bands having nourishment ministered, and knit together, increaseth with the increase of God"* (Colossians 2:18-19).

The nature of man is to worship that which is more glorious and splendorous than he. We see accounts in the Bible where men tried to worship the angels who delivered messages to them. Every time, the angels demanded they not worship them, but worship God only.

No matter how amazing an angelic visitation may seem, you cannot give angels the worship due to God alone. To bow before an angel would mean you would have to negate the lordship of Jesus in your life. You never, ever want to do such an abominable thing.

Do not let any man or any story cause you to believe you should ever worship angels, and never seek to rule over them. Let God be God. He is completely capable of ruling the angelic hosts on your behalf.

ANGELS AND THE BIRTH OF JESUS

The Bible account of the birth of Jesus contains some of the most well-known stories of angels heralding messages to men and women. Though you have heard these stories before, let me share them once more.

It was a dark night, and a young woman named Mary stood perfectly still in the middle of her room. There was someone standing directly behind her, she was sure of it, but she was too afraid to look and see who it was. Finally, he spoke: *"Hail, thou that art highly favoured, the Lord is with thee: blessed art thou among women."*

Mary turned slowly to see who had spoken those strange words, and there he stood, the angel Gabriel. As Mary struggled to make sense of what she was seeing and hearing, Gabriel spoke again: *"Fear not, Mary: for thou hast found favour with God. And, behold, thou shalt conceive in thy womb, and bring forth a son, and shalt call his name Jesus. He shall be great, and shall be called the Son of the Highest: and the Lord God shall give unto him the throne of his father David: And he shall reign over the house of Jacob for ever; and of his kingdom there shall be no end."*

So, there it was. The message to end all messages. How was a young woman supposed to react to this whole thing? She had been minding her own business, not bothering anyone, when this angel comes in the room and tells her she is going to have a baby. Hello! Weren't angels supposed to bring good news? Mary could not contain herself, and so she asked, *"How shall this be, seeing I know not a man?"*

Gabriel calmly answered her: *"The Holy Ghost shall come upon thee, and the power of the Highest shall overshadow thee: therefore also that holy thing which shall be born of thee shall be called the Son of God."* Then he went on to tell Mary about her cousin Elizabeth's pregnancy, almost as if to give her something tangible to hold onto after the encounter was over and more questions began to arise in her mind.

Mary lowered her head and considered the entire message from beginning to end. It was shocking, there was no denying that. A virgin, still planning her wedding, was going to give birth to a son, and not just any son, but a great son who would reign over the house of Jacob forever. All of this was supposed to happen supernaturally, without so much as knowing a man. This was not going to be easy to explain to Joseph, or to her mom and dad, or to anyone she knew, for that matter. Who had ever heard of such a thing?

Gabriel stood waiting patiently for Mary to respond, and finally, she knew what she had to do. Only when she could muster true assurance, she raised her head and said, *"Behold the handmaid of the Lord; be it unto me according to thy word"* (see Luke 1:26-38).

This is undoubtedly the most amazing angelic story ever told. Not only would it affect Mary and her entire household, but it would impact all of humanity for all time.

Notice Gabriel said, *"Fear not."* As we noted before, fear will derail angelic activity in our lives. So, Gabriel told Mary to have faith, and then he told her the most incredible thing ever said to a human being, that she, a virgin, would conceive and give birth to a child.

Even when Mary questioned how it would happen since she had never had sex with a man, Gabriel was not moved, but answered her question and told her exactly what she needed to know. Mary discerned that Gabriel was sent by God and accepted what he said without doubt, even though his message was completely illogical from a human standpoint. Mary believed the angel because Mary believed God.

Joseph, Mary's fiancé, had his own encounter with an angel soon after Mary's visitation, though in this instance the angel appeared in a dream. At the time, Joseph was considering whether he should put Mary away after she told him she was pregnant. Joseph was a righteous man, but he loved Mary very much, and so this whole situation put him in a very tough spot.

Here's what the angel said to him: *"Joseph, thou son of David, fear not to take unto thee Mary thy wife: for that which is conceived in her is of the Holy Ghost. And she shall bring forth a son, and thou shalt call his name Jesus: for he shall save his people from their sins."*

Now it was Joseph's turn to discern what he had just heard. Was Mary telling the truth? Had an angel come and given her a divine appointment with God, one that would change their lives forever? Could they really be responsible for raising this special child together?

Joseph had a big decision to make, and he had to make it fast. People would begin to talk soon, and he had not only his family to think about, but Mary's, and that of the son she was carrying. Joseph pondered, and I imagine he prayed fervently. At last, he discerned that the angelic dream was indeed from God, and he decided to stay with Mary (see Matthew 1:18-21).

Nine months later, a multitude of angels appeared to a group of shepherds in the fields near Bethlehem on the night that Jesus was born. In Luke 2:8-12, we read that first the angel of the Lord appeared and told them about the birth of Jesus, including this well-known statement: *"For unto you is born this day in the city of David a Saviour, which is Christ the Lord."*

88

Then verses 13-14 record: *"And suddenly there was with the angel a multitude of the heavenly host praising God, and saying, Glory to God in the highest, and on earth peace, good will toward men."*

In this case, the shepherds saw one angel who gave them the most exciting message they had ever heard, and then, if this wasn't enough, a multitude of angels were made visible in the sky above them praising God. Angels are by nature worshipers, so it is no surprise to have found them praising God in the heavenlies when such a momentous event was taking place. The angelic beings were busy doing what they do best, but it was not until God opened the shepherds' eyes and ears that they were able to see and hear what was going on around them.

These three stories are amazing, but they are not as uncommon as you may think. Angels are always busy in the heavenlies and working all around us, but it is only at God's discretion that you and I will be allowed to see and hear them. This is why the more we know and understand about angels, the more ready we will be, should God ever choose to let us peek behind the curtain and catch a glimpse of angelic activity. We are not all Mary or Joseph or the shepherds in the fields, but we all can see and hear what God allows us to.

ENTERTAINING ANGELS

We read in Hebrews 13:2: *"Be not forgetful to entertain strangers: for thereby some have entertained angels unawares."* Here we find something unusual. Angels can, at God's discretion, take upon themselves the appearance of men and physical matter.

This is why Hebrews 13:1 tells us: *"Let brotherly love continue."* You never know when the homeless guy you pass on the way to the mall might be an angel. These heavenly beings don't always show up in all their splendor and glory, riding in limousines and wearing diamonds on their hands.

Jesus didn't arrive this way, so we shouldn't be alarmed if an angel's appearance is not what we expect it to be. We always need to be ready, because we never know when we may encounter an angel without our knowledge.

Remember, this is only at God's discretion. Angels cannot appear in human form on their own. They do not have the right or the power, but they must be given access by God into the natural world. Then and only then will you see and hear them with your natural senses.

Abraham had this kind of experience in Genesis 18:1-16. He was sitting at the door of his tent one day when he saw what he thought were three men approaching. Abraham recognized they were not ordinary men, so he ran to greet them, and as was the custom he bowed down and offered to wash their feet. This was a sign that Abraham accepted their visit and wanted to make them feel at home.

Abraham asked them to sit down under a tree, and then he prepared a meal. He served them food, and they ate it. Their form was such that they could act like a man in every way, although they were only in this form temporarily.

We know from further study that two of the men were angels and one was an Old Testament appearance of Jesus. They came with a message for Abraham and Sarah, telling them Sarah would bear a son even though she was well past child-bearing age.

Later in Genesis 19, the two angels went on to Sodom and Gomorrah and spent time with Lot before destruction fell. In this account, it is made clear they were indeed angels, but their human form was so real, the ungodly men of that city wanted to have sex with them.

Both Abraham and Lot took good care of these heavenly beings. We, too, should be hospitable to strangers just in case, some day, God sends an angel to check up on us.

This may never occur, yet it may—and you be unaware because you are uninformed. So, get educated! Find out what God says about angels, and be ready.

PETER AND THE ANGEL

Acts 12:6-10 records the story of Peter's escape from prison: *"And when Herod would have brought him forth, the same night Peter was sleeping between two soldiers, bound with two chains: and the keepers before the door kept the prison. And, behold, the angel of the Lord came upon him, and a light shined in the prison: and he smote Peter on the side, and raised him up, saying, Arise up quickly. And his chains fell off from his hands. And the angel said unto him, Gird thyself, and bind on thy sandals. And so he did. And he saith unto him, Cast thy garment about thee, and follow me. And he went out, and followed him; and wist not that it was true which was done by the angel;*

but thought he saw a vision. When they were past the first and the second ward, they came unto the iron gate that leadeth unto the city; which opened to them of his own accord: and they went out, and passed on through one street; and forthwith the angel departed from him."

This angel came with a purpose and a message. The purpose was to set Peter free from prison. The message was simple: "Follow me." Since we know that angels did not change from the Old Testament to the New, we also understand they have not changed from Peter's day until now. Angels are still active, still being sent with a purpose for our good, and they still speak the messages of God.

In this case, the angel must have taken on human form because Peter felt pain in his natural body when the angel hit him on his side. Which brings me to an interesting question. This prison was tightly closed and Peter was behind several sets of doors and gates, so how did the angel get beyond the metal doors and gates if he was in a human form?

He was able to do this because angels are not subject to human matter even when they appear in human form. What's amazing in this story is that while in the presence of the angel, Peter was also not limited to human capabilities and was able to exit the prison right alongside the angel.

We see from the scripture that the first and second wards in this prison had gates and doors that Peter and the angel passed through supernaturally. Then when they came to the outer gate, it opened all by itself and they walked right out of the compound.

Angelic visitations can be full of supernatural activities like this one, or they can be simple conversations where an angel delivers his message without fanfare. Whatever the case, it is essential to remember that angels only do what God has allowed and instructed them to do.

IN SPIRIT AND TRUTH

Please understand that Abraham's story and also Peter's are not necessarily the norm. Most often, when angels speak or appear, they will do so as spiritual beings.

You are spirit, soul and body. You have five natural senses, and you also have certain spiritual senses. You can hear in the spirit realm, and you can see there, both at God's discretion.

Unless he has taken on human form, when an angel speaks to you or is allowed to be seen, you are no longer hearing and seeing with your physical senses, but with your spiritual senses. It may seem strange to say such a thing, but it is absolutely true.

Let me prove it. In Luke 16:19-31, Jesus related the story of Lazarus and the rich man. Notice Jesus never called this account a parable, which is a made-up story used to teach a principle. In this case, Jesus said, "There *was* a certain beggar named Lazarus." This story is real and illustrates my point perfectly.

Lazarus, a righteous beggar, died and went to Abraham's bosom. Soon after, an ungodly rich man died and went to hell. In hell, the rich man looked up and saw Lazarus with Abraham and asked that Lazarus be sent to cool his tongue with water. Abraham answered back that there was a great gulf fixed between them and neither could cross over to the other.

Notice, the rich man saw, heard, talked and felt discomfort while he was in hell. Where was his body? In the grave. So how did he see, hear, talk and feel? He did it in the spirit. This proves we have spiritual bodies which resemble our natural bodies. The rich man clearly recognized Lazarus when he asked for his help. Evidently Lazarus looked very similar to the way the rich man remembered him when he sat begging outside his door.

The point I am making is that according to this story, we can see, hear, communicate and feel in the spirit realm. It also reveals that we can think and reason. So we know we operate in the spirit realm in much the same way we do in the natural, only without the limitations of our natural bodies.

Most often, when someone sees an angel and hears him speak, that person is seeing and hearing with his spiritual senses, generally by the discerning of spirits, which we will learn about later. In the end, the message an angel delivers is what matters most, not how we see or hear him. It makes little difference if the angel appears in bodily form or as a spirit, because his message will be of a spiritual nature, just as the Word of God is spirit and truth. Don't ever let the "how" of an experience draw your focus away from its purpose. God has a message, so be sure to pursue what He has to say.

THE ROLE OF ANGELS

Let's go back to Hebrews 1:14 which asks: *"Are they not all ministering spirits, sent forth to minister for them who shall be heirs of salvation?"*

We looked at this verse earlier and discussed the fact that angels are servants and ministering spirits, agents between God and man. They are dispatched by the Lord to help righteous people. They do have God-given access to earth and to Heaven, and they are intermediaries, but they are not mediators.

Here's what I mean. Angels travel between God and man at His discretion. They carry messages and bring help when needed, but they do not mediate, or take a place as a negotiator between God and man. Jesus is the only such mediator, and His mediation took place on the cross.

The role of angels is limited. They do not and cannot answer prayer. That is not their place or their right. They are very active in the Kingdom, but their assigned role is to help the saints carry out and fulfill God's will and purpose. They only do what they do when God gives the order.

It's also important to note that if you ever see or hear an angel, it will not be because you are so much more spiritual than another person might be, rather, at that moment in time, it is the method God decides is the most suitable for you in your situation.

Let me pose this question: Could God have sent Peter a dream to set him free from prison? No, He couldn't because Peter needed the angel's supernatural power to pass through the doors and open the gates to let him out. God sent an angel because it is what Peter needed at that particular moment.

If the Lord sends you an angel, it will be for a similar reason. He will do so because He needs to, or because He simply chooses to. Do not read more into angelic visitation than is intended by God. Angels deliver messages and help righteous people, but they do not act of their own accord. They are servants, not heroes.

If you understand the role of angels and base your reaction to them on that understanding, when you do encounter an angel you will behave appropriately and open the door for more visitations when needed. But if you react inappropriately and behave improperly toward an angel, God will not likely send you another.

Let me add one more warning: Sin will completely disqualify you from angelic visitation. Let me say that again: *Sin will completely disqualify you from angelic visitation.*

God will not send an angel into a household where sin abounds. If your house is full of anger and strife, or if you are given to worldly influences by way of television or the internet, do not expect to see an angel any time soon. Angels hate sin and will avoid it at all costs. They come from Heaven where holiness is required, so they do not understand when sons and daughters of God allow sin to reign in their homes. The Father simply will not send angels to righteous people who act like the unrighteous.

If you want angels to have access to your life, you will have to live sin-free—to be holy as God is holy. You don't have to be perfect, because no man is perfect in his own power, but you do have to be sincerely striving to walk uprightly before God by the power of His Spirit. Then and only then will you prepare a place for angelic access. Keep your hands, your eyes and your ears clean. Run from sin, and one day, you may find yourself running straight into an angelic visitation.

JUDGE WHAT YOU HEAR

Angels are sent for your good, so if you do encounter a messenger you think was sent from Heaven, just remember the words of an angel are not more powerful than the Word of God. In fact, you should judge what every angel says according to the Word. Hold the message to the light of scripture and make sure it can stand the test.

You don't want to be led around by false angels or seducing spirits. Always judge what you hear by the Word of God, no matter how dazzling and brilliant the messenger may appear to be. A true angel from Heaven will bring a word that confirms and builds upon that which you already know from the Bible. Angels never deliver new words or new doctrine. They simply bring a message for the moment, direction for the situation at hand, or guidance to help you overcome.

Remember these words from the Apostle Paul: *"But though we, or an angel from heaven, preach any other gospel unto you than that which we have preached unto you, let him be accursed. As we said before, so say I now again, If any man preach any other gospel unto you than that ye have received, let him be accursed"* (Galatians 1:8-9).

The message of an angel from Heaven will agree with the Word of God in every way because it is God-sent, and it will be the Lord's words flowing out of the mouth of the angel. No angelic visit will ever draw you away from the Bible. It will never push you toward a new doctrine or a new way of thinking, because there is nothing new under the sun (see Ecclesiastes 1:9).

There is no new gospel, no last minute addition to the scripture that God just remembered. The Word is complete and entire as it is. Nothing will be added, ever. Nothing will be changed or altered, ever. Nothing will be removed, ever!

In today's world there is a great fascination with angels. You can find books and angel figurines almost everywhere. People carry angel pins as if they are some sort of lucky charm that will protect them and make them succeed. The world's view of angels is far removed from the truth of the Bible, so be careful to steer clear of the ungodly wisdom concerning angels that is so prevalent today.

We are living in a supernatural time which is advancing us toward the end of God's plan. It is a time where hunger and thirst for spiritual things will continue to increase. Men and women are running all over the earth today seeking truth, searching for a messiah, trying to find a connection to God. We realize that Jesus Christ is the only link to God. He is the Messiah. He is the Truth, the Way and the Life (see John 14:6).

We must be more vigilant than ever before to judge everything that passes before our eyes and makes its way into our ears. The Bible tells us he that is spiritual judges all things (see 1 Corinthians 2:15). Don't just swallow everything you hear because it has a spiritual label on it.

The Bible says the world will wax worse and worse as we approach the time of Jesus' return (see 2 Timothy 3:13). Doctrines of devils will rise and draw many away. Some of those false teachings will come through the mouths of fallen angels masquerading as Heaven-sent beings. So be careful. Be wise. Compare spiritual things with spiritual (see 1 Corinthians 2:13). Compare the Word with the angelic message. If the message falls short, throw it out and get away from the situation that drew you into the false encounter in the first place.

Second Corinthians 11:13-15 says: *"For such are false apostles, deceitful workers, transforming themselves into the apostles of Christ. And no marvel; for Satan himself is transformed into an angel of light. Therefore it is no great thing if his ministers also be transformed as the ministers of righteousness; whose end shall be according to their works."*

Notice that not only will the devil begin to transform himself and make false appearances today, but his ministers, the fallen angels who do his bidding, will also transform themselves into angels of light. They will look attractive, but the things which proceed out of their mouths will be corrupt and vile, nothing more than doctrines of devils. One example is the manifestation of familiar spirits.

Familiar spirits are known by this title because they are familiar with the activities of certain men and women. They have followed them and know the details of their lives, so when called upon by a spiritualist or by a foolish man or woman, these spirits can produce what seems like credible information that draws men and women after them.

Some of these spirits masquerade as known figures, such as Mary, the mother of Jesus. Today, there are dozens of people who claim to have witnessed appearances of Mary where she instructed them to do certain things so that now, they believe she is equal with God. In fact, there is a big push in certain churches to make Mary the fourth part of the God-head. This is an abomination! I believe without a shadow of a doubt that these poor, misled souls have encountered a familiar spirit who preached a false gospel to them. Unless they see the light and repent, they will be eternally cursed.

Nearly every founder of a false religion or cult based his doctrine on the visitation of an angel who told him there were other books and other doctrines besides the Bible. Whenever anyone, man or angel, begins to move you away from the Word, you can bank on it, that man or angel is not from God. Don't be a fool. There is no other gospel besides that which Paul preached, and that is Jesus Christ and Him crucified.

The end of angelic messages sent from Heaven to earth will come one day when we see Jesus face to face. No longer will we be separated by our earthly flesh, but we will be like Him and know Him, as we have been known by Him. Until that great and wonderful day, we must rely on God to speak to us in many different ways. An angelic messenger is only one of those ways. So keep your eyes on Jesus and rely on His Word to judge every word spoken by an angel.

Never let yourself be caught up in a moment to the detriment of your eternity with Christ. Be mindful of everything you see and hear, and pass it all under the microscope of God's Word. Only then can you be sure that what you heard is, "Thus says the Lord." Only then can you prosper and have good success.

CHAPTER 6

THE AUDIBLE
VOICE OF GOD

Young Saul was furious. These Christ followers were blaspheming God, and he had had enough. He pondered what a mess they had made of his life as he and his like-minded friends traveled the road to Damascus. They were on their way from the office of the high priest having picked up letters that gave them permission to capture and detain every blasphemer they encountered. They were going to get them off the streets once and for all.

Saul had been pressed into service to rid the world of the disciples of Jesus, a task he did not relish, but one he felt responsible to perform. He had witnessed some unsettling things lately, like that blasphemer Stephen who stood perfectly still as he was stoned for proclaiming Jesus was the Messiah. Saul cringed when he thought of how Stephen not only took the stoning like a brave man, but he actually claimed to have had a vision of Jesus standing up in Heaven, ready to greet him. Enough was enough!

Saul could not bear it anymore, and he let his friends know just how much he hated these people. The entire trip to Damascus was nothing but one long tirade, one irate discourse on why Jesus could not be the son of God, but had to be some imposter whose death mysteriously only added to His fame.

As he marched down the road in an angry fit, suddenly a light flashed around him, and he was instantly surrounded by an intense beam of light that appeared to come straight from Heaven. Saul was no dummy. Even as angry and disgruntled as he was at the moment, he knew when he was licked by a power mightier than he, so he hit the deck hard and fast.

Just as he landed, a voice said, *"Saul, Saul, why persecutest thou me?"* Trembling and recognizing this must be the voice of one sent from Heaven,

Saul replied, *"Who art thou, Lord?"* The voice continued, *"I am Jesus whom thou persecutest: It is hard for thee to kick against the pricks."*

Saul was shaken to the core. No! How could this be? Jesus was surrounding him with light and speaking to him from Heaven? Jesus, the man he hated so much for calling Himself the Son of God, was there talking to him on the road to Damascus? Saul hoped he was having a dream; a very, very bad one.

As realization began to flood Saul's mind, and he began to understand how wrong he must have been about this man from Galilee, he quietly asked, *"Lord, what wilt thou have me to do?"* Filled with compassion, Jesus told him to go into town and wait until someone came to tell him what to do next.

The light went out, and the men with Saul stood speechless and terrified by the fact they had heard a voice, but they had not seen anybody. Saul stood up carefully, shaking and coming to the realization he had been blinded by the light. He quietly asked his friends to lead him by the hand into Damascus. When he arrived in the city, he got himself a room, and like a good, frightened man, he went on a three day fast (see Acts 9:1-9).

Of course you know this was the way God chose to call the apostle Paul to preach. Not bad. I would say that Jesus made His point quite well, judging from Paul's obedient response. The story ends with Ananias coming to Paul and laying hands on him to restore his sight. The Bible does not say what went on during the three days Paul spent alone, fasting in the dark, but I suspect they were days filled with revelation as Paul came to be saved and know that Jesus was the Christ, the Son of the living God. Truly, God's audible voice came for a purpose, and judging by Paul's writings in the New Testament, this purpose was surely fulfilled.

DISCOVERING GOD'S VOICE

When I was first called to preach in the living room of my humble ranch home over 25 years ago, I did not immediately understand that I was called to be a pastor. I knew for certain that God had called me, but where and how I was to preach was a bit of a mystery to me.

One day, I was in a church service when the preacher called me out and prophesied that I was called to be an evangelist. Being young in the Lord, I thought, "That's it! I'm an evangelist!"

Again and again I would attend church services and person after person would tell me I was an evangelist. Trouble was, God had not given me this direction personally, so when I tried to be an evangelist, no one wanted to hear me.

I gave it my all trying to be a mighty evangelist, and I did my best to get churches to preach in. One pastor did let me hold a three day evangelistic crusade, but as time went by no one else called me to preach. I was failing and losing hope fast. I was frustrated, but I kept on trying.

After a year or so, I was praying, and I began to approach God about my lack of invitations. I said, "You called me to be an evangelist, so why haven't the doors opened for me?" God gave me this astounding reply, "I never called you to be an evangelist. Others did." The conversation ended abruptly, and I did not hear another word for over three months.

One day, when I was in the shower, (about as humble as a man can be), I heard the audible voice of God again. He told me to kneel down, and then He told me He was anointing me to be a teacher and a pastor to the Body of Christ. I remember it as if it happened yesterday, and I also recall the shock I felt, and how I wished I had known before I had spent all of my time and energy trying to be what God had not called me to be.

I had been listening to men, when I should have been listening to God. It was not the fault of those who had prophesied over me. They weren't the devil, but were just human vessels seeking to be used of God and trying to discern my zeal and passion for the Lord. The fault lay directly at my doorstep, because I was supposed to judge all things.

Once I recovered my senses I told my wife, and we both cried. We wept because I did not think I wanted to be a pastor, and my wife definitely did not want me to be one. Her father had been a preacher, and she knew exactly how difficult it could be. We cried and cried, but then we settled down and agreed that we had to do what God had called us to.

From that moment of agreement, I have been a pastor. Today, I am blessed to lead a wonderful congregation in a growing church. I am blessed to travel to other nations and preach the gospel with signs following. I am so happy I did what God instructed instead of doing what others told me to do.

How did I get from there, a place of failure, to here, a place of success? It was only by turning away from the false prophecies and allowing God to speak to me personally and write His word of direction on my heart. Only by the audible voice of God did clarity come and direction show me the way.

Since that day I have never turned back, and I never will. As far as I am concerned, I will be pastor at my church until the day I die. I'll never leave because God wrote it on my heart and inscribed it on my spirit. His voice has been infused in me, and I will never, ever turn back.

It's called staying true to what God tells you to do. There is no sense in crying out to the Lord for an answer, hearing it when He gives you one, trying it for two weeks, then going back and crying out for something else.

When God tells you to do something specific, you don't have the option to give in to murmuring just because things get tough. And they will get tough; it's just part of the process. Your job is to stick with it and stay the course. Your only option is to do what God tells you to do.

I don't ever have to ask God again about being a pastor. His voice was loud and clear then, and it remains clear to this day. Now, it's up to me to continue on and be faithful. I have to keep going, even when things get difficult.

I cannot do anything other than what God has told me to do. I would be afraid to because I know that if I do anything else I will remove myself from the covering and protection of my heavenly Father, and I will be on my own. This is not a place I am willing to be. I have determined that I will fulfill the audible call of God on my life, and I will pastor and teach the people He has placed under my care all of the days of my life.

THE VOICE OF HEALING

God has an audible voice today. I know because I heard it in the shower on that morning so many years ago, and I have heard it numerous times since.

In truth, God has been vocal since the beginning of time. He used a resounding voice at creation when He said: *"Let there be light."* He still had His voice when He spoke to Abraham, and later to Moses. God was able to speak just fine when He spoke to Solomon in a dream and asked him what he desired.

God was still vocal when He spoke to David and told him how to conquer the Philistines. His voice was heard when He spoke to Jonah and explained why He had mercy on Nineveh. He had no trouble talking when He spoke to Jesus, or to Paul or Ananias, or to Phillip or Peter.

And many people today still hear God's voice audibly. One of my congregation members wrote me this wonderful testimony of her experience from years ago:

"God spoke to me in an audible voice as I lay in a hospital bed one night back in 1977. I was 24 at the time, had been in an auto accident, and was in the intensive care unit with a broken neck.

"I was paralyzed from the neck down and had no feeling in my body at all. I was very aware of what was going on around me, though.

"The doctors told me I had a 50/50 chance of gaining any feeling back in my body, but they admitted they really had no idea if I would ever be any better than I was as I lay there. I was in a hospital far from home, and my family could only visit me briefly, so I felt very lonely, helpless and frustrated.

"One night as I lay alone, I cried out to God, although I was not yet saved at the time. I told Him I could not live like this because it would not be a life at all. I did not want to be a burden for anyone, and I could not stand the thought of being unable to help myself.

"I told God I wished I had died in the accident. (I had gone down the tunnel towards the light so many people talk about, but was called back.)

"As I poured out my heart to God, suddenly I heard a voice say, *'Don't worry, everything will be alright. You'll walk out of here.'* Immediately, a sense of peace came over me, and I just knew it would be okay.

"I was moved to another room about a week or so later and began therapy. Sure enough, I did get back on my feet. Once I was up, I could not stay in bed. I would walk the halls at night and visit with the nurses when I couldn't sleep.

"One night, a nurse named Flo gave me a little Gospel of John booklet and told me to read it sometime. I still cherish that book today.

"Two and a half months later, I walked out of that hospital on my own and returned home. The doctors were amazed at my quick recovery. It took more therapy, but I know how I made it. God healed me."

What a testimony of the Father's great mercy and love toward this woman, still a sinner on a bed of affliction, and yet God took the time to speak a healing word to her that ultimately led to her salvation. The Lord always has a purpose when He speaks which is far more important than what we initially understand.

Yes, God was concerned for this woman's recovery, but He was far more concerned for her soul. By getting her attention with His audible voice, He opened the door for a godly nurse to plant the seed of the gospel into a heart that was prepared. Then, God got the increase, as He always does.

GOD'S VOICE IN THE BIBLE

When God spoke audibly to people in the Bible, they did an incredible thing. They listened.

An early example is the life of Abram. He was minding his own business one day (Genesis 12) when God spoke and told him to leave his father's house and move to another land. Abram immediately packed up and left, just as God instructed.

In Genesis chapter 15, the Lord spoke to Abram again, this time in a vision, and made a covenant with him which included the promise of a child to be his heir, and the promise of land for his inheritance. In Genesis chapter 17, when Abram was 99 years old, God again spoke audibly and changed his name to Abraham. Not long after this name change, Isaac was conceived and God's long-awaited promise was fulfilled. Because Abraham obeyed the voice of the Lord without question, he was blessed in every area of his life.

As we read in chapter four, God spoke to Moses after he was banished from his childhood home and living on the backside of the desert, herding sheep for a living. One day the angel of the Lord spoke to Moses from a burning bush.

When Moses turned to look and see, God spoke from that same bush in an audible voice and called Moses to deliver His people from the hand of Pharaoh. After some amazing signs and wonders were revealed, Moses was finally convinced to go and do as God said.

Later, when the children of Israel were wandering in the wilderness, Moses continued his unique relationship with God. Exodus 33:11 states: *"And the Lord spake unto Moses face to face, as a man speaketh unto his friend."*

This relationship struck fear in the hearts of the children of Israel because they could not imagine having a personal relationship with the Lord. To them, God was far away and impersonal, but to Moses, God was his friend.

God and Moses remained close right to the very end. In fact, just before Moses died, the Bible says the Lord took him up on a mountain top to see the Promised Land. He stayed with Moses until he did die, and incredibly God buried him with His own hands (see Deuteronomy 34:1-6). This was more than a friendship; it was a covenant relationship that endured the good times and the bad.

Of course you know God often spoke through the prophets and the godly priests. His Word was delivered to the people through these serving agents all through the Old Testament. The Lord warned, taught, encouraged, admonished and corrected, just as He longs to do for you today.

When Jesus arrived on the scene and the New Covenant was ratified and established by His blood, everything changed, though in many ways it remained the same. God still spoke to people audibly, as He did before, but He no longer limited His speaking to prophets, priests and men and women of high standing. After the resurrection of Jesus, God spoke to sons and daughters. Every believer could hear the audible voice of the Lord, if He chose to speak that way.

There are many examples in the New Testament of God speaking to His people in an audible voice. He spoke to Philip in Acts chapter eight and told him to go to a certain place to meet an Ethiopian eunuch to answer his questions and point him to Jesus. And don't forget Ananias. God spoke to him and told him to go and see Paul, still named Saul at the time. As far as Ananias knew, Saul was in town to imprison Christians, but he obeyed and went anyway.

In encounter after encounter, God spoke audibly all throughout the New Testament. Thankfully, God never changes, and His voice is still being heard today. Now, we all have the opportunity to hear from God any time we need Him because Christ bridged the gap for us on the cross and made us sons and daughters of the Most High.

If you will take the time to allow God to speak to you personally, you will experience the same results that Moses and others did. Your relationship with Him will mature and develop into something much more than a distant acquaintance. It will become a sonship relationship which is based on His love for you and your response to that love.

GOD'S VOICE TODAY

The voice of God in our generation is as strong as it ever was to the men of old. Their lives are examples to us, not only of suffering, but of living by faith and hearing what He said. God's audible voice to them was the mark of their office, the seal of His approval. Today, we already have God's blessing, but we still need to hear His voice.

The men of old lived in treacherous times while we live in relative ease in comparison, yet they were not afraid to obey and testify of what God said to them. We should be as courageous and live by what we hear just as boldly as they did.

Today, many Christians think God has stopped using His audible voice. The truth is, God does not have laryngitis, but many Christians do have "lack-of-faith-itis". They simply do not believe God speaks out loud anymore; therefore, they cannot hear His voice. Believers like this will only have the opportunity to hear His voice when they finally ignore the voice of religion that denies God speaks today.

Remember, faith comes by hearing, and hearing by God's Word. If you never hear or understand that God speaks audibly, you will have no faith in His ability to do so, and you will never experience God's voice this way. Don't let unbelievers, scoffers, and critics steal the revelation that God does still speak today as He did in the Bible.

I have listened to many testimonies over the years of folks who have heard the audible voice of God. My own experience began before I was even saved. When I was a sinner, I was involved in activities which took me to very bad places. Sometimes, an extremely annoying thing would happen to me right in the middle of one of those bad situations. God would talk to me and tell me to stop what I was doing.

It irritated me so much, I would talk back. I would even yell and tell God to stop bothering me. You may think that's quite bold for a mere man, but I was dedicated to my lifestyle of sin, and I did not want anybody, not even God, messing it up.

My story is not an isolated case, as I learned from one of my church members. Here's her story in her own words:

"My son was attending Ohio State University in Columbus years ago when I had an urgency to pray for him one night. At that time, if he and his friends had to go out at night, they had to do it in groups because the area they lived in was so dangerous.

"On this particular evening, he and a friend had gone out and were about to enter a certain building. Halfway from the car to the building my son heard an audible voice that told him to stop and leave.

"He looked around to see who had spoken and saw no one around, so he continued toward the building. He took a few more steps when he heard the voice again, *'I told you to get out of here!'* This time, a little fearful of what was happening, he turned around, and he and his friend got back in the car and left the area.

"Several days later when I asked him what had happened that night at a certain time, he was silent for a moment, then he told me the story. He said he found out the next day that an armed robbery was taking place in that very building at the time I was praying for him, which was also the very moment he heard the audible voice tell him to leave.

"My son was pretty shaken because he realized he could have been killed had he and his friend interrupted the robbery. I told him I had been praying for him and that God had spoken to him in order to spare his life."

This is an amazing story of the Father's infinite love for sinners and saints alike. God loved this woman so much, He was willing to speak to a sinner to get his attention, and He loved this young man so much He was willing to keep after him until he obeyed and left the scene, sparing his life.

Another church member wrote this testimony: "Once, about twenty years ago, as I was driving home from work, I was praising God for the wonderful day He had given me. I said, 'Father, I thank You for such a great day.' Much to my surprise, I heard a voice as plain as if someone was sitting next to me say, *'You're welcome.'* I was so blessed! I will never forget it."

Our heavenly Father is so kind to us. He meets us right where we are and takes us to where we need to be. I guarantee this woman never will forget the sound of His voice. Even though the message was simple, it let her know God was listening, and that He appreciated her heart of thanksgiving.

One more testimony of God speaking audibly came from another of our church members: "The first time God spoke to me, it was on a Sunday morning as I was getting ready for church. He spoke audibly. I stopped what I was doing and looked around, and then I realized it was God.

"Two years went by and I hadn't heard anything. We began attending church at Only Believe Ministries. After attending for a couple of months, I began to hear a gentle leading.

"Since that time, for the last three years, there has been an open communication. Sometimes when I pray, I will be quiet. That's when God speaks to me. Sometimes He speaks audibly, as He did that very first time, and at times He speaks through the Holy Spirit in my spirit."

Once again, God's love directs His speaking. How often we could avoid the pitfalls of life if we would do as this young man does and take time to listen when we pray, instead of always doing all the talking.

A RUNNER HEARS FROM GOD

Jacob was the younger of Isaac's twin sons, and because of the birth order, his brother Esau was entitled to the double portion birthright given to eldest sons. Jacob and Esau were as different as night and day. Esau was a hunter, a man who liked to wander in the wild and bring home big game for dinner. Jacob, on the other hand, was a bit of a mama's boy, and he preferred to hang around the tent.

One day, Jacob was in the tent as usual, cooking a pot of stew. Esau came stumbling into camp at the end of a long day of hunting, and he was starving. Esau asked for some stew, but Jacob hesitated. In a moment of what he perceived was divine inspiration, Jacob told Esau that he could have the whole pot of stew, if he would sell him his birthright. Esau was so hungry, he told Jacob he could not care less about a birthright, and so he swore to sell it to Jacob for the pot of stew.

You know what happened next. Sometime later Jacob and his mother plotted to get Isaac to bless Jacob with the firstborn's blessing while Isaac was sick and bedfast. When Esau found out, he was furious, and he swore he would kill Jacob.

Fearing for his life, Jacob's parents sent him to live with his uncle for awhile, but before he left, his father blessed him with the blessing of Abraham, the blessing of promise. Though Jacob had connived and purchased the birthright from Esau, it was Esau's to give up, and so Isaac honored the birthright blessing.

This put Jacob on the run, fleeing everything he knew and loved, while he headed for a destiny he could not comprehend. As Jacob made his way to his uncle's house, he stopped for the night in the wilderness, and he made himself a bed of stones to sleep on. While he slept, God spoke to him audibly in a dream. (How God does this, I have no idea. I just know that's what the Bible says.)

God said: *"I am the Lord God of Abraham thy father, and the God of Isaac: the land whereon thou liest, to thee will I give it, and to thy seed. And thy seed shall be as the dust of the earth, and thou shalt spread abroad to the west, and to the east, and to the north, and to the south: and in thee and in thy seed shall all the families of the earth be blessed. And, behold, I am with thee, and will keep thee in all places whither thou goest, and will bring thee again into this land; for I will not leave thee, until I have done that which I have spoken to thee of."*

When Jacob woke up he was so moved by what God had spoken, he took the stone he had laid his head on, and he set it up as a pillar. Then he poured oil on it to signify his dedication to the voice of God. Jacob prayed at the pillar and vowed a vow, saying: *"If God will be with me, and will keep me in this way that I go, and will give me bread to eat, and raiment to put on, so that I come again to my father's house in peace; then shall the Lord be my God. And this stone, which I have set for a pillar, shall be God's house: and of all that thou shalt give me I will surely give the tenth unto thee"* (see Genesis 28:10-22).

What I want you to see here is two-fold. First, even when we fall short by man's standards, when the call of God is on our lives as it was on Jacob's, the promises of God will come to pass, not because of us, but because God is faithful. Second, I want you to notice how Jacob reacted to the voice of the Lord. He immediately responded in faith, and he made a memorial there.

This is so important. When God speaks to you, I believe you should always obey, but I also believe you should go a step further and make some sort of memorial. You may choose to write down exactly what God said in a journal so you can refer to it later. Or you may choose to make an audio recording so you can listen to it again and again.

Whatever you do, mark the place and time, and make it a special remembrance for you and the Lord. Don't ever take the audible voice of God for granted, because not everyone will hear it on earth. If God chooses to speak to you this way, be grateful, and be sure to do exactly what He commands.

I can remember every word God has ever said to me with an audible voice, because I have made a record of it, and I have made a memorial in my heart. I will never forget, and I will not allow myself to fall short of what God has told me to do.

I encourage you to build your own memorials, and remember in your own way, but make sure you do something tangible, as Jacob did, which will last for generations to come.

GOD SPEAKS TO A TEENAGER

Sometimes people believe age or experience has something to do with whether or not they hear from God. It is simply not true. My daughter Nicole has a great story from her teenage years that proves God is no respecter of persons. It does not matter how old or how young you are; if you are alive on this earth, you are a candidate to hear God's audible voice. Here's Nicole's story in her own words.

"I was sixteen and a half years old. Yes, that half a year is very important when you are a teenager, and I was proud of it. My mom and dad were out of town for a few days, and they asked a family friend named Janice to come stay with me. I may have been 16 and a half, but in my parent's eyes I still needed to be looked after. In hindsight, they were probably right.

"I had a 9:00 P.M. curfew at that time, and of course mom and dad gave me 'the speech' before they left, reminding me what would happen to me if I tried to pull the wool over Janice's eyes and stay out past my time. I rolled my eyes and assured them I would behave.

"One night, around 10:30 P.M., I was sitting in my room and minding my own business when I suddenly felt that God wanted me to go to the mall in a town about 20 minutes away. I knew the unction was from God, but I had no clue how I was going to convince Janice that God had told me to go. She was a great lady who loved the Lord and heard from Him quite a bit, but I figured it would be a stretch for her to believe me, a mere teenager, especially since my boyfriend just happened to live in the same town.

"I approached Janice in the living room and said, 'Janice, I think God just told me to go to the Piqua mall.' She looked at me for a moment, trying to evaluate my words even as she judged the expression on my face. After a few seconds she repeated my statement back to me. 'You think God told you to go to the Piqua mall?' I nodded. 'Okay,' Janice said, 'If God told you to go, then go.'

"I couldn't believe my ears, but I didn't wait for her to change her mind. I ran for the car and headed for the mall as fast as I could go. When I arrived, I suddenly felt very foolish because I realized I had no idea why I was there or what I was supposed to do.

"The mall was closed, and things were not the way I expected them to be. It was dark, and the parking lot seemed huge and kind of creepy. Driving around in circles made me even more nervous, and I began to imagine myself trying to explain this whole thing to mom and dad when they returned. It wasn't a pretty picture in my mind, so I stopped the car and prayed as hard as I could for God to tell me why I was there.

"As I prayed, the only thing I perceived was that I was supposed to wait, and so I did. After awhile I got cold and decided to fire up my Audi diesel and drive around the parking lot with the heater on to warm up. As I turned a corner at the back of the mall, I saw a truck I thought I recognized. I drove past slowly, keeping my distance, but sure enough I saw my friend inside the truck with her boyfriend. I wondered if this was why I was there, but again, I felt that I was just supposed to wait some more.

"I parked several rows away and shut the car off so they wouldn't hear my diesel engine rumbling nearby. Several more minutes passed, and I still had no idea what to do. Just when I began to wonder if God was ever going to tell me why I was there, He spoke to me in an audible voice. Without warning, a voice as big as all outdoors said, 'Now!' I didn't have to ask for ID. I knew it was God, and I knew I had to go to my friend in the truck as fast as I could. The only trouble was my car didn't get the message.

"My old diesel was one of those that delayed the start-up until the glow stick reached a certain temperature, and of course it was taking a whole lot longer than I thought it should. I smacked the steering wheel and yelled at the car, 'He said now!' Finally, the engine fired up, and I floored it. I screeched to a halt bedside the truck, jumped out and tapped on the driver's side window. I said a big, 'Hi! What are you guys doing here?' but I didn't really have to ask after what I saw.

"My friend, wearing a mini skirt, was sitting on her boyfriend's lap. Thankfully, they were still fully clothed, but I knew by the shocked look on her face that they had not intended to keep it that way. I used my cheeriest voice and said to my friend, 'So, maybe I should take you home now.' She climbed off her boyfriend's lap and replied, 'No, I think I got the point already.' Then she looked her boyfriend straight in the eye and said, 'I think *you* better take me home now.'

"When I returned to the house I excitedly told Janice what had happened. She said, 'See, honey, you were used of God tonight.' That was it. No fanfare or trophies, just a little pat on the back for hearing God's audible voice. As I went to bed that night, I thought about whether I should tell mom and dad right away or save it until later. Thankfully, I decided to tell them the first thing after they crossed the threshold. Amazingly, they didn't even mention the whole curfew thing, which was an even greater miracle for a teenager learning to hear from Heaven!"

I still vividly remember this story. Phyllis and I were so proud of Nicole for not only hearing God's voice, but for being brave enough to act on it. It really does no good to hear the Lord speaking unless we are willing to act on what we hear. When God speaks, we need to obey immediately. His voice is always a "now" voice, not a "when I get around to it" voice. It's all about obedience in the Kingdom of God, and it's no different when it comes to doing what God says to do, when He says to do it.

If you hear God's voice loud and clear, you better put the pedal to the metal, just like Nicole did, and start doing what God told you to.

YOU CAN HEAR GOD'S VOICE

God should not have to convince Christians He is the same yesterday, today and forever (see Hebrews 13:8), and that He still speaks with an audible voice today. As believers, we should keep an open heart to hear Him and be prepared to obey.

As you can see from the various stories in this chapter, the time and place mean nothing to God. He will speak to you at any hour and in any location. What matters to Him is that you have a listening ear.

Most of us have one not-so-useful skill down pat. We can "listen" to a person and do something else at the same time. Some of us practice this every day when our spouse talks to us.

"Yes, dear. Whatever you say, dear." That's not really listening. To truly listen, you have to give them your undivided attention. You have to turn the TV off, close the blinds, put the newspaper down and look your spouse straight in the eye. Then and only then will your spouse see how valuable his or her voice is to you.

God deserves at least our full attention. He does not need to have to yell over the evening news, or shout over your shoulder as you read the sports section. God should not have to wait for you to give Him 30 seconds before you go to sleep. It should be possible for Him to get your attention any time He wants, day or night.

Does God have this kind of access to your heart? I wonder how many of us can honestly say, "Yes"?

It takes a conscious choice to allow God access to your eyes, ears and your heart, just as it takes a conscious choice to listen to your spouse after a long, hard day. Sometimes we just need to be heard. I am sure God feels this way, too, because He has the heart and love of a father.

I encourage you to consider at what point the Lord could get your attention in an average day. Could He speak in the morning when you wake up? Could He reach you at noontime?

Would God dare to talk during prime time TV? Could He grab your attention for ten minutes before you drift off to sleep? How about during the night? Would God dare to wake you up to say something? He is more than willing to speak. The question is, are you more than willing to listen?

It's time to be honest with yourself and make the changes necessary to give God time to speak to you.

"What if I never hear His audible voice?" you may ask. That's okay. It doesn't matter *how* you hear, but *that* you hear. God may choose to speak to you in a myriad of ways over a lifetime, but if you are not listening, you'll never hear any of them. Remember the words of a young Samuel: *"Speak, Lord, for thy servant heareth."* (1 Samuel 3:9).

I challenge you to let those words flow out of your mouth and ring in God's ears. They will be for Him a sweet, satisfying song, and an unexpected delight from you whom He loves and watches over. Remember I Peter 3:12: *"For the eyes of the Lord are over the righteous, and his ears are open unto their prayers: but the face of the Lord is against them that do evil."*

God is listening, waiting to hear your voice. Can He say the same about you?

PART TWO

FIVE GIFTS
FROM HEAVEN

CHAPTER 7

THE PERFECTING OF THE SAINTS

Isaiah lay prostrate before the Lord, and the glory of God was heavy upon him. As in times past, he knew that the message God was giving him was a timely admonition for Israel, a prophetic utterance which he would be responsible to deliver to God's people. Isaiah also knew by the tone of the message that the Lord was not pleased with them.

When he felt released, Isaiah stood to his feet, took in a deep breath, and went out to deliver the word of the Lord at an appointed time. What he was about to say, as recorded in Isaiah 58, was going to be a bit harsh, a kind of wake-up call for the nation. As he stood before Israel, Isaiah said: "You seek the Lord daily and delight to know His ways, as if you are a nation that does righteousness, and forsakes not the ordinance of their God. You ask of the Lord the ordinances of justice, and you take delight in approaching God."

So far, so good. He had the people's attention, but he knew their expectant countenances were about to change. Isaiah continued: "You say, 'Wherefore have we fasted, and God does not see? Wherefore have we afflicted our souls, and God takes no knowledge?' I will tell you! Behold, in the day of your fast you find pleasure, and exact all your labors. Behold, you fast for strife and debate, and to smite with the fist of wickedness. You do not fast as you do this day, to make your voice to be heard on high.

"Is that the kind of fast that God has chosen? Is it a day for a man to afflict his soul? Is it to bow down his head as a bulrush and to spread sackcloth and ashes under him? Will you call this a fast, and an acceptable day to the Lord?"

The people looked dumbfounded, unable to understand why they were being rebuked on a day of fasting. Isn't that what God wanted from them, that they bow down before Him and afflict themselves? Isaiah went on: "Thus says the Lord, 'Is not this the fast that I have chosen, to loose the bands of wickedness, to undo the heavy burdens, and to let the oppressed go free, and that you break every yoke? Is it not to give your bread to the hungry, and that you bring the poor that are cast out to your house? When you see the naked, that you cover him; and that you hide not yourself from your own flesh and blood?'"

Isaiah could see they were beginning to get it, and so he pressed on: "Then shall your light break forth as the morning, and your health shall spring forth speedily: and your righteousness shall go before you, and the glory of the Lord shall be your reward.

"And if you draw out your soul to the hungry, and satisfy the afflicted soul; then shall your light rise in obscurity, and your darkness shall be as the noonday. And the Lord shall guide you continually, and satisfy your soul in drought, and make fat your bones. And you shall be like a watered garden, and like a spring of water, whose waters fail not.

"And they that shall be of you shall build the old waste places. You will raise up the foundations of many generations; and you will be called, 'the repairer of the breach,' 'the restorer of paths to dwell in.'

"If you turn away your foot from the sabbath, from doing your pleasure on My holy day; and call the sabbath a delight, the holy of the Lord, honorable; and shall honor Him, not doing your own ways, nor finding your own pleasure, nor speaking your own words; then you will delight yourself in the Lord; and I will cause you to ride upon the high places of the earth, and feed you with the heritage of Jacob your father: for the mouth of the Lord has spoken it" (see Isaiah 58:1-14).

The people rejoiced, and Isaiah breathed a sigh of relief. It wasn't what they had expected, no doubt, but it was what God had given him, and so Isaiah did what prophets do, he obeyed, and he delivered the unvarnished word of the Lord. Hopefully, it would empower them to change their ways.

GOD SPEAKS THROUGH MEN

God clearly spoke through the prophets of old; through men like Isaiah, Jeremiah, Ezekiel, Daniel and all the rest. The prophets of the Old Covenant were the main way the people of Israel heard from God. They did not have access to a personal copy of the law, so they had to depend on the prophets, priests and kings of the day to pass on what the Lord was saying to His people.

Today, we have several copies of God's Word in our homes. And we have access to study aids and teaching materials that would astound our Old Covenant brothers and sisters. So, the question is, does God still have need of prophets and others to speak to us today?

In Ephesians 4:7-12, we find the answer: *"But unto every one of us is given grace according to the measure of the gift of Christ. Wherefore he saith, When he ascended up on high, he led captivity captive, and gave gifts unto men. (Now that he ascended, what is it but that he also descended first into the lower parts of the earth? He that descended is the same also that ascended up far above all heavens, that he might fill all things.) And he gave some, apostles; and some, prophets; and some, evangelists; and some, pastors and teachers; For the perfecting of the saints, for the work of the ministry, for the edifying of the body of Christ."*

It's obvious from this passage of scripture that God does still speak through prophets, just like He did in the Old Covenant. Now, though, He also uses apostles, evangelists, pastors and teachers. God's voice is not less evident in our world today, but is much more readily available through many more avenues, because we are in a new dispensation of the Lord dealing with man.

In the opening verse of this passage, we see that we have each been given a measure of grace, a divine ability implanted in us at the new birth. This measure of grace allows each of us to be set in a specific place in the Body of Christ to perform a particular work for the Kingdom of God. When you and I complete our works as we should, those around us will be able to complete their assigned tasks, and the church will be edified.

There is an intricate dynamic within the Body of Christ, one part working with another (see 1 Corinthians 12:12-27; Romans 12:4-8). There are different abilities given to each of us so we can all be what we have been called to be, and so we can complement and help one another.

Verse seven tells us about the grace given to all, but the remaining verses in this passage of scripture refer to specific gifts for specific people—gifts through which God speaks to all of us.

THE FIVE-FOLD MINISTRY GIFTS

In Ephesians 4:11-12, we discover what we call the five-fold ministry gifts. Let's look at the verses again: *"And he gave some, apostles; and some, prophets; and some, evangelists; and some, pastors and teachers. For the perfecting of the saints, for the work of the ministry, for the edifying of the body of Christ."*

Jesus has given us specific gifts in the form of five different measures of grace that minister to and build up the church. These gifts are assigned to certain people for the edification of the Body of Christ, and they are used by God to deliver messages to His people, just as He did through Isaiah long ago.

Notice verse 11 says, *"and he gave some,"* indicating there are not many who will operate in these gifts, but only a certain, designated few. The five-fold ministry gifts are not man-made, but these individuals are divinely equipped and called by God. They are gifts to the church and are supernaturally endowed with certain abilities which allow them to do what they are called to do.

You cannot decide to be a part of the five-fold ministry. You are either called by God, or you are in the wrong business. Those who are truly called will treat their gift with respect and give their lives to fulfilling the call. In turn, we who benefit from the five-fold gifts should treat them with the same respect we treat any present given to us. We should honor the gifts and those who bear them.

No man of God should be set upon a pedestal, but the gift he has should make room for him, and he should be honored if he attends to his office well (see Proverbs 18:16; Romans 13:7). (You understand that when I say, "man of God," I am referring to women of God also.)

No five-fold minister should ever try to puff himself or his office up in order to gain respect. Such respect should be given only when that minister earns it by his love, his sacrifice, and by his godly behavior both in the church and outside it.

As a pastor and teacher, a part of the five-fold ministry, I do not expect anything from my congregation. They owe me nothing, but I do owe them my utmost. I hope I will earn their respect, even as I respect them, so that through this mutual regard God will be able to move through us and fulfill His call for our church.

THE PURPOSE OF THE FIVE-FOLD GIFTS

Now, I want to look at a verse which is very precious to me. Psalm 68:18

118

says: *"Thou hast ascended on high, thou hast led captivity captive: thou hast received gifts for men; yea, for the rebellious also, that the Lord God might dwell among them."*

Ephesians 4:11 tells us Jesus gave the five-fold ministry gifts to men, but this verse tells us about when the Father gave the five-fold gifts to Jesus. I want you to grasp what this means.

When Jesus ascended to Heaven, He did so having all power in Heaven and earth at His disposal (see Matthew 28:18). Having this power, He still lacked something which was necessary for His work on earth to continue. Jesus went to Heaven to receive the five-fold ministry gifts so He might give them back to men and women who would be empowered to raise up others to carry out the work of the ministry.

He knew that the plan of the true church could not be accomplished until He had men and women on earth He could trust with the five-fold ministry gifts—men and women who would in turn deposit the fruit of their gifts into others who would be edified and carry out the plan and purpose of God.

The five-fold ministry is a mainstay in the foundation of the church, and it is an extension of the cornerstone, Jesus Christ. In Ephesians 2:19-22 we are told: *"Now therefore ye are no more strangers and foreigners, but fellowcitizens with the saints, and of the household of God; And are built upon the foundation of the apostles and prophets, Jesus Christ himself being the chief corner stone; In whom all the building fitly framed together groweth unto an holy temple in the Lord: In whom ye also are builded together for an habitation of God through the Spirit."*

Verse 20 talks about the church's foundation. We all know that a foundation is a level platform which is laid down before a structure is built. Whether it is made of concrete, cement blocks, or whatever, the house cannot be built until the foundation is in order.

Jesus is the cornerstone, the very first block to be laid, and the five-fold ministry is the completion of this foundation. First, the apostles and prophets laid their doctrine. Then, the other five-fold gifts have reinforced the foundation, and the church has been built upon it. According to this scripture, where there is no five-fold ministry, the foundation is incomplete.

Notice, the church is not built with strangers and foreigners, but is established with those who are believers, also known as saints. Believers in turn invite and encourage strangers and foreigners to come, get saved and join

119

the household of God. The five-fold ministry, beginning with the doctrines established by the apostles and prophets, works with those new saints who have been led into the fold, teaching them, praying for them, encouraging them, building them up and leading them in the way that they should go. In this way, the church is built, and Jesus is glorified.

THE DIVINE CONNECTION

Ephesians 1:22-23 says it this way: *"And hath put all things under his feet, and gave him to be the head over all things to the church, Which is his body, the fulness of him that filleth all in all."*

This scripture is talking about Jesus, the head and ruler of the church. Since Christ is the head, you could say that the five-fold ministry is the neck. The head and neck are in intimate relationship, and the one cannot function well without the other.

Just ask someone who's had their neck in a brace. When the neck is not well, the head is impaired and limited in what it can do. Worse yet, if the head ever becomes separated from the neck, it's all over, because the body cannot function without the head.

The neck is the natural connection between the body and the head. Likewise, the five-fold ministry is the divine link between the church and Jesus.

Try this test to prove a point. Stand up, hold your body still, and try to move your head. When your head moved, did your body automatically move with it? No. Your neck moved with your head, but your body remained still. It is possible for the head and neck to move as one while the body is completely out of sync with both of them. This is too often true in the Body of Christ.

Jesus, the head, gives divine commands. The signal comes from the head, but it passes through the neck on its way to the body. If the signal is hindered on its way to the body, the body will not be able to function properly.

The head is the place where corporate vision, counsel, instruction and direction are established, but in order for the body to benefit from them, they must pass through the neck. Without the divine connection between the head and neck, the head cannot get anything done. The head needs the neck, and the body does, too.

So, we see the importance of the five-fold ministry in establishing church doctrine, order and vision. Jesus, the head, declares divine vision, establishes counsel and instruction, and institutes direction for the body. These things pass through the five-fold neck and are deposited in the body so that all things may be orderly in the church.

My arm never told my head what to do, but my head tells my arm what to do all the time; in fact, *every* time. My arm is not a free agent; it needs my head and my neck. Without them, it would be a dead limb going nowhere and doing nothing.

Unfortunately, this is what so many foolish Christians try to be. They say things such as, "I don't need to go to church. God is everywhere, so I can have church wherever I am."

Cut your arm off once and see if this is true. You will last outside the safety of the church and away from the five-fold ministry about as long as your arm will last apart from your body. You need the head and neck, but you also need the rest of the body to protect you (see Hebrews 10:25; 13:7).

My wife has a great saying, and it goes like this, "The banana away from the bunch is the first one peeled." It's the same for limbs away from the body. They'll be the first ones to shrivel up and die.

Don't be a foolish Christian. Understand the order of the church, accept and work within it to accomplish what God has called you to do (see Romans 13:1-5).

Jesus will never establish divine order apart from what He already established in the Word, so you will never find a time when He says, "Oh, I think I'll do it different for Sister Knowitall." No, Jesus will work within the confines of His established order. If you will stay there too, you will benefit and become all you are called to be.

SUBMITTED TO A LOCAL CHURCH

I want you to see another important point in Acts 13:1-2: *"Now there were in the church that was at Antioch certain prophets and teachers; as Barnabas, and Simeon that was called Niger, and Lucius of Cyrene, and Manaen, which had been brought up with Herod the tetrarch, and Saul. As they ministered to the Lord, and fasted, the Holy Ghost said, Separate me Barnabas and Saul for the work whereunto I have called them."*

Notice Saul (Paul) and Barnabas were functioning in and submitted to the local church. They were fasting and praying right alongside the other men in this gathering. They were not out on their own somewhere when God confirmed their five-fold offices, but they were in a church, submitting themselves to the leadership there.

Paul and Barnabas were there to learn, grow and prove themselves before God made their calls public knowledge. I personally believe that not only did Paul and Barnabas know about their calls before the prophecy came forth, but the local leaders knew about them too. They were watching Paul and Barnabas, and proving them until the time came for the Holy Spirit to send them out (see 1 Thessalonians 5:12).

The local leadership did not call them to the five-fold ministry; verse two says the Holy Spirit took credit for that, but the local leadership did confirm their calls through a prophetic word and sent the men on their way as an outreach from the church. This is significant for a number of reasons.

I firmly believe the next profound move of God on the face of the earth will come the same way the first move of God came when it was birthed on the Day of Pentecost. The church was the birthplace of the move of God then, and it will be the birthplace of the end-time move of God to come. God will speak through men and women anointed by His Spirit, and the voice of the Lord will be heard all over the earth.

Over the years, we have had great men and women of God minister around the world. Through these individuals we have had moves of God that affected specific areas at a certain time in history. In these last days, I believe the Lord will move in every Spirit-filled, Spirit-connected church nearly simultaneously before Jesus returns.

The church is so strategic in the plan and move of God that I believe we are going to experience great manifestations in our local congregations in the coming years as we have never experienced before. We will see things the early church only dreamed of.

This is why it is expedient that local churches begin to gather the remnant of those who remain outside the church to prepare for this end-time move of God. Those outside will not experience the end-time move. Only those divinely connected to the head through the five-fold ministry in the local church will see what God has in store for us in these last days.

If you are not established in a local church, I encourage you to get connected. Get in your place so you don't miss what God is about to say to the church as the time of Christ's return approaches. Never allow past experiences or past hurts to derail God's plan for you, and don't be rebellious against authority. This is the nature of carnal people, not those like you, who are spiritual.

If you've been separated from the church for a season, I encourage you to get back in the fold and watch God move. I guarantee you won't be disappointed. But if you choose to stay on the outside, you will be there all alone, looking in as the Body of Christ grows and prospers, hearing the voice of the Lord as His return draws closer still.

Now is the time to get in the place that God has for you in the local church, so you can receive from the five-fold ministry gifts. There are so many great pastors and teachers in our world today, and there are many great evangelists whose ministries are based in local churches and who go forth as representatives of these local bodies. There are true prophets who are recognized in local churches, and are therefore accountable for what they say. There are great apostles establishing local churches around the world in preparation for the coming harvest of souls. They are all there for you, and they are ready to impart into your life. The church is the place to be these days, so I encourage you to get in and get ready!

THE FIVE-FOLD OFFICES WORKING TOGETHER

Jesus held and operated in every office of the five-fold ministry before He ever gave them to men. We see Jesus the Apostle in Hebrews 3:1 which says: *"Wherefore, holy brethren, partakers of the heavenly calling, consider the Apostle and High Priest of our profession, Christ Jesus."*

Jesus the Prophet is discussed in John 4:19 which says: *"The woman saith unto him, Sir, I perceive that thou art a prophet."* We see Jesus the Evangelist in Luke 4:18 which states: *"The Spirit of the Lord is upon me, because he hath anointed me to preach the gospel to the poor; he hath sent me to heal the brokenhearted, to preach deliverance to the captives, and recovering of sight to the blind, to set at liberty them that are bruised."*

We recognize Jesus the Pastor in I Peter 5:4: *"And when the chief Shepherd shall appear, ye shall receive a crown of glory that fadeth not away."* Then we see Jesus the Teacher in John 3:2: *"The same came to Jesus by night, and said unto him, Rabbi, we know that thou art a teacher come from God: for no man can do these miracles that thou doest, except God be with him."*

Jesus carried all five divine implants of God. With them He was able to develop His disciples to carry on His earthly ministry of the revelation of an invisible God. Just as Jesus walked the earth and told the disciples, *"...he that hath seen me, hath seen the Father"* (John 14:9), the five-fold ministry also carries a similar revelation that enables the church to minister in its fullness, one to another, so that as people see the church, they see Christ in action.

The pastor does not carry a complete revelation of Jesus by himself. The teacher does not carry it by himself. Neither does the prophet, apostle or evangelist. Only in the fullness of all five gifts can we see a full revelation of who Jesus is.

This is why it is imperative that the local church and those ministries who operate outside the church be divinely connected. The bottom line is, the five-fold purpose is not to build ministries, but to build saints.

When a prophet comes into a local church and confirms the word of the Lord, it builds up the Body of Christ. When an evangelist comes into a local church and exhorts and stirs people to tap into a supernatural lifestyle, it edifies the church.

The only way the church can be touched as Jesus touched the disciples is for the five-fold ministry to operate together. Without Jesus carrying the five divine implants, He would not have been able to touch men as He did. In the same way, if we are ever going to affect and change lives according to the divine plan, directive and will of God, it will be through a cohesive, unified five-fold ministry.

Each gift reveals one facet of God's character, personality and ability. So, a pastor will reveal one side of God, an evangelist another, an apostle another and so on. Each one brings to the church a more precise picture of the invisible God, but each is incomplete without the other.

Now, there are certain men and women, who by reason of need, have more than one five-fold gift operating in their ministries. According to 2 Timothy 1:11, Paul carried more than one office: *"Whereunto I am appointed a preacher, and an apostle, and a teacher of the Gentiles."*

Paul's primary office was that of an apostle, but he also operated in the office of the teacher. James, the brother of Jesus, is another example. He was an apostle, but he was also a pastor in the Jerusalem church.

There will be times when God will call a man or woman to multiple offices because of the work He needs carried out, such as pastors with the teaching anointing, which we will discuss in the next chapter. God will always give us what we need. What we must remember is that no man or woman, no matter how many offices they occupy, is a complete expression of Jesus, and only Jesus was a complete expression of the invisible God. We all need one another.

SPIRITUAL RELATIONSHIPS

Every five-fold minister you come in contact with has been sent to you as a spiritual minister of spiritual information; therefore, relating to the five-fold ministry gifts in a spiritual manner is very important.

So often today, Christians tend to focus on the soulish aspects of five-fold ministers rather than on their spiritual roles in their lives. When we identify with men and women of God for what we like about their personalities, for example, or for what we enjoy about their delivery style when they preach, more than for what they say, we are establishing soulish relationships with these ministers rather than spiritual ones. What is a soulish relationship? It is one which benefits our senses rather than our spirit.

In 1 Thessalonians 5:23 we read: *"And the very God of peace sanctify you wholly; and I pray God your whole spirit and soul and body be preserved blameless unto the coming of our Lord Jesus Christ."*

You are first of all a spirit, someone birthed by God to be connected to His Spirit. Second, you have a soul (your mind, will, intellect and emotions), and finally, you live in a body. You need all three parts to function in this world, but when you deal with the five-fold ministry, you need to focus on the spiritual benefits of their ministries rather than on the things that tickle your ears.

There's nothing wrong with enjoying the style of a certain minister, but if you are moved more by his delivery and his ability to make you laugh than you are by the meat of his message, you may miss what God is trying to say to you. I love to make people smile, don't get me wrong, but I love to impart spiritual truths so much more.

When you relate to a five-fold minister, make sure you are seeing him or her as one sent by God to deposit spiritual impartations into your life, not as merely a man or woman sent to entertain you. You would be surprised how many Christians lack spiritual soundness even though they listen to tons of teaching CDs and read dozens of books every year. It's not about how much they put in, but about how they treat what they put in.

If you will give the five-fold ministers God has placed in your life the honor and respect they are due, and place more importance on receiving the word God sends through them, rather than on their personality traits or delivery style, you will be surprised how much more you get from their messages (see 1 Thessalonians 2:13).

Jesus stated these valuable words in Matthew 10:41: *"He that receiveth a prophet in the name of a prophet shall receive a prophet's reward; and he that receiveth a righteous man in the name of a righteous man shall receive a righteous man's reward."*

If you will receive five-fold ministers as spiritual gifts bearing spiritual impartations, you will receive a full reward from Heaven, but if you see them as mere men and women, you will only receive from them what mere men and women can give.

I encourage you to consider carefully how you accept the men and women of God who operate in the five-fold ministry in your life. Be careful not to lower their value by receiving them as less than they were sent to be. Respect them and their place in your life, and allow God to speak to you with fresh manna from Heaven, the Word of the living God imparted into your heart and mind for His glory.

RESPECTING ONE ANOTHER

In this opening chapter on the five-fold ministry gifts, we have established that no man is an island, so we need to respect one another, knowing we will be required to work together both now and in eternity to come. Understanding this, I want to make a few statements concerning how the five-fold ministry should operate in the Body of Christ today.

First, every five-fold minister should be prepared and willing to submit to the one who has invited him to minister, and to whom the responsibility of maintaining the order of a service has been given.

As any five-fold minister operates in his office and ministers in the pulpit of a local church, for instance, he does so without stepping into or superceding the pastoral anointing. Instead, he submits himself to the covering of that local pastor and operates within the confines of established order in that particular church. No man should ever think so highly of himself that he would dare go over the head of the pastor who invited him to minister and do things he knows are not accepted in that pulpit.

When I go to another man's church, although I am a pastor, I do not stand before that man's congregation as a pastor. I stand there in whatever capacity the pastor allows me to operate.

If he has invited me for a miracle service, I will honor his request and the service will go in that direction. If he has invited me to teach, I will teach. I do not choose what his people receive, but the pastor does. This is simple respect for the other five-fold gifts. We should always strive to work together and help one another, not hinder one another.

Second, no five-fold minister should try to induce a following from another man's ministry or pulpit. We should never take sheep from one fold and sneak them off into another. I have sheep which have been given to me, and another man has his own sheep for whom he is responsible.

The apostle has his responsibilities, the prophet and evangelist have theirs, and the teacher has his job in the Body of Christ. This is vital, especially as we come closer to the return of Jesus. If the leadership cannot work together, how can the people of God ever expect to come into the unity of the faith?

When the five-fold ministry works as one, respecting the boundaries established in the Word, then the body will become one. God is waiting for this very thing before He sends Jesus back to receive us unto Himself. This is what I long for the most, and it is what will shortly come to pass. How soon is strictly in our hands (see Ephesians 4:3).

Third, understand that you can know the five-fold ministry by their fruits (see Matthew 7:16). If you can't see pastoral fruit in the life of a man or woman claiming to be a pastor, you better beware. They may not be what they think they are.

True shepherds, or pastors, can only be shepherds, but sheep can be three things. They can be true sheep, goats who think they are sheep, or wolves in sheep's clothing.

A church without a true pastor will endanger the sheep and place them at the mercy of the wolves and goats. This is dangerous, so be very careful about who you hold in high regard. Make sure the shepherd is who he says he is.

A prophet should bear the fruit of a prophet, an apostle the fruit of an apostle and so on. Don't be drawn into a false ministry by verbal claims only.

Look for the fruit you would expect to find and don't be led by enticing words alone.

It is not a disrespectful thing to ask questions before you receive from any ministry. What is the five-fold minister like in public life? What about his home life? The Bible makes it clear that a man or woman in leadership must keep their house in order (see 1 Timothy 3:1-7).

Does the prophet keep his word? Does what he says in a prophetic utterance come to pass, or does he have to make excuses because he misses it half the time? Does the pastor keep order in his church according to the precepts he teaches from the Word, or does he do it by his own set of rules? The five-fold ministry gifts should operate according to the Word of God, not according to the doctrines of men or organizations. Always let the Word be your guide, and remember, you will know them by their fruit.

BEWARE OF WOLVES

Finally, I believe it is necessary for me to end this chapter with a word of warning for churches everywhere. As I said before, I believe the Lord is going to birth the great end-time move of God and the last great revival out of the local church. That said, it stands to reason that if there's anything the devil wants to hinder, damage or destroy right now, it is the local church.

Most often, the enemies of the church do not come from those who are without, but from those who are within. Wolves are not from the outside, but from inside the Body of Christ.

In Acts 20:29-31, Paul states something significant concerning dealing with wolves: *"For I know this, that after my departing shall grievous wolves enter in among you, not sparing the flock. Also of your own selves shall men arise, speaking perverse things, to draw away disciples after them. Therefore watch, and remember, that by the space of three years I ceased not to warn every one night and day with tears."*

Paul spent three years warning this church with tears about the destructive manner of wolves. Notice Paul said the wolves and perverse men would rise up from within. Understand, these wolves and others were people who had once been in right relationship with their church. They had been a part of the body and benefitted from the five-fold ministry.

Paul knew by the Spirit of God that, for whatever reason, when he left some would turn their backs on sound doctrine to attack the very shepherd who cared for them. He knew they would rise up to try to take positions of authority not belonging to them, and would eventually devour the sheep who had once been their friends.

Paul had been with this church for a long time, teaching, warning and preparing them for his departure. Even though he had poured so much of himself into these believers, he knew it would not be enough to keep the wolves at bay.

In even greater danger today is the church where there is no authoritative structure of God laid down, where the five-fold ministry is not understood, and where there is no clear truth settled. Here, error can be birthed at any time.

People will always challenge the truth through carnality and wrong motives. This is really what a wolf is—a sheep with wrong motives. He wants his following and his own thing to override structured authority.

Hear me. Your "own thing" is not important if it is disconnected, unedifying and shrinking the borders of your local church. God is not about ministry building, but He is about the Body of Christ being built upon the foundation of the five-fold ministry.

So here's my warning. There is coming a time when those who set themselves up against the church and against God's established five-fold structure will perish.

The Bible is full of examples where this very thing happened. In Numbers 16:1-35, we read the story of Korah, a man who gathered others unto himself against God's established authority under Moses. He did this because he considered himself more superior than God had called him to be. As a result of his pride and disobedience, he and his men, and all of their households, were swallowed up by the earth in an instant of time. Evidently, God was not happy with this kind of behavior.

We find another Old Testament example in Numbers 12:1-16 where Miriam and Aaron spoke against Moses because of the woman he had chosen to marry. Once again, we see how God was not pleased with people who stood up against His appointed authority. This time they did not die for their sin, but Miriam became leprous as a result. Aaron quickly repented, and Moses prayed for Miriam. Thankfully, God had mercy and healed her, but it cost her a week in the wilderness all alone.

In the New Testament, in Acts 5:1-10, we read the story of Ananias and Sapphira who set themselves against the vision and plan of God. As they stood before the apostles and lied, they each dropped dead instantly and were buried together, because they disrespected God's established authority.

God is not a respecter of persons. I truly believe the consequences which came upon men and women of the Bible will befall others living in like sin in these last days. God is restoring holiness to His church, and I believe a godly fear will return which will birth revival.

When Korah and his men were swallowed up by the earth, fear came on the camp and people began to live right. When Miriam became leprous, it led to repentance and respect for God's chosen leader.

When Ananias and Sapphira died, it birthed revival, not mourning. There came an awe (or fear) in the church, a reverence and respect for a holy, separated, consecrated people who were dedicated to serving God. The church gained much honor and respect during this time and multiplied greatly. I believe this same respect and honor will be restored in these last days, which will come before the final great harvest revival.

So, we need to be wary of wolves entering in, but we also need to beware that we do not become a wolf in sheep's clothing. Do not open the door to offence, jealousy, back-biting and name-calling that mark the life of a wolf.

Wolves breed more wolves, just as sheep breed more sheep. You will become like those you hang around with, so don't associate with wolves. Run from them and warn everyone around you to get away, too. Be like the boy in the children's story and cry, "Wolf!"

You can only be sure of one person going to Heaven, and that is you. You can be assured of your own redemption, but you cannot be certain of anyone else, because we are all responsible to work out our own salvation with fear and trembling (see Philippians 2:12).

Years ago I wrote very strong letters to all of my friends who were backslidden and out of church. I lovingly warned them to get back in right standing with God and reestablish themselves in a local church before it was too late. I could send the warning, but only they could give heed to my concern.

I'm sending you this warning, but it's up to you to respond. Run from wolves if they come around you, and guard your heart so that you do not become a wolf yourself. Your eternal reward, or lack of it, lies in the balance.

CHAPTER 8

THE CARING PASTOR

I sat at the oak table in the breakfast nook of our 100-plus year old farm house. It was early Sunday morning, and the wind was blowing on this winter day. Every so often the back door would blow open, and as always I would grab the snow shovel and remove the snow drift that would form on our sagging floors.

The wood stove was trying its best to keep up with the cold, but I was chilled as I sat and thought about how the Lord had blessed us with this home. My wife Phyllis and I were in a time of learning and growing with God. We had used our faith to buy this old house, and to us it was a blessing beyond measure, even with the creaks and groans of the old brick structure. We were in a learning process in our church, too, as it was also creaking and groaning in the spirit while we and our congregation grew and stretched our borders for Jesus.

As I sat and pondered the goodness of the Lord in our home and in our church, I had a vision. I saw a wheat field, golden and ripe for the harvest. The wind was blowing softly over the slender stalks, and it looked as if the hand of God was gently stroking the wheat. I watched in amazement for a moment, and then God posed a question. He asked, "Who will build a barn for the harvest of the wheat?" I instantly knew He was giving me direction for our church. It was time to build and expand our borders once more. It would require faith, unity and sacrifice from every person in our congregation, and the stretching we had been experiencing was about to become even more intense than it had ever been before.

I knew the need would never outweigh the benefit, but I also knew we had come to the end of our ability to expand where our church building was currently located, and we would have to launch out to buy land if we were to grow another inch. We had already expanded three times prior to this day, so

I realized this fourth expansion would take not only an enormous financial blessing, but also a major injection of faith to keep us strong when the times got tough. We had been through times of testing before, so I had every confidence God would be more than enough, no matter how trying things might become.

As the pastor of a young and growing church, I had been given a directing vision, and now it would be my responsibility to carry out the vision and keep the people focused as we moved into a new realm of possibilities. Even as a shepherd cares for his sheep and leads them to new pastures, I would have to step up to a new level of leadership and take my "sheep," the people of our church, to a whole new level in Christ. I knew it would not be easy, but I also knew we had to go where we were led.

After conferring with my wife, my co-pastor and confidant, I presented the vision to our congregation, and they immediately began to respond by giving sacrificially. They joyfully gave their finances, but more than that, they gave of themselves. So many beloved friends stepped up to the plate and gave their time and effort to bring the vision to fruition.

Today, having just completed the seventh major construction project in our over 25 year church history, I can look back at the moment when God first challenged me to build and reminisce with a heart-felt gratitude for everything God has done for our church family over the years. I recall all of the miracles it took for that expansion to come to pass, and the many other expansions since then, each one challenging us to rise to a new level of faith and confidence in the provision of our God.

I no longer remember the struggles of that time of stretching and change, but I do remember the victories. I remember the triumphs and the awesome day of praise when we settled into our new facility, and the glory of the Lord came down upon us. The barn was raised, and now it was time to bring in the harvest of souls.

THE GIFT OF THE PASTOR

The pastor is the main gateway to the local church congregation. It is his responsibility (and of course it could be her responsibility, too) to impart the Word of God into the lives of his people on a continuing basis. The pastor establishes the doctrine in his church, according to the Word of God, and he sets the order in each service. He is responsible for maintaining that order and for allowing the move of the Spirit each time his congregation comes together.

In John 21:17, Jesus talked to Peter and gave him insight into the ministry of the pastor when He said: *"...Feed My sheep."*

Pastors are men and women who are committed to God, and who day after day, week after week, and year after year, feed and care for their sheep. They teach them, pray for them, counsel them, marry and bury them, and stand by their sheep through thick and thin.

Feeding and caring for sheep is no small task. They don't just eat once in a while and go in the strength of that food for weeks, but they have to be fed a well-rounded diet regularly. They need stable, balanced nourishment with a variety of spiritual foods.

Pastors also perform the important duties only a shepherd would tackle. They not only feed the sheep, but they clean them up, too. If you've ever been around sheep on a farm, you know they are a mess and need constant attention. They have to be dipped, clipped, and de-nastified, if that's a word. Sheep cannot clean themselves, so all the muck and yuck they are around clings to their wool, and they are easily infected if they are not kept clean.

Being a pastor requires a lifetime of patience and understanding because some sheep learn, while others do not, so the shepherd sometimes has to clean up the same messes year after year after year. We see just how valuable the role of the shepherd is when we realize that sheep who are not well-fed and cared for die. This makes the responsibility of the pastor heavy and not to be taken lightly.

You already read of my personal call to the ministry and my initial reaction. I did not think I wanted to be in the ministry in those first moments when God spoke to me, because I knew what that meant. I knew I would be responsible for the spiritual well-being of my people. I would have to feed and care for them, and I was not sure I could.

I knew I would be responsible to teach them the Word, to give them godly counsel, to rebuke them when necessary, pray for them always and give an account for my actions when the end of my time on earth would come.

James 3:1 tells us: *"My brethren, be not many masters, knowing that we shall receive the greater condemnation."*

This is not a weight I would have chosen for myself, but because it was chosen for me, God has given me the measure of grace I need in order to do what I am called to do. Without this grace, I would not be a pastor, nor would anyone be able to fulfill His call on their own.

The gift of the office of the pastor is a divine implant with abilities and insight no man or university could provide. The call of a true pastor will be verified not by academic achievements, but by the fruit the pastor bears. A true pastor will have a well-fed, growing flock who are bringing more sheep into the fold. Sheep birth sheep, so an authentic pastor will always have new sheep to care for even as he cares for the adult, faithful sheep of his pasture.

The pastor is the one office that should not change in a local church. The shepherd should be growing, yes, but not wavering. The members should have every reason to be confident their pastor will be a constant source of sound doctrine, godly wisdom and divine counsel. Without these, the people will scatter and the flock will perish. This is not an acceptable outcome in any church.

FEED THE FLOCK

We read in 1 Peter 5:1-3: *"The elders which are among you I exhort, who am also an elder, and a witness of the sufferings of Christ, and also a partaker of the glory that shall be revealed: Feed the flock of God which is among you, taking the oversight thereof, not by constraint, but willingly; not for filthy lucre, but of a ready mind; Neither as being lords over God's heritage, but being ensamples to the flock."*

It is interesting to note that the word pastor is only mentioned in the New Testament one time, and that is in Ephesians 4:11. In the passage of scripture above, however, the word "elders" refers to pastors. We know this because Peter exhorts them to, *"feed the flock of God which is among you,"* which is the primary job of the pastor.

"Feed the flock" means to teach them truth so they will arrive at a productive place with God. Mothers and fathers feed their children for the same reason. They want them to grow, mature and become productive in life.

It would be very odd to find a thirty year old sucking on a bottle, so we know that over time, moms and dads have to adjust what they feed their children. Babies start out on milk, but as they grow they are expected to be able to swallow cereal, then strained foods, until eventually they can eat off the table and digest the same things mom and dad eat.

It's the same with pastors. While they have to adjust their messages according to who is in the house, they should not have to serve the same

134

warmed-over milk thirty years from now. Growing Christians should be able to handle meat when the time comes, and every pastor should be able to serve up the meat of the Word (see Hebrews 5:12).

Let's look at Ephesians 4:11 again: *"And he gave some, apostles; and some, prophets; and some, evangelists; and some, pastors and teachers."*

I want you to notice the punctuation in this verse. Each of the five gifts is separated by a comma except for "pastors and teachers." I find this very interesting.

My personal belief is that a teacher can be a teacher without being a pastor, but a pastor cannot be a pastor without the teaching anointing. Every pastor needs such an anointing to impart truth and cause his people to grow in it. A pastor must lead by example and by teaching.

Sheep without a teaching pastor will never be fed with the depths of revelation, but will be surface grazers, living on surface truths. They will be relegated to the brown tips of the grass, when what they need is the depth of the dark green stems hidden below, because nutrition is the strongest near the root where earth and plant meet.

A pastor must be able to offer the deep things of the Word to his people in order to assure the greatest growth in his congregation. He must be a shepherd, leading his sheep in the way they should go, and a teacher, instructing them in the ways of life. This is how he "feeds the flock."

GOD SPEAKS THROUGH THE PASTOR

God speaks through the office of the pastor in many different ways:

- God speaks through sermons, which are messages brought before the people and meant for all to receive.
- God speaks through counsel, where one or two need to hear a specific word.
- God speaks through the gifts of the Spirit, sometimes in a service where everyone benefits, but other times one on one where an individual needs direction.
- God speaks through signs and wonders, healings and miracles.
- God speaks through the pastor's lifestyle, through his prayer, study and fasting, and through the fruit of the Spirit evident in his life.

135

- God speaks through the pastoral relationship in acts of kindness and care for the people of his or her church.

Jesus is the primary example for how a pastor, also known as a shepherd, ought to care for his people, allowing God to speak to them through him. Jesus personally cared for the disciples. He taught them, trained them, rebuked them when necessary and expected them to follow Him.

Jesus spoke to Peter concerning how to carry out the duties of a pastor in John 21:15-17: " *So when they had dined, Jesus saith to Simon Peter, Simon, son of Jonas, lovest thou me more than these? He saith unto him, Yea, Lord; thou knowest that I love thee. He saith unto him, Feed my lambs. He saith to him again the second time, Simon, son of Jonas, lovest thou me? He saith unto him, Yea, Lord; thou knowest that I love thee. He saith unto him, Feed my sheep. He saith unto him the third time, Simon, son of Jonas, lovest thou me? Peter was grieved because he said unto him the third time, Lovest thou me? And he said unto him, Lord, thou knowest all things; thou knowest that I love thee. Jesus saith unto him, Feed my sheep.* "

Jesus seemed to say the same thing to Peter three times, but if we do a word study, we discover subtle differences.

The first time Jesus addressed Peter, He said: *"Feed my lambs."* The word translated "feed" here simply means to cause to graze. We know that when sheep graze, they grow, so we see Jesus instructed Peter to teach His people the Word, which would cause them to grow and develop.

We also see that Jesus called the people, "My sheep," which tells us men and women in the church are precious to God, and that no pastor should ever deal with them outside the confines of the Bible, because God takes it very personally when His people are mistreated.

The second time Jesus addressed Peter, He said: *"Feed my sheep."* This time the word "feed" means to instruct, and to have rule or dominion over. Here, Jesus was talking about taking a place of supervision over the people.

So, we see that the shepherd feeds the sheep for growth, but he also instructs and takes a supervisory role over them, a position of spiritual leadership ordained by God. In other words, a pastor instructs, directs, judges and corrects his people according to God's Word. Not all sheep will receive this kind of instruction and correction, but all sheep need it.

Let me give you a natural example to explain. I heard about a news story

136

where someone had taken video footage of a small flock of sheep that had frozen to death in less than two feet of water. This little stray flock had wondered into a flooded area, and rather than move out of the water as the cold of night came on, they stood in that water until they died of exposure.

The video footage was incredible because it showed that if the sheep had moved just a few steps in either direction, they would have saved themselves. They were standing in a relatively small amount of water, but because they had no shepherd to lead them to safety, they died there.

It's like that in the Body of Christ sometimes. There are moments when Christians find themselves in cold, dangerous waters, often because of mistakes they have made, and on other occasions because of the attacks of the enemy. It doesn't matter how they got there, what matters is what they do once they have arrived.

In the middle of the flock, in the middle of the night, it's not always easy to know what to do, but God has anointed your pastor to lead and guide you. If you will listen to the word of the Lord given through him each time he teaches and preaches, and if you will heed his instruction and warnings, you will be able to find your way to safety.

I'm not talking about a pastor ruling over every detail of your life or forcing you to do anything, but I am referring to allowing God to speak through him as he teaches, trains and leads you in paths of righteousness and safety. I am talking about following his example.

I guarantee the shepherd was heart-broken when he found this frozen flock of stray sheep, because he could have saved them with one simple call. He could have led them to dry ground and safe keeping.

"Follow me as I follow Christ" is what Paul said (see 1 Corinthians 11:1). This is what a true pastor wants you to do, just follow Him as he follows Jesus.

PASTORS ARE EXAMPLES

Let's look again at 1 Peter 5:3, which says: *"Neither as being lords over God's heritage, but being ensamples to the flock."*

An example is an instructor and a leader. If you are a role model to someone, they will follow you and do as you do. That's why sheep follow the shepherd, because they have trusted him before and believe he will lead them to green grass and safe waters.

In like manner a congregation should not be afraid to follow their pastor. They should be confident that his anointing will lead them to revelation of God's Word, and that when he stands in the pulpit and says, "Open your Bibles," what he is about to say is inspired of the Lord.

Pastors are also to be an example to their congregations in word and in deed. When a pastor preaches the Word, he should be delivering just what God directed him to deliver. And when he challenges his people to do something, it should only be as far as he is willing to go and do himself.

If God asks me to challenge my church in some way, I will be the first in line to show them I am every bit as committed as I expect them to be.

I remember a time years ago when I asked our people to build a church in another country. This was a great challenge for us because it would cost us $7,000 to put up a basic structure for a congregation in a third world nation. The amount seemed very large in our eyes at the time.

I remember specifically as I sat on the platform about to take up the offering, God spoke to me and told me to give the first $1,000. Now, you have to understand, this was all my wife Phyllis and I had. We had saved for 17 years to accumulate that much money, so it was going to be an extreme act of faith on our part.

My reaction at first was, "Do what?" I looked at Phyllis for any sign of confirmation, but she immediately turned her head and looked away from me. I was on my own, so I prayed and said, "God, you better tell my wife because I'm going to do it." I stood up and told my congregation that Phyllis and I would give the first $1,000."

When I got in the car after the service I quickly told Phyllis, "Honey, God told me to do this." She said, "I know. He told me at the same time, I just couldn't bring myself to look at you to confirm it."

We laugh about it now, but that was a very big deal for us, one we will never forget. Since then we have asked our congregation to build over 70 churches in other nations, and each time we always step up to the plate first because we want to be an example in word and in deed. We want our congregation to be able to follow us, and not have to push us along.

In the same way, I will always be the first one to commit to a fast before I ask my congregation to join me. I will always fast more often than I ask them to because I want to lead as a good example and with a pure heart.

How men of God can ask more of their people than they are willing to give themselves is beyond me. I believe pastors should always be the first to do the most in every situation. This is leadership, and what God expects of true pastors.

THE PASTORAL RELATIONSHIP

When we speak of pastors, we are talking about the one office of the five-fold ministry that actually builds personal relationships with people. Apostles, evangelists, prophets and teachers blow in and blow out of a local church, while the pastor is left to deal with his people on a daily basis.

Don't get me wrong, I honor and respect every five-fold minister, and I open my pulpit often to their ministry gifts so my church will be well-rounded. But this doesn't change the fact that no evangelist will ever bury any of my congregation members. No prophet will ever marry a couple in my church. No apostle will ever sit down for one-on-one counseling with any of my people. Those are my jobs, and I am happy to carry them out because I have established personal relationships with my church family, and I am constantly working to nurture them.

God will speak to you through your personal relationship with your pastor. I'm not talking about having him over to lunch every Sunday, but I am referring to the fact that you know him, and he knows you. You have watched and listened to him over the years, and you have developed a trust in him which helps you in the hard times.

Your pastor has also watched you go through seasons in your walk with Christ. He knows your strengths and weaknesses, your gifts and your calling, where you are doing well, and where you need more help.

Your relationship with your pastor is a spiritual one, governed by the Word of God. In many ways, the connection between you and your pastor reflects your relationship with God.

No godly pastor wants his own will for your life, but he desires God's perfect will to come to pass for you and your family. He wants you to develop your spiritual gifts and become the person God intends you to be for your family and for your church.

With this in mind, it is easy to understand why God will speak through your pastor to direct, correct and lead you in the way that you should go. Notice I said *lead*, not push or force. Just as good parents know their children and lead them to develop their God-given gifts, so pastors who know their people will help them grow the spiritual gifts placed in them.

As I said before, no other five-fold ministry gift has the same personal, day in and day out relationship with you that your pastor does. And no other five-fold gift will be there for you when you need them. This does not make the pastor more important, just unique in that God has placed him or her in your life to be a constant source of spiritual input.

Spiritual relationships are essential to our Christian walk because it is through these bonds God can lead us, correct us and direct us to be all He has destined us to be.

In Hebrews 13:7 we read: *"Remember them which have the rule over you, who have spoken unto you the word of God: whose faith follow, considering the end of their conversation."*

I know discussing someone having rule over you is not what causes most Christians to shout. The Bible tells us one sign of the end times will be that people will despise government, or rulership (see 2 Peter 2:10). This means not only natural government, but also church government.

So many Christians despise anyone who tells them what is right or wrong. Some have even told me that as a pastor, I have no right to tell them what to do. My response is always the same, "You may not think I have a right, but I do have an obligation."

I will not leave my people to their own devices when I see them heading for destruction any more than a parent will leave his child headed for a busy highway. It is the pastor's responsibility to intervene, correct and if necessary rebuke when someone is going the wrong way, because it is his duty to protect his people, just as it is the parent's job to protect his or her child.

Hebrews 13:17 makes it even clearer that we are to listen to our pastors: *"Obey them that have the rule over you, and submit yourselves: for they watch for your souls, as they that must give account, that they may do it with joy, and not with grief: for that is unprofitable for you."*

Your pastor is responsible for watching over your soul. Every pastor takes his call seriously, and invests much time and energy in prayer and study so that he will always be ready for whatever comes along.

Of course I understand it is not possible to watch over someone who does not want accountability. People who rebel cannot be supervised. They can be dealt with in a spiritual manner, but it is impossible to watch for their souls.

Such individuals always think they are smarter than their spiritual fathers, and more intelligent than spiritual government. They think they are wiser than the rule God has established in the Kingdom and believe they know everything and have need of nothing.

This kind of attitude misses the whole point of the pastoral relationship. In ministry, rulership is not about intelligence or collective knowledge, but it is about an appointment by God to carry out the pastoral call.

God calls pastors to lead, guide, nurture, exhort, correct, rebuke, encourage and feed. No man or woman could carry out such a call apart from the grace and anointing of His Spirit. This is what makes the pastoral relationship so unique. We each get to partake of this special anointing as we receive the word of God through our pastors.

THE HEART OF A PASTOR

We learn in 1 Thessalonians 2:4: *"But as we were allowed of God to be put in trust with the gospel, even so we speak; not as pleasing men, but God, which trieth our hearts."*

We do not want ourselves or our pastors to be men-pleasers, or even us-pleasers. Men-pleasers have unstable churches where everyone is vying for their own rights and their own way. It is dangerous to have such a pastor in the pulpit. One who is ruled by men rather than by God will ultimately find his church split right down the middle and his people divided and destroyed.

Pastors ought to please God and God alone. They should allow Him to speak plainly and openly to their people each time they preach. They should not attempt to please their congregations with messages that tickle their ears without ever telling them the truth. Often, what God has to say through a pastor will make a direct hit on his congregation's toes.

Look at how Jesus treated the disciples. He was frank and honest with them, never pulling punches or trying to stroke their egos. Jesus always told the truth, correcting them when they were wrong and teaching them how to do things the right way. This is called speaking the truth in love, and it is what God speaks through a true pastor.

People love easy-going messages as much as sheep love lollygagging around in the same old pasture, but it's not good for either of them. People need to hear the meat of the word along with the stuff that is easier to swallow, just as sheep need rousted out of their slumber and made to move to a new pasture when the old one begins to run out of grass.

141

In 1 Thessalonians 2:5-11, Paul goes on to say: *"For neither at any time used we flattering words, as ye know, nor a cloke of covetousness; God is witness: Nor of men sought we glory, neither of you, nor yet of others, when we might have been burdensome, as the apostles of Christ. But we were gentle among you, even as a nurse cherisheth her children: So being affectionately desirous of you, we were willing to have imparted unto you, not the gospel of God only, but also our own souls, because ye were dear unto us. For ye remember, brethren, our labour and travail: for labouring night and day, because we would not be chargeable unto any of you, we preached unto you the gospel of God. Ye are witnesses, and God also, how holily and justly and unblameably we behaved ourselves among you that believe: As ye know how we exhorted and comforted and charged every one of you, as a father doth his children."*

These verses lay out the heart of a pastor for his people perfectly, and they also show us the heart of God toward us. Remember, each of the five-fold ministry gifts reveals a glimpse of our heavenly Father, so what we see our pastors do for us, we know God desires to do even more.

As verse seven says, God desires to speak through your pastor gently, even as a nurse cherishes her children. This does not mean that what He says will always be comfortable and easy to bear. The truth, even when spoken tenderly, can sometimes be hard to take, just as medicine is difficult for a baby to swallow, but so necessary for that child's health and well being.

In verse eleven, we see God will speak through your pastor to exhort, comfort and charge you, as a father does his children. The words of a godly father are always for the good of the child, but again not always what the child wants to hear.

Sometimes dads get to play with their kids in the back yard at the end of a hard day, but other times they have to correct and discipline. It's called relationship, and this is what also happens between you and your pastor.

There will be Sundays God will allow him to speak a pleasant word for your life, one that will edify and comfort. But then will come the Sunday when God will ask him to speak a word of correction and give you a charge to do things differently. We need to receive both as words delivered from the throne of God, through our pastor, and for our good.

An honorable pastor will not rule from a place of forced authority, but from one which is forged by the love and compassion he has for his people.

Respect should be earned, not demanded or required simply for the sake of authority.

True pastors do not manipulate or try to control people, but they do what they do because they are striving to fulfill 1 Thessalonians 2:8 which says: *"So being affectionately desirous of you, we were willing to have imparted unto you, not the gospel of God only, but also our own souls, because ye were dear unto us."* This is the heart of a true pastor.

GOD SPEAKS FAITH

In the book of Jude, verse three, we are told: *"Beloved, when I gave all diligence to write unto you of the common salvation, it was needful for me to write unto you, and exhort you that ye should earnestly contend for the faith which was once delivered unto the saints."*

When God speaks through a pastor, He will speak words that will stir you to contend for the faith delivered to you. This means every pastor should be teaching his people about faith and encouraging them to walk by faith. No pastor should ever preach anything that strips hope and comfort from his people, but should always be diligent to teach them to walk by faith and not by sight (see 2 Corinthians 5:7).

There is nothing simpler or more needful than the message of faith. We are saved by grace through faith, we live by faith, we walk righteously by faith and we are justified by faith (see Ephesians 2:8; Romans 1:17; 3:22, 28). We speak by faith, we stand by faith, we abound in faith, we increase in faith and we are children of God by faith (see Romans 6:8; 11:20; 2 Corinthians 8:7; 10:15; Galatians 3:26).

Jude verse 4 explains why it is so crucial for the pastor to teach us faith: *"For there are certain men crept in unawares, who were before of old ordained to this condemnation, ungodly men, turning the grace of our God into lasciviousness, and denying the only Lord God, and our Lord Jesus Christ."*

Faith makes us able to stand up against those who creep into the fold to do us harm. Every shepherd watches for wolves, but sheep need to be prepared to encounter and deal with them, too. We are prepared when we contend for the faith, and it is our pastor's job to teach us how to do this.

I remember the year 1999 and the scare that had everyone spending lots of time, energy and money trying to prepare for the "doomsday" computer crash which was predicted to befall the world at 12:01 A.M. on January 1, 2000. Y2K, as it was affectionately known, was going to cripple financial institutions all over the planet, interrupt food supplies and wreak havoc with one click of the second hand at midnight on that dreaded date.

All around the world everyone predicted gloom and doom for months on end that year. Chicken Little could not have been more proud of the cries of "the sky is falling" that went up everywhere. Newspapers, internet sites and newscasts predicted the crash of all crashes if we did not prepare and sacrifice to correct our computer calendars. Most believed that even if we did everything we could to prevent it, disaster was inevitable.

When well-known church leaders jumped on the bandwagon and began to publish their own crisis predictions, each claiming to have a word from the Lord, I decided I could not allow my congregation to feed on the lies anymore. One Sunday, I stepped up to the pulpit and told them that I had complete assurance that we were going to be fine. I believed God had said nothing major would happen, and so I told my people not to fear, but to trust in Him. Some believed me, but others continued to worry about the coming New Year.

Sure enough, when the glittering ball dropped and the year 2000 officially began, an amazing thing happened: Absolutely nothing! The lights stayed on. The planes stayed in the air. The food trucks kept on cruising. The computers kept on computing. Everything continued at 12:01 A.M. just as it had at 11:59 P.M. the day before.

As I look back I am amazed that none of the "doom and gloom" preachers offered a money-back guarantee for their failed predictions, false prophecies and deceptive books that made them a ton of money. As far as I know, not one person ever held them accountable for what they had said. Once the day came and went, all was forgotten, and the world went on as it had before, only a little lighter in the pocket and a little wiser for the experience.

As always, God knew what would happen, and He had given me a sense of peace I could pass on to my people, even as a shepherd who encounters a stormy situation infuses a sense of calm into his flock. Though my words ran contrary to practically every noteworthy report from sinner and saint alike, we remained peaceful and steadfast, and we actually enjoyed our New Year's Eve celebration. By resisting fear and going against the flow, we were able to trust

God during those days of the unknown, and He prevailed on our behalf. The Lord was faithful, and when challenged, the message of faith sustained His people.

When God speaks faith through your pastor, you will be built up, encouraged, and equipped to stand against the wiles of the devil, too (see Ephesians 6:11). You will be ready for anything Satan can send your way, and you will stand steadfast, no matter what the world around you says. The gospel is good news to each of us, and faith runs like a golden thread through the entire gospel message. Every time God speaks faith through your pastor, He speaks the good news and builds you up to live as children should live— blessed, faithful and secure.

GIVEN TO THE WORD AND PRAYER

Let's go back to 1 Peter 5:2 which says: *"Feed the flock of God which is among you, taking the oversight thereof, not by constraint, but willingly; not for filthy lucre, but of a ready mind."*

One who takes oversight is one who leads, and such a person must be able to see where he is going, so a pastor must be a man of vision. If a pastor does not have a vision, he and his people will perish (see Proverbs 29:18).

A pastor must be able to see clearly, and this unclouded sight or vision will only come from being a man or woman of prayer. Any pastor who tries to complete his ministry without much prayer will never see the true vision of God for his church. This vision only comes through time in prayer and fasting, and through building a relationship with the Holy Spirit who shows us things to come (see John 16:13).

A pastor, as the leader of a church, must be able to see with the eyes of God and have the Lord's plan and ability at work in him in order to allow the Father to speak through him.

Acts 6:1-4 records: *"And in those days, when the number of the disciples was multiplied, there arose a murmuring of the Grecians against the Hebrews, because their widows were neglected in the daily ministration. Then the twelve called the multitude of the disciples unto them, and said, It is not reason that we should leave the word of God, and serve tables. Wherefore, brethren, look ye out among you seven men of honest report, full of the Holy Ghost and wisdom, whom we may appoint over this business. But we will give ourselves continually to prayer, and to the ministry of the word."*

Notice verse two: *"Then the twelve called the multitude of the disciples unto them, and said, It is not reason that we should leave the word of God, and serve tables."* James and Paul both held more than one of the five-fold offices, so we know this passage of scripture applies to *every* five-fold office.

God has set the pastor in the church as a visionary, to be in the Word and prayer, and to set the course for his church. He is not called to carry out every activity created by that vision by himself.

The Lord has placed men and women in every church to be a help to every pastor. If we would allow these helpers to develop and be used according to the scripture, every pastor would be freed to pursue the vision for his church without the weight of the world on his shoulders, and every congregation would be blessed as a result.

If God is ever going to be free to speak through pastors as He desires, they must be able to spend hours in prayer and study every day, rather than spending hours "serving tables."

I encourage you to free your pastor to pursue God's vision for your church so that the Lord can speak freely through him every time he stands behind the sacred desk and delivers the Word to your congregation. Let your pastor fulfill verse 4 by giving himself *"continually to prayer, and to the ministry of the word."*

Then, God will speak through him in messages from the throne, in wisdom and knowledge, in acts of kindness and caring for His people. Through him will come God's divine counsel, gifts of the Spirit, signs, wonders and miracles. The Lord will speak volumes through him in a lifestyle filled with the fruit of the Spirit.

Your pastor can deliver the word of the Lord only as he is allowed to receive it in times of prayer and study, times of pulling away to fast, times spent alone with the Spirit of grace and truth who will fill him with *"the spirit of wisdom and revelation in the knowledge of Him: The eyes of his understanding being enlightened; that he may know what is the hope of His calling, and what the riches of the glory of His inheritance in the saints,"* so that your pastor may declare *"what is the exceeding greatness of His power to you who believe, according to the working of His mighty power"* (Ephesians 1:17-19).

Give your pastor the gift of time for the Word and prayer, and God will speak to you through him. Of this, I have no doubt.

CHAPTER 9

HEAR THE TEACHER

I was teaching on a Wednesday evening in our mid-week service, and I had no idea if the message was having an impact on the congregation or not. They were unusually quiet, which is always a bit unnerving for someone standing behind a pulpit expecting to change lives with a word from the Lord, but I pushed on despite the lack of response, and I delivered what I thought was a good message.

It was the second in a series of teachings, and I was excited about the subject because I really believed that if people would catch hold of it, they would be changed—which is always my target when I teach the Word. Change is what will cause believers to mature and grow in the things of the Lord. Being a man, however, I am also looking for a clue that will tell me if I am reaching my goal.

When I arrived home later that night, my wife said something I will never forget. She commented, "I knew that, but I've never really seen it until tonight." Revelation! This was what was happening in the crowd during the message. They were receiving revelation. So, instead of lots of "Amens," I heard a deafening silence, but the people were being impacted, just as my wife had been. I did not really need the encouragement, but I enjoyed it anyway.

Sometimes preachers think those in the congregation aren't getting what they're preaching, when in reality they are seeing something in the Word they've never seen before. When the light of revelation enters a prepared heart, the Word of God changes that life forever. This is why revelation is the goal of every Bible teacher. There is no more precious treasure on earth, and there is no other prize in the eyes of the five-fold teacher. When a teacher hears "I got it!" from a hungry listener, it is reward enough. The job of the teacher has been completed, and the Word of God has been exalted. How much better could it be?

THE GIFT OF THE TEACHER

When God called me to be a pastor, He also called me to teach His people. As a man who carries both the office of the pastor and the office of the teacher, I do not take my responsibility lightly. I truly believe that all pastors need the teaching anointing to establish sound doctrine in their churches.

The five-fold teacher is so important to every believer because the teacher is the man or woman who digs deep into the Word of God and extracts revelation, and he imparts this revelation line upon line, precept upon precept, taking complex thoughts and ideas, and breaking them down into bite-sized morsels which people can digest and understand.

The Bible is very simple, yet many find it difficult to grasp, so the job of the teacher is never-ending. There will always be precepts to teach, doctrines to establish and life-lessons to impart. Every church is made up of believers at various stages of life and spiritual understanding, so the role of the teacher will be ever-changing as people change and grow, and yet some things will always remain the same.

Teachers will always stick to the Word like glue. They will never stray, because to them the Word is the single most precious thing in the world. They would never want to dishonor God by teaching doctrine that is man-made or humanistic in any way. A five-fold teacher will proclaim the Word and the Word only, and he will fight you tooth and nail if you try to convince him scripture is not true and accurate.

In the eyes of the teacher the Bible is absolute, eternal, perfectly ordered, unchanging, complete, without error, infallible and one hundred percent the Word of God. Of course we know this is all true, but no one understands or believes it more than a five-fold teacher. He trusts what he reads in the Word more than he trusts anything else in the entire world.

There are two categories of five-fold teachers who do not carry the pastoral anointing. The first is made up of those who have a training ministry which requires them to travel from church to church and from venue to venue, ministering specific words to multiple groups of people. These have their ministry offices established outside of a local church, but most of them are still connected to a local congregation in some form or fashion.

The other category is just as important. Their offices are established in local churches, and they travel from venue to venue as an outreach of that church. Even as they travel, they are rooted in and remain active in their home congregation. I believe as we approach the end of the last days, more and more ministries will anchor themselves to a local body of believers, which I feel is God-ordained.

Whatever their base of operation, teachers are called by God to deliver messages to believers everywhere, revealing hidden truths and uncovering nuggets of revelation to edify the Body of Christ.

THE TEACHER'S PLACE IN THE BODY

Every office in the five-fold ministry has equal value, but I believe that the teacher is one of the more misunderstood gifts in the church. Let's be honest. Most of us were raised up by preachers of the Word, not by teachers. We grew up under men and women who could "preach a good preach" and "shout a good shout," but oftentimes they did not impart much truth into our lives.

I've talked to people who are attracted to such ministries (as I was in the past, to be honest). After they leave a service, most of the time they cannot even identify what the message was about, they just know they feel better having heard it. That's okay, sometimes. There are services when we need an exhortation, a good shouting message that will fire us back up and set our feet on solid ground again.

There's nothing wrong with being stirred up and sent on your way, but if we want to come to the fullness of the stature of Christ, we need the teacher to be active in our lives. We can gather all the preaching and shouting tapes that we want, but if this is all we ever hear, we will be lacking in the balances of maturity and left without a clear understanding of our purpose.

There are some Christians who stay away from teachers because they have the mistaken idea that they are somehow less significant than those who stir with their preaching. Nothing could be further from the truth. Teachers may be different in the way they deliver their messages, but they are not of lesser value than any other five-fold gift. They are anointed and appointed by God, just as much as the shouting, sweating, stomping, fist-banging preacher is.

A woman left our church years ago because she said I was no preacher, I was just a teacher. In her mind, she had to be stirred to an emotional frenzy every week in order to receive something from God. As a pastor and a teacher, this was not my style. Now, don't get me wrong. I like to shout with the best of them, and there are times when God will loose me to crank out a shout-filled message, but most of the time I am content to teach line upon line, precept upon precept, here a little and there a little (see Isaiah 28:10).

I am content for two reasons, because I know my calling, and because I understand the benefit of sound doctrine in the church. I am a pastor, but I am also a teacher, so it is essential for me to speak words of revelation that set people free.

Others in the Body of Christ mistakenly believe teachers are boring, and so they refuse to listen to them. They envision history class in ninth grade and the nap that always followed. They think that Mr. History has been called to the office of the five-fold teacher and placed behind a pulpit in their church, just to torture them.

I can assure you that teachers are not dull, but they do deliver the Word in a different way. They make sure that every point they present is backed up with scripture reference after scripture reference. They never stray from the Bible, and they never attempt to give you their own opinion unless they have first given you a warning. A teacher will recharge you with the Word, and he will stir you, not by shouting and fist-banging, but by revelation and inspiration. He will edify you with the words he speaks, and will challenge you by the way he lives. In the end, it's the Word that brings results, and the Word is never boring.

The Body of Christ has been through many phases over the years. They have clamored for one type of ministry in one decade, and then despised it and demanded something else in the next. Today, hopefully you are of the opinion that men and women who are called of God should simply be who they are called to be. It's time we are more concerned about the message than we are the style of the messenger. Stylistic mannerisms should never rule who or what you listen to. Just because the teacher teaches line upon line rather than shouts, don't run off and hide. Allow God to speak through the teacher. You might just learn something!

DIGGING FOR HIDDEN TREASURE

The teacher has a divine eye that allows him to see beneath simple black and white. He has a supernatural ability to see the things which are in between the crossing of the 't's and the dotting of the 'i's. He is able to see and explain what the Spirit of God meant when He wrote something in the Word. The

Bible is a book of profound simplicity. Every verse can be taken at face value, but then there is always a deeper truth, something below the surface. The teacher is the one called and empowered by God to dig it out.

Teachers dearly love the words of the Bible. They spend hours looking them up in the original language and checking their meanings in the dictionary and the concordance. They love study aids, and they can't wait to run references to see what else God said about certain things in the Bible. Teachers strive to probe into the deeper things in the Word of God, and they work hard to penetrate down below the surface of every verse to glean every last nugget of truth they can find. Teachers also work very hard to lead people into their own study of God's Word.

When I teach, I ask my congregation to turn to a whole list of scriptures, because I want to make sure that they see the Word for themselves and become candidates for revelation. It is most gratifying to me when a person really sees a truth for the first time, and then goes a step further and actually does what they see. This is the heart of the teacher—to not only impart truth, but to see that truth change lives. This is what God always has in mind when He anoints and appoints someone to one of the five-fold ministry offices.

Teachers will always stick to the Word, and they will encourage you to look for yourself and not just believe everything they say just because they said it. This is the mark of a true teacher, one who is willing to withstand the scrutiny of questions and individual study of the Bible. A teacher will never shy away from being asked to explain something, but will in fact enjoy explaining what the Bible means.

Some of my most treasured times with my congregation are those when I lay aside my notes for the evening's message and just spend an hour allowing my church family to ask me questions about whatever is on their heart. I am amazed at the in-depth questions I receive, and I am equally amazed at the teaching that flows out of me, the Spirit of God reaching down to touch people with personal answers about real life issues. This is one aspect of teaching that is unique. It can be very personal even while it touches the hearts of so many in the room. Only God can speak in this supernatural way, delivering one answer that will satisfy multitudes of questions.

SOUND DOCTRINE

Paul tells Timothy: *"As I besought thee to abide still at Ephesus, when I went into Macedonia, that thou mightest charge some that they teach no other doctrine"* (1 Timothy 1:3). Five-fold teachers will teach foundational truths and stay true to established doctrine. While they impart the Word that will bring revelation, it will always be intertwined with foundational truths which have already been established (see Hebrews 6:1-2).

First Timothy 1:4 tells us: *"Neither give heed to fables and endless genealogies, which minister questions, rather than godly edifying which is in faith: so do."* Teachers will pop the bubbles of false doctrines and the traditions of men. They will erase fables from your mind and challenge you, because they will teach truth instead of what mama taught, or what papa said.

In Hebrews 5:12 we learn: *"For when for the time ye ought to be teachers, ye have need that one teach you again which be the first principles of the oracles of God; and are become such as have need of milk, and not of strong meat."* An effective teacher will realize where his audience is coming from and tailor his message to meet their needs. If he is teaching a group of babies, he will grind his meat into tiny, bite-sized portions so they can digest what he says. If he's teaching a group of meat-eaters like himself, then he can go deeper and slice the prime rib for them.

However he prepares and delivers his message, you can rest assured it will be doctrinally sound and will stick to the written Word. There will be nothing new, but there will always be something fresh. Ecclesiastes 1:9 tells us there is nothing new under the sun, but this does not mean God cannot uncover revelation which makes the old seem new again. This is one of the great things about teachers. They have the knack to take a basic truth and offer it in such a way as to help you see something you've never noticed, even while they stay true to established doctrine and previously taught truths.

Many of the teachers I know today are very diligent to make sure they do not divert their messages away from basic doctrine. Even when they bring forth a revelation which many have not heard before, they will always take it back to the foundational truths we all rely upon, because they do not want to mislead anyone, or have any listener mislead themselves, which can happen.

As scripture declares: *"For the time will come when they will not endure sound doctrine; but after their own lusts shall they heap to themselves teachers, having itching ears"* (2 Timothy 4:3). Such people are those who want to hear a message that will make them shout, but they don't want to hear the part about personal responsibility and living a sin-free life. Itching ears want the blessing, but they don't want the work. They desire the fruit, but they don't want to dig in the dirt and plant anything.

People with itching ears are a danger to themselves, and they actually mislead themselves into doctrines of devils, not even realizing it. This is why we need to be very careful what we give our attention to. Make sure the voice of the Lord is not skewed by the voice of men who are striving to make themselves a name, instead of seeking to bless the name of the Lord.

GOD SPEAKS IN DIFFERENT WAYS

The Lord communicates through the teacher in many different ways. God can speak through him in a message taught from a pulpit in a local church or in another setting. God can speak through him in conferences, or in single lessons. He can also speak through a teacher when he writes books or other teaching materials.

I have written several books. Sometimes, I take a teaching or a concept I have preached over the years, and I re-work that teaching into written form. In the process I have discovered that the written word is very different from what I speak. When I deliver a verbal message, I can be very animated and even use props to get my point across. But when I write, I have to create word pictures and order my teaching in a slightly different manner.

This is a good thing, because some people are quite verbal and process information better when a message is delivered in person, but others are very word oriented and learn more when they read the teaching than when they hear it. God made us all unique individuals, so it is good the Lord can speak through teachers in a variety of ways so we can each receive in the manner best suited for our individual needs.

There is one more place God speaks using a teacher, and that is through one-on-one counseling. I love to teach when I counsel. This is my opportunity to take my time and pour into someone who is hurting, or one with a question or a need. In those times, God can deliver a word of wisdom for that individual, which we will cover in a future chapter, and give that person just what he needs to deliver himself from the snare of the enemy.

Counseling sessions allow for eye to eye contact, and up-close and personal interaction. Not only will revelation flow in these sessions, but messages will sometimes be born which will later be delivered to the entire church. I love this about the Spirit of God.

The Lord can also speak through a teacher in life messages. Watch how a teacher lives and what he says in certain situations. Allow God to speak to you and encourage you to do what you see. As we read before, *"Follow me as I follow Christ"* was Paul's basic message all through his letters to the New Testament churches. Following the instruction and the lifestyle of a teacher can be an effective way for you to hear from God.

The primary method God will speak through the teacher is through revelation, because revelation is the Word illuminated and the Word made real to you. Remember the fine diamond and how you can see different colors and facets when you look at it from different angles? Teachers love to be the one to point out the varying colors and show you hidden facets.

Teachers want you to receive revelation that will cause you to know the truth, so the truth can make you free (see John 8:32). They want to deposit revelation that will shine a bright light on a verse or a passage of scripture so you can see it clearly, as if you've never seen it before. They will want you to hear God speak to you by His Spirit through the revelation that comes as they lay line upon line, and precept upon precept. They love the satisfaction of seeing a verse jump out at you as they teach, knowing the revelation they have delivered will make the Word come alive in your life.

DOERS OF THE WORD

In our Christian lifetime, most of us have heard enough messages to sink a ship, but the majority have been doers of only a small fraction of what we've heard. A teacher will not be satisfied until His audience is doing what he is teaching; therefore, he will go over and over and over it until he sees results. This is the heart of the Father speaking through the teacher.

If you have children, you understand why I make this comparison. I do not remember ever telling my daughter something only one time, but I do remember telling her things repeatedly. Children rarely clean their room the first time you tell them. (And how many wives will say the same about their husband's garage!) Parents usually have to ask Tommy or Susie three or four times before the room finally, miraculously, gets cleaned.

Our heavenly Father knows our frame. He understands we are as weak as our children, and that we need to be told over and over before we finally stand up and become doers of the Word. So, God speaks through the teacher, through someone endowed with godly patience to repeat a message as often as necessary, until God says, "They got it!"—and lets the teacher move on.

I've told my congregation many times, "You may think you've heard this message before, but you really haven't because God told me to preach it again." Hearing with the human ear and hearing with the spiritual ear are two entirely different things. Physical hearing requires you to process the sound, but not necessarily understand the noise. Spiritual hearing requires understanding before it counts.

This is why the Bible tells us: *"So then faith cometh by hearing, and hearing by the word of God"* (Romans 10:17). Faith does not come by simply processing the sound waves; it only arrives when understanding occurs. Teachers are used by God to help bring this understanding. Having said that, we also need to realize faith does not come by hearing the teacher only. The teacher opens the door, but you must by your own hearing and understanding walk through that door before faith will truly come alive.

A teacher wants you to see what he sees and understand what he understands because he is so in love with God's Word, he wants you to be also. A teacher will tell you one thing in ten different ways because he wants you to comprehend it just as he does. Why is a teacher this way? Because Jesus is this way. Remember, Jesus carried all of the five-fold gifts in His ministry. When Jesus taught, He taught with a purpose, to get His Word into the hearts of men and women who were seeking to receive.

Jesus never forced revelation on anyone. Most of the time, the disciples had to track Him down privately if they did not understand what He taught the crowds. Jesus wanted them to get it, but He refused to force on them what they did not want to receive. When they came seeking privately, though, He always took the time to go over and over it until He was sure they understood. When you see a teacher, you catch a glimpse of Jesus on the mountainside teaching the disciples. You see His love and care for you, and you see His Word made alive.

TEACHERS AND MIRACLES

Let me tell a story that will show you a side of teachers you may not have experienced before. One evening Paul was teaching a group of disciples in the city of Troas. He had been there for several days, a pit stop of sorts on his way to Macedonia. Paul was planning to depart the next day, and so it was his desire to leave behind as much of himself as he could before he was gone.

155

We know Paul was an apostle, but he was also a teacher of the Word. The teaching anointing must have been on him quite strong that evening because his message continued until midnight. The place was packed, and every eye was glued to Paul, except for a young man who had been dozing on and off all night, way up in the highest loft of the room.

The longer Paul spoke, the heavier this young man's eyes became, until at last he could not take it anymore, and he fell into a deep sleep. It wasn't long before he lost his balance and fell to the ground with a loud thud. The people gasped, but Paul was not deterred. He ran to the young man and knelt down close. Paul detected that life was still in him, although barely. The apostle grabbed him and embraced him in prayer, and then he said to the people, "Don't worry. He'll be fine."

The moments seemed to pass like eternity, but suddenly the young man drew in a quick breath, then he opened his eyes and sat up, blinking and trying to figure out where he was. The disciples helped him to his feet, and then incredibly they all sat down to a meal, rejoicing for what God had done. Ever the diligent teacher, Paul continued his discourse until dawn (see Acts 20:6-12). This incident brought much joy and comfort to the church, and it also showed them something they did not know before, that teachers are also miracle people. Did you know that?

John 3:1-2 records: *"There was a man of the Pharisees, named Nicodemus, a ruler of the Jews: The same came to Jesus by night, and said unto him, Rabbi, we know that thou art a teacher come from God: for no man can do these miracles that thou doest, except God be with him."* Jesus was a teacher, and as our example He was most definitely a Man of miracles. In fact, Nicodemus recognized that Jesus was a teacher, an instructor of God, because the gift of miracles accompanied Him wherever He went.

If you are a teacher, you need to know there is a gift of miracles residing in you that will confirm the Word preached with signs following. The teaching ministry, when it came with the equipment necessary to be a teacher, also was given with the divine appointment and ability to work in miracles.

In Luke 5:17, we find a very powerful verse: *"And it came to pass on a certain day, as he was teaching, that there were Pharisees and doctors of the law sitting by, which were come out of every town of Galilee, and Judaea, and Jerusalem: and the power of the Lord was present to heal them."*

On this particular day there were Pharisees in the room who knew the law.

They were experts on the scripture, but did not live by its power. As Jesus taught, the power to heal was present with Him, and there was an anointing to bring forth miracles. The power was present because of the Word preached, but the Pharisees did not benefit from it because they had no real understanding of the Word, and they had no faith.

Teachers today, just like Jesus, have this same anointing for miracles present with them when they teach the Word. God greatly desires to speak through teachers in healings and miracles, confirming His Word with signs following, because there is no better way to teach than to offer visual evidence of the spoken word. A teacher can give you a thousand pages of notes on healing, but it will never be as effective as one simple miracle before your eyes.

Signs following are the greatest teaching tools and object lessons there are. People can scoff at what you say, but they cannot deny what you do. When you show them what you teach, you have changed them for life.

HELPERS

Let me conclude this chapter with an important key to the success of every church. As a pastor who is also a teacher, I am very aware I cannot do it all alone. I cannot personally teach every class in my church, nor oversee every outreach or event by myself. This is why God has so graciously given me helpers, as he does every pastor, who can shoulder a portion of the burden and assist me.

We find these helpers in Romans 12:4-8: *"For as we have many members in one body, and all members have not the same office: So we, being many, are one body in Christ, and every one members one of another. Having then gifts differing according to the grace that is given to us, whether prophecy, let us prophesy according to the proportion of faith; Or ministry, let us wait on our ministering: or he that teacheth, on teaching; Or he that exhorteth, on exhortation: he that giveth, let him do it with simplicity; he that ruleth, with diligence; he that sheweth mercy, with cheerfulness."*

God has given some a gift that makes them able to teach, not in the five-fold capacity, but in the helps capacity. These folks are blessed, humble people who recognize their gifts and also their limitations. They can and do assist me by teaching a class of adults on a given subject, or by taking a position to teach once a month in children's church. They are not full-time ministers, but they are equipped and *"apt to teach,"* as Paul said (see 1 Timothy 3:2).

These teachers are a great blessing to a local church. While they do not establish doctrine or teach outside the confines of what they have been assigned, they do relieve the pastor of the entire responsibility of teaching basic doctrinal truths. People often have questions I cannot answer from the pulpit, but if I get enough similar questions, I can ask one of the trusted teachers in my congregation to prepare a class that will dig into those issues and offer answers to a smaller group of people, in a more personal setting. This is a vital ministry, one for which I am personally grateful.

Understanding there are different levels of the teaching anointing will help you distinguish between those called alongside to help the pastor, and those called to minister to the Body of Christ. Making this distinction helps us all fulfill our personal ministry calls without stepping out into areas where we are not equipped, and therefore cannot succeed. God has called every one of us in some capacity in the Body of Christ. If we will remain faithful to His plan and carry out our purpose, the Body will be blessed and our churches will grow.

The five-fold ministry gifts are here for your benefit. They are present to teach, bless and edify the Body of Christ so we can be all God has called us to be. As we join together to receive everything the five-fold gifts have been designed to give, each of us taking our place and building upon the work of the other, we will come unto the measure of the fullness of Christ, unto the stature of a fully developed, fully functioning body, each supernaturally supplying what the others need, and all becoming one in Him.

CHAPTER 10

THE STIRRING EVANGELIST

"**Y**ou don't have any trouble! All you need is faith in God!!" I had heard it before, but it still thundered in my spirit. As the evangelist preached on I listened to his words of simplicity, and I marveled at how the level of faith in the room seemed to rise up several degrees in just the first few minutes. Soon signs, wonders and miracles were evident all over the sanctuary, and the name of Jesus was magnified.

Perhaps you know the evangelist, R.W. Schambach. This great man of God has traveled the world several times over, preaching the gospel of Jesus Christ, and in every city signs and wonders always follow his ministry, just as they did the ministry of Jesus. I am honored to call R.W. Schambach a dear friend, and I am ever so grateful to God for bringing us together.

Over the years, I have observed him preach what seems like hundreds of times. It never ceases to amaze me how God uses him in such mighty ways. His preaching, though different each time, always carries a simple message of faith, an exercise of power and authority, and of course, a good dose of the Holy Ghost. By the time his faith-filled, Jesus-exalting message is over, the gift of faith will have risen up strong, and miracles will invariably follow.

I do not believe I have ever met another evangelist whose message is confirmed with the gift of faith quite like it is in this man's meetings. The gift that manifests as he preaches always brings mighty miracles, great healings, powerful deliverances, amazing signs and wonders, and of course life-changing salvation to so many.

I have been privileged to preach myself in several countries: India, Brazil, Cuba, Nigeria, Honduras, Haiti, Kenya, the Philippines, Colombia, Canada, Mexico, Ecuador and Russia, to name a few. No matter where I have been, I do not remember one time I ever mentioned the name of R.W. Schambach that it did not bring a wealth of testimonies of the powerful impact his messages have brought to the nations. Lives have been touched, faith has been sparked and multitudes have been changed forever.

As an evangelist, Brother Schambach has stirred the nations with the gospel of Jesus Christ, and his ministry is still shaking the world today. What he has planted in city after city and nation after nation has grown and flourished, and it is bearing so much fruit.

I count it an honor to know him, and our mutual friendship is a great blessing. He and his family are loved by my family, and we are sharpened by their influence on our lives. While the stories in the Bible are incomparable, and there are so many amazing evangelists at work in the world today, I do not believe any other gift of the evangelist has shaped the nations with any more impact than that of my dear friend, R.W. Schambach.

THE GIFT OF THE EVANGELIST

Each five-fold ministry gift brings us a different revelation of who God is in our lives. Some think the evangelist is limited to a revelation of salvation, but this is not true. God is much more complex than this, and the ministers He has appointed to carry His good news throughout the world are equally complex.

In Mark 16:15, Jesus gives us the basic job description of the five-fold evangelist: *"...Go ye into all the world, and preach the gospel to every creature."* This verse encompasses so much because the gospel is different things to different people at different times, understanding that the word gospel in its simplest form means "good news."

What is good news to a sinner? "Jesus died for you." But what is good news for a sick man? "Jesus is a healer." How about good news for a man who has suffered loss? "Jesus is a restorer." And what about for the man who is depressed? "Jesus heals the broken-hearted."

Luke 4:18-19 gives us the clearest understanding of what the word gospel means. Here, Jesus said: *"The Spirit of the Lord is upon me, because he hath anointed me to preach the gospel to the poor; he hath sent me to heal the brokenhearted, to preach deliverance to the captives, and recovering of sight to the blind, to set at liberty them that are bruised; to preach the acceptable year of the Lord."*

The word evangelist means "to show forth good news," so the evangelist will always preach the good news, but each message will reflect the crowd he or she is preaching to. He may preach salvation one night, and healing the next; he may preach end-time signs and wonders in one crusade, and holiness in the next.

The evangelist may exhort people to tap into the supernatural and stir them to action, as Brother Schambach does time and time again, or he may encourage the weary to get back up and do the Word. He may preach a million sermons in a million ways, but they will all boil down to one thing in the end, "I have good news for you, and His name is Jesus."

Evangelists should be honored for what they do, for stirring and inspiring people, and reminding them what the good news gospel is all about. They should be utilized in the local church and allowed to exercise their gift, but they should never be expected to do more than they are called and equipped to do.

THE WORK OF THE EVANGELIST

It is important to understand that the evangelist is not charged to teach doctrine, but to preach the good news. Though it may seem a little confusing at first, there is a difference you need to grasp. We'll start by reading Matthew 28:19, which says: *"Go ye therefore, and teach all nations, baptizing them in the name of the Father, and of the Son, and of the Holy Ghost."*

Notice the word "teach" I have underlined. We have mistakenly called Matthew 28:19 the Great Commission, when in reality, it is not. The Great Commission is given to every believer, to witness and tell others about Jesus, but we are not all called to teach sinners spiritual truths. In fact, it is not even possible to teach sinners spiritual things; you can only preach the simple gospel to them.

This is where so many believers miss it in their personal attempts to witness. They try to teach spiritual truths to a spiritually dead person, which will never succeed. When we witness, it is about one thing only: Jesus Christ and Him crucified (see 1 Corinthians 2:2). Our personal testimony is a great starting point for opening the conversation, but when all is said and done, if we win someone to Jesus we will have done it by preaching the simplicity of the cross. Arguing doctrine will never win a soul to the Kingdom; only the simple message of the crucifixion and resurrection will get the job done.

Likewise, when God speaks through an evangelist, He does so to preach the good news, not to teach doctrine. The evangelist will always proclaim a revelation of redemption; how to be saved, how to be healed, how to be delivered, and a host of other things, but every message will always come back to the simple message of the cross.

Preaching good news is so valuable to the Body of Christ, and of course to every sinner who hears and accepts it. I will never diminish the office of the evangelist, but I will also never expect what he or she is not anointed to deliver. Evangelists preach good news, but they do not teach doctrine. There is a great difference that if honored, will bless the church more than asking ministers to cross over from one calling to another. We should let God be God, and allow the gifts He has given to flourish among us.

In Acts 8:4 we find another significant distinction between the office of the evangelist and personal ministry. It says: *"Therefore they that were scattered abroad went every where preaching the word."* What were these scattered people preaching? Of course they were proclaiming the good news of Jesus. Did this make them evangelists? Absolutely not. We have all been called to share the good news, but we are not all five-fold evangelists.

Our call as believers is found in 2 Corinthians 5:18-19: *"And all things are of God, who hath reconciled us to himself by Jesus Christ, and hath given to us the ministry of reconciliation; To wit, that God was in Christ, reconciling the world unto himself, not imputing their trespasses unto them; and hath committed unto us the word of reconciliation."*

It is essential to understand the difference between a true evangelist and the rest of the Body of Christ called to the message of reconciliation. The evangelist is directed by God to deliver the gospel to specific churches, people groups, and even nations, while the message of reconciliation is generally carried out one by one, person to person.

Door to door witness, one on one sharing of the good news, street preaching, handing out tracts—these are all admirable activities that win souls, and they are the fruit of the ministry of reconciliation, but they are not necessarily the mark of an evangelist. The message of reconciliation is of the utmost importance, but everything we say when we minister to an individual will not necessarily be, "Thus says the Lord."

Let's look at Philip the evangelist in Acts 8:4-8 to see the difference between the ministry of reconciliation and the office of the evangelist:

162

"Therefore they that were scattered abroad went every where preaching the word. Then Philip went down to the city of Samaria, and preached Christ unto them. And the people with one accord gave heed unto those things which Philip spake, hearing and seeing the miracles which he did. For unclean spirits, crying with loud voice, came out of many that were possessed with them: and many taken with palsies, and that were lame, were healed. And there was great joy in that city."

In verse four, the scattered people preached everywhere, but their results are not listed. When Philip the evangelist preached to a city, though, the results which followed completely changed the inhabitants. Here we see the difference: corporate change. Evangelists bring great transformation to churches, cities and even nations. This corporate change is the mark of the office of the evangelist. The message he preaches will meet the needs of the people he is ministering to, and it will bring break-through change to all who receive it.

Does this mean our one on one ministry is not necessary? No way! But it does tell us that only those evangelists sent by God will affect a city or a region. Every believer can touch lives one at a time through the ministry of reconciliation, but only the evangelist can change the world. In other words, we can all evangelize, but we will not all be five-fold, world-shaking evangelists.

STIRRING THINGS UP

Philip is our best biblical example of how God speaks through an evangelist. We first see him mentioned in Acts 6:5: *"And the saying pleased the whole multitude: and they chose Stephen, a man full of faith and of the Holy Ghost, and Philip, and Prochorus, and Nicanor, and Timon, and Parmenas, and Nicolas a proselyte of Antioch."*

These were the seven men chosen by the disciples to serve tables and take care of the hands-on work of the early church. Though Philip was called to be an evangelist, we do not see him work in this capacity until the story we just mentioned in Acts 8:4-8.

There, Philip preached Christ to the people in Samaria as an evangelist and stirred them up. There were great signs and wonders, miracles and deliverance from demons, and there was much joy in the entire city. This is a classic example of the anointing an evangelist carries, because he is a "stirrer." He shakes up sinners to repentance, and he stirs up believers to rekindle the fire of their relationship with Jesus.

Later in Acts chapter eight, we see the work of a stirring evangelist in action again in the life of Philip, but this time in a more unique way. Beginning in verse 26, we read how the Spirit of God sent Philip to the desert to minister to one man, an Ethiopian eunuch who worked for a queen. The man was confused about the book of Isaiah, and he asked Philip to explain what it meant. Philip was happy to do so, and then he preached Jesus to him.

The man believed, received Christ and was baptized, and then an amazing thing happened in verses 38-40: *"And he commanded the chariot to stand still: and they went down both into the water, both Philip and the eunuch; and he baptized him. And when they were come up out of the water, the Spirit of the Lord caught away Philip, that the eunuch saw him no more: and he went on his way rejoicing. But Philip was found at Azotus: and passing through he preached in all the cities, till he came to Caesarea."*

Think of it! Philip baptizes this man, but when they rise up from under the water Philip disappears and is translated to another city to preach Jesus there. Talk about a quick trip! Philip literally went from one place to another instantly by the supernatural power of the Holy Spirit. When he landed, Philip simply took up right where he left off with the eunuch and preached Jesus some more. This is what I call stirring things up!

Philip's focus shows us the heart of evangelists. No matter where they are, they have one thing in mind, and that is preaching Jesus. No matter who they are with, their purpose is never altered. Evangelists have a one-track mind; they preach Jesus wherever and however they can.

They edify, astound, encourage and stir because the call of the evangelist is a call to action. We know God speaks through these men to spur activity because action is what the life of faith is all about. God does not want us to be hearers only, deceiving our own selves, but doers of what we hear, pleasing Him in everything we do (see James 1:22; Hebrews 11:6).

Action that produces profound life change is the fruit of a true evangelist. If you will listen and do what he says, you will be changed, just as one lone eunuch was, and just as the people of an entire city were transformed, by the ministry of a stirring evangelist.

THE CONVICTION OF THE EVANGELIST

The word evangelist is only mentioned three times in the entire Bible. In fact, Philip is the only man in scripture who is actually called by this name. Philip did not even realize he was operating in the office of evangelist at the time because the revelation of the office did not come until later when Paul wrote his letter to the Ephesians, but Philip still operated in the gift flawlessly. He was unaware of the gift he had, but he knew he had been sent by God with a word in due season for those in need. God spoke through Philip, and lives were changed forever.

The people in Samaria were touched by the work of the evangelist in different ways at the same time. Some were saved, others were healed and delivered, others had their joy restored, and still others experienced miracles, signs and wonders. God spoke one message through a single evangelist, and His anointing brought manifold blessings to every hearer. This is what makes the evangelist so special, because his ministry call encompasses a wide variety of opportunities.

Preaching salvation to sinners is a part of the call of the evangelist. Wherever he goes, he must preach the cross. Whether he stands before a crowd in a stadium or behind the pulpit in a local church, he has one goal in mind—preaching the good news and bringing people to Jesus.

The evangelist is also charged with edifying the Body of Christ, reminding believers what the cross means to them and exhorting the church to do what is right in the eyes of God. This takes courage and conviction, the kind that does not come from a mere man, but from the call and anointing of God.

Jude was a person in the Bible who spoke with just this kind of conviction. He exhibited consistency, faithfulness and courage. Jude is interesting because, although he was the half-brother of Jesus, he only identified himself as the brother of James. This proves he was humble, and one who desired no esteem for himself, but only glory for the Lord.

In the book of Jude, we catch a glimpse of the man and his message. Though he was never called an evangelist in the Bible, he certainly carried the passion of one. Jude began his writing by explaining the purpose of his message, which was *"to write unto you of the common salvation."* This reveals the desire of every evangelist, to be wholly devoted to preaching Jesus and the cross.

Jude went on to say: *"It was needful for me to write unto you, and exhort you that ye should earnestly contend for the faith which was once delivered unto the saints. For there are certain men crept in unawares, who were before of old ordained to this condemnation, ungodly men, turning the grace of our God into lasciviousness, and denying the only Lord God, and our Lord Jesus Christ."*

Here we see Jude's concern for the integrity of the gospel. He did not want any false doctrine to creep in that would lead men and women astray, and so he reminded them they needed to contend for the faith that brought them salvation.

Jude continued by giving an overview of the history of the gospel, and how God delivered His people out of Egypt and destroyed His enemies. Then he talked about Sodom and Gomorrah, and the judgment which resulted because of their sin. He went on to talk about how true believers will not despise authority, but will obey the word of the Lord without question.

Then Jude moved to the meat of his message, to the people who were defiling the gospel and blaspheming God. Of them Jude said: *"These are spots in your feasts of charity, when they feast with you, feeding themselves without fear: clouds they are without water, carried about of winds; trees whose fruit withereth, without fruit, twice dead, plucked up by the roots; raging waves of the sea, foaming out their own shame; wandering stars, to whom is reserved the blackness of darkness for ever."*

Jude was not happy with these individuals, and he wanted to warn the Body of Christ about their presence in the church. He said they were *"murmurers, complainers, walking after their own lusts; and their mouth speaketh great swelling words, having men's persons in admiration because of advantage."* (This describes a wolf if I ever saw one.)

Finally, Jude offered an exhortation for believers to do right and stay away from sin when he preached: *"But, beloved, remember ye the words which were spoken before of the apostles of our Lord Jesus Christ; how that they told you there should be mockers in the last time, who should walk after their own ungodly lusts. These be they who separate themselves, sensual, having not the Spirit. But ye, beloved, building up yourselves on your most holy faith, praying in the Holy Ghost, keep yourselves in the love of God, looking for the mercy of our Lord Jesus Christ unto eternal life"* (Jude 1-25).

This shows us the focus and passion of an evangelist. It is a heart of compassion for the church, but a heart of anger toward those who try to defile it. This is why evangelists are sometimes called preachers of fire and brimstone, because they love people so much, they do not want to see them led astray by false doctrines or consumed by wolves who masquerade as sheep among them. They preach Jesus, but they also protect His message with all their might. Evangelists never leave a job half done; they complete the work of the ministry with great zeal and conviction.

If the evangelist does his job well, he will allow God to speak through him with passion while he ministers the good news to everyone in his audience. He will leave some edified, encouraged and refreshed; others will be chastised as he comes against sin when needed; and of course he will win souls, because it is his primary calling.

There is no cookie cutter form an evangelist must fit into, which makes this gift very unique. Evangelists come in all sorts of packages, but their messages remain consistent in this one thing. "There is good news in the world, and His name is Jesus. Live right and follow Him."

SIGNS FOLLOWING

Just as in the ministry of R.W. Schambach, when an evangelist speaks the word of the Lord under His direction, that word will be confirmed with signs following: *"And the people with one accord gave heed unto those things which Philip spake, hearing and seeing the miracles which he did. For unclean spirits, crying with loud voice, came out of many that were possessed with them: and many taken with palsies, and that were lame, were healed"* (Acts 8:6-7).

Notice the people heard and saw the miracles. What do you hear when you see a miracle? You hear that God is alive and well, and that He cares enough to intervene in your life. You hear God is the Healer, the Deliverer, the One who sets you free from every bondage.

When the divine anointing of an evangelist is evident, no matter what he says, God will do something special with every word he utters, and the signs which follow will speak as loudly as the truth he delivers. Remember, when Philip preached, Samaria was turned upside down by one man fulfilling his five-fold call and delivering a simple gospel message.

You have to understand the persecution which was upon the church at the time to realize the full impact of Philip's preaching. Stephen, one of the men called along with Philip to attend to the daily affairs of the church, had just been taken before the high priest and stoned for preaching in the name of Jesus.

For a period of time, Christians had scattered and were feeling extremely vulnerable. This is when Philip decided it was time for an evangelistic crusade in Samaria. It took great courage to do what he did, and because he fearlessly, efficiently and effectively declared the good news, the people put faith in what he said, and signs and wonders followed.

This is what I love about evangelists. It amazes me when I watch them preach a simple, but heart-felt message, and then I watch God use what they say to produce mighty signs and wonders, confirming His Word. As a teacher, I want my messages to have a long list of scriptures and pages full of notes before I think I'm ready to go, but the evangelist will step up to the pulpit, preach on one passage of scripture and stir a crowd to signs, wonders and miracles.

To me, that is a great blessing which shows us the heart of the Father and how much He desires to amaze us. He wants nothing more than to invade our lives with His presence, and He uses the ministry of the evangelist to show us it is not our words of wisdom which bring His power, but simple faith in Jesus.

Obviously, the most important thing God will ever speak through an evangelist is, "Jesus Christ died for your sins on the cross, and He rose again so that you might receive eternal life and have a relationship with Him eternally." This central theme of the gospel message will never change. It is the basis of our faith, and it is the same message that will turn cities upside down and change people forever today, just as it did so long ago in Samaria. God is still speaking the gospel through evangelists to deliver hope, change lives, bring miracles and save souls. These signs are powerful stuff for men and women of God called to minister simple truth, and they are designed to stir and shake us to the very core.

A SERVANT'S HEART

You can rest assured, God is speaking through evangelists every day with as much power and glory as He did in the early church. I have had the privilege of inviting some of the most well-known evangelists in America to minister to my congregation, and God has blessed me to become their friends; men including T. L. Osborn, Oral Roberts, Jesse Duplantis, and of course Brother Schambach.

In these relationships, what impresses me most is their unshakeable desire and intense focus on preaching the gospel. These men are some of the most well-known people in the Christian world, but they are also some of the most humble human beings I have ever met.

They, like Paul in 1 Corinthians 2:2, prefer to be known for nothing except: *"...Jesus Christ, and him crucified."* I admire this in any minister, but it is especially unique that evangelists who are known around the world could remain so humble and kind, preferring others above themselves, and still be so successful in the work that they do.

I believe this is a direct reflection of who Jesus is. He declared that we are not called to be served, but to serve (see Matthew 20:26-28). When I see great men and women of God fulfill that verse and carry out their ministry with a servant's heart, it gives me renewed hope for the Body of Christ.

As an example, let me tell you about a lady evangelist I know who operates in the purity of the gift more so than any man or woman I have ever seen. When she preaches what we would call a deep or revelatory word, she never makes more of it than is necessary. She simply exhorts the people and gives her testimony of how she was once bound by legalism, and how God freed her. Every message she preaches is profound, and yet so simple.

Too often, people try to make more of their messages than they ought to. They attempt to go so deep no one can follow them. If the congregation can't keep up with the revelation, it's safe to say they won't be able to use what is being preached. In my opinion, if people can't grasp and hold onto what the preacher is proclaiming, it is useless. This is why I count it an honor every time someone tells me what I preached was simple enough to understand and put to work. For me, this is the greatest compliment of all.

This woman I know preaches just that way: Simple. She is down to earth, and the people love her. It's as if she is trying to preach to a ten year old each time she stands behind the pulpit, but somehow she manages to reach all of us with her simple message of good news. Of course we know it is the anointing that empowers her, and this is why so many people are blessed, stirred and set free, but to me it is the greatest thing since the discovery of white sugar, and I love her messages!

I enjoy reminiscing about the many occasions she stood on our platform and preached up a storm. Every time she came, the people in our church would shout and dance, and her tapes would sell out night after night—all because of a simple gospel message that anyone could understand. And when she would begin to move in the gifts of the Spirit, watch out! Miracles, healings, prophecies and words of knowledge would just flow. In the natural, the way the people reacted, you'd have thought that Elijah had returned.

I still stand in awe of her obedience to the simplicity of the gift, and I marvel at the power of the anointing evident in every service. I do believe her ministry is the one of the purist operations of the office of the evangelist I have ever seen.

Now here is my point. If I wrote her name, you would not even recognize it, but that is what makes her truly great. She is not an evangelist trying to become well-known; but she is just a person trying to fulfill the call of God on her life. Her clear messages of God's love and hope allow her to be an individual who is greatly used by God, even while she is an obedient servant. This is why I esteem her ministry so highly. Would that we could all be so simple and obedient, so used of God and still so down to earth.

Christians are supposed to be ordinary men and women of God who live in the world, yet who do not live of it. We should take the example of this great woman and live just as powerfully as she does. She has never been above us, but she has always caused us all to come up with her in the anointing. This is what the office of the evangelist is all about—bringing people up into the things God desires them to experience, and being a true example of His love and mercy manifested in our lives.

EVANGELISTS TODAY

Today, the work of the evangelist encompasses so many areas the evangelists of old never dreamed of because of the technology available to us. Evangelists can literally bounce their messages off of satellites in space and send them to the other side of the world in an instant. What Philip did when he was translated was tremendous, but that did not happen every day. In our world, evangelists do not need to wait for the supernatural move of God to take them from place to place in an instant. They can do it via television and radio waves every minute of every day.

This is what makes the work of today's evangelists so exciting. They could literally preach to the entire world at one time with the right satellite feed. I believe this technology is no accident. Though television is misused by many, I believe God ordained it to help His five-fold ministers, and evangelists in particular, deliver the gospel to more people in more ways than anyone in the early church ever dreamed possible.

Using today's technology, God is speaking through evangelists to people globally, appealing to them to come to Jesus before it is too late. I believe this manifestation of the end-time gospel message will literally win millions of souls before Jesus returns.

In my opinion we should never be afraid to launch out and use the tools available to us to preach the gospel. New things are not always the best things, but when it comes to preaching the Word and getting souls saved, I am all for the newest and the best, because the message of God's love deserves to be heard by every man and woman on the planet.

I am definitely for using whatever it takes to get this life-changing message to the most people in the shortest time possible. If it means shooting more satellites in the air, then this is what we will do. If it requires doing a better job of capturing the attention of men and women on the Internet, that is what we will do. If it means working harder than ever before, we are ready!

It's time for the Body of Christ to take the limits off of God and let the gospel message shine forth in every way, all of the time, in all of the world. Every evangelist I know thinks this is exactly how it should be.

CHAPTER 11

THE ROLE OF THE APOSTLE

Paul had been in prison for two years, waiting for his case to come before the court. Finally, the day arrived when he stood in the highest court and made his case to King Agrippa. Because of his Roman citizenship, however, the king could not rule, and so he decided to send him to Caesar.

Paul was taken by ship on the long journey to Rome. Along the way they encountered bad weather, and Paul came on deck to prophesy. As recorded in Acts 27, he said: *"Sirs, I perceive that this voyage will be with hurt and much damage, not only of the lading and ship, but also of our lives."* In other words, "It's time to put into port until the stormy weather passes; otherwise, we're all going to take a dip in the sea that was not planned."

Unfortunately, the centurion in charge of the voyage believed the master and the owner of the ship instead of Paul, so they sailed on. Despite the coming of winter the weather pattern changed, and the winds died down for awhile, deceiving the captain into believing he had been right after all.

However, it wasn't long until the wind returned with violent fury. It was so strong they gave it a name, *"Euroclydon"* (Acts 27:14)—just as we name hurricanes today. The force of the storm was extremely fierce, and the ship was in danger of sinking fast.

The crew tried everything to save themselves, but nothing worked. It was the perfect storm, and it threatened to take their lives. Fearing for the worst, they began to toss everything overboard, including the ship's tackle. The wind pounded mercilessly for days and days until all hope was lost.

In the midst of the tempest, back came Paul with another word of the Lord. This time he said: *"Sirs, ye should have hearkened unto me, and not have loosed from Crete, and to have gained this harm and loss. And now I exhort you to be of good cheer: for there shall be no loss of any man's life among you, but of the ship. For there stood by me this night the angel of God, whose I am, and whom I serve, Saying, Fear not, Paul; thou must be brought before Caesar: and, lo, God hath given thee all them that sail with thee. Wherefore, sirs, be of good cheer: for I believe God, that it shall be even as it was told me."*

This was good news to Paul, but the men on the ship were not so sure. On the fourteenth day of the storm they finally approached land, and they anchored just off the coast, trying to avoid crashing onto the rocks. Once again, Paul stepped forward and spoke to the men, saying: *"This day is the fourteenth day that ye have tarried and continued fasting, having taken nothing. Wherefore I pray you to take some meat: for this is for your health: for there shall not an hair fall from the head of any of you."*

Paul picked up a piece of bread, gave thanks to God for it and began to eat in front of them. A cheer went up, and they all joined him. After they ate, they decided to lighten the ship once again, and they threw the rest of the food overboard, expecting to reach land the next day.

To make a long story short, they all safely made it to dry land. However, the ship was lost in the process, as Paul had prophesied it would be, but not one man drowned, not even any of the prisoners on board. So, what is the point of this long story?

God needed the apostle Paul to go to Rome. No matter what faced him on his long journey there, Paul was pre-determined to make it, unhurt and unscathed. The Lord went so far as to save an entire ship of ungodly men, over 270 of them, just to make sure Paul made it to his destiny. This is the life of an apostle, one of fulfilling destiny against all odds, and at any cost. It's the life of words from Heaven being delivered to men, and of supernatural intervention bringing forth divine destiny.

THE GIFT OF THE APOSTLE

The apostle is probably the least known of the five-fold gifts, primarily because his work is less often publicized than the other gifts. Most apostles are too busy completing the work God has set before them to promote themselves and their ministries. Apostles go and do; they do not go and boast.

In 1 Corinthians 1:1 we read: *"Paul, called to be an apostle of Jesus Christ through the will of God..."*

Apostles, like the other five-fold gifts, are of course called by the Lord. You cannot work your way into apostleship because of your long track record of ministry deeds, and you cannot be promoted there by some board. You do not earn the office of apostle as a lifetime achievement award. You are either called by God, or you are not an apostle.

This office can be seen most readily in the life of Paul. In Acts 26:16-18, Paul describes his call on the road to Damascus. Here, Jesus is speaking to Paul: *"But rise, and stand upon thy feet: for I have appeared unto thee for this purpose, to make thee a minister and a witness both of these things which thou hast seen, and of those things in the which I will appear unto thee. Delivering thee from the people, and from the Gentiles, unto whom now I send thee, to open their eyes, and to turn them from darkness to light, and from the power of Satan unto God, that they may receive forgiveness of sins, and inheritance among them which are sanctified by faith that is in me."*

Jesus Himself interrupted Paul on his way to do harm to Christians and called him to be an apostle, a *"minister and a witness"* to *"open their eyes, and to turn them from darkness to light."*

Notice Paul was sent to a specific people with a specific message. This is a good description of the office of the apostle. They are called by God, sent by Him to deliver a message as a minister and a witness, to open the eyes of those blind and in darkness, and to turn them toward faith in Christ.

THE WORK OF THE APOSTLE

The word apostle means "one sent from God, a messenger." The apostle is sent with a divine anointing to go to specific places at specific times for specific purposes to deliver specific messages. An apostle does not have a command to minister in the anointing of his office all over the world, but is given particular assignments.

He is also gifted to operate in miracles. Every believer can lay hands on the sick and the sick will recover, but the apostle, as part of the five-fold ministry, will use his gift to benefit the multitudes.

Notice what Paul said about his office in 2 Corinthians 12:12: *"Truly the signs of an apostle were wrought among you in all patience, in signs, and wonders, and mighty deeds."*

We already learned that signs and wonders have a voice and what they say. They announce, "God is real. He is here. He loves you and is reaching out to you." They may also say, "Wake up! The Lord is here, so you better pay attention!"

The apostle was the first five-fold gift established in the church. The eleven disciples (having lost Judas) were appointed as the first apostles in the church, and then Paul was called to be an apostle at a later time when Jesus appeared to him on the road to Damascus.

The doctrines of the early apostles, now scripture for us, are to be the foundation of everything we teach and preach today. We are never to leave the basic principles found in the Word, but are to teach, train, edify and admonish based on this Word, without wavering.

Ephesians 2:20 tells us: *"And are built upon the foundation of the apostles and prophets, Jesus Christ himself being the chief corner stone."*

In 2 Timothy 3:16 we learn: *"All scripture is given by inspiration of God, and is profitable for doctrine, for reproof, for correction, for instruction in righteousness."*

This settles it forever. The written Word, inspired by God and penned by the early apostles and prophets, is our doctrine. This is what we build the Body of Christ on today, nothing more, nothing less.

There is no new doctrine as far as we are concerned because the Bible is God's Word, and it is our only measure of truth. Whatever was written is for our benefit, and it stands as our established doctrine, directing our steps and creating order in our churches.

So, apostles are sent by God. They deliver messages to specific people, and they establish sound doctrine based on scripture which leads to divine order. Now let's look at each characteristic in detail.

SENT BY GOD

Remember, apostles are sent by God. In Acts 16:9-10, we see Paul being commissioned to preach in a certain area: *"And a vision appeared to Paul in the night. There stood a man of Macedonia, and prayed him, saying, Come over into Macedonia, and help us. And after he had seen the vision, immediately we endeavoured to go into Macedonia, assuredly gathering that the Lord had called us for to preach the gospel unto them."*

Paul was assigned to a specific place at a specific time for a specific purpose. This is always the case with an apostle. They do not choose where they go, but they wait until they are sent by God, knowing they will only be successful under the anointing His sending provides.

When Paul reached Macedonia, some amazing things took place. Paul was traveling with Silas, and they stirred up the city by casting the devil out of a servant girl. Once her masters realized she had been set free, they demanded Paul and Silas be sent to jail.

Well, you probably know the story. Paul and Silas were singing and praising God at midnight while confined to a filthy prison cell. God came on the scene and the place was shaken, so much so that the prison doors popped open, and Paul and Silas walked out untouched. Once again, God moved Heaven and earth in order to keep an apostle on the road to his appointed assignment.

Apostles are often sent where no one has gone before. In Romans, 15:15-16, we see Paul's primary purpose as an apostle: *"Nevertheless, brethren, I have written the more boldly unto you in some sort, as putting you in mind, because of the grace that is given to me of God, that I should be the minister of Jesus Christ to the Gentiles, ministering the gospel of God, that the offering up of the Gentiles might be acceptable, being sanctified by the Holy Ghost."*

Paul was sent to a people largely unreached until he came on the scene, the Gentile world. He broke fresh ground and delivered most of his New Testament doctrine while ministering to his newly established Gentile churches.

Apostles in today's world are also founders of churches, just as Paul was. They are sent to preach the gospel where it has not been proclaimed before, and out of that ministry they establish churches which will follow up and carry on the work of raising up, maturing and equipping saints.

The apostle will place a pastor over each new church and watch over him while the congregation goes through the stages of growth and change. He will come back periodically to encourage and edify the people, but eventually, if he has done his job well, he will leave the church as a self-sufficient entity.

John G. Lake is a great example of this aspect of the apostle's office. Brother Lake founded an organization called Apostolic Faith Mission of South Africa which started over 700 churches in that nation in the early part of the 20th century. These churches became centers for healings and miracles, which were the life-blood of Brother Lake's ministry.

It is no surprise to find the stamp of the founder on an apostolic work. What the apostle lives and breathes will be what the churches he establishes live and breathe also. This makes the apostle a very unique gift. It is not just a matter of sending him to open buildings and attract people to come, but it is placing the very heart of the man into the hearts of the people who will continue the work once the founder moves on.

Brother Lake began this remarkable work while raising seven children. It's no wonder he nearly exhausted himself, but after a time he was able to hand the reins over to capable men who carried on to fruition what God inspired him to begin, just as the apostle is supposed to do. (Details found at www.jglm.org).

No man can begin and complete a church-building work alone. It takes an army of men and women to carry out such a task. This is why God raises up great pastors to follow great apostles in the work, pastors who will equip saints for ministry. Every ministry needs a strong founder, but it also needs continuing support to carry on the vision after the founder moves on. As apostles are sent with a specific purpose to advance the Kingdom of God in a specific place, their success edifies the Body of Christ, and the work of the ministry goes forward.

DELIVERING MESSAGES

When an apostle is sent somewhere, he will go equipped with a particular message for that place. Sometimes it will be delivered as doctrine, as Paul delivered to so many churches in the New Testament. Other times it will come in the form of instructions for church order. We see this repeatedly in Paul's letters.

On occasion the apostle has to bolster the pastor or other five-fold minister, just as Paul encouraged Timothy in his second letter to him. He may be required to deliver a word of warning or correction as we see in the letters to the Corinthian church.

Paul described how he delivered his messages in 1 Corinthians 3:10: *"According to the grace of God which is given unto me, as a wise masterbuilder, I have laid the foundation, and another buildeth thereon. But let every man take heed how he buildeth thereupon."*

Paul's messages were foundational. They laid a sure foundation of the gospel, and then they allowed for the work of others to build upon them and to finish what God desired for that place. When Paul built a church, he did what every good apostle will do. He continued in prayer for them, gave sound

178

doctrine, encouraged and visited them, but finally it was up to them, to men like Timothy and Titus, to build the building and finish the work.

So, we see that the apostolic message will be a beginning, a starting place, and a foundation upon which others will build. The message may take on different forms for different places, but it will always begin at the cross and end at the church.

The apostle consistently lays a foundation of sound doctrine, beginning with Jesus Christ and Him crucified, and he establishes church order and structure, which we will see in a moment. Then the offices of the pastor, teacher, evangelist and prophet build upon this foundation and the work of the ministry is completed.

In many respects, an apostle is a seed planter, allowing God to send another man to water his message, but in the end the Lord will get the increase. Paul established this principle when he said: *"Who then is Paul, and who is Apollos, but ministers by whom ye believed, even as the Lord gave to every man? I have planted, Apollos watered; but God gave the increase"* (1 Corinthians 3:5-6).

Apostles are not overly concerned who gets the credit for a work of the Kingdom, as long as God gets the glory for the messages he sends them to deliver. When they speak the word of the Lord and it is received, this is all that matters to an apostle.

ESTABLISHING DIVINE ORDER

Apostles deliver sound doctrine which leads to church order. Today's apostles will never create new doctrine, but they will only build on what is established.

The very first apostles had the privilege of writing inspired scripture that added to and completed the writings of the prophets in the Old Testament. Paul's writings and others explained the gospel message from the vantage point of this side of the cross and became the doctrine of the church.

Today's apostles will establish church order based on that doctrine found in the written Word, but they will never, ever write new doctrine. That part of the apostolic anointing is no more. The Word of God is complete and accurate, just as it stands today. We do not need to look for anything new.

When an apostle begins to set a church in motion, he will bring it into divine order. You cannot have a solid body of believers without establishing standards and procedures. Structure and order are what keep a building standing, and every good church will rest upon this same type of order.

Let me explain further. If a contractor tried to build a house without a blueprint, he would end up with a complex mess of boards, wire and plumbing supplies, all brand new and ready for service, but none connected or useful. The blueprint, which is a plan for structural integrity, brings order to the pile of 2 x 4s, the bundle of PVC pipe and the spools of wire stacked on a job site. Without it, the house will never stand.

In the same way, divine order, based on the blueprint of established doctrine, brings structural integrity to the church. A written, detailed design shows a contractor how to build, and in like manner, sound doctrine tells the apostle how to build within a new church.

In every building, you can trace every beam, every rafter, every 2x4 back to the foundation, because in one way or another, they will all be connected. Some boards are directly attached, while others are connected to those directly attached. There are no free-standing boards in a building, and there are no free-standing doctrines in the church. All we have in the church today and all we rely upon can be traced back to the doctrine of the very first apostles.

Everything you read in the New Testament is the result of the work of the office of the apostle. You could not even be saved had not an apostle written: *"For by grace are ye saved through faith; and that not of yourselves: it is the gift of God"* (Ephesians 2:8). This fact alone makes the office of the apostle extremely valuable.

Apostles are very orderly. In the early church, whenever a dispute arose among the disciples, they took the matter to James, the brother of Jesus. His was a very important role, and he settled the matters to the satisfaction of the other apostles. Although the works of Paul are more well-known, James had a significant impact on the early church because he made sure that the original doctrine and church order were maintained, and that all matters were settled accordingly. Even the other apostles willingly obeyed whenever James set a standard and made a judgment.

The order of the early church should be an example to the church today. We need to acknowledge the authority God has set in the church and give ear whenever they speak. We are not all James, or Peter, or Paul, but we all have our designated place in the body, and we should all be willing to submit one to another.

Apostles do not speak of their own accord, but they speak revelation from Heaven. Paul said in 2 Corinthians 12:7: *"And lest I should be exalted above measure through the abundance of the revelations..."* Apostles deliver doctrinal messages of divine order, not in their own strength, but in the strength of the revelations given them by the Holy Spirit. Every apostle carries this ability to receive divine revelation and interpretation of scripture to keep things in order.

You may say, "Well, if God can tell him, He can tell me, too." Not necessarily. The apostle is divinely equipped by God to receive revelation that believers in general are not equipped to receive. That's why God set them in the church—to deliver those revelations to you.

God will speak to you through apostles to deliver divine instructions for godly order for your life, and for the life of your church. This is the wonder of the office of the apostle, that it could have such a profound effect on individuals even as it does on the church as a whole.

Future generations, should Jesus tarry, will look back upon the apostles of our generation and give them honor for their work among us, just as we give honor to the apostles of old. Today's apostles no longer write scripture, but they still go as those sent by God to deliver specific messages to specific people, and they still help us maintain sound doctrine and divine church order. For this, they are to be respected and honored.

GOD SPEAKS THROUGH THE APOSTLE

Apostles today are sent to many places at many times, but their messages will be the same wherever they go. The truth does not change, so the message of the apostle will not either.

When a true apostle speaks, what he says will be inspired of God because he will not dare weaken the foundation he is building upon with personal ideas. He will always maintain a solid, functional basis upon which the work he has been sent to establish may rise and flourish.

Apostles are foundation-conscious because they realize that if they fail to prepare the proper groundwork, God's work will fail. This reality makes his work so critical, and his call and appointment so significant. This is also why no man should ever try to mimic or copy the work of an apostle, because not only will his vain attempts fail, but the people who follow him and attempt to build upon his sandy foundation will also crumble.

Every five-fold ministry gift carries a penalty for failure, but I believe none is so devastating than when an apostle fails. This is why only God knows who to call, who to trust and empower, and who will succeed.

Romans 1:11 reveals the very heart and soul of an apostle: *"For I long to see you, that I may impart unto you some spiritual gift, to the end ye may be established."*

The apostle has no greater desire than to see people and churches established and grounded in the Word. Apostles speak the word of the Lord, and they long for people to receive and understand what they say. They pray to be received as one sent by God, but more than anything they long for their words to be received as sent from Heaven. When the words of the apostle are received as those spoken by God, He will confirm them with signs following, and they will release the blessing of the apostle for the good of the people.

DEFINED BOUNDARIES

In Romans 15:20-21 we read: *"Yea, so have I strived to preach the gospel, not where Christ was named, lest I should build upon another man's foundation: But as it is written, To whom he was not spoken of, they shall see: and they that have not heard shall understand."*

Even as the apostle speaks the word of the Lord, he will not invade another man's territory, because he is not sent to that location. Every apostle has his own specific territory for which he is responsible, and he will not try to override the boundaries God has established for him.

Apostles often go into unreached lands on foreign soil and break new ground for the gospel. They carry a divine anointing to preach the Word, and then establish an ongoing ministry, a local church or groups of churches which will continue the work there. They prepare the foundation, and then the other five-fold ministers build upon it and equip the saints. As engineers of structural soundness, apostles equip authority, and then they go on to another place to build again. (This is why the office of the apostle is more difficult to recognize in America, where most have heard the gospel and where there are multiple churches established in every city.)

Apostles may also be called to raise up a great work right in their own homeland. An example is the story of a young soldier in the Indian army who met Jesus one day, and his life was never the same. The young man answered the call to preach not long after this encounter, and he and his wife and baby went to a place in India where no other Christians lived. The man was P.G. Vargis, and he and his wife Lilly began a great faith adventure which has birthed congregation after congregation in an un-churched region of the world. For decades this dedicated couple has traveled all over India, living up to their ministry motto to "reach the lost at any cost."

Today, the churches P.G. Vargis and his wife have founded are thriving all over India, and the lost continue to be won daily. His ministry includes a children's home, missions, counseling, technical schools, Bible training, and seminars and crusades that impact pastors from around the country. Each and every year thousands of souls are saved, and lives are changed for eternity.

P.G. Vargis has a heart for his country, the part of the world God has empowered him to impact with the glorious gospel of Jesus Christ. As an apostle, he watches over India's largest church-planting organization, and his churches are doing the work of the ministry with him, still "winning the lost at any cost." His amazing life and ministry show us God can send the apostle anywhere in the world, including his own back yard! (Details found at www.pgv.com).

THE LIFE OF PAUL

I want to conclude our study of how God speaks through apostles by looking a little closer at the life of Paul. No apostle is more well-known than he is, and no man today will ever match his impact on the Body of Christ, so his life is one that should be studied and honored.

The account of the ministry of Paul in the book of Acts reads like an adventure novel. Shipwrecks, snake bites, stoning and resurrection, standing before kings, prison breaks, preaching to the masses, carrying divine appointment, and traveling the world.

It all sounds so glamorous and exciting. Then you realize that the ministry of Paul did not take place in a few months time, but over the course of some 56 years. Paul was not running from adventure to adventure, as we think he was when we read the stories in Acts, but he was in fact living a normal-paced life, facing daily hardships and struggles, just like you and I do.

The difference was this: Paul's life was one long race, one continuing push to fulfill the call given him by Jesus on the road to Damascus. Everything Paul did was directly connected to that call.

Paul traveled from city to city, at God's direction, establishing churches in some, and giving direction to existing churches in others. He set pastors in churches and taught them how to lead. He encouraged and helped those pastors throughout his ministry, making sure he returned to visit them as often as possible, and he sent written messages when he had to be away. Paul cared for those who served with him, and made sure they had all the resources they needed to become all God had called them to be.

One example is the ministry of Titus, one of the lesser known characters in the Bible. When Paul was released from prison in Rome, he and Titus established churches in several cities on the island of Crete. Paul went on to other works, but he left Titus in charge on the island and instructed him to complete the order of the church.

Crete was a difficult place in which to begin a work of the Lord, so Titus had his work cut out for him. Daily life in Crete was immoral, at best, and the lazy, lying, gluttonous inhabitants of the island were a handful for Titus. I'm certain that when Titus received his letter from Paul, which is one of the New Testament books today, he was relieved, because it spelled out how to continue the work on the island and succeed. With Paul's blessing, Titus had authority to take control of the situation and drive out false teachers and correct erroneous doctrines. Without this authority, Titus would have quickly found himself in a sinking ship.

Paul also helped Timothy in his second letter to him. Here, Paul had to exhort a weary young preacher to continue in the fight of faith. This is what an apostle does best, exhorting, encouraging and watching over those who serve with him. Timothy had his own struggles to contend with, and apparently word of his discouragement had reached Paul. The apostle was kind to Timothy, but he also reminded him of the prophecy which had confirmed his call, and told him that sometimes we have to fight the fight of faith using our prophetic words to undergird us when we grow weary.

Paul was also instrumental in establishing the doctrine of the church as a whole. Two-thirds of the New Testament is attributed to the writings of this apostle. God spoke through Him, and the gospel message was established, explained, expounded upon and delivered to the rest of the Body of Christ. It was the job of the five-fold ministers of his day to deliver the message to the people, and to make sure the church began to function as one unified body.

Over the years, Paul traveled several thousand miles in his journeys, all on foot, or by the occasional beast of burden or ship. There were no jets, no comfy motel beds; just the dusty road and the open sky at night. He did what he did without the creature comforts we are so used to today, because he was empowered by God to reach the nations in his generation.

No one man will ever accomplish as much as Paul did in his lifetime, but every five-fold minister can achieve all the Lord desires using the same kind of faith that Paul lived by. Today's men and women of God are equipped for our generation just as Paul was equipped for his. No one can be Paul, but all can follow him as he followed Christ.

While the journey of Paul demonstrates how amazing the life of an apostle can be, it also shows us it is God speaking to us through anointed men that makes the work of the Kingdom possible. These individuals, called and appointed by God, can do great and mighty things through weak and human vessels when they walk by faith and not by sight (see 2 Corinthians 5:7).

Let us hear them and give God glory for this wonderful gift, and let us honor the offices and the authority the Lord has established in the church.

CHAPTER 12

THE VOICE
OF THE PROPHET

I sat in the back of the room, listening to a young minister for the first time. His name was Timothy Bagwell, and he was preaching up a storm, dedicating a new church in Mt. Gilead, Ohio. I listened intently, drinking in every word like a thirsty man. Little did I know that his life and mine would soon cross paths, and that his gift would impact me and my ministry in a very unique way.

Fast forward to a warm summer morning in my own church. It was Sunday, and I had invited Brother Bagwell to take my pulpit for the day. I did not do this very often on a Sunday morning, so it was a special occasion for all of us. As the service progressed, Brother Bagwell moved into the prophetic flow, as he does so often in his ministry. On this day, however, my life was about to change forever.

Brother Bagwell looked me dead in the eye and prophesied that I would begin to move into the miraculous. I bowed my head and listened hard, fully aware that my life and ministry were about as far away from fulfilling his words as it was possible to be, but my heart cried out for the very things he said would come to pass for me. To the natural eye, I did not appear to be a candidate for signs, wonders and miracles, but God had a different plan in mind.

Year after year, it seemed, Brother Bagwell would stand in my pulpit, and he would prophesy the same things to me. Sometimes I felt like he was using the exact same words, repeating again and again that the miraculous would manifest in my ministry. I longed for and prayed for the manifestation of the prophecies with all of my heart, but it did not seem to be happening with any speed at all.

The words of the prophet became a sign post which said, "Don't give up. Your desire will come to pass. Just remain steadfast and diligent, and you will become all that I have destined you to be." Over time, Brother Bagwell's words from Heaven instilled faith, changed me, and birthed a hunger and thirst which God used to form and mold me for His glory. His words prepared me for what I am today.

The many prophecies God gave Brother Bagwell for me have come to pass now, and I can look back with gratefulness for the persistence of the Spirit of God who spoke through him. He prophesied that I would go to the nations of the world with the miraculous, seeding nations for miracles and revival, and these have come to fruition in every way. His words birthed great expectations, but my life has far surpassed them. This is why I thank God with my whole heart for the office of the prophet.

When you come to know him, it's easy to understand why I call Brother Bagwell the prophet of our church. He stands in this office and confirms so many gifts in our congregation, and he moves in the gifts of the Spirit and gives godly direction for our church body. I have heard him prophesy to person after person, and then I have watched the prophecies come true. For these fulfilled prophecies and for my own personal journey into God's destiny for my life, I am very thankful, but I am most grateful to the Lord for bringing me into relationship with this great man of God.

Tim Bagwell is my dearest and best friend. I have come to love him, his family and his church over the years, but it is much more than a mere friendship. Ours is a covenant relationship. I have relationships with some of the greatest preachers and prophets of our time, but no one is as dear to me as Tim Bagwell, not just because of the gift that encouraged me to pursue God's destiny for my life, but because of who he is, a godly man who lives for Jesus with his whole heart, soul and mind. I am truly privileged to know him.

THE GIFT OF THE PROPHET

The five-fold ministry gift of the prophet is intended to be a tremendous blessing to the church. His gift allows him to confirm the word of the Lord, edify, comfort and exhort individuals and congregations alike, and show us things to come in the Body of Christ.

With this wonderful opportunity for good, however, comes a great opportunity for error and misunderstanding. Nothing brings as much blessing to a church as a true prophet who is allowed to function in his five-fold role. By the same token, nothing produces quite as much misinformation in a church as a false prophet who is allowed to run amok among the people. With this in mind, I want to establish a few basic points, then move on to address certain misunderstandings and error in the church today.

The first thing I want to state is that there is a distinct difference between the prophets of old and today's five-fold ministry prophets. In our generation the five-fold prophet is best known as the man or woman who stands before a congregation and declares, "Thus says the Lord!" God speaks through the five-fold prophet for specific purposes, some of which are the same as the prophets of old, and some of which are strikingly different.

The Old Testament prophets brought a revelation of the Lord to the people. They were men of God set in their office for a specific time period, and they spoke to the entire nation of Israel. What the Old Testament prophet spoke to the people became the declaration of the rhema word of the Lord. He then inscribed the inspiration of the Lord in logos form, and it became scripture.

Writing scripture was an important part of the office of the Old Testament prophet, but that part of the prophet's office has been done away with because we are no longer allowed to add to scripture (see Revelation 22:18). This being said, nearly every other function of the Old Testament prophet is in action today in some form or fashion in the ministry of the New Testament five-fold prophet.

The prophets of old could foresee and foretell future events. Today's prophets still tell us of things to come by the Holy Spirit (see John 13:16), and they warn, reveal, confirm and lead as they did in old times. The prophet's place in the Kingdom of God still encompasses the power gifts which operated in the lives of the prophets of old.

Though they are similar in activity, we cannot judge New Testament prophets by Old Testament rules. This would be like trying to fix a jet airplane using the manual for a station wagon. It won't work because the parts won't fit. There is a thread which makes them the same, and yet today's prophets operate in a dimension that unveils something about God which is entirely different than the Old Testament prophets knew.

Those prophets often delivered bad news for Israel because the people had strayed from God. New Testament prophets, however, living on the other side of the cross, usually have better things to talk about. They generally have specific things to say to specific people or specific churches.

Every prophet will have a different personality and different strengths which God will use to speak to us and show us who He is. For example, Moses was a prophet who delivered Israel. When God spoke through Moses He said, "I am the Deliverer."

Jeremiah was known as the weeping prophet, showing us that God is a God of compassion and emotion. Hosea, whose name means "salvation," was called to marry a prostitute in order for God to show Israel how great His mercy and longsuffering were toward them. Nehemiah was a prophet who rebuilt the temple, reminding us that God is a rebuilder of our lives; no matter what the devil does, the Lord can rebuild and strengthen you, and make you better than you were before.

New Testament five-fold prophets, like their forefathers, also have very unique traits which reveal distinct characteristics of God. Not only does each personality reflect a different side of the Father, but the way each prophet functions in his ministry shows us how God desires to touch us personally.

I have been in services where the five-fold prophet called people out and told them their names and the names of the streets they lived on. Why would this be important? Evidently, the Lord needed those people to realize that He knew who they were, where they lived, and just what they were going through. When God speaks through a prophet in this manner, it brings great comfort and opens people up to hear the rest of what, "Thus says the Lord." Other five-fold prophets operate differently.

Here is a prime example. I openly identify Tim Bagwell as the recognized prophet of our church, because although he has his own church, when he ministers here he does not come as a pastor, but as our prophet. When he speaks, he confirms certain gifts that have been set in our church. He will call people out and speak a word over them that generally reaffirms what I already know about them, but when that word is spoken publicly it edifies and exhorts the person and confirms what he felt stirring in his spirit. Brother Bagwell also speaks words which establish direction for our entire church. He has a knack for hitting our people right where they live, and he encourages them to keep on keeping on. He confirms vision even while he inspires us to press on to completion. No other prophet impacts our church as he does.

God sets prophets like this before certain people to be a reflection of His ways to them. Remember how God set Moses before the people, and they saw God mirrored in his face? In the same way, as the prophet stands before us and confirms the word of the Lord, we see God reflected in him, and in turn reflected in us.

PROPHETS BY GRACE

We are all given a measure of grace to carry out the works of the Lord. Romans 12:6 tells us: *"Having then gifts differing according to the grace that is given to us, whether prophecy, let us prophesy according to the proportion of faith."* Even the five-fold gifts operate according to the measure of grace given unto them; therefore, each prophet will operate in different dimensions by that grace.

No two prophets are alike. Each functions according to the grace given, and according to the assignment made. Some are prophets for certain churches, while others are prophets for certain regions, and still others are prophets for certain nations. God speaks through each as He wills. We see this concept in Deuteronomy 1:15, where Moses was subdividing the oversight of certain matters in Israel. He said: *"So I took the chief of your tribes, wise men, and known, and made them heads over you, captains over thousands, and captains over hundreds, and captains over fifties, and captains over tens, and officers among your tribes."*

Were those assigned to watch over groups of 50 any less important than those assigned to watch over 1,000? No. They each operated in the measure of grace assigned to them, so as long as they each did their work well, they were considered successful in the eyes of the Lord. In the same way, a prophet to the nations may receive higher regard in our eyes, but in God's eyes, as long as the prophet called to minister to five churches operates in the level of grace given him to the best of his ability, he is pleasing to the Lord.

God knows you intimately. He knows your call and gift, but He also knows your frame. He knows your strengths, weaknesses, limits and boundaries. The Lord will never ask more of you than He knows you can handle. If you develop yourself in the grace you are given, then you will be changed from glory to glory. We can each grow in God to the highest level possible for us personally. My highest may not be as high as someone else's, but as long as I reach the top of my rungs, I am doing all I can, and God will be pleased.

It's the same for prophets. You should not belittle the man who travels to the same twelve churches every year to deliver a word of encouragement for their congregations. If he is doing all he is called to do, he is pleasing God. So don't compare prophet with prophet. When a prophet stands in your pulpit, give him the honor he is due and receive from his gift, but don't judge him by the gift of another.

One prophet may come and read everybody's mail, so to speak. Another may only minister to one person individually, but his corporate message could be outstanding. Each has been set in the church for a specific time and a specific purpose. I encourage you to do as God says in 2 Chronicles 20:20: *"...Believe in the Lord your God, so shall ye be established; believe his prophets, so shall ye prosper."*

EDIFICATION, EXHORTATION AND COMFORT

There is a second distinction which must be made about today's five-fold prophet, and it has to do with the simple gift of prophecy described in 1 Corinthians 12:10. This, one of the nine gifts of the Spirit available to every believer, is not the same as the five-fold office of the prophet.

We read in 1 Corinthians 14:3: *"But he that prophesieth speaketh unto men to edification, and exhortation, and comfort."* This verse shows us what the basis of all prophecy is about. Its main purpose is to edify, exhort and comfort believers. Whether in the form of a simple prophecy delivered by a believer under the operation of the gifts of the Spirit, or as a corporate word delivered by the five-fold prophet under a completely different manifestation, prophecy will never stray far from this basic premise. It will always edify, exhort and comfort.

The main difference between the simple gift of prophecy and a prophetic utterance given by a prophet is this: The simple gift of prophecy is limited to edification, exhortation and comfort, period. It will never include anything other than one or more of these three elements, ever.

While the simple gift of prophecy is limited in its scope, the five-fold prophet can do many things to bless the Body of Christ. He can warn. He can reveal or confirm callings, as God did for Paul and Barnabas. A prophet can also lead and show us things to come in the future. A five-fold prophet is distinctly different from one who operates in the simple gift of prophecy. It is important that you be able to distinguish the difference.

Prophets are five-fold ministers, called and appointed by God for a lifetime, while those who prophesy under the operation of the gifts of the Spirit are simply believers releasing a temporary anointing to edify, exhort and comfort a congregation during a church service, or an individual in a one-on-one setting.

You cannot become a prophet by repeated use of the simple gift of prophecy. Only God can call and establish someone in the five-fold office of the prophet—which is a calling, not a job you can earn.

PROPHETS WARN

If a prophet declares, "Trouble is coming to the earth," He is not saying it to terrify the Body of Christ, but to warn us so we can take appropriate action and prepare for God's supernatural provision. When a five-fold prophet is sent by God to deliver a word of warning, he will not leave you hopeless and helpless, but will show you the way of escape even as he warns you of an impending storm.

We see this in Acts 11:27-29: *"And in these days came prophets from Jerusalem unto Antioch. And there stood up one of them named Agabus, and signified by the spirit that there should be great dearth throughout all the world: which came to pass in the days of Claudius Caesar. Then the disciples, every man according to his ability, determined to send relief unto the brethren which dwelt in Judaea."*

The prophet's news was not encouraging. Famine was coming to the land, but notice the disciples did not leave the meeting discouraged, but were empowered and determined to help those who would be most affected by the drought.

The prophetic, no matter how it is administered, will always end in edification, exhortation and comfort of the church. It will call us to prepare, and it will show us the way of escape because every prophetic declaration is accompanied by grace that allows us to see God.

I do not put much stock in so-called prophets who never speak anything but words of doom and gloom. This is not the God of the New Testament I know and read about in the Bible. Yes, God did warn in the New Testament, but He never gave a warning without encouraging them to pursue the way of escape.

Remember, the basis of every prophecy is to edify, exhort and comfort. Even godly warnings do not leave us helpless and hopeless, but point us in the direction of victory.

PROPHETS REVEAL, CONFIRM AND LEAD

Let's look closer at the prophecies of Agabus, an established New Testament prophet. We find two distinct stories in Acts 11:27-30, which we just looked at briefly, and in Acts 21:10-13. Agabus brought a word of the Lord which revealed a future event in one case, and confirmed a personal word to the Apostle Paul in another. In each instance, his words came from God just as surely as the written Word did.

In the first story, when Agabus prophesied of a drought and famine that would come upon the land, the church believed the voice of the prophet, rallied together, got their finances in order and sent relief to the areas that were going to suffer the most during this troubled time. Here, the prophet revealed and foretold a world event that ordered the steps of the church.

Later, Agabus confirmed a personal word to Paul which warned him of trouble in Jerusalem. Paul already knew about it and was prepared to give his life for the name of Jesus, so this word did not alter Paul's plans, but it did confirm to him what was coming in his very near future.

Agabus operated in his office by divine design. He said only what God told him to say, no more, no less. His words were received, and because they were, the church was prepared in one instance, and Paul was made even more determined to do the will of the Lord in the other.

While the simple gift of prophecy does not lead or guide, the word of the prophet may do just that. In Acts 13:2, the Holy Spirit spoke through the prophet and told Saul (Paul) and Barnabas it was time to go and do what they were called to accomplish. That word did not give them a call, but it did confirm it, and directed them to get up and go immediately. This prophetic word led Paul and Barnabas to begin doing the work God had already called them to.

There is a great difference between confirming a call and creating one. If you've not heard of the call a prophet describes, you can bank on the fact he missed it. Prophecy confirms, but it does not call. It may direct you to go and do what you have been called to do, but it will not direct you to go and do something you know nothing about.

When Tim Bagwell prophesied to me concerning moving into the realm of the miraculous, it was not new information for me, although it was not yet manifested. His words verified the very things I desired and longed for with all my heart. Those desires were given to me by God to draw me to the place of completion and fruition. The prophecies simply confirmed the desires and gave me strength to keep pressing in and pursuing what God had in store for me.

My encounters with the prophet of our church in this instance were much different than those early on with the so-called prophecies which nearly caused me to give up in the process of trying to be something God had not called me to be. But once I heard my call directly from God and moved toward it, I have never been the same. Now I rejoice at words of prophecy confirming what God has already birthed in my heart, and I reject anything that does not.

In today's world, many are running to and fro, looking for someone to give them a personal word from the Lord. Most of these seekers have itching ears rather than truly open hearts. They are looking for a man or woman of God to call them into the ministry, or to give them a special revelation which only pertains to them, but this is not how the Lord designed the office of the prophet to work.

I believe Christians who run from prophet to prophet, seeking personal words, are doing so at their peril. A true call will be established first in your heart, and will then perhaps be confirmed by a prophet, but don't look for more than a prophet is called to deliver. Only God can speak to you and give you what you are looking for.

Let me take a short rabbit trail for a few paragraphs to show you some things about your personal destiny. When God gives you a destiny or a call, it is a divine treasure, the wealth of the fulfillment of your life. No one can tap into the destiny of any person except that individual.

The devil does not know your full destiny. If he did, he would destroy it. He may see signs of certain gifts in you that he has seen before, but God does not allow him to know the fullness of all He has for you. This is personal, private information to be shared by you and God alone. Your destiny is laid up in Heaven, and it is only deposited in your life when you use the keys which extract it from its place of rest. If you do not use the keys, you will go through life without ever knowing your true destiny.

No man or five-fold minister, nor even your pastor, can hear from Heaven for you. Your pastor may hear a word which will confirm what you heard, but God will not allow you to possess the treasure of your destiny until you pay the price it takes to obtain it yourself. No other man or woman—pastor, prophet, apostle, evangelist or teacher—can discover your destiny treasure for you. This is a personal journey only you and God can fulfill together.

No one else can fast for you. No one else can pray in your place of authority. No one else can study to show that you are approved, a workman who does not need to be ashamed (see 2 Timothy 2:15). Your spouse, your pastor, or a friend can fast with you, and they can pray for you, but ultimately you have to pay your own price to hear from Heaven.

The treasures which are laid up for you above are kept there for your own protection. There, neither moth nor rust can corrupt. There, no thief can break through to steal (see Matthew 6:19-20). God will never extract the treasures of a man's destiny and place them in the hands of another man, leaving the individual without accountability, responsibility or payment for what God has laid up for him. We all work out our own salvation with fear and trembling (see Philippians 2:12). We do not depend on others to do this for us.

Having established this, we return to the five-fold prophet and realize he does not have the capacity to give you a destiny, but he does have the capacity to confirm it. Remember, the steps of a good man are ordered of the Lord, and we as children of God are led by the Spirit, not by people (see Psalm 37:23; Romans 8:14). The prophet may confirm and encourage you in your call, but he will never determine your call. Only God can do that. So, be very careful and prove every prophecy before you take off and attempt to do something beyond the ordinary. If you don't know about the call before the prophet proclaims it, it's probably not a real call.

If you are called, you will know it long before the prophet does. Your pastor will likely know, because he knows you, but even he will not single you out to confirm this and send you forth until and unless God tells him to. Never follow the word of a man unless the Lord has truly called you and told you already. Even then, as I discovered in my early years, men can be close, but still miss God's direction for you.

Don't try to be an evangelist if you are a pastor, like I did. And don't try to be a five-fold minister unless you are truly chosen by God for this purpose.

196

If you have to ask, you're not called; or maybe you're like me and know there is a call, but you don't have specific direction yet. Be patient and let God be in control of your destiny. Remember, clarity comes in stages of growth and preparation, and the prophet helps make your vision and destiny clear. He can also strengthen faith, and sometimes even unveil the timetable of Heaven.

BE CAREFUL WHO YOU HEAR

There is an interesting story in Acts 21 involving Paul and some disciples eager to help him. In verse four it says: *"And finding disciples, we tarried there seven days: who said to Paul through the Spirit, that he should not go up to Jerusalem."*

Who sent Paul to Jerusalem? According to Acts 18:21, God did because Paul states: *"...I must by all means keep this feast that cometh in Jerusalem: but I will return again unto you, if God will..."* If Paul was determined to go to Jerusalem by any means, we can conclude he was on a mission from Heaven. No matter what, Paul had to go.

Tracing Paul's steps, we see in Acts 19:21 that he still had his face set toward Jerusalem, although he had not yet been able to begin the journey. This verse says: *"After these things were ended, Paul purposed in the spirit, when he had passed through Macedonia and Achaia, to go to Jerusalem, saying, After I have been there, I must also see Rome."*

A timetable was set in Acts 20:16, which tells us: *"For Paul had determined to sail by Ephesus, because he would not spend the time in Asia: for he hasted, if it were possible for him, to be at Jerusalem the day of Pentecost."*

In this we finally see confirmation that Paul had indeed been sent to Jerusalem by God: *"And now, behold, I go bound in the spirit unto Jerusalem, not knowing the things that shall befall me there: Save that the Holy Ghost witnesseth in every city, saying that bonds and afflictions abide me"* (Acts 20:22-23). Paul was going to Jerusalem *"bound in the spirit."* In other words, he had been sent by God, so the trip was non-negotiable.

I've taken the long way around to return to Acts 21:4, which again says: *"And finding disciples, we tarried there seven days: who said to Paul through the Spirit, that he should not go up to Jerusalem."*

A disciple is one who has been taught by another. So, these men were not ignorant of the things of God, but neither were they prophets or leaders in the

197

church. They had no right to do what they did, but they did it nonetheless. Though they were not prophets, they stepped outside the boundaries of established order and prophesied a directive word to Paul anyway. Their simple prophecy did not edify, exhort or comfort, but it gave specific instructions.

What does this tell us? The word was not from God. Even though they said, "Thus says the Lord," they were not speaking the truth, nor were they speaking the word of the Lord. How do we know they missed it? In verse 11, the prophet Agabus came to Paul sometime after the disciples prophesied, and he gave him a true word from the Lord, one of warning concerning what was awaiting him in Jerusalem.

Agabus said: *"...Thus saith the Holy Ghost, So shall the Jews at Jerusalem bind the man that owneth this girdle, and shall deliver him into the hands of the Gentiles."* Notice Agabus never tried to direct Paul away from Jerusalem; he only told him what was waiting for him there. There is an enormous difference between what the prophet declared and what the disciples before him said.

In verse 12, after the prophetic message was delivered, the men in leadership with Paul begged him not to go to Jerusalem, but look at Paul's answer in verse 13: *"Then Paul answered, What mean ye to weep and to break mine heart? For I am ready not to be bound only, but also to die at Jerusalem for the name of the Lord Jesus."*

Here we discover Paul's focus. God had directed him to go to Jerusalem. Although he was hindered and delayed, Paul's heart was set to obey, no matter what. Though the disciples tried to intervene, Paul ignored them. Even when the prophet proclaimed what awaited him in Jerusalem, Paul stuck to the call of God, even unto death, if that's what it meant. (This is a true call of God, one which will cause you to desire to fulfill it more than you desire life.)

We see Paul vindicated in Acts 23:11: *"And the night following the Lord stood by him, and said, Be of good cheer, Paul: for as thou hast testified of me in Jerusalem, so must thou bear witness also at Rome."*

Jesus Himself confirmed He had indeed called Paul to go to Jerusalem, and then to Rome, just as Paul knew all along (see Acts 19:21).

What is the moral of this long story? Be very careful who you listen to. Not everyone who says he is a prophet is one, and not everyone who says, "Thus says the Lord" has a clue what the Lord is saying. Always weigh out what you hear by the Word of God first, and also by what you already know in your spirit by God's Spirit. The Lord will not change His mind and tell you different things at different times. What God says stays firm, no matter what changes around you or what others say or think.

IMPERFECT VESSELS

So what happened with the disciples of Acts 21:4? They missed it, plain and simple. The Bible says they prophesied "through the Spirit," but they still managed to miss the message. Every gift is perfect, but the man or woman who delivers the gift is not perfect. It is possible for someone to prophesy out of his own desire or his own understanding, instead of by the Spirit of God.

It's like this: We are vessels of clay. When God sends an utterance through us, it has to pass through the clay, like water in a clay pitcher would. Sometimes, if the pitcher is not properly fired, the pure water of the message will get mixed up with the clay of the vessel on the way through, so what is poured out will be cloudy and imperfect.

Does this mean we throw out those who make mistakes? No, we don't discard disciples. But we do have a higher standard for five-fold prophets. Notice Paul simply ignored the disciples who missed it, but when the church leaders in Acts 21:12 tried to stop him from fulfilling his call, he openly rebuked and chastised them. Anyone who has ever raised a child will know why Paul treated one mistake differently than the other.

The disciples were babies, still dragging their diapers around with them, sucking their thumbs while they tried to prophesy. If you've ever had a toddler in the house, you know to expect the loss of some of your household treasures when your bundle of energy runs through the room. It's the same with baby Christians. If you get around them, you're likely to suffer a little loss, but that's okay. We know they'll grow out of it, just as babies do, so we suffer through these times and help them grow up as quickly as possible.

However, if your teenager or young adult child comes crashing through the house making a mess of things, you're going to grab him by the nape of the neck and say, "Hey! Knock it off!" It's no different in spiritual matters. The leadership with Paul was expected to know better than to try to direct an apostle. But they did it anyway. So Paul rebuked them and made sure they understood he did not appreciate their behavior.

You need to be cautious and always remember that disciples are learning, so be very, very careful when you hear a word from them. And even leaders sometimes miss it, so you have to be watchful and compare everything to God's Word, even as you try and prove those words by the passage of time.

Prophetic utterance can be one of the greatest tools of encouragement, exhortation and comfort, but it can be one of the greatest destructive tools if it is not of God. The words of the prophet should be judged just as we judge the words of every other five-fold gift. They must line up with the written Word of God.

No prophet should ever establish a new doctrine or a new way of interpreting the Word. When someone goes that direction, red flags should pop up everywhere, and sirens should sound. The words of the prophet, if truly from God, will line up with the Word, encourage you to go to the Word for further instruction, and deepen your dependency on God.

As a final check, look to see if the words of the prophet lift up the name of Jesus. A true prophet will always exalt God's Son and lead people to Him. Though not in the same way as the evangelist, the ministry of the prophet will always lead people to Jesus in some form or fashion.

Prophets have been set in the church by God as part of the foundation of the Body of Christ. They are pillars of maturity, teaching and revelation, and their gifts are eternally established. They do not diminish in power, nature or in purpose over time. As long as the Body of Christ is on the earth, the five-fold prophets will be here for our edification, exhortation and comfort.

BEWARE OF FALSE PROPHETS

With every true manifestation of God, there is an opportunity for erroneous manifestations to creep in. In no other office is this more prevalent than in the five-fold prophet's office.

In Deuteronomy 18:20-22 we learn how God feels about false prophets: *"But the prophet, which shall presume to speak a word in my name, which I have not commanded him to speak, or that shall speak in the name of other gods, even that prophet shall die. And if thou say in thine heart, how shall we know the word which the Lord hath not spoken? When a prophet speaketh in the name of the Lord, if the thing follow not, nor come to pass, that is the thing which the Lord hath not spoken, but the prophet hath spoken it presumptuously: Thou shalt not be afraid of him."*

This is very serious business. On one hand, the false prophet will reap his own reward of death. On the other hand, those who hear from such men should not give them a second thought. This is what the last verse means when it tells us, *"Thou shalt not be afraid of him."* In other words, don't pay any attention, and do not regard him with respect because he has not earned any.

Here again, we see a distinct difference between how God regards the office of the five-fold prophet and how He regards the simple gift of prophecy. The five-fold prophet who speaks presumptuously and misleads people will not be tolerated by God. This man or woman will be punished severely. But, if a man (or a woman) prophesies in a church service with the simple gift of prophecy and speaks from his own head instead of by God's Spirit, that man should be corrected by his pastor, but not necessarily banned from prophesying ever again.

The gifts of the Spirit require use and correction before we become skillful in their operation. Paul's letters to the Corinthians offered many such corrections, but they also clearly encouraged the operation of the gifts in every service.

The five-fold prophet, however, is not given such a wide path. He who is called had better know when to speak and when to be still. He should never speak out of turn or infuse his own opinion in the mix. The five-fold office of the prophet is not to be taken lightly. Every prophet should be very careful to weigh his words before he ever says, "Thus says the Lord."

So, beware of false prophets, but do not fear them. As with every single one of the five-fold ministry gifts, judge what the prophet says by the written Word of God. Let time prove the words given and the people giving them. As we discovered before, the Word should be the judge and jury in every case.

If you will judge what you hear when you receive the ministry of a prophet, you will avoid false prophecies, and you will hear the voice of God and be blessed in all you do.

SCHOOL OF THE PROPHETS

I want to touch briefly on a specific phenomenon in the Body of Christ today known as the School of the Prophets. At this writing, if you go online and search under that title you will find page after page of web sites devoted to this subject. I generally do not challenge the ministries of other men, but in this case I believe it is so dangerous that I would be wrong if I did not give it some space. While not every web site under this category will fit what I am about to write, most did in some way.

The online offering consisted of everything from one seemingly legitimate site, to a place that promised you could apply and register to become a prophet. Some were nothing more than what I call new-age wooey-land sites. There was even one which was devoted to Joseph Smith, the founder of the Mormon church and most definitely a false prophet.

Some promised to "raise up prophets and the five-fold ministry." Others promised to "teach and train you to become a prophet." Some advertized you could join a class where you would practice giving and receiving words, one to another. And finally one site promised to train you in all seven religions of the world. It was quite a strange mix of nonsense, for the most part.

It is sad to see sincere believers get mixed up in these things innocently, and there are far too many Christians who are attracted to these kinds of "ministries" because they are actively seeking a personal word from the Lord. They will go to great lengths to get that word, rather than rely on the written Word first. These individuals are not operating in a true spirit of hunger and thirst for the things of God, but are led astray under a cloak of ignorance and self-motivation.

Some of the various forms of the School of the Prophets seek to teach people how to become prophets, to foretell and foresee. We already established thoroughly that the five-fold offices are not available for any man or woman to decide to pursue. You are either called, or you are not. There is no training that will qualify you for the five-fold ministry. Only God can call and qualify you—not man, or a school, or a registration fee.

A five-fold office cannot be learned or earned. It cannot be bought and paid for. It cannot be raised up or transferred to you. It can only be implanted in you by God. Besides this, you do not want to try to invade some place the Lord has not anointed you to go.

So, certain seeking people, having presumptuous ideas about themselves, sign up for a School of the Prophets. Rather than exit as prophets, they usually exit as people who are more ignorant than they were when they entered. I admonish you not to try to mimic or copy a prophet. If you've got it, you've got it; and if you don't, you cannot learn it from man.

It's hard enough to operate in the five-fold ministry when you are called, appointed and anointed. To try to operate there in your own ability could be life-threatening. Ask Aaron's sons and Korah. They were all killed for venturing to go where God had not sent them. What God appoints in the five-fold ministry is sacred. You cannot choose to invade that territory, nor do you have a choice to apprehend its giftings and abilities.

Even those in the School of the Prophets arena where they try to teach you to operate in the simple gift of prophecy have no right to go there either, because the gift is a supernatural utterance just as tongues is a supernatural utterance. You cannot teach someone to speak in tongues, and you cannot teach them to prophesy.

The place for learning is in the local church where the pastor can judge, not only what is said in the simple gift of prophecy, but also the person doing the prophesying. None of the Schools of the Prophets online have any intention of developing relationships with their students, but a pastor knows you, and therefore knows whether what you are operating in is of God or of your own will. Your pastor understands that everyone grows, and every office and gifting matures, so he will correct you when you need correction, and he will encourage you when you need encouragement.

Surfing the web for your call and anointing is like surfing the ocean for lunch. You're going to get tossed on the beach and be left alone, hungry and soaked to the bone—if you're not eaten by sharks before that! Be careful and stay away from the hype and false promises so prevalent in today's society, and let the written Word of God and a good dose of common sense be your guide. Get rooted in a church where you can grow and mature in your gifts, and where you can experience spiritual things in a safe, nurturing environment under the watchful eye of a caring pastor.

LET THE WORD PREVAIL

I end this chapter with a reminder. No matter how exciting a supposed prophecy may sound when it comes forth, and no matter how many people run to pat you on the back after you receive it, always, always check it with the Word before you rush to do anything. Seek counsel from those you are submitted to, and allow the Word of God to complement true prophecy, and confirm and provide you with more direction after the fact.

True prophecies are a treasure, and they are needful in our fight of faith (see 1 Timothy 1:18). Having said that, they should never drive us away from established doctrine, or away from the counsel of those who watch for our souls.

Scripture tells us: *"Where no counsel is, the people fall: but in the multitude of counsellors there is safety"* (Proverbs 11:14). Trust your pastor, if he is a man who understands prophecy, and trust those who have the benefit of years in the Body of Christ to help you discern whether what was spoken as, "Thus says the Lord," was truly from Him.

No prophet will ever be offended if you check with the Word and trusted counsel before you go and do something, especially if it is extraordinary. True prophets expect their words to be compared to the written Word and welcome your caution and your proving.

I encourage you to exercise the wisdom God gave you and be careful not to run off and sell all that you have just because a prophet told you to. Remember, prophets are used by God to confirm what He has told you in your own quiet times with Him, so a true prophecy will not be a surprise, but a welcome confirmation you are on the right track.

Prophets are great men and women of God. Let's not bring shame to true prophets by allowing ourselves to be led astray by *"every wind of doctrine"* (Ephesians 4:14). After all, this is one of the things God established the five-fold ministry gifts to combat.

Let the Word of God be your guide in everything you do, even in your receiving of the prophetic word of the Lord, and you will find yourself blessed, stable and doing well in the Kingdom of God.

Part Three

Spiritual Gifts

CHAPTER 13

ENDUED FROM ON HIGH

P eter stood talking to a very prominent Gentile, a man who was intriguing—as much for what Peter did *not* know about him, as for what he *did* know. Peter knew his name was Cornelius, and he knew God had brought him here by a supernatural visitation, but what was about to happen next was going to take Peter by surprise.

As they strolled into the living quarters of Cornelius' lavish home, Peter realized he was not alone in his invitation. There were several other people in the main foyer, and they all seemed to know one another. Suddenly, Peter felt very alone.

A little overwhelmed, he blurted out his innermost thoughts to Cornelius, saying, "You know that it is an unlawful thing for a man who is a Jew to keep company with someone of another nation. God just recently spoke to me and showed me that I should not call any man common or unclean, and this is the reason I came without question, but I must ask, why am I here?"

Cornelius was only too happy to tell his story, one of an angelic visitation which had compelled him to send men to find Peter. Smiling broadly Cornelius replied, "Now we are all here present before God, to hear the things you are commanded to say by God."

This was all it took, and the preaching commenced. Peter spent the next several minutes explaining the gospel in its most basic terms. He concluded with this word of the Lord: "To Him give all the prophets witness, that through His name whoever believes in Him shall receive remission of sins."

And then it happened. Just as on the Day of Pentecost, the Holy Spirit fell on every person in the room. Peter and the men who came with him were completely astonished because they saw and heard something they never dreamed they would. A room full of Gentiles speaking in tongues and magnifying God, just like the 120 in the Upper Room had done not so long ago.

Peter watched in disbelief for a moment, and then he said, "Can any man forbid water, that these should not be baptized, since they have received the Holy Spirit the same as we have?"

The vision God had given him suddenly seemed crystal clear. The Gentiles were going to be engrafted into the Body of Christ right alongside the Jews, and they were going to receive every benefit, including the infilling of the Holy Spirit. It was a miracle! (see Acts 10:27-48).

THE GIFTS OF THE SPIRIT

The infilling of the Spirit in this notable story opened the door to the gifts of the Spirit being manifested in this Gentile family. Truthfully, the gifts of the Spirit are some of the most overlooked ways through which God can speak. We find these gifts in 1 Corinthians 12:7-11: *"But the manifestation of the Spirit is given to every man to profit withal. For to one is given by the Spirit the word of wisdom; to another the word of knowledge by the same Spirit; to another faith by the same Spirit; to another the gifts of healing by the same Spirit; to another the working of miracles; to another prophecy; to another discerning of spirits; to another divers kinds of tongues; to another the interpretation of tongues: But all these worketh that one and the selfsame Spirit, dividing to every man severally as he will."*

We see in verse seven that the gifts of the Spirit are given for our benefit. They are nine dimensions of God revealed to humanity, and the Lord uses them to give us a glimpse of who He is and what He desires to do in our lives.

For instance, when a word of knowledge is given to you, God says, "I am an all-knowing God." When a word of wisdom shows you what to do, it reminds you that the Lord is the one who leads and directs your steps. When the discerning of spirits is in operation, it shows you there is nothing hidden from the eyes of the Lord. The gift of faith reminds you that faith is what pleases God. When the Father speaks through the gift of prophecy, you are reminded it is God who edifies, exhorts and comforts you.

God speaks through gifts of healing to confirm that He is a healing God. The working of miracles unveils that there is nothing impossible with Him; His hand is not too short, but is extended to you in great acts of mercy. Speaking in other tongues reminds you God speaks in a language no man can understand; He speaks mysteries to help you and build you up on your most holy faith. Interpretation of tongues teaches you that all interpretation belongs to the Lord, and that the spirit of man is the candle of the Lord, revealing the meaning of hidden mysteries.

The essential thing to understand about the gifts of the Spirit is the fact they are available to all of us, to every believer, for our profit. God desires to speak through the gifts of the Spirit, but it is up to you to hear and grow in Him.

Again, 1 Corinthians 12:7 tells us: *"But the manifestation of the Spirit is given to every man to profit withal."* The word *profit* means to live in completeness for the service of the Kingdom, for the partaking of life and it more abundantly in every area. The gifts of the Spirit are not just for your profit in church services, but they are for your profit in your walk with Christ.

Jesus benefitted by using the gifts of the Spirit in His everyday life. He used the gifts for the good of the disciples and for the multitudes in order to reveal who He was—the only Truth, Way and Life.

Jesus said in John 17:12: *"While I was with them in the world, I kept them in thy name: those that thou gavest me I have kept, and none of them is lost, but the son of perdition; that the scripture might be fulfilled."* The disciples were in a spiritual battle, and Jesus kept them supernaturally by operating in the gifts of the Spirit in their midst.

God's Son also used the gifts of the Spirit when He ministered to the multitudes that followed Him everywhere He went. Jesus operated in the gift of faith, in gifts of healing and the working of miracles when He healed the multitudes, multiplied the loaves and fishes, walked on the water, moved through a crowd without being seen, calmed a storm and a host of other examples (see Matthew 14:15-21; Mark 4:35-41; Luke 4:40).

Jesus operated in words of knowledge and wisdom when He told people things He could not have known in the natural. He operated in the discerning of spirits when He cast out devils, and when He rebuked the Pharisees for harboring evil thoughts in their hearts (see Matthew 12:14-15, 24-37; 17:14-18; Luke 7:39-48; John 1:43-51). Jesus operated in and profited from the gifts of the Spirit every day, and He is our ultimate example for the way we should live our lives.

The gifts of the Spirit are given to every believer who is filled with the same Spirit who filled Jesus (see Matthew 3:16). This means that the gifts are not just given to accompany the five-fold ministry, but they are given to all who will receive them. You can benefit from the gifts of the Spirit in your everyday life, too.

How specifically do you profit from spiritual gifts? Well, if you need knowledge, the word of knowledge will profit you. If you need healing, the gifts of healing will be beneficial. If you need wisdom, a word of wisdom will be profitable, and so on. Hearing God's voice through the gifts of the Spirit is one of the most readily available ways through which you can hear Him in your own personal life. God is not withholding anything from you, but has established so many avenues for you to hear from Him because He loves you and wants to speak to you daily.

WHO ARE THE GIFTS FOR?

Here are two frequently asked questions concerning the gifts of the Spirit: "Are the gifts really for today?" and "Are they for me?" To find the answers, let's see what Jesus said just before He departed into the clouds and was received into glory: *"But ye shall receive power, after that the Holy Ghost is come upon you: and ye shall be witnesses unto me both in Jerusalem, and in all Judaea, and in Samaria, and unto the uttermost part of the earth"* (Acts 1:8).

Surely the last thing on Jesus' mind before He ascended to Heaven would be the most important thing—what He needed the disciples to understand the most. I'm sure as He spoke they remembered His words from John 14:16-17: *"And I will pray the Father, and he shall give you another Comforter, that he may abide with you for ever; Even the Spirit of truth; whom the world cannot receive, because it seeth him not, neither knoweth him: but ye know him; for he dwelleth with you, and shall be in you."*

Jesus wanted to make sure the disciples understood now was the time for them to receive the fullness of what He had promised in this scripture and what He had revealed to them through His life. The moment had arrived for them to be filled with the Spirit so they could be His witnesses.

The very first infilling of the Holy Spirit was received by the 120 who tarried in the Upper Room in obedience to Jesus' final command. After ten days of waiting and praying, what is described in Acts 2:2-4 took place: *"And suddenly there came a sound from heaven as of a rushing mighty wind, and it filled all the house where they were sitting. And there appeared unto them cloven tongues like as of fire, and it sat upon each of them. And they were all filled with the Holy Ghost, and began to speak with other tongues, as the Spirit gave them utterance."*

This outpouring of God's Spirit was a direct fulfillment of John 14:16-17 and Acts 1:8, along with a host of other scriptures, including Joel 2:28 and Acts 1:5 (see also 2 Corinthians 6:16-17 and 1 Corinthians 6:19). Notice the result of the Spirit of God filling those 120 faithful men and women in the Upper Room. They began to speak with tongues as the Spirit gave them utterance, the first evidence of a dramatic change in their lives.

This utterance was not man made. It was not born of intellect or education, but it was a gift given by God as a confirming sign that the Holy Spirit had come upon them as Jesus had promised. It also confirmed He had given them special gifts, later identified as the gifts of the Spirit in 1 Corinthians 12:7-11. This is why we call speaking in tongues the evidence of being filled with the Spirit, because it was the very first sign to be seen and heard on the Day of Pentecost.

So, back to the questions, are the gifts for today, and are they for you? The answers are found in scripture. In Acts 2:38-39 we read: *"Then Peter said unto them, Repent, and be baptized every one of you in the name of Jesus Christ for the remission of sins, and ye shall receive the gift of the Holy Ghost. For the promise is unto you, and to your children, and to all that are afar off, even as many as the Lord our God shall call."* Here we see that the promise of the infilling of the Holy Spirit was not only for those in the early church, but also for *"those that are afar off"*—including you and me.

Then in Luke 11:11-13 we find: *"If a son shall ask bread of any of you that is a father, will he give him a stone? Or if he ask a fish, will he for a fish give him a serpent? Or if he shall ask an egg, will he offer him a scorpion? If ye then, being evil, know how to give good gifts unto your children: how much more shall your heavenly Father give the Holy Spirit to them that ask him?"* According to this scripture the only requirement needed to qualify to ask for the infilling of the Holy Spirit is for you to be a child of God, one who calls Him, *"Father."* If you are saved, a child of the living God, you can ask and be filled with His precious Holy Spirit.

We can also look for confirmation in 1 Corinthians chapters 12 and 14 where God gives us instructions concerning spiritual gifts and their operations. Why would the Lord give us such in-depth instructions if the gifts were to fade and pass away? I don't believe He would.

There's no doubt in my mind that the infilling and gifts of the Spirit are for today, and that they are for you. Remember, Jesus promised *"another Comforter,"* one who would take His place. The work of the Holy Spirit in our lives is vital because His presence keeps us today just as Jesus kept the disciples when He walked with them on earth.

The infilling presence of the Holy Spirit also gives us access to all of the nine gifts of the Spirit, as He wills and as we need them. These two benefits alone are great blessings, but there is so much more to the infilling of the Holy Spirit, so much for us to learn.

FILLED WHEN SAVED?

If you study the events in the Upper Room, you will notice that no one spoke in tongues until after they were filled with the Spirit. There was a distinct connection between the infilling of the Spirit and the manifestation of the gifts of the Spirit. Since it is clear that we must be filled with the Spirit before we can access the gifts of the Spirit, it is important to know how and when we can be filled.

Unfortunately, there are many today in the Body of Christ who no longer believe in the infilling of the Holy Spirit or in the gifts of the Spirit. They teach that we receive some manifestation of the Holy Spirit when we are saved, but there is no second experience, there are no active gifts, and the work of the Holy Spirit today does not include signs and wonders. Others preach that you receive all there is to receive when you are saved. Let's go back to our source, the Bible, and find out what God says about this.

Acts 19:2-6 states: *"He said unto them, have ye received the Holy Ghost since ye believed? And they said unto him, we have not so much as heard whether there be any Holy Ghost. And he said unto them, unto what then were ye baptized? And they said, unto John's baptism. Then said Paul, John verily baptized with the baptism of repentance, saying unto the people, that they should believe on him which should come after him, that is, on Christ Jesus. When they heard this, they were baptized in the name of the Lord Jesus. And when Paul had laid his hands upon them, the Holy Ghost came on them; and they spake with tongues, and prophesied."*

Why do you suppose Paul asked, *"Have ye received the Holy Ghost since ye believed?"* Evidently, the apostle understood it was possible to believe, and yet not be filled with the Spirit. Paul recognized that these men did not have the fullness of God which had been promised to them, and so he did something about it.

Since they only knew about the baptism of John, the first thing Paul did was show them the way of salvation in Christ. Once they believed and received salvation, then he baptized them, baptism being an outward sign of their inward change. After this was accomplished, he laid hands on them, and they were filled with the Spirit and began to speak with tongues and prophesy. Nowhere in the Bible do we find people being born again by the laying on of hands, but we do see them receiving the infilling of the Spirit by this physical act time and again. So, this story reveals it is possible to believe but not have the infilling of the Holy Spirit, showing us once again they are two separate acts of faith and receiving of grace.

We also see the reason these men had not been filled with the Spirit is because they lacked knowledge about His infilling presence. It may be the same for you today. Perhaps you have never heard you can be filled with the Spirit and access the gifts of the Spirit in your life through faith. Maybe you have been unaware that there is more to your walk with Christ than you were told before.

Ignorance is not sin, but it will keep you from the benefits of being filled with the Spirit, and it will keep you from the fullness of all God has for you. So often, ignorance is why Christians fail to hear God's voice. The Bible assures us that the infilling and gifts of the Spirit are for today, for our benefit, and they are for you. Now that you know, let's dig a little deeper.

WHY TONGUES?

Being filled with the Spirit is so much more than speaking in tongues, which is the one gift that causes controversy in many churches today. There should be no contention because Jesus said in Mark 16:17 that speaking with new tongues would be a sign available to all believers. Personally, I want everything that Jesus wants me to have. Don't you?

To help take away a little of the mystery, it is important for you to understand that the word "tongues" is simply an old English word which means "languages." It's that easy. When you speak in other tongues, you are speaking in other languages you have not learned and do not know. You speak in the spiritual languages of the Kingdom of which you are a citizen. Why shouldn't you speak in the languages of your Homeland? If God can lead us by His Spirit, don't you think He can lead us into new languages the same way? Of course He can.

While speaking in tongues is not the only gift of the Spirit, it is the first evidence of the infilling of the Spirit. In fact, it is the gift that accompanied the infilling of the Spirit in the Bible as immediate evidence over and over again. Let's look at a few more examples.

We already read of the account in Acts 2:4 where the very first infilling of the Holy Spirit took place, and they all began to speak with tongues as the Spirit gave them utterance. This is a powerful example. The first time the Holy Spirit filled people after the resurrection of Jesus, every person in the room spoke in tongues. Since God never changes, we should expect the same evidence when the Holy Spirit fills us today.

Continuing on in the book of Acts, in chapter ten we return to the story of Cornelius and his connection with God. In verses 45-46, we once again see the undeniable sign of the infilling of the Holy Spirit: *"And they of the circumcision which believed were astonished, as many as came with Peter, because that on the Gentiles also was poured out the gift of the Holy Ghost. For they heard them speak with tongues, and magnify God."*

How did Peter know these people were filled? He knew because he heard them speak in tongues, just as he had heard in the Upper Room. These believers did not glow. They did not float. They simply spoke in a language they had not learned, manifesting a supernatural utterance given to them by the Spirit of God, and by this sign Peter knew they were filled.

The story we just read in Acts 19 is another example, and we know from Acts 9:17 the apostle Paul was filled with the Spirit. Let's see what Paul said about tongues in 1 Corinthians 14:18: *"I thank my God, I speak with tongues more than ye all."* Then in 1 Corinthians 14:39 Paul counsels: *"Wherefore, brethren, covet to prophesy, and forbid not to speak with tongues."*

Paul also said, *"Be ye followers of me, even as I also am of Christ"* (1 Corinthians 11:1). Did Paul speak in tongues? Was he filled with the Holy Spirit? Did he receive that infilling after he was saved? If the answers are yes, yes and yes, (and they are), then we are to follow his example.

We believe the gospel of salvation Paul preached is for us today, and we willingly follow Paul in his belief. We should be just as willing to believe that what he preached about the Holy Spirit is for us today, and we should also be ready to follow him in this same doctrine. What Paul said about tongues is just as true as what he said about the good news of salvation, and we should follow him in both.

Speaking in other tongues is just one of the gifts of the Spirit. While it is the first to be manifested, it will not be the only evidence that the Spirit of God has touched your life. The nine gifts of the Spirit are all available to you, having been deposited in you when you received the infilling of the Spirit. While speaking in other tongues is the first evidence of the infilling, you also have access to the other gifts. They are waiting to be manifested in you to touch you, your family, and the world around you. By allowing the first evidence of the infilling of the Spirit to manifest in your life, a big step of faith for some Christians, you open the door to the working of the other eight gifts, which is a benefit worth striving for.

STRONG IN THE LORD

Before we discuss how you can be filled, I want you to understand why you *need* to be filled. Second Corinthians 4:7-8 shows us the importance of being filled with the Spirit of God. This scripture says: *"But we have this treasure in earthen vessels, that the excellency of the power may be of God, and not of us. We are troubled on every side, yet not distressed; we are perplexed, but not in despair."*

As Christians, we go through the same struggles others do, but our outcome is different when we have the Holy Spirit in us, because He not only brings us victory, but He makes our victories billboards to the world about our redemption. When the world sees you delivered from a situation with joy unspeakable and full of glory, even though you encountered the same problems they did, they will wonder, and they will ask you why. Then you will have the opportunity to minister to them and be a witness of the goodness of God, which will lead them to repentance (see Romans 2:4).

In our world, there is a spirit of anti-Christ at work and increasing in activity every day. It is opposed to you and your Christianity—and opposed to the anointing which has been sent by Christ to remove every yoke. The spirit of anti-Christ is here to keep you bound, and if he is successful, there will be no voice of hope for others in Christ.

We can thank God for this promise: *"Ye are of God, little children, and have overcome them: because greater is he that is in you, than he that is in the world"* (1 John 4:4). Certainly, there is an onslaught of the adversary against the church and every believer, but it will never be greater than the Holy Spirit who fills you. You may not be a match for the devil in your own strength, but you are more than a match when you trust in the Spirit of God.

Paul, while bound in chains, said: *"For I know that this shall turn to my salvation through your prayer, and the supply of the Spirit of Jesus Christ"* (Philippians 1:19). Though it looked to the world like Paul was finished and the enemy had him bound for sure, he knew the Spirit of God was more than enough to turn his situation around and bring deliverance and salvation.

Paul knew two things were needed for this turn-around—the intercession of believers and the supply of the Holy Spirit. Even though Paul was bound by natural chains, he believed the Holy Spirit could overcome, reverse and break him free from every plan of the enemy, so that his deliverance would shine as a light in a dark world and stand as a testimony of the goodness and grace of God.

In Ephesians 6:10 we are told: *"Finally, my brethren, be strong in the Lord, and in the power of his might."* This power is available through the infilling of the Holy Spirit. Our battles are not with flesh and blood, but they are with an unseen enemy whose principalities and powers are more than mere men can manage, but they are not more than the Holy Spirit, partnering with you, can handle. Jesus used the power of the Spirit to defeat Satan, and you can do the same thing when you are filled, because He is the strong one in and through your life (see Matthew 12:28-29).

You are toe to toe and nose to nose in confrontation with the devil. In your own strength, you cannot win. In your own power, you will fail, but you don't have to depend on your own strength. You can allow the Spirit of God to fill you, and you can become strong in the Lord through Him. The choice is yours.

YOU CAN BE FILLED

We've learned why we should be filled with the Spirit, and what the initial evidence will be. Now, I want you to see just how easy it is to receive this infilling. You can be filled with the Spirit just as easily as you were saved. Let me prove it.

You did not have all knowledge about salvation when you prayed the sinner's prayer, but you did have just enough understanding for faith to break through and salvation to come. With what you've just read in the Bible concerning the infilling of the Holy Spirit, you now have enough knowledge (that God gave you) for faith to do its work, this time for the infilling of the Spirit (see Romans 10:17). When you receive the Word for yourself personally, you receive the faith it takes to manifest your answer, so all you have to do is ask.

Remember what Jesus said in Luke 11:13: *"If ye then, being evil, know how to give good gifts unto your children: how much more shall your heavenly Father give the Holy Spirit to them that ask him?"* God cannot lie. If He said to ask for the Holy Spirit and you would receive, that's just what He meant for you to do.

If you would like to be filled with the Spirit of God and receive all of the benefits His indwelling presence brings, including speaking with new tongues and the other gifts of the Spirit, you can pray at any time and ask God to fill you. Your prayer might be something as simple as this:

Father God, I come to You as Your child. You said in Your Word that if I would ask for the Holy Spirit, You would give Him to me, to fill me and empower me to be a witness. I ask You right now to fill me to the full with Your precious Holy Spirit. Give me an utterance that I may glorify You in new tongues and pray in the Spirit according to Your Word. I receive this gift right now in Jesus' name. Amen.

Do not worry about receiving a counterfeit gift, and know for certain that Satan cannot give you anything. Your mind will not deceive you, either. The Lord said He would give you this gift, so whatever words come to your mind or out of your mouth, trust they are from God (see Acts 2:3-4). Just begin to praise Him, not in English anymore, but in the new language and the utterance the Holy Spirit gives you. Don't try to figure out or understand it, but trust God that He is faithful to His Word, just as He was when you asked to be saved.

Allow the new words, no matter how many or how few, to pour forth from your spirit, by God's Spirit. After all, Jesus said of the Holy Spirit in John 7:38-39: *"He that believeth on me, as the scripture hath said, out of his belly shall flow rivers of living water. (But this spake he of the Spirit, which they that believe on him should receive: for the Holy Ghost was not yet given; because that Jesus was not yet glorified.)"*

Don't question or try to understand with your mind. Jesus said: *"The wind blgweth where it listeth, and thou hearest the sound thereof, but canst not tell whence it cometh, and whither it goeth: so is every one that is born of the Spirit"* (John 3:8). You may not always understand, because the Holy Spirit is beyond your understanding, but though you do not comprehend everything, you can know you are experiencing the effects of His infilling in your life, just as you recognize the effects of the wind.

Allow the river to flow. Let the Holy Spirit do a work in and through you as you pray in the Spirit, even as you have prayed in the understanding. First Corinthians 14:15 tells us this is exactly how we should pray, both in the Spirit (in tongues), and in the understanding (in our own language). Here's the verse for you to see for yourself: *"What is it then? I will pray with the spirit, and I will pray with the understanding also: I will sing with the spirit, and I will sing with the understanding also."*

You need to allow time for prayer in your own language, petitioning God for the things you need and making intercession for others, but you should also allow the Spirit of God to pray through you in other tongues. We're going to look at this in depth in the next chapter, but right now I want you to see a glimpse of what you have received by asking to be filled with the Spirit.

No longer are you limited to what your mind can pray or your own spiritual knowledge, but now you can allow the Spirit of God to pray through you in other tongues. You are no longer earth-bound, but now you can have a supernatural connection to Heaven like you've never experienced before. You can stir yourself up daily and keep your fires burning. You can build your strength to overcome the wiles of the devil. You can enter the presence of the Spirit of God and learn to communicate with Him every day.

Learning to talk with the Spirit of God is a process, just as everything else is in your Christian walk. It will become more natural to you as you become accustomed to spending time with the Holy Spirit this way, and it will become easier as time passes and your mind begins to relax. Remember, for your spirit to rule in your life, it will depend on not only the Holy Spirit, but on the choices you make to act in cooperation with Him (see 1 Corinthians 14:15).

As you are diligent and faithful, you will begin to experience the many benefits of praying in the Spirit, such as the promise of Jude verse 20, which says: *"But ye, beloved, building up yourselves on your most holy faith, praying in the Holy Ghost."* When you pray in the Spirit, this verse will manifest in your life, and you will be strengthened to face the issues of each day.

Most important, you will become confident that because you are now filled, all of the gifts of the Spirit are waiting to be manifested in you and flow through you. Let's discover more about the amazing gifts you have received.

SUPERNATURAL HELP

As a reminder, the gifts of the Spirit are listed in 1 Corinthians 12:7-11, and they are: Tongues and interpretation, discerning of spirits, the word of knowledge, the word of wisdom, prophecy, gifts of healing, the working of miracles and the gift of faith. Many Christians believe these manifestations of God's Spirit are only for church services on rare occasions. Neither of these ideas is true. They are not just for church services, and they are for far more than just rare occasions. These gifts are for you and your family to benefit from in everyday life.

I personally believe that when God places children in our homes, He expects us to protect them with supernatural manifestations of the gifts of the Spirit. My daughter Nicole can testify to how often my wife and I knew what she was up to as a teenager before she ever breathed a word to us. If we suspected something, we would tell her, "You can 'fess up now, or you can wait until we pray and the Holy Ghost tells on you, but either way we're going to know what you're doing." Nicole was not involved in anything out of the ordinary for teenagers. She was a good kid, but she was also facing the same temptations every child her age wrestled with.

My wife and I prayed, heard from God and intervened when necessary. By doing so, we saved Nicole from many teenage troubles by the gifts of the Spirit operating in our lives. I believe my daughter is a blessed woman of God who is living for Jesus today because my wife and I were diligent to seek God's voice about her life when she was young.

Teenagers are in a battle against temptation every day of their lives, and they need you to hear from God on their behalf to protect and help them avoid the pitfalls so common for their age group. No matter how wonderful you may think your kids are, they will face temptation. Even Jesus had to face temptation, so your child will not be the exception. It's best to prepare for it now, pray for discernment, and be ready to intervene when necessary.

Your children, like our daughter, may not welcome your intervention at first, but I know today Nicole is grateful her parents were praying and hearing from the Spirit of God to help her make it through the teen years unscathed. This is what the gifts of the Spirit are for, in a nutshell, to help us overcome the challenges we face daily as Christians who desire to live holy and pure in a world that is corrupt and impure. We cannot accomplish this alone, but with the empowerment of the Holy Spirit we can live our lives more abundantly (see John 10:10).

THE GIFTS IN EVERYDAY LIFE

As Christians, we are dealing with an enemy who is determined to kill us, steal from us and destroy our lives, so it should come as no surprise that God would equip us with nine divine implants of grace to empower us to overcome his devices. The Lord knows exactly what the enemy is up to, and He wants you to know too, but it is up to you to recognize how God speaks, and then to get in position to hear when He does.

Paul says: *"Now concerning spiritual gifts, brethren, I would not have you ignorant"* (1 Corinthians 12:1). I believe God would speak to us every day through the gifts of the Spirit, but too often we are ignorant and do not allow Him to do so.

This may be the first time you have heard that God could use the gifts of the Spirit outside of a church service, and you may be a little reluctant to believe He would desire to speak to you personally, in your own home about everyday issues, but let me assure you that the Lord desires to speak to you more than you can imagine. Let's consider what would happen if the gifts of the Spirit were only allowed to operate in the weekly church service, as some have been taught, and were not intended for you to access in your personal life.

Let's just suppose that the only time the gifts of the Spirit could operate was in a packed church, in front of hundreds or even thousands of people. If that was so, how could God ever reach you with the gifts of the Spirit for a personal matter? How could He override 1 Corinthians 14:5 which says that tongues and interpretation of tongues in a church service is for the benefit of all? And how could He ignore 1 Corinthians 14:27 which tells us tongues and interpretation of tongues in a church service is to be limited to two or three at a time?

Under those circumstances, if the gifts were only for church services, I don't see how it would be possible for them to profit all. I could see how God could speak a word using the gifts that might edify you as it edifies the church, but He most likely could not speak to your specific issue in front of the congregation through tongues and interpretation, because He simply would not have time with the limit of two or three per service. Imagine how long it would take to get one message to each person in your church family.

The point is this: The gifts of the Spirit which operate in a church service are designed primarily for the benefit of the whole body, though on occasion one or more individuals may be called out with a word of knowledge or a prophetic utterance. If our churches are attended by hundreds or even thousands, the only way we can each profit is for the gifts of the Spirit to be operational in our personal lives and in our homes.

You cannot spend your life waiting for your pastor or a guest minister to call you out in a service to hear from God. If you wait, it may be too late. You have to access the gifts for your personal benefit on your own. This is what God intended, that the gifts of the Spirit be for the church, yes, but also for you, the individual believer.

More than this, imagine how great it would be for you to be able to demonstrate to your children the miraculous in their own home so they can believe, not by your words of persuasion, but by your acts of demonstration. If you will live a godly life and allow the gifts of the Spirit to have a place in your family, your children will be drawn to live godly by the same Spirit who is manifesting Himself in you.

God truly cares about our everyday lives, about our normal routines and our usual ways, but He does not leave us to deal with normal life in our own strength. I am truly grateful the Father loves us so much He made the gifts of the Spirit available for each of us in our own homes and lives, so we can run the race and reach the victory line with joy and peace together.

COVETING THE GIFTS

"Now that I am filled with the Spirit, how do I access the gifts of the Spirit?" I'm glad you asked. First Corinthians 12:31 says: *"But covet earnestly the best gifts: and yet shew I unto you a more excellent way."* The gifts of the Spirit can be manifested in your life by coveting them, and they can be activated by faith. As a believer, you can operate in some dimension of the gifts of the Spirit if you will simply covet the gifts and pursue them, doing what it takes to activate them in your life.

The gifts of the Spirit are the only things we are instructed to covet in the Bible, and we are instructed to covet the *"best gifts."* But what *are* the best gifts? They are whatever you need at a particular moment, or whatever is needed to reach into the lives of others to reveal Christ. If you need wisdom, the word of wisdom is the best gift right at that time. If you need healing, the gifts of healing are the best for that situation. If you need comfort, the gift of prophecy will be best, but if you need a miracle, the working of miracles is what you need.

To covet, or desire, is to have a hunger and thirst for, to have a passion for, and to seek after with great intensity. There is a price which must be paid to walk in the gifts of the Spirit on a regular basis. It cost Jesus a trip to the wilderness before He could return *"in the power of the Spirit"* (Luke 4:14).

There will be times in your life, in your household, when you will need a supernatural visitation, demonstration and manifestation. It will be up to you to pay the price to put yourself in a position to see it happen for your family.

We pay a price to raise our children in the natural, and also to raise them in the supernatural. What is the price? Time. How much time? How ever long it takes. It takes time in the Word, and time in prayer and fasting to open ourselves to the power and activity of the Holy Spirit. Jesus prayed and fasted to move in the power of the Spirit. We should expect that it will take no less than prayer and fasting for us to move in our homes in the power of the Spirit. God is not resisting you, but the flesh, the mind, reason and Satan himself are pressing against you every day (see 1 Corinthians 9:27; Galatians 5:16-17).

Paul said of his attempts to visit the saints in Rome that there were times when even he was hindered by Satan (see Romans 1:9-13). Though we face resistance, God tells us not to fall behind, so we can be sure He will always provide a way of escape for us so that we will be able to activate the gifts no matter what is going on around us (see 1 Corinthians 1:4-7; 10:13). We should never be in need or fall behind due to a lack of the gifts.

We are told in Ephesians 6:13-14 that having done all, we should stand. Stand in what? Stand in our spiritual operations. It doesn't matter if you fast a portion of every day for six weeks, if you fast every other day for six months, or if you fast one day a week for a year. Whatever it takes, you engage in spiritual activity, knowing God is faithful to reward you and do what He said He would.

If you covet, desire and do what it takes for the gifts of the Spirit to be active in your life, you can be assured, they will operate in your home, your work place, and of course, in your church, and you will hear the voice of God through them.

Spend time in the Word, building your faith in the release of the gifts. Spend time in prayer, loosing the gifts and praising God for allowing them to manifest through you (see Matthew 16:19). And spend time fasting, setting yourself apart to hear the voice of God and to open the door for spiritual manifestations in your life. It will be worth every minute and every sacrifice. God has challenged me to draw closer to Him this way for years now, and I do not regret one single moment of time in prayer, or one meal missed as I fasted and set myself apart to hear His voice. I don't believe you will regret it either as you begin to see the gifts flow through you and bless your loved ones greatly.

PERFECT? NOT SO!

You do not have to be perfect for the gifts of the Spirit to operate in your life. If your house is a mess, you are still a candidate for a supernatural manifestation. Why? Because the Lord desires to intervene in our messes.

God spoke to Abraham in the middle of a big mess in Genesis 21. God told Abraham to put Hagar and her son Ishmael out of the house as Sarah had asked. Why was this word of wisdom needed? Because in chapter 16, thirteen years earlier, Abraham had made the mistake of trying to help God give him a son by joining himself with Sarah's handmaiden, Hagar.

What confusion it caused. Abraham listened to his wife and conceived a son with Hagar, then later when Isaac was born, Sarah regretted it and asked Abraham to put both Hagar and the child out of the house. God spoke to Abraham in the middle of this chaos, not because Abraham and Sarah were perfect, but because they were people of faith even though their home life was in trouble. In the midst of the strife that resulted from Abraham's temporary unbelief, God spoke to him and told him what to do to fix the situation.

Your life may be in a mess, equal to or worse than Abraham's. Your family life may be in turmoil, and your home may seem to be upside down. Your finances may be lacking, or something on your job may be causing you trouble. It doesn't really matter what the problem is. If you will buckle down, get serious with God and turn back to the foundation of faith your life was once founded upon, the Lord will visit your household, and He will speak to you through the gifts of the Spirit to help you, even as He helped Abraham.

These gifts are here for your benefit and to bring a godly outcome to even the most difficult situations. God wants to tell you what to do in the midst of your problem, but what He needs before He can is your coveting, listening ear.

The gifts of the Spirit have been given to you for your profit—to show you things to come, reveal hidden truths and give you wisdom in tough situations. They have been made available to you so God might always have an avenue by which He can speak to you as often as He desires. He can also speak to the world through you, because the gifts are the voice of the Spirit that reveals God and His will, and Jesus and His lordship.

It's important for me to make one qualification here. God wants you to pursue the gifts, but He wants you to seek them for the right reason. In most chapters in Part Three, I insert a word of caution, and so we have come to that point in this chapter.

It is perfectly okay to benefit from the gifts of the Spirit when you have a need, but too often, Christians seek to activate a gift in order to give birth to a call or an office. When they have this motivation, they will soon be hurt and disillusioned, because they will convince themselves they have a call when in reality what they have is a manifestation of a gift which is available to all.

The gifts of the Spirit do not qualify you for a call, but they do accompany every call. You must recognize the difference. If you are called to the five-fold ministry, you will need the gifts of the Spirit in your ministry, this is true, but operating in the gifts in no way qualifies you to occupy a call. Active gifts do not make you a five-fold minister, but they do make you a believer who has been empowered by the gifts of the Spirit so you can do the works that Jesus did. You cannot be who Christ was, but you can work the works that He worked (see John 14:12).

As we established in previous chapters, only God can call us to our destiny and ministry. We cannot earn, work for or pray ourselves into a call of God. Let's not be deceived into thinking we are more than we are just because a gift manifests in our lives.

A gift cannot be earned. It is not a reward for longevity in the Kingdom or a benefit received for acts of service. A gift is just a gift, something given to you for the benefit of yourself or another. Don't be puffed up by it or misread God's intent in giving it to you. If you are called, you are called by God, not by manifestations of spiritual gifts. Keep this in mind when the gifts manifest through you, and you will remain balanced in your Christian walk.

REVEALING WHO GOD IS

I want to conclude this chapter by reminding you what the gifts of the Spirit are for. Ultimately, the gifts of the Spirit empower us to demonstrate who God is to our families, our churches and the world.

The word of wisdom unveils that God is the God of infinite wisdom, through whom unending wisdom flows. The word of knowledge unveils He is the God who knows everything, and there is nothing hidden from His eyes. The discerning of spirits reveals that God knows the thoughts and intents of our hearts more so than we know them ourselves. The working of miracles says God is a miracle-working God; He can change all things, do all things, and all things are possible with Him.

The gifts of healing tell us God is a God of healing, a God of restoration and wholeness. The gift of faith reveals God is a faith God; it takes faith to please Him, and it takes faith to be saved and walk with Him. Tongues and interpretation of tongues reveal that God is a God of the supernatural, and He empowers us with an utterance which takes us beyond our human limitations.

Prophecy shows the world that God is the God of the prophetic; He edifies, exhorts and comforts, and He unveils things not seen by the eye of man.

The nine gifts of the Spirit reveal the Lord to the world in a way our preaching does not. Manifestations of the gifts are an undeniable voice, establishing who Jesus is and bringing great blessing to those who receive them. The gifts of the Spirit establish faith that cannot be overthrown. They are voices which amplify what we preach, and are a portion of the signs that follow and confirm the Word (see Mark 16:20).

There are so many ways the gifts of the Spirit can profit us. God may speak through you to help another, or He may speak through someone else to help you. There are also times when God will speak directly to you using the gifts of the Spirit. No matter how He uses them, when God speaks through the gifts of the Spirit, He does so for your profit.

In the next few chapters we will look at each gift in-depth, discovering from the Bible how God spoke through the gifts of the Spirit in days gone by. We'll also learn from testimonials how God continues to speak through the nine gifts of the Spirit today.

Chapter 14

A Heavenly Language

The room was packed to capacity. One more body and the place would go from cramped to unbearable. They had been waiting for ten days, but no one in the room knew exactly what they were waiting for; they just knew that Jesus had told them to stay until they were endued from on high. They had been praying and fasting for the entire ten days, the only sure things they felt comfortable doing while the time passed, but impatience was just around the corner.

Without warning it came, a blast of wind that blew across the room like a tornado; only they were inside, so how could this be? The room began to shake, and then, incredibly, they began to see fire, shaped like a human tongue, hovering over one another's heads. They didn't know whether to run from the room screaming, or bow down and worship.

Just when it seemed too incredible for human minds to grasp, all at once every person in the room began to cry out in languages they had never heard before. Louder and louder, the voices began to blend like a symphony of pure joy. What was this thing? Was this what Jesus had told them would come? Was this the empowerment from on high? Only time would tell.

Overwhelmed by the sheer intensity in the room, many began to run into the streets, no longer able to contain themselves. Those poor souls on the city's sidewalks that day were astounded by what they saw and heard. Men and women, shouting and praising God and speaking loudly in other languages, were running up and down the street like unhinged fools.

Some thought the men and women of the Upper Room were drunk, but others were amused by the whole spectacle. One after another the people of the city began to recognize their native languages coming out of the mouths of the "crazy people," and they wondered.

227

How could lowly fishermen know the languages of other countries? How could unlearned women speak them so fluently? And how could men and women from so many different nations hear their own native tongues spoken in the same place, at the same time, in the middle of what seemed like chaos? It was a great mystery that day. It was a great secret (see Acts 2:1-15).

THE SECRET PARTNER

What happened is no longer a mystery, and it is not intended to be kept a secret. In fact, the secret was revealed over 2,000 years ago by Jesus Himself when He said: *"And I will pray the Father, and he shall give you another Comforter, that he may abide with you for ever; even the Spirit of truth; whom the world cannot receive, because it seeth him not, neither knoweth him: but ye know him; for he dwelleth with you, and shall be in you"* (John 14:16-17).

Of course He was talking about the Holy Spirit. When the Holy Spirit came to fill the crowd in the Upper Room on the Day of Pentecost, God revealed the times had changed. No longer was He a distant dictator, as some had thought, but now He was available for intensely intimate fellowship. The Holy Spirit was waiting to fill men and women who were ready to be filled; men and women who had been born again and wanted to receive the fullness of all God had for them; men and women like you who desired to be empowered to witness for Jesus.

You do not have to go through life alone, or live the Christian life under your own power. The Holy Spirit, your secret partner, longs to fill you and leave behind the same evidence He left on the Day of Pentecost. He wants you to speak with other tongues as He gives the utterance, and He wants you to experience victory, the victory only His indwelling presence can provide.

All of the great men and women of God who have gone before us, those in the Bible and those in our church history, have one thing in common. They all depended upon the Holy Spirit to fill, teach, guide, empower, lead and use them for God's glory. These men and women did what they did because they were accompanied by the Holy Spirit, their secret partner, who brought a strength which was not available to mere unsaved men.

The victory experienced by those who have gone before us did not come at their own expense, but was bought by their faith through the strength of the Holy Spirit. This same Spirit has great victories available for you too, things that will transform you, but you have to access them by faith, just as you do every other promise in the Bible.

You can become another man or another woman by the infilling of the Holy Spirit and a new dependence upon your secret partner. You can be transformed and empowered with spiritual gifts others cannot access or enjoy.

The reason I like to call the Holy Spirit your secret partner is because His presence and power will be manifested in you, but will not be seen or understood by the world. They will see the results of His infilling in your life, but they will not see Him. They will witness your transformation, but they will not recognize the One who transformed you. They will hear a new language flow from your lips, but they will not understand the sign they hear.

The Holy Spirit wants to be your better half, your collaborator, your right-hand man and your yoke-fellow. Everything in your life can benefit from the supernatural strength that comes through the Holy Spirit as He comes alongside to help you achieve your goals. He is the Helper, the Comforter, and He can be your personal friend just as Jesus was to the disciples when He walked the shores of Galilee.

The Holy Spirit has been the strength of the church since the time of its birth. In fact, Jesus told those who followed Him not to go anywhere until they had gone to Jerusalem and were endued with power from on high (see Luke 24:49). If you have been filled with the Holy Spirit, you have been endued with that same power. You may not use it to its fullest extent, but you have power nonetheless.

The Secret Partner abides *in* you and desires to work *for* you so that Christ can be glorified *through* you. God wants to speak to you and to the world through tongues and interpretation of tongues, just as He did on the Day of Pentecost. He has much to say, and He needs willing vessels through which He can speak.

NO LONGER MERE MEN

The apostle Paul said: *"But if the Spirit of him that raised up Jesus from the dead dwell in you, he that raised up Christ from the dead shall also quicken your mortal bodies by his Spirit that dwelleth in you"* (Romans 8:11).

Paul realized that Christians who have been filled with the Spirit of God are no longer mere human beings, but are empowered and accompanied by One who embodies all of the power of the God-head in them. This amazing enablement of the Holy Spirit and the life of the supernatural demonstration of God are yours for the asking. Though you might feel weak and may have many frailties and insecurities, you must remember it is not by man, but by God's Spirit that victory is born in the life of a believer (see Philippians 4:13).

Your alliance with your secret partner will baffle the understanding and confound the wisest of mere men. Think of King Ahab when he took off in a hurry toward the city of Jezreel. Off he went, beating the backs of his horses as he raced to the gates, not knowing that Elijah would arrive before him on the power of his own two feet. How did Elijah do that? It was by the power of the Holy Spirit, by the power that made him a new man (see 1 Kings 18:45-46). Ahab had no idea what had happened, but we do. We know it was the power of the Spirit of God in Elijah.

There is a supernatural strength we cannot explain. It is a secret thing, one not obvious to human eyes, nor understood by human ears. It cannot be interpreted by human senses, but we are confident that the power of God's Spirit is with us and in us, and it enables God to speak through us.

Think of prophecy, tongues and interpretation, and even the language of faith which is born of this empowering, enabling presence of the Holy Spirit in you (see Romans 4:17-20; 2 Corinthians 4:13). God desires for the world to see and hear, through you, how much He loves them so they will be drawn to Him. Remember, Romans 2:4 says: *"Or despisest thou the riches of his goodness and forbearance and longsuffering; not knowing that the goodness of God leadeth thee to repentance?"*

When God's goodness is manifested in your life, it will spill over into the lives of those around you. You won't just witness in word only, but you will also witness in the way you live your life, and in the way God blesses and empowers you to overcome in every situation. When you are endued from on high, you are a light to the world, a city set on a hill that no one can hide. Tongues and interpretation is just one sign revealed on that hill that will show the world God is still alive and well, and working through men today.

SPEAKING IN OTHER TONGUES

The sign of speaking in other tongues has mystified many in the Body of Christ over the years. This gift was never intended to be a mystery to believers, but was intended to strengthen each of us as we join together with the Holy Spirit and become dependent upon His power instead of on our own.

The Bible talks about divers kinds of tongues, the many different tongues available to us when we are filled with the Spirit of God, but for this purpose I want to focus on two. There is the tongue that will be used in a worship service, in the sight and hearing of all, and there is the tongue which will be a prayer language for you and God to hear. What most people know about the gift of tongues and interpretation is what they have experienced or heard about taking place in church.

In a worship service, it is possible that God will desire to give a special message to the congregation, and He may choose to use tongues and interpretation of tongues to deliver this message. In this case, someone may rise to their feet or approach the altar to indicate they have a message from Heaven. If they have the tongues part, they will speak out when they are given permission by the pastor or whoever is in charge of the order of the service that day (see 1 Corinthians 14:33-40).

Once the tongue is delivered, then someone else, or sometimes the same individual, will give out the interpretation in English for all to hear. When these two gifts function together, they have the same benefit as prophecy. They edify, comfort and exhort the body.

In this instance, there are certain rules concerning how many messages may be delivered. Paul wrote about the limitations in his first letter to the Corinthians: *"If any man speak in an unknown tongue, let it be by two, or at the most by three, and that by course; and let one interpret. But if there be no interpreter, let him keep silence in the church; and let him speak to himself, and to God"* (1 Corinthians 14:27-28).

These are the only limitations placed on the use of tongues and interpretation of tongues, but so much has been said about mistakes of the past that many churches have decided to push it to the side rather than deal with the truth. The Bible is very plain on how this great gift is to be used, so there should be no reason to ignore it.

It's true that there have been times when someone who was young in the Lord or ignorant of spiritual things misused the gift of tongues, or spoke out of turn, but we should not throw the baby out with the bath water. Pastors need to correct mistakes if need be, but not limit the gifts just because someone missed it. We have all made mistakes at one time or another, but if we threw out biblical truths just because someone misinterpreted or misused them, we would limit what God wants to accomplish in our services (see 1 Thessalonians 5:19-20).

It's time for the Body of Christ to throw off carnal thinking and allow the Spirit of God to be in charge of our services again. He should be allowed to do whatever He sees fit to do every time we come together. The created ones should never, ever limit the Creator.

PRAYING IN THE SPIRIT

There is the gift of tongues to be used in public worship, but we may also use this gift in private for our own benefit. When we talk about praying in tongues, the Bible sometimes calls it praying in the Spirit, so for this teaching that's what I will call it to help you see the difference between the manifestation of the gift in public and its use in private.

The Bible has much to say about praying in the Spirit. Let's begin with what the apostle Paul taught: *"Likewise the Spirit also helpeth our infirmities: for we know not what we should pray for as we ought: but the Spirit itself maketh intercession for us with groanings which cannot be uttered. And he that searcheth the hearts knoweth what is the mind of the Spirit, because he maketh intercession for the saints according to the will of God"* (Romans 8:26-27).

When you are filled with the Spirit of God, there is a new prayer language available to you that you could not access before. This is what the Apostle Paul is describing in these verses. When you pray in the Spirit, the Spirit of God prays through you in other tongues according to the perfect will of God. You don't understand the words you are praying, but the Holy Spirit prays just what is needed.

Here's why this is so important: Jesus was the disciples' prayer partner when He was on the earth. He prayed for them daily, and they knew they had a connection with Him whereby they could have any need met at any time by simply asking Him. When Jesus told the disciples He would send another Comforter (see John 14:16), He was telling them He would send someone to do what He had been doing for them all along. He would send someone to continue to keep them in prayer, and to be as close to them as He had been. In essence, the Holy Spirit would take His place in their lives.

This is what the Holy Spirit does for you as you pray in the Spirit. He acts just as Jesus did and keeps you in prayer. He longs to pray for you as you allow Him to pray through you. When you join with Him in prayer, He will help you, teach you and direct your steps. He will also strengthen and empower you to overcome, and He will deal with things beyond your knowledge. Remember, Jude 20 says: *"But ye, beloved, building up yourselves on your most holy faith, praying in the Holy Ghost."*

When you pray in the Holy Spirit, you build yourself up in faith and enter into intimate fellowship with the Father. As you do, you allow the Spirit of God to give you an utterance in other tongues which will edify, comfort and exhort you. You allow Him to speak great mysteries about your future, and to pray for things you cannot know in the natural (see Hebrews 4:13).

Praying in the Spirit allows you to prepare yourself for things to come, for what no eye has seen nor has any ear heard. You prepare as David did for the lion and the bear, so when the giant stands before you, you will not fear, but will depend on the Spirit of God to deliver you once again.

The choice is yours. You have to make an effort to pray in the Spirit and invite His help. Too many of us think we're too busy, and we try to deal with things on our own. Others of us are convinced we can reach victory through steps and principles. These may be fine, but sometimes there are hindrances we cannot see and a "hinderer" who is at work behind the scenes. There is a spiritual battle raging you cannot see with your natural eye. It is for this battle you need the help of the Holy Spirit. Earthly weapons will not work against the devil, but you need to engage in a spiritual battle against your spiritual enemy. And you need the battle array of the Holy Spirit on your side.

Here's what I mean. In Bible times when men went out to fight, the armies set themselves in battle array against their enemies. This meant they set themselves in combat order, side by side, shoulder to shoulder and prepared to fight the conflict. They were covered in battle armor and carrying their banners of victory. Sometimes their sheer numbers, all aligned in orderly rows as far as the eye could see, would be enough to send the enemy armies running for their lives.

When you pray in the Spirit, the devil does not see you arrayed for battle alone anymore, but he sees the Spirit of God arrayed alongside you. Even better, when you speak, he hears the voice of the Lord speaking instead of just a man. The devil sees you as more than a conqueror through God who loves you, and when he sees the orderly arrangement of the Spirit of God covered in heavenly armor and set to do battle for you, he knows his days are numbered in your situation, and he will do the only thing he can—which is flee. This is what makes praying in the Spirit so powerful and so necessary for our Christian lives.

ENTERING THE REST

God has given you the Holy Spirit, and it doesn't matter what the devil or any man has done or can do; the Holy Spirit is greater than all. When He fills you, He will take up where your weaknesses leave off, and He will give you a supernatural rest.

In Isaiah 28:9-12 we read: *"Whom shall he teach knowledge? And whom shall he make to understand doctrine? Them that are weaned from the milk, and drawn from the breasts. For precept must be upon precept, precept upon precept; line upon line, line upon line; here a little, and there a little: For with stammering lips and another tongue will he speak to this people. To whom he said, This is the rest wherewith ye may cause the weary to rest; and this is the refreshing: yet they would not hear."*

Some have said that stammering lips is baby talk that no one can understand, but 1 Corinthians 14:20-22 interprets this passage of scripture for us: *"Brethren, be not children in understanding: howbeit in malice be ye children, but in understanding be men. In the law it is written, With men of other tongues and other lips will I speak unto this people; and yet for all that will they not hear me, saith the Lord. Wherefore tongues are for a sign, not to them that believe, but to them that believe not: but prophesying serveth not for them that believe not, but for them which believe."*

The "stammering lips and another tongue" Isaiah wrote about refer to praying in the Spirit. It may seem like stammering to those who do not realize it is a gift of the Spirit, but those who know and believe will recognize it is the voice of the Holy Spirit as on the Day of Pentecost.

I want you to notice Isaiah 28:12 again: *"To whom he said, This is the rest wherewith ye may cause the weary to rest; and this is the refreshing: yet they would not hear."*

Praying in the Spirit can bring rest and refreshing. It can restore your strength and cause you to relax comfortably in even the most trying situations. Praying in the Spirit brings the rest spoken of here, and in Hebrews 4:11, which says: *"Let us labour therefore to enter into that rest, lest any man fall after the same example of unbelief."*

Praying in the Spirit is a part of the laboring we do to enter that rest in the

234

Spirit where we become dependent upon Him and His direction, instead of on our own limited abilities. Though you do not understand what the Holy Spirit is praying through you, it's worth the labor of stammering lips and other tongues to enter into the rest of the Spirit. It's worth pressing past the limitations of your mind and body to reach into the depths of His peace.

Resting in Him is so much more than physical relaxation. It is a rest from your own human labors and from trying to help God do what only He can do. To rest in Him is to end your own futile attempts to succeed and depend instead on God. This will only come when you finally conclude you can do nothing alone, but can do all things through Him who strengthens you. The rest of the Spirit is the only true rest in this world.

SUPERNATURAL WISDOM

Jesus tells you: *"But when they deliver you up, take no thought how or what ye shall speak: for it shall be given you in that same hour what ye shall speak. For it is not ye that speak, but the Spirit of your Father which speaketh in you"* (Matthew 10:19-20).

When you face issues beyond the scope of your natural wisdom, God's wisdom is waiting to be accessed by praying in the Spirit. It is supernatural and born of the Spirit of God.

In Proverbs 2:6-7 we read: *"For the Lord giveth wisdom: out of his mouth cometh knowledge and understanding. He layeth up sound wisdom for the righteous: he is a buckler to them that walk uprightly."*

There is wisdom laid up for the righteous, along with knowledge and understanding. And in scripture we find wisdom for spiritual matters, but also to deal with the everyday affairs of life. This supernatural wisdom comes from the mouth of God.

In my opinion, wisdom for everyday living is what is lacking most in the Body of Christ. Christians have faith, but they don't know how to use it on a day to day basis. Just because you have faith does not mean that you will be successful in using it. You need the wisdom of God to put your faith to work effectively.

Let's say you are praying about a wayward teen. You have tried everything you know to do, and still you seem to be failing in your attempts to reach her. You don't know how to help her find her way, so you go to the bookstore in search of an answer. You find the best-selling author of the month and buy his most recent child-rearing book entitled, "How to Reach Your Wayward Teen."

You think you've hit the jackpot because the subject matches your need perfectly, so off you go to read and find wisdom to reach your struggling child.

While this author may be a great Christian, no matter how much human wisdom he has, it will not be enough to reach your teenager and truly solve her problems. His knowledge and understanding is not your answer, but the wisdom of God is. The reason his wisdom will not fit your situation perfectly is because every child is different, as is every situation. No single answer can solve every problem in every family, because every child is individually made by God and is uniquely attacked by the devil.

Where can you find the wisdom to build a bridge to your wayward teen? You will receive it, not from man, but from God. He knows exactly what makes your child tick. He knows her frame, her weaknesses, how she got into this mess, and He knows exactly what it will take to get her out of it permanently.

So, which would you say would be the best source for your help? A book of generalities, or God's specific wisdom for your specific situation? The answer is a no-brainer, of course, so the real question is how to obtain the wisdom of God in the day to day world.

UNLOCKING WISDOM

We find the key to unlocking hidden wisdom in 1 Corinthians 14:13, which says: *"Wherefore let him that speaketh in an unknown tongue pray that he may interpret."*

You can access this hidden wisdom by praying in the Spirit, and then praying for the interpretation. This way, you will hear the voice of God as He shows you what you were praying, and you will receive wisdom which will help you deal with your issues. We learned to interpret our dreams and visions and signs and wonders the same way—by asking God to give us the interpretation.

Remember, you pray in tongues as the Spirit gives the utterance. It is your mouth that provides the sound, but it is God's mouth that provides the words. If you will invest time in extracting the wisdom of God and hearing His voice as you pray in the Spirit, you will find the wisdom and the answers you need.

There is no more personal way for you to hear the voice of God than to pray in other tongues in your prayer closet, and then ask Him to interpret what you prayed so that you might hear His voice and walk in His wisdom. Tongues and interpretation of tongues is a language from God's mouth to your ear. It is God's wisdom to your understanding.

Paul goes on to say in 1 Corinthians 14:14-15: *"For if I pray in an unknown tongue, my spirit prayeth, but my understanding is unfruitful. What is it then? I will pray with the spirit, and I will pray with the understanding also: I will sing with the spirit, and I will sing with the understanding also."* When you pray in the Spirit, your mind does not understand automatically, but if you ask the Holy Spirit to allow you to interpret, then your understanding becomes fruitful, and you are able to extract the wisdom flowing through you from the mouth of the Spirit of God.

It's time to begin to practice praying in the Holy Spirit and asking for the interpretation. "Well, what if I get the wrong thing?" you may ask. My answer is, what if you get the right thing? You won't know until you try.

Misinterpreting is not failure; it is learning. Only by trial and a little error will you begin to recognize the voice of the Spirit and be able to distinguish it from your own inner voice, but you will never learn to tell the two apart if you never try. You have to exercise yourself in spiritual matters and step out by faith before you can ever succeed. You will not be perfect, but you will be moving forward, and it's much easier for God to steer a moving vehicle than one parked by the side of the road. You have to begin to trust God.

"But what if it's just my mind?" You'll prove what is the truth. You will compare it with the Word of God and decide if it is God or not. "But what if it's the devil." You'll discover this by practice. If you refuse to launch out and try, you will never go anywhere. You will stay right where you are, in the same trouble, the same hardship and the same circumstance because you are afraid to try.

Let me ask: Did you come to recognize your spouse's voice by ignoring him or her? No, you learned to distinguish that special voice by spending time together. You do the same with the voice of the Spirit of God. Spend time praying in the Holy Spirit, then ask for the interpretation and wait until it comes. Trust me. It will be worth the time and effort.

Wisdom, knowledge and understanding are in the mouth of the Lord. What a privilege that He gives you a way for these things to be deposited in your mouth, heard and understood by your ear, and then brought to pass in your life. God desires to speak to you personally and directly, and He desires for you to hear and understand. Give Him your tongue, your ear and your time. In return, you will receive more than you ever dreamed of.

THINGS TO COME

In John 16:13 we are told: *"Howbeit when he, the Spirit of truth, is come, he will guide you into all truth: for he shall not speak of himself; but whatsoever he shall hear, that shall he speak: and he will shew you things to come."*

The Holy Spirit sees what awaits you in your tomorrows. He knows the plans of God, and He also knows the plans of the enemy. Do you think He wants you to know, too? According to this verse He does. When you pray in the Spirit and then ask for the interpretation, the Holy Spirit will show you things to come, future situations and circumstances you are about to face, so you can be prepared and know what to do when the time arrives.

Let's look at an example. *"And when they drew nigh unto Jerusalem, and were come to Bethphage, unto the mount of Olives, then sent Jesus two disciples, saying unto them, Go into the village over against you, and straightway ye shall find an ass tied, and a colt with her: loose them, and bring them unto me. And if any man say ought unto you, ye shall say, The Lord hath need of them; and straightway he will send them"* (Matthew 21:1-3).

Jesus knew what to tell the disciples to look for, and He even knew what they should say. The entire situation was laid out before Him so that no hindrance could keep Him from fulfilling scripture and entering Jerusalem riding on the back of a donkey, just as it had been prophesied of Him in Zechariah 9:9. How did Jesus have this information? He received it because He was filled with and connected to the Holy Spirit (see Luke 4:1). Praying in the Spirit and expecting to hear the interpretation gives you this same connection.

Though Jesus received His information through a word of knowledge, the Spirit of God is not limited to this method only. He can show you things to come using any of the gifts of the Spirit, or any of the other ways we have learned that God speaks to us today. In fact, the Holy Spirit gives us what to say as Jesus did for the disciples.

When we pray in the Spirit and ask for the interpretation:

- It may come through the avenue of any of the gifts of the Spirit.
- It may come through a word of knowledge or a word of wisdom.
- It may come through the discerning of spirits or prophecy.
- It may come in a still small voice, or in a dream or a vision.
- It may come immediately, or it may be later.

Don't ever give up just because you pray in the Spirit and do not seem to receive an instantaneous response. God may choose to speak now, or He may wait until you are better able to hear later. Whatever the case, He will get the interpretation to you, and will show you things to come so you will be prepared for what lies ahead, just as Jesus was. As you build your faith, working with the Holy Spirit, then He will bring you into other dimensions of who He is so you can become more active with Him, doing more and partnering with Him for the good of the Kingdom of God.

SPEAKING MYSTERIES

Jesus tells us: *"Lay not up for yourselves treasures upon earth, where moth and rust doth corrupt, and where thieves break through and steal: But lay up for yourselves treasures in heaven, where neither moth nor rust doth corrupt, and where thieves do not break through nor steal"* (Matthew 6:19-20).

And we read in Psalm 139:13-17: *"For thou hast possessed my reins: thou hast covered me in my mother's womb. I will praise thee; for I am fearfully and wonderfully made: marvellous are thy works; and that my soul knoweth right well. My substance was not hid from thee, when I was made in secret, and curiously wrought in the lowest parts of the earth. Thine eyes did see my substance, yet being unperfect; and in thy book all my members were written, which in continuance were fashioned, when as yet there was none of them. How precious also are thy thoughts unto me, O God! How great is the sum of them!"*

Before you were ever born, even before you were conceived or thought about with human minds, God equipped you with certain gifts, abilities and anointings to fulfill His purpose for your life. They are treasures which are laid up for you in Heaven. No one else can go to Heaven to find all God has for you; only you can discover the things the Lord has hidden for your life and ministry. If *you* will seek, *you* will find (see Matthew 7:7).

Paul writes: *"For he that speaketh in an unknown tongue speaketh not unto men, but unto God: for no man understandeth him; howbeit in the spirit he speaketh mysteries"* (1 Corinthians 14:2).

When you pray in the Spirit, you speak hidden mysteries about your future (see Isaiah 41:22-23). Your future is not only hidden from the world, but also from the devil, and in part it is hidden from you until you are ready to receive it and things are prepared for you to enter into it (see Isaiah 42:9).

There is much God wants to do in your life and many things He wants to tell you personally. You will discover this if you will pray in the Spirit and ask Him to reveal what He has said about you, what gifts He has given you, and what things He wants you to do for your family, for your church and for the world around you.

So many Christians wait for a prophecy to reveal their gifts and calling, when what they should do is pray in the Spirit so that God can speak to them directly. Prophecies may come to confirm what you hear and release you into your call, but until you hear what God has to say in your private time with Him, no prophecy will be needed.

In earlier chapters I told you about my mistake in this area, how I was convinced I was an evangelist in my baby Christian years. I had several men prophesy to me and tell me I was an evangelist, so I did my best to become one. A few months later, I still had no place to preach, and was tempted to give up and quit.

One day, as I was praying about having nowhere to preach, God spoke. He said, "I never told you that you were an evangelist." I responded, "But God, those men..." Before I could finish the sentence God told me, "So go see those men." And that was the end of that conversation.

How would you like to think you were called to be an evangelist, then one day God speaks and tells you He had never given you that call? And then to top it off, He just stops talking? This is how it was for me at that time.

It wasn't until much later and much prayer in the Spirit that God continued the conversation in my shower and said this, "I have called you to be a teacher and a pastor to My people." I replied that I didn't want to be a pastor, but God convinced me that I did, so I knew I had to teach, and I had to be a pastor.

Your gifts and calling are laid up in Heaven for you, and they will be revealed to you, not to others. I encourage you to avoid my mistake. Don't bank your future on a prophecy if God has not already spoken to you personally, but spend time praying in the Spirit to discover the mysteries God has in store for you.

KEEP YOURSELF

Let's look at Jude verses 18-21 again: *"How that they told you there should be mockers in the last time, who should walk after their own ungodly lusts. These be they who separate themselves, sensual, having not the Spirit. But ye, beloved, building up yourselves on your most holy faith, praying in the Holy Ghost, keep yourselves in the love of God, looking for the mercy of our Lord Jesus Christ unto eternal life."*

Notice that some are separated because of their sensual nature, because of the lust of their flesh and mind. They are separated from the things of God, but this is not who you are. You can pray in the Spirit and build yourself up on your most holy faith, and you can keep yourself in the love of God. Praying in the Spirit will also keep you strong in Him so that you won't fall into the sensuality that births sin.

Paul tells us: *"For we know that if our earthly house of this tabernacle were dissolved, we have a building of God, an house not made with hands, eternal in the heavens. For in this we groan, earnestly desiring to be clothed upon with our house which is from heaven: If so be that being clothed we shall not be found naked. For we that are in this tabernacle do groan, being burdened: not for that we would be unclothed, but clothed upon, that mortality might be swallowed up of life. Now he that hath wrought us for the selfsame thing is God, who also hath given unto us the earnest of the Spirit"* (2 Corinthians 5:1-5).

Notice the word "groan." We groan to deal with our earthly tabernacle so we can finish the race and obtain another tabernacle. When you pray in the Spirit, you become strong spiritually to raise a standard of morality in your life. If you have moral weaknesses that so easily beset you, start praying in the Spirit. If you keep doing this, you will be built up to overcome them in time because you mortify the deeds of the flesh through the Spirit (see Romans 8:13).

There's more. Proverbs 18:4 instructs us: *"The words of a man's mouth are as deep waters, and the wellspring of wisdom as a flowing brook."* And Jesus said: *"He that believeth on me, as the scripture hath said, out of his belly shall flow rivers of living water"* (John 7:38).

Do you know how powerful the flow of a river is? A strong current can rip trees from their roots and knock houses down. How much stronger than a natural river do you suppose the river of the Spirit is? Its force is unimaginable, and it is waiting for you to unleash the flow into your situation by praying in the Spirit.

When you pray in the Spirit, you are tapping into the wellsprings of God's power, and you can draw from this whenever you desire. You don't need to be without help because the wellsprings of the Spirit are always available whenever you pray in the Spirit, just waiting to break loose and take you over the top to freedom from sin.

BREAK FREE!

Let's look closer at Romans 8:26-28: *"Likewise the Spirit also helpeth our infirmities: for we know not what we should pray for as we ought: but the Spirit itself maketh intercession for us with groanings which cannot be uttered. And he that searcheth the hearts knoweth what is the mind of the Spirit, because he maketh intercession for the saints according to the will of God. And we know that all things work together for good to them that love God, to them who are the called according to his purpose."* We all know this passage of scripture, but how many of us live it?

Too many Christians are bound by things they need not be held captive by. You may have a pure heart for God, but you may also have some "old man" baggage clinging to you and hindering you, the stuff that still sticks to you from before you were saved. You need to break free, and you do this by applying what verse 26 says, allowing the Holy Spirit to make intercession through you for those things you cannot see.

The weight you are carrying may be too heavy for your faith alone to handle, and you may not be skillful enough to use the faith you have to bring about victory. Your knowledge and understanding may not be developed enough to break the yoke of bondage that has been attached to you for so long it feels like it's a part of you.

Sometimes it takes skillful surgery to disconnect yourself from the baggage of the past. You can't always rip it off and leave the flesh intact. Sometimes it takes the skillful hand of the Holy Spirit to handle the scalpel and deal with the issues that beset you.

Too many of us have struggled with the same problems for years and years. I know I used to struggle with certain things until I realized that the Holy Spirit was there to partner with me to overcome them.

I remember in the first year of my pastorate, a lady came to me and told me I was too dumb to be a pastor, so God had called her to replace me. I calmly told her that I knew God had called me to my church, and because of that I believed the Lord may have called her to go to a different church! She was miffed at my rebuke, so she and her husband left my tiny congregation.

At that moment, I looked very composed on the outside, but inside I was crushed. My insecurities from childhood were trying to rise up and confront me. A voice in my head said, "See, you're not good enough. You've never been good enough. You will never make it."

I went home, closed myself in the bedroom, and cried. I cried for days. My friends would call and ask for me, and Phyllis would have to tell them I was locked in the bedroom crying. She'd tell them I just could not get over the hurt that encounter had caused.

When I came out of the room after several days of crying and praying in the Spirit, I had a revelation. I never again shed tears over opposition, over people who could not accept me or work with me, or over those who did not want to stand with me.

I never wept over those things again because I came to realize that the Holy Spirit was my partner. I discovered He was my help, so I was no longer available to offense, strife or division. I hung an invisible sign around my neck after those days in my room that said, "No Vacancy." With the help of the Holy Spirit, I overcame hurt and insecurity. With His help, you can overcome, too.

The Holy Spirit will take up your battle when you submit yourself to His strength by praying in the Spirit. When you come to the end of your faith and knowledge, you are not left to die, but you have an advocate, a helper, a secret partner who can go to the throne of grace with you and help you overcome. You may reach the end of your possibilities, but you will never come to the end of the Holy Spirit's possibilities.

Too often we try to struggle in our own might, and we get nowhere. The Holy Spirit is the stronger one. It is He whose finger cast out devils through Jesus. It is He whose strength liberates the bound, sick and diseased. It is He who blesses and turns financial problems around. It is not by the power of mere men, but by the Spirit of the Lord.

When the Holy Spirit gives you an utterance, the battle is no longer yours, but it is the Lord's. Let Him be your shield and buckler (see Psalm 91:4). Let Him pray through you so He can raise up a standard and release His sword, placing it in your hand (see Ephesians 6:18). He will enter into the battle with you, and just as Jesus spoke the Word and Satan turned away, likewise when the Spirit prays through you, the devil will turn and run (see Luke 4:1-13).

Let's allow Him access. Let's give Him our tongues (see 1 Corinthians 2:13). Let's allow Him to speak through us an utterance that will deliver us from the hand of the enemy and set us free to be all that God desires us to be.

Praying in the Spirit will lead you from faith to faith, from glory to glory, and from victory to victory. It will change you into another man or another woman, one who is empowered by the Spirit to conquer and break free. It's time to build ourselves up on our most holy faith and reveal Jesus to the world!

CHAPTER 15

DISCERNING OF SPIRITS

The sun was out, and the sky was crystal clear. A gentle breeze was blowing, and all in all it was a great day to be alive. My wife Phyllis was driving her white BMW down a city street without a care in the world. Traffic was very light, and for the moment she was the only car on her side of the street. She was humming a carefree tune when suddenly the Spirit of God spoke within her and told her to switch from the left lane to the right. He was very emphatic and said, "Get in the right lane now!"

Knowing no one was behind her or beside her, Phyllis immediately cranked the steering wheel hard to the right and switched lanes without hesitation. She entered the right lane just as she passed under a traffic light, and as she did she heard a tremendous crash. She looked in the rearview mirror and saw something quite unexpected. The traffic light lay in a heap in the left lane. It had crashed onto the pavement at the exact moment she would have passed under it had she not obeyed the voice of God.

Phyllis was astonished at what she saw, and began to thank God for saving her. She praised Him for speaking to her and giving divine direction in just the nick of time. After a few moments of praise, she thought about what would have happened had she not been in tune with the voice of God. Suppose she had not discerned His voice at that moment in time? She knew she could have lost her life, or at the very least been severely injured.

How many of us have been in similar situations, but for one reason or another we did not hear the voice of God on a particular day, at a particular time? How many needless injuries have we suffered because we did not discern God's voice when we needed it the most? For most of us, it is safe to say it happens too often.

This is why I believe the discerning of spirits is one of the most important gifts in the walk of every believer. It is vital in your personal life, in your home and business, and in your church. The ability to discern the voice of God or the intentions of someone you encounter is a valuable gift. When we are left to discern without the help of God, we are often mistaken in our judgments.

Just imagine how much better your marriage could be if you could discern the thoughts and intents of your spouse. I'm not talking about reading minds, but rather understanding what your mate really means, not just what you think he or she said.

I know how often I have counseled married couples who seem to have never had a conversation together in their lives. At least that's what you would think when they get together in my office.

"I never said that."

"Oh, yes, you did!"

"Oh, no, I didn't!"

This could go on and on for hours because they have never really heard one another. They've been in the same room in the middle of the same conversation, but neither has understood a word the other said. It would have been far better if they had each retreated to the prayer closet and asked God to interpret what the other was saying before the fight broke out, but this didn't happen, so they ended up in a counseling session instead. Don't get me wrong, counseling is beneficial, but sometimes it could be avoided if we would simply take time to listen to God first before we try to listen to each other.

The Bible tells us: *"Wherefore, my beloved brethren, let every man be swift to hear, slow to speak, slow to wrath"* (James 1:19). We need to be quick to hear not only each other, but the voice of the Spirit of God, too.

The discerning of spirits is one way to hear God speak and to allow Him to give you a sense of what is going on behind the scenes in your situation. This gift empowers you to recognize whether what you are dealing with is of God, of the spirit of man (his calling, gift etc.), or if it is of the devil. It can also help you understand the spirit or motive behind what others do.

MAKING GOOD DECISIONS

When we face crucial decisions, we need the discerning of spirits to show us what to do. One example is choosing a college for your graduating teenager. Have you ever helped a young person choose a college before? This is a very critical decision in his or her life, and in yours, as the one who will likely pay a large chunk of the bill. Would the decision have been easier if the Holy Spirit had shown you the motivating spirit behind your son or daughter's school? Of course it would.

There are great universities in this nation whose only intention is to give a good education and help young people achieve in life, but then there are those who mask a hidden agenda behind beautiful campuses and advertisements of their successful graduates. Higher education involves so much more than new dorm rooms or wireless internet. It is about molding sons and daughters into productive men and women. It's also about enhancing or destroying the ground work you have labored to lay in your child's life.

Only God knows the true intention of the colleges and universities your child is considering. Only He knows the heart and motive of each professor and how the campus life will affect your son or daughter in the long run. Wouldn't you like to know, too? You can by the discerning of spirits. Pray and ask God to reveal the true heart and motive of the campuses your son or daughter is considering.

When the Lord speaks through the discerning of spirits, He may only give you a sense regarding a certain place, a feeling that it is just not right, or He may give you the sense a specific school would be the perfect fit. You may not hear an audible voice when the discerning of spirits is in operation, but you will know in your spirit how to advise your child. The discerning of spirits is not a wooey-land experience, but it is a very real gift which can flow through you to benefit your family in tangible ways.

There are other places where the discerning of spirits can be valuable. For instance, how else can you know which kind of spirit is behind the person you're thinking of hiring in your business? Life could be so much easier if we would listen to the One who knows everything about everyone and every situation, rather than rely on our own knowledge or our own human instincts. Knowledge is good, and instincts in business can be a wonderful asset, but no one can top the information the Holy Spirit can give.

I encourage you to stop and listen to what the Spirit of the Lord is trying to say. Don't just brush off that inner nudge you feel inside. It might very well be the voice of God showing you how to save your life.

DISCERNING GOD'S SPIRIT

The spirit realm is alive with activity all around us every second of every day, but most of the time people have no clue because they are unaware, untrained and sometimes just plain ignorant. I see it in church services continually. We may be in a time of prayer and ministry where the Spirit of God is moving and people are being touched. Right in the middle of this precious move of the Spirit, some dear ignorant person will stand up and leave the sanctuary. This is dishonoring the Holy Spirit.

Why would someone treat Him this way? Because they did not discern His presence. When Christians do not recognize the Lord is working—that faith is being coupled together with a promise; that God is ascending and the Holy Ghost is raising people up; that Jesus Christ is becoming involved in this faith union—they miss the move of God and dishonor His works around them.

The discerning of spirits enables an individual to see openly, and to become aware of and fully sense God. It may be by His voice, by a vision, or by one's senses. Have you ever had the hairs on the back of your neck stand up? When this happens, you need to stop and pray because your senses are discerning something, and you need to find out what it is.

We need the discerning of spirits so we can recognize and honor the presence of God in our churches, but we also need to sense His presence in our homes, cars or workplaces. When we know God is in a situation, we can rest assured that the outcome will be for our good, but if we are unsure, we may do the wrong thing and find ourselves in a bad situation.

Is God in the business deal? Is He in the purchase of that new home? Is the Lord in the move to a new city, or is it your humanistic idea to pack up and go? It is essential to discern if God's Spirit is in a situation before making any big, life-changing decision.

You need to discern the Spirit of God when you are trying to interpret a dream, a vision, or a sign or wonder. How can you know if the interpretation you think you heard is from God? You can only know this with the discerning of spirits, because this is what enables you to recognize God's voice (see 2 Corinthians 11:13-15; 1 Corinthians 14:10).

This is not a "sweet by and by" gift, but one that is useful in every situation, every day of your life. I do not want to go where God has not gone before me, so I always desire to know if the path I'm on is the correct one. Am I going in the right direction and doing the right thing in ministry? Am I leading my household in the things of God as He would have me to do? Only by the discerning of spirits will I be able to discover the answers and find the conviction and courage to carry on.

DISCERNING MAN'S SPIRIT

Another vital aspect that will protect you from many mistakes in life is the discerning of the spirit of man. You need to be able to recognize the source of every individual's intent. Is what a man says from God? Is it from the devil, or is it from humanistic thoughts? Knowing which is which can save you from much difficulty.

Discerning the spirit of man will also help you when you see someone struggling, so you can act in a way that will truly help them. God can tell you where the trouble is rooted. If the problem is the person's own fault, he can be rebuked, instructed and directed down the right path, but if a man's trouble is the result of an attack of the enemy, you can show him how to resist the devil and flee to victory.

Have you ever noticed someone across the room in tears and did not know what to do? Next time it happens, why don't you pray and ask God to show you what's going on so you can be a help and not a hindrance? The Lord can tell you why they are crying. Are they depressed? Are they under conviction? Are they under the attack of the enemy?

If we would operate in the discerning of spirits when we deal with other people, we would save ourselves the embarrassment of assuming the wrong thing. We could eliminate tired clichés and actually help someone in their time of need if we would simply wait for the discerning of spirits to show us how to approach hurting people.

There is nothing more frustrating than to be in a mess and have someone throw some tired old Christian cliché at you. This is not what I want to hear. I want the Spirit of God to tell you what to say or do to help me. I believe it's what you want, too.

How much better could you be as a parent if you could discern what was going on in that brick-covered teenage mind? Young people put up walls to keep you out, but the Holy Spirit can give you a kind of x-ray vision to see right through the snide remarks to the heart of the matter. Understanding your teenager is about much more than catching on to the latest trends or being their best friend. It involves getting to the core of their being and understanding who they are beneath the surface attitude. You need to discern the spirit of

249

your teenager, not just outward manifestations.

Discerning the heart of man is imperative in our homes. Knowing by God's Spirit what's going on inside your spouse or your children can save you from a multitude of mistakes and make you a much more effective intercessor for them. You can be a better spouse, a better parent, a better friend, a better co-worker, a better son or daughter and a better believer if you will allow God to speak to you and lead you through the discerning of spirits before you act.

DISCERNING ANGELS AND DEMONS

God can speak to you through the discerning of spirits to show you the work of angels and demons. There will be times when you need to know about both. When an angel is in your church or in your home, do you discern his presence? Do you perceive what the Lord is trying to do in your house or in your sanctuary? God is always trying to do something to help you, and sometimes His work involves sending an angel to assist you or to deliver a message, but if you never discern an angel's presence, you will miss what God has to say through him.

Discerning of spirits will also reveal the work of demons when you need to know what they are up to. I remember vividly the first time I experienced this. I had just opened our first church building, and the crowds were thin. Two of my most faithful members were my wife Phyllis and our niece Dreama, who later became our church receptionist. (My wife told me years later she wouldn't have come if she wasn't married to me!)

I wasn't exactly making a huge impact for the Kingdom, but I knew God had called me, and I refused to give up. After about a year and a half of very slim growth (we had around 10 people), I decided I had had enough. I told my wife I was going to lock myself in the church to fast and pray, and I was not coming out until I had an answer. So off I went to fulfill my promise.

I walked and prayed, and prayed and walked. I did everything I knew to do to hear from the Lord. After a few days, and I really do not remember how many, suddenly God opened my eyes to discern what was going on in the spirit realm. It was as if the Lord peeled back the roof of our church and I could see straight up to the sky, but instead of fluffy white clouds, what I saw was an ugly demon perched on a throne above our building. By the discerning of spirits, I immediately knew what I had to do. I began to contend with this spirit in the name of Jesus, and I did not stop until he finally got off the throne and left.

From that day on, our little church was filled to capacity. We went from ten members to standing room only in four days time. From a Wednesday evening prayer meeting to a Sunday morning service, our congregation was changed forever. It was a great miracle, but one that would have never happened had God not shown me by the discerning of spirits what was going on in a realm I could not see with my natural eyes.

What the Lord did for me, He desires to do for you. God wants you to succeed more than you do. He has gifted and empowered you to do certain things for His Kingdom, and He does not want you to stand helplessly by while the devil prevents you from fulfilling your destiny. The Lord desires for you to know what's going on, and He wants you to contend where you need to, but it's up to you to covet the discerning of spirits and put yourself in a position to hear and receive.

GROWING SPIRITS

Our spirits grow. Did you know that? In 1 Peter 2:2 we are told: *"As newborn babes, desire the sincere milk of the word, that ye may grow thereby."* You aren't growing physically when you drink in the milk of the Word, but you are developing spiritually. The Word of God is the Bread of Life, not just for your mind, but for your spirit.

When you are born again, your spirit is made alive and new, and you are in a covenant relationship with God, but you've still got to grow in the fruit of the spirit. You have to change and mature spiritually, not just be transformed mentally. This is why we have to treat one another as unformed spiritual beings. We are not what we are going to be, and we will not become what God wants us to become until we are molded into that which we are called and equipped to be.

If you can discern who your spouse and children are now, and who they are meant to be, you can ask God to help you mold them into vessels of honor ready for the Master's use, and you can become a tool the Father uses to develop your family in the ways of the Lord. God can show you the giftings in your children so you will know how to use wisdom to raise them to be all God has planned. You can discern the spirit in your spouse in order to know how to speak to him or her and give the things needed in the good times and the bad.

I encourage you to allow the discerning of spirits to help you raise your children in the nurture and admonition of the Lord, growing godly spirits in blessed, happy children. I also encourage you to allow God to speak and show you who your spouse really is so you can walk by their side as a faithful helper who is determined to believe the best, pray for the best and expect the best in your mate.

We cannot ever accomplish what God wants us to unless we are willing to do it His way. When God calls and equips us, He expects us to use faith to fulfill that call. Part of the life of faith is the life of growth and increase, both in our spiritual lives and in the use of the gifts of the Spirit in our families.

Do not take the discerning of spirits for granted, but be a grateful, willing vessel, and God will use you to help your family become all He wants them to be. Over time, you will rejoice as you watch the spirits of your children and spouse increase and grow to be used in the Kingdom of God for great and wonderful things.

DISCERNING YOUR CHILDREN

The one area where so many long to hear the voice of God is in the attempt to raise godly children. Countless parents feel overwhelmed by society's influence in their children's lives, and they believe they are not educated enough in spiritual things to overcome the world and make a difference. Nothing could be further from the truth.

If you are born again, you are a supernatural person with the Spirit of God always at the ready to help you. You are His child, and you have the capacity to hear His voice, even in the midst of a temper tantrum in a play room, or in the middle of a screaming match with a stubborn teen on the other end of a cell phone. God wants you to know how to raise your children in the nurture and admonition of the Lord, so He has given you the gifts of the Spirit, and discerning of spirits in particular, to empower and help you bring them from glory to glory, raised in the image of God.

We each possess a spirit which is unique to us alone. I'm not talking about God's Spirit in us, or a demonic spirit influencing us, but I am speaking of our personal human spirit that is designed by God for a specific purpose. If parents are ever going to succeed in molding a child's spirit to be all God has destined him or her to be, they must learn, not by books or magazines, but by the discerning of spirits what type of spirit their child has.

In Proverbs 14:29 we read: *"He that is slow to wrath is of great understanding: but he that is hasty of spirit exalteth folly."* This is just one type of spirit you as a parent may need to deal with—a hasty spirit.

I have such a tendency in me which I have to watch over carefully. If I do not rule my spirit, I can quickly end up on the wrong side of an issue. So, I do not allow it to control me, but I rule it and mold myself to overcome the weakness a hasty spirit presents in my everyday life. You have to do the same in the lives of your family members.

Talebearers often have hasty spirits. They want to hear and tell a story quickly, without any regard for the truth or for the consequences of repeating rumor. They need to be rebuked and instructed, even when they are tiny talebearers.

A strong-willed child has another type of spirit which must be molded to glorify God. He or she may be destined to be a leader in some capacity, so this molding will need to teach the young person to lead with humility. There are other children who will always be followers. This is okay because we need leaders and followers in the Kingdom of God, but if a parent misreads a child and tries to make a leader out of a follower, or vice versa, the parent will have a problem on his hands.

There are haughty spirits that must be humbled by the Word of God. Hasty spirits must be controlled and taught to slow down to think before they act. Prideful spirits must be taught how to submit, and strong-willed spirits need to learn how to lead as Jesus did, as a servant of all. The Word of God is full of insight for every type of spirit once you identify what you are dealing with. Every variety of human spirit can be taught, educated and controlled when submitted to the Word of God.

Don't let your children develop bad habits they will regret for a lifetime. Pray and ask God to show you what spirit is driving your child, and when you discern, begin to put a diligent watch over it to mold, lead and direct your child, and to teach him how to control his spirit and submit it to God.

DISCERNING A BROKEN SPIRIT

Nowhere is the discerning of spirits more necessary than when you deal with people in times of great struggle. We are each a triune being. We are a spirit, we have a soul, which is made up of our mind, will, intellect and emotions, and we live in a physical body (see 1 Thessalonians 5:23). If any one of those parts is damaged or unbalanced in any way, it will affect us in every other area.

The Bible tells us: *"A merry heart doeth good like a medicine: but a broken spirit drieth the bones"* (Proverbs 17:22). It is possible for your human spirit to become broken, and when this is the case, it will affect you in your soul and body.

Bones provide strength and stability. Dried bones are the result of a broken spirit, and they make people unstable, weak and unable to meet God's goals for their lives. The only way to know if someone has a broken spirit is through the discerning of spirits.

Let's say you have been praying for your spouse or for your children, and you seem to be getting nowhere. Why don't you ask God to show you the condition of their spirits by the discerning of spirits? You may be surprised to discover you have been praying for the wrong thing. You've been praying, "God convict my husband and turn him around," when what you needed to pray was, "God heal his broken spirit so that the fullness of your Spirit can reside there. Help him to trust again, and to show love and receive love from You and me."

A broken spirit is leaky. What goes in cannot stay there, so it has no lasting effect. Your husband may put the Word in, but he can't seem to keep it there for very long, and off he goes back to his old habits. If you really want to help, I encourage you to ask God to show you what caused the leak so that you can pray more effectively.

You need to realize that your spouse and children are spiritual beings, and their spirits can be broken by a multitude of things that happen to them at work, at school and at home every day. A spouse browbeating a spouse, for instance, or school yard put-downs repeated over time can cause a spirit to break in half.

Too much chastening or harsh correction can also crush a child's spirit. Colossians 3:21 says: *"Fathers, provoke not your children to anger, lest they be discouraged."* Less angry yelling and much more targeted nurturing may work wonders in your household. Only the Spirit of God can tell you when your child's behavior toward you is rebellion, and when it is the result of a broken spirit. You can't treat cancer with a band-aid, and you can't heal a broken spirit with punishment. You need correct spiritual information to pray and act in the right way, and this information is only available by the discerning of spirits.

If your children have fractured spirits, they may see who they are and mentally assent to what God has empowered them to do, but never act like it because the fractures cause them to be negative, always believing the worst in themselves. When your children are negative, they will reap more negativism. Unless they allow God to intervene and heal the brokenness, they will never fulfill destiny and be who God has called them to be.

Unfulfilled dreams can break the human spirit, too. As Proverbs 13:12 tells us: *"Hope deferred maketh the heart sick: but when the desire cometh, it is a tree of life."* Realizing when someone's brokenness is caused by unfulfilled dreams can mean the difference between restoration and backsliding. Restoration will come if you discern the cause and help them rediscover their dreams, but backsliding may be the unfortunate result if you miss it.

You also need the discerning of spirits when you attempt to comfort those who have lost loved ones. At this time of grief, their spirits may be severely broken. This is why you should pray first and discern what they need before you start unloading all of your favorite clichés at them. They've already heard "I'm so sorry" a million times, and they haven't believed it yet.

Why not show up at the funeral home with a word of true comfort born of your time spent in prayer to discern what they really need? Sometimes people want to hear something totally opposite of what we think they need to hear. Let the Lord lead and tell you what to say.

God is the healer of the broken-hearted, so if He speaks to you through the discerning of spirits and reveals brokenness in a loved one, it is your responsibility to intercede, intervene with encouraging words, and make sure the healing process is allowed to go forward so your loved one can grow into God's vision for them.

HEALING BREAKS AND WOUNDS

In my personal life, I realized one of my most vulnerable areas was a feeling of failure born of a broken spirit from my childhood. It's not that I did not have fun in life, but I never felt as if I succeeded as a child.

If I made the baseball team, I was put on second string. When I made the track team, I was the last guy selected. When I made the basketball team, they told me I might play, if they needed me. It seemed as if everything I ever did was somehow secondary to the other kids. What this instilled in my young mind was that I was not quite good enough to succeed, and I would somehow always be second rate.

These experiences burned in me a fear of failure, of falling short, and a fear of never achieving. When I did begin to achieve something later in life, I would not stick it out to completion because I was afraid somebody better than me would show up, and I would lose my place just like I did when I was young.

It produced in me a failure mechanism which acted as a protection against the brokenness I experienced as a child. I convinced myself if I never truly succeeded, I could not truly fail. So, I became a young man who took no risks or chances, had no vision or purpose, and fulfilled no goals in life. It was only through the intervention of God that I ever made it over the hump and allowed myself to achieve something for Him.

This kind of brokenness can also happen to you or your loved one. If you know about it through the discerning of spirits, you can become a healer of brokenness through intercession. You can begin to restore a merry heart, and to speak an encouraging word which will mend the broken spirit.

Scripture tells us: *"The spirit of a man will sustain his infirmity; but a wounded spirit who can bear?"* (Proverbs 18:14).

A healthy spirit is like healthy skin. It protects you and keeps out what is trying to infect you. However, a wounded spirit makes you vulnerable. Just like a wounded body is susceptible to infection, a wounded spirit will open the door to the nastiness that lies in wait all around you. This explains why certain people are offended so easily. It's because they are wounded, and every little thing that comes near their wound makes them hurt even more, so they build walls to protect themselves. If you discern their wounds by the Holy Spirit, you can begin to help them understand why they do what they do, and pray with them for their healing.

People with wounded spirits respond to others the same way someone with a wounded hand responds to people in a crowded room. They will be over-protective and cast a suspicious eye toward any person who attempts to come close.

You don't want to shake hands with anyone, no matter how important they are, when your hand hurts, and similarly, you avoid interacting with anyone on a spiritual level, no matter how much you would like to, when your spirit is hurting.

This is why when someone is wounded, regardless of how kind you are to them, they may respond in a confusing way. By allowing God to show you the problem through the discerning of spirits, you can become a part of the answer instead of a part of the problem, a repairer of the breach instead of one who adds to it and widens the gap.

We can't always tell what's going on in the spiritual realm by watching an individual with the natural eye. Many times we mistake a spiritual struggle for a natural one because we misread the signs. If the disciples had exercised the discerning of spirits when Jesus was in the Garden of Gethsemane, they would have realized He was in a great spiritual battle and could have come to His aid, instead of sleeping through what was taking place (see Matthew 26:37-46).

Discerning of spirits will enable you to perceive the spiritual well-being, or lack thereof, of those you live with, giving you precious insight which will help you assist the ones you love. Take the time to find a real solution to a very real problem, and allow the Spirit of God to show you both how to act toward the one with the wound, and how to pray. People need our intercession, but they also need our personal touch to help them heal. Be like Jesus, and become a mender of the broken-hearted.

DISCERNING SPIRITUAL CONDITIONS

Did you know God wants to speak to you through the discerning of spirits about the condition of your own spirit? You may have prayed and prayed concerning a certain aspect of your life, not realizing that all the while your spirit has been broken in this area and everything you have tried to put in has leaked out as a result. Only God knows, and only He can tell you.

Discerning of spirits will also enable you to determine if you are going through a spiritual struggle or a mental one; if you have a personality weakness or are being chastened of God; if you are in an emotional battle or just a changing season that will pass. It is important to discern the passing seasons in our spiritual lives, not only so we can be sensitive to those around us, but so we can discern what we are personally passing through. Seasons come and go in our spirits just as they do in the natural:

- Perhaps you are in a season of temptation, just as Jesus was in the wilderness.
- Perhaps you are in a season of dormancy before the time to sow arrives, just as winter dryness comes before the spring planting.
- Perhaps you are in a season of attack from the enemy, a time when he will attempt to destroy your destiny.
- Perhaps you are in a period of growth where you will experience great revelation of the Word.
- Perhaps you are in a season of planting, or maybe you are in a season of harvest.
- Perhaps you are in a season of fire where God's presence will seem hot and exciting to you.
- Perhaps you are in a season that is cool and quiet where God your Father will mold you in times of intimacy.
- Perhaps you are in a season of correction and chastening.
- Perhaps you are in a season of sharpening in preparation for the next stage of "from glory to glory" (see 2 Corinthians 3:18).

You need to understand what is transpiring in your life so you will know how to react to situations, and how to stand and pray. For this reason, you need the discerning of spirits to operate in your life every day.

In Acts 8:18-23, we find a story of how God spoke to Peter through the discerning of spirits about the spiritual condition of another man: *"And when Simon saw that through laying on of the apostles' hands the Holy Ghost was given, he offered them money, saying, Give me also this power, that on whomsoever I lay hands, he may receive the Holy Ghost. But Peter said unto him, Thy money perish with thee, because thou hast thought that the gift of God may be purchased with money. Thou hast neither part nor lot in this matter: for thy heart is not right in the sight of God. Repent therefore of this thy wickedness, and pray God, if perhaps the thought of thine heart may be forgiven thee. For I perceive that thou art in the gall of bitterness, and in the bond of iniquity."*

This encounter brought great conviction to Simon, and he asked Peter to pray for him in the next verse. Peter discerned Simon's fault through the discerning of spirits, dealt with it scripturally with a rebuke, and then God moved on Simon and he repented.

In Simon's defense, he had just come out of witchcraft, idolatry and sorcery where spiritual powers were for sale. Had Peter dealt with his fault incorrectly, he could have lost Simon forever. Thank God Peter rebuked and corrected him, allowing God's conviction to fall upon him and bring repentance. Because Peter discerned Simon's spiritual condition, he realized his ignorance was leading him into places where he would perish for his lack of knowledge, and he was able to rescue him with a godly rebuke.

It would be wonderful if we could discern the spiritual condition of one another so we could help each other reach a place of repentance and reconciliation instead of condemning each other to eternal damnation. This is too often what happens in the break-up of a marriage. One spouse fails to discern the lukewarm spiritual state of the other that leads to sin. If discovered in time, intercession could have been made before sin was birthed and the marriage was destroyed.

Does this make it your fault that your mate failed? No, but it does make your intercession and discernment imperative. How much better could your marriage be if you would become one who discerns and prays instead of one who reacts and prays?

Marriage is a spiritual covenant which is under the attack of a spiritual adversary, but it is also protected by two spiritual, born again beings who are helped by God's spiritual input. If one falls alone, he is no match for the adversary, but if he falls while under the watchful eye of a discerning mate, he can be helped back up and sustained to victory.

Discerning the spiritual conditions of ourselves and of others can lead to repentance and restoration, to rescue and recovery—the very things God desires to manifest in your family.

DISCERN AND PRAY

In Luke 22:31-34, we see an interesting story of the discerning of spirits in action in the life of Jesus: *"And the Lord said, Simon, Simon, behold, Satan hath desired to have you, that he may sift you as wheat: But I have prayed for thee, that thy faith fail not: and when thou art converted, strengthen thy brethren. And he said unto him, Lord, I am ready to go with thee, both into prison, and to death. And he said, I tell thee, Peter, the cock shall not crow this day, before that thou shalt thrice deny that thou knowest me."*

Jesus was able to tell what spirit was operating in Peter's life by the discerning of spirits. Through this gift Jesus saw how Peter was under an attack from Satan, one which was meant to separate him from Jesus for good.

Peter expressed what his desire was, but Jesus knew he would not be able to fulfill his desire in his own strength because the attack of the enemy would be too much. Jesus told Peter He had prayed for him, that he would be turned around, and when he was restored he would strengthen those around him.

The discerning of spirits should always lead us to prayer. When we come before the Lord we should pray that God will have His complete work and will in the lives of the people we are praying for, and that the Lord will strengthen them. Then we bind, come against, rebuke and draw lines against the devil, and we begin to proclaim what God said would happen to the brother or sister in the midst of the battle. We should always speak God's Word over the person we are praying for and expect the Lord's best for them.

When we are given knowledge concerning an individual and know a fall is coming, we should be wise enough to pray as Jesus prayed and allow His Spirit to work as He did in Peter. What we don't need to do is criticize and try to be the chastening of the Lord ourselves. Notice, Jesus did not rebuke Peter on this occasion, but He instead gave him words of encouragement he could hang onto when he fell short of what he intended to do. Thank God, Jesus recognized Peter was in the battle of his life and interceded for him to make it through.

Many times, when we see people struggle, we automatically conclude they are under the chastening of the Lord, and we think less of them as a result. We should never walk away from the struggle of another, especially if it is happening in the life of a family member, but we should be willing to sacrifice and intercede until discernment comes to show us how to pray.

We need to be able to discern the difference between the chastening of the Lord and the attack of the enemy. If we don't, we may leave our loved ones to fend for themselves when they need us the most. When it comes to your loved ones, start praying. Ask God to show you the source of their trouble, then intercede for them and allow God to move and reconcile them to Himself.

I need to offer a word of caution about the discerning of spirits, because I know that many who are reading this book may be new to this realm. I understand what it takes to covet and pursue the gifts. You have to set yourself to times of prayer and fasting, often for months on end, before they fully manifest in your life. You have to be dedicated and diligent to pursue them at such a great cost, without giving up. Because it costs you so much to hear from God in this manner, don't you think it would be wise to handle what you have with the greatest care possible? I do.

When we covet, pursue, seek after and receive a gift, that gift is a very valuable thing we must carefully watch over. When Paul said we should covet the best gifts, it was for good reason, because they are precious, wonderful treasures which should be treated with the utmost respect. The gifts of God should not be mishandled in any way, although it is very easy to do just that out of ignorance mixed with zeal.

So, here's my word of warning. Just because God gives you discernment about someone, it does not mean this information should be made public knowledge. It should not be shared with your prayer team at church, or your closest friend. Take it to your prayer closet instead, and keep it there.

If God gives you discernment concerning an individual, that word is a sacred word, an intimate thought from God toward the person, and it should be treated with the greatest of care. Things were said to Mary the mother of Jesus which she never proclaimed to others. Instead, she kept them hidden in her heart because they were too precious and too personal for her to reveal. We should be as wise as Mary.

Some things God will tell you about your family member or a loved one are not for anyone else to hear, including them. There are times you are given discernment for the sole purpose of intercession. If this happens, you should tell absolutely no one. God is entrusting you with revelation which will be life-changing for that loved one, so you need to treat it with discretion. Pray in private, and God will reward your loved one in the open.

Paul tells us in 1 Corinthians 14:32: *"And the spirits of the prophets are subject to the prophets."* In other words, we are each responsible to control what the Lord gives us. You need to make sure that you rule your gift and that your gift does not rule you. So, when you break through and the gifts begin to move in your life, be very discreet and wise about their use. There will be times to use them privately, and times to use them publicly, but if you handle them wrongly, you may do great damage, which is why you must be very careful.

261

Never release information about another which comes through the discerning of spirits; don't disgrace yourself or your loved ones this way. Be like Mary and keep it to yourself, hidden in your heart. Pray and intercede, encourage and edify, but do it all in the love of God.

The discerning of spirits is a vital gift that can help you in every area of life. I encourage you to treat it as a precious possession and allow God to mature you in its use for His glory.

CHAPTER 16

THE WORD OF KNOWLEDGE

It was the first day of unleavened bread, the day when they killed the Passover lamb. Jesus was resting with His disciples in the morning when someone posed the question of where they should have the Passover meal prepared for the evening. Without hesitation, Jesus chose two of the twelve and told them exactly what they needed to do.

Jesus said, "Go into the city. When you arrive there, you will see a man carrying a pitcher of water. Follow him. When he enters a building, find the landlord of that place and tell him I need to know where the guest room is, the room prepared for Me to eat the Passover with My disciples. He will show you a large upper room that is completely furnished and prepared. Make your arrangements for the meal to be taken there and made ready for us."

The two disciples hurried to the city, not knowing what to expect. When they rounded the corner on a certain street, there he was, a man carrying a pitcher of water. The disciples looked at one another, a little surprised at what they saw, and they ran to catch up to him.

They followed him for several blocks, and then he entered a building. The disciples went in after him and asked to see the landlord. Just as Jesus said, he had a room fully prepared for them, as if he was expecting them to come. Without hesitation, the disciples made dinner arrangements, and later that evening they all sat down to the Passover meal together (see Mark 14:12-16).

How do you think Jesus knew about the man with the pitcher and the room that was ready just for Him? Was it a good guess, or did He have some inside information? Based on this account of the story, it came through a word of knowledge.

Jesus could not know about the man with the pitcher or the room that was ready and waiting by any natural means, but He could know by the operation of the Spirit of God. Notice, Jesus did not know anything other than when and

263

where the man would be carrying the pitcher of water, and that he would be able to lead the disciples to a prepared room for their Passover meal. This shows us a word of knowledge is just that, a single word, or a portion of the whole. It is not complete knowledge about a given subject or situation, but is just enough information to get the job done.

We know that every manifestation of the gifts of the Spirit is for our benefit. In this case, the word of knowledge brought divine provision, which is something we all need and enjoy. God spoke through this gift of the Spirit, this operation of the manifestation of the Holy Spirit working on earth, and Jesus and His disciples were blessed.

LED BY THE SPIRIT

One of my church members, a man named Bob, wrote me a letter and shared this amazing testimony of how God led him by the word of knowledge to accomplish an important work. It is such an incredible story because it shows not only how God speaks to us by the word of knowledge, but it also shows us how vital it is for us to obey what we hear. Here's Bob's story in his own words:

"I had been visiting and witnessing to a man named Chester for three months. Chester was 86 years old, and he was not saved. His wife had been born again on her death bed, but Chester was still not ready to make a commitment. Chester and I had great times together, reminiscing about his life. Sometimes he would say he wanted to receive Jesus as his personal Lord and Savior, but he would never follow through.

"One day, a Tuesday around 4:30 P.M., I was on my way home from work, and I had my evening all planned. I was remodeling my house and wanted to spend the entire evening on a certain project. As I drove, I heard God speak inside my spirit as clearly as if He had been sitting in the passenger seat beside me. God said, 'I want you to stop and see Chester tonight.'

"I groaned, 'No!' but headed my car toward Chester's house anyway. By the time I got to his road, though, I had talked myself out of stopping, and I drove right on past.

"Again, I heard very distinctly, 'I said tonight.' I immediately stopped the car and turned around right in the middle of the road. I drove straight to Chester's house and told him I needed to speak with him. After talking with him frankly, he finally got saved that night.

264

"Well, the story doesn't end there. I read of Chester's death in the newspaper just two days later. I quickly called his son and discovered that Chester had passed away as he ate breakfast the very next morning after my visit. As far as I know, I was the last person to see him alive!

"I was so happy to be able to deliver the news to his son that his dad was in Heaven with his mother. When I visited the family at the funeral, I could see a look of peace on Chester's face that had not been there before. He was home, and I was so glad I had listened."

This story is a great illustration of the word of knowledge in action. Just as Jesus sent the disciples to a certain place at a specific time, so Bob was sent to Chester's house on a certain day for a very important purpose.

This word of knowledge was simple, "Go see Chester." It did not give any more details than a simple, "Go now." Again, a word of knowledge is a single word, not all the knowledge there is about a situation, but enough to get the job done.

All Bob needed to know was to go. God had the rest under control, knowing Chester's heart was finally ready, and knowing his time on earth was about to draw to an end. Think of how awful Bob would have felt if he had continued to ignore God's voice. Think of how Chester's eternity might have been different if not for Bob's obedience. When a word of knowledge comes, no matter how little information is offered, we need to obey and do whatever God instructs.

There are other words used in the Bible to describe this leading of the Spirit. Acts 16:18 tells us: *"And this did she many days. But Paul, being grieved, turned and said to the spirit, I command thee in the name of Jesus Christ to come out of her. And he came out the same hour."* What was this "being grieved" all about? It's not that Paul was sad, but that he was moved by the Spirit of God to do something. God gave him a word of knowledge without ever speaking a single syllable, and Paul delivered this girl from her torment.

In Acts 17:16, we find another example. This time the verse reads: *"Now while Paul waited for them at Athens, his spirit was stirred in him, when he saw the city wholly given to idolatry."* Here, the word of knowledge came by way of a stirring inside Paul which made him want to act. This word led Paul to begin to dispute with the Jews in the synagogue and to teach the Word of the Lord from place to place. Ultimately, it led to the opportunity to preach before a great crowd, and many lives were changed.

In each instance, God needed Paul to do something specific, and in each case the Lord chose to send His message, not by words, but by an inner conviction, or an inner stirring which caused Paul to act as God wanted him to act.

There will be times when the word of knowledge will come in the form of actual words in your spirit, as it did for Bob, but at other times you will "just know" you need to do something, as Paul did. Either way, it is God speaking to you to go and do, and so you better obey—and go and do!

DIFFERENT WAYS TO RECEIVE

I want to return to the story of Cornelius and Peter from Acts 10:1-48. (I encourage you to read this passage of scripture before you continue on.) We've looked at this story from two different angles so far. The first time we looked at it, we focused on Peter and his vision. The second time we studied the story, we looked at Cornelius and how his family was saved and filled with the Holy Spirit.

This time, I want you to see how Peter and Cornelius each received a word of knowledge, though the messages came in two very distinct ways. God used two different manifestations of the word of knowledge to bring two very different men together for one important purpose—the salvation of many. One word came by way of a vision, while the other came through the mouth of an angel, but both were life-changing events for these men, and for Cornelius' entire family.

This is necessary to understand because the word of knowledge is not something that can be limited in any way. It may come in a dream or a vision, as it did to Peter, but it may also come through an angelic messenger, as it did to Cornelius. It may come as that still, small voice in your spirit, as it did in the story about Chester and Bob, or it may come as a stirring inside, as it did for Paul. However the word of knowledge is given to you, it comes from the Spirit of God.

One more thing I want to point out about Cornelius: I believe the reason this man was in a position for such a divine intervention is because he was busy doing what he knew to do. He didn't know everything, but he did as much as he knew. Cornelius was aware from his understanding of the Old Covenant how God required men to pray and to give to the poor, so he set about doing just that. Cornelius did not know about Jesus or about the New Covenant based on His shed blood, but he did as much as he knew to do, and God honored it. This shows us we should be doers of the Word and not hearers only if we want to hear from Heaven.

We can't be lazy, constantly watching the world go by on a 36" TV screen and expect God to swoop down upon us for no reason. We need to be active in what we know, which will allow God to give us more knowledge. Why would He say anything to a lazy man, knowing such a man will continue to be a hearer only? Hearers never get anything done for the Kingdom, but doers produce much fruit.

If we sit on the sidelines, God cannot do what He wants to do for us, or say what He wants to say to us, but if we will persevere in doing what we know, then God will bless us and give us additional instructions. It's that simple. Doers become doers of more, but hearers will not hear more if they do not take action.

God rewards those who diligently seek Him (see Hebrews 11:6). If you will become consistent in prayer and giving, I believe God will make your household a supernatural place where the gifts of the Spirit will flow, and you and your house will be blessed, just as Cornelius and his household were so long ago.

AN OLD TESTAMENT WORD

Certain people in the Old Testament were allowed to benefit from the gifts of the Spirit in limited fashion. While these gifts did not operate in many, they were available in a limited degree to the prophets and others who served the Lord faithfully.

We see this in a story found in 2 Kings 6:8-12. Here we read how God gave Elisha a word of knowledge which revealed where a warring king was planning an attack on the children of Israel. Elisha sent word to the king of Israel and warned him of the coming attack so that the army was prepared and avoided the encampment of the enemy. This happened more than twice, by this account, making the king of Syria very angry with his men because he thought he had a traitor in the camp.

In verse 12 his servants told him what was going on behind the scenes: *"And one of his servants said, None, my lord, O king: but Elisha, the prophet that is in Israel, telleth the king of Israel the words that thou speakest in thy bedchamber."*

We know that Elisha did not sneak into the king's bedroom at night and spy on him. Elisha had no natural ability to know what was going on in the enemy's camp, but God knew—and He told on the Syrian king so that He could protect His people.

God can hear what the righteous man says, but he can also hear what the wicked man says in secret. The Bible tells us that in the day of judgment we will all give an account for every idle word that we speak (see Matthew 12:36). There is nothing that goes on outside the confines of God's knowledge.

The Lord simply passed on, by a word of knowledge, what He knew about the plot of the Syrians, and because Elisha was faithful to pass it on to the king of Israel, God delivered Israel from the hand of their enemy—and He can speak to you in the same way today and deliver you from your adversaries. The Lord knows where you are, where your adversary is encamped, what the enemy has planned for you, and He desires for you to be delivered from it.

Wouldn't you tell a child if a big, ferocious dog was waiting for him behind a tree in your back yard? Of course you would. You'd shout until your child heard and moved away from the danger. But, if your child was not listening, he may walk into the trouble anyway.

It's the same in spiritual matters. God wants you to know what the enemy is up to, but the key is for you to be quiet long enough on a given day for Him to be able to get His message through to you. God can't speak if you never take the time to be quiet and listen. I encourage you to always allow time to hear from the Spirit of God each and every day, because you never know when the message you hear will save you from great hidden danger.

A WORD IN A VISION

We already touched on the story of a disciple named Ananias in Acts 9:10-19, but I want to go a little deeper. Ananias was a disciple who lived in Damascus at the time when Paul was on his way to that city in a huff. As Ananias sat praying one day shortly after Paul's encounter with Jesus, the Lord spoke to him in a vision.

Jesus appeared to the man and said, "Ananias." A little shocked at what he was seeing and hearing, the man replied, "Behold, I am here, Lord." Jesus continued: "Arise, and go over to the street called Straight. When you arrive, inquire at the house of Judas for a man named Saul of Tarsus. He is praying there, and he has seen in a vision a man named Ananias coming in to visit him and lay hands on him so that he might receive his sight."

Ananias was unnerved when he heard the name, because Saul of Tarsus was pretty well-known in Christian circles, and what they knew about him struck fear in their hearts. Bravely, Ananias responded, "Lord, I have heard of this man, and I know how much evil he has done to the saints at Jerusalem. In fact, he has been given authority from the chief priests to capture anyone who calls on Your name."

Jesus was not moved by Ananias' hesitation, but said, "Go on your way now, for this man is a chosen vessel, and he has been called to bear My name before the Gentiles, and before kings, and even to the children of Israel. Don't worry, for I will show him how great are the things he must suffer for My name's sake." This calmed Ananias, and the vision ended.

Ananias immediately stood up and went his way. When he arrived at the house, he went inside and found Saul (Paul), just as Jesus had said he would. He quickly laid hands on him and told him: "Brother Saul, the Lord, even Jesus, who appeared unto you on the road; He sent me so you may receive your sight, and so you can be filled with the Holy Spirit."

In the blink of an eye, something fell from Paul's eyes, a sort of scaly substance, and he was able to see again. Paul asked to be baptized right away, and that's what happened. After that, he joined the disciples at Damascus and became known as a true brother in the Lord.

The vision Ananias had was the manifestation of a word of knowledge. We know this because it gave him specific information about things he could not know any other way than by the Spirit of God. This word of knowledge gave him instructions that led to another man's instant healing and deliverance, and eventually resulted in the establishment of many Gentile churches years later.

Ananias may have had previous knowledge of where the house of Judas was located, and he may have been down the street called Straight many times before, but he had no idea Paul was staying there, or that Paul was praying and expecting his visit because God had also given him a vision that showed a man would come lay hands on him so he would receive back his sight. Paul's vision was also a word of knowledge that instilled faith in him to receive his healing and to be filled with the Spirit.

The word of knowledge often leads people to act in faith and receive something they could not receive without it. I see this in miracle services all of the time. God will show me something about an individual I will think is insignificant, but to the person, it means the world that God would reveal an intimate detail about his or her life. When people see the Lord truly does love them, and knows what they're going through, it will usually increase their faith, and they will receive their miracle.

One such incident stands out in my memory. It was the night when I stood before a prayer line made up of folks who were deaf in one or both ears. The Spirit of God had instructed me to call them forward, and I was led to a certain man in the middle of the line.

I put my right forefinger in this man's left ear, and when I did, I had the sudden urge to pray in the Spirit. I stood and prayed, feeling totally foolish to be honest, and wondering what this man must be thinking. Here he was, standing in front of a crowd of people, probably nervous already, and the preacher had his finger jammed in his ear while he prayed in tongues very loudly.

I prayed for one minute, and then two, and then I decided I better stop, but the Spirit of God told me not to, and so I continued, my finger still stuck in this fellow's ear. The longer I continued, the more foolish I felt, but I knew I had to obey and keep going. Finally, I felt released.

I started to pray as I usually do for deaf people, but God stopped me in my tracks and directed me to do something totally different. In order to confirm what I sensed in my spirit, I asked this man if he had been involved in a war on an island. He looked surprised and answered yes. I then asked him if he had been near a big blast, and if that was when his hearing was lost. Again he responded in the affirmative.

I confidently told him that God had showed me all of this while I prayed, and that He showed me that a deaf devil had come on him while he was on the island. I also explained that the reason God had me pray in the Spirit for so long was because I was addressing that devil in the native tongue of the island. With that, the deaf devil left the man, and in an instant of time, his hearing was completely restored!

The word of knowledge directed me to minister to this man in exactly the way God needed me to. Once he realized God knew what had happened to him and had revealed it to me, his faith soared, and the miracle he needed was instantly manifested right before our eyes.

The Spirit of God is always trying to cultivate faith in our lives so He can give us what He desires for us to have. The word of knowledge is a great tool which can open the door of faith and allow a miracle to be loosed in your life, too.

WORKING FOR A MANIFESTATION

The word of knowledge will not always come to us in an instant of time. There are occasions we will have to wait for and work for the word we need. I remember an incident a few years ago that illustrates this point very well.

One day my son-in-law Randy discovered he had misplaced his leather coat. In that coat he had his billfold with all of his personal identification and credit cards. Randy came to me distressed, saying, "Pastor, I've looked everywhere. What should I do?" I said, "I want you to loose the gifts of the Spirit, and I want you to believe that God is going to help you find your coat."

So, Randy loosed the gifts of the Spirit, and he prayed, "God, I need you to show me by a word of knowledge where my coat is."

Days passed and nothing seemed to have happened. He came back and asked me how long he had to wait before something broke loose. I told him to keep thanking God that when he prayed, God had loosed the word of knowledge, and it had revealed to him where his coat was.

More time passed, and Randy became frantic. Finally, one morning as he was praying, he had a vision. He came to me and excitedly told me that as he prayed he saw the name of a restaurant, and then he saw his coat hanging in a corner of that restaurant. Randy was convinced he had his answer.

Later that day he called the restaurant, but they told him they had no such coat. So back he came the next morning disheartened and said, "Man, Pastor, I thought that was God, but they don't have my coat." I told him to go back to his prayer closet and keep thanking God.

Weeks later Randy got a call from a hostess at the same restaurant. She told him she had been trying to reach him for some time. Apparently, the manager had gone into a back room in the restaurant, found the coat, remembered Randy's call and asked her to return it.

To me, this was a miracle, but one that required work on Randy's part.

271

Suppose Randy had not loosed the gifts, or suppose he had not acted on the vision and made the initial call. Worse, yet, suppose he had given up and failed to stay with it long enough to see the vision come to pass. He could have ended up defeated, but because he stuck it out and worked the gift, the gift worked for him.

The Bible is filled with stories just like Randy's, accounts of men and women who refused to give up until the promise came to pass; stories of people willing to work the gifts until the gifts worked for them.

Jesus worked the gifts, too. Remember when He sat at a well with a woman who had been married several times and was currently living with another man? Jesus did not know everything about her, but He got a glimpse from God, and then He worked the word of knowledge until He received all the information He needed.

Jesus asked this woman questions, leading her to the place God needed her to go. He must have had an inkling the Father wanted to do something in this woman's life, but He had to work a little to discover just what it was that she needed.

Because Jesus persisted until He got to the bottom of the issue, the word of knowledge was loosed, and He was able to tell her things He could not know in the natural. When He did, her spirit was opened, she received the gospel, and she went and preached it to everyone she knew.

Don't ever be discouraged just because your answer takes a little while to manifest. You need to trust that when you prayed, God answered, and the word of knowledge you need has been loosed for you. Until you hear what God has to say, do what the Bible says and *"...having done all, to stand. Stand therefore..."* (Ephesians 6:13-14).

A WORD FOR A MIRACLE

We discovered in the beginning of this book that we can live under an open Heaven, and we can hear the voice of God. The word of knowledge is just one key to receiving from this open Heaven, but it is a vital key, one I have witnessed in miracle services and crusades over and over again.

Let me share this story from an overseas crusade that will show you one way the word of knowledge opens the door to miracles, signs and wonders.

We were in Cuba a couple of years before this writing, and we were holding a week long conference for young people. So many had been healed already, and we were witnessing miracle after miracle in every service. God was truly showing Himself strong on the behalf of the oppressed people.

When Sunday morning rolled around, the church we were ministering in was packed to capacity. A group of deaf folks sat together over against the wall, and many of them were also mute. As the service progressed I began to think about them. I wondered if God would heal them all on that great day. I had witnessed just such a miracle in Russia, where, as I mentioned earlier, an entire deaf school was healed in one night, so I knew this would be no problem for God, but I also knew I could not move until He spoke and gave me direction.

I watched them throughout the service, and I wondered when God would tell me who to pray for first, and who had faith to be healed and freed. In myself, I certainly had no way of knowing, but I was sure that God knew, and that He is always so faithful to lead me, speak to me and reveal what I need to know so that others can be blessed, healed and saved.

As we approached the end of the service, I walked over to this group of deaf people, and it was then the Lord revealed what I needed to do. I just knew that I knew what I should pray for, and who I should pray for. I looked straight at a woman who appeared to be 65-70 years old, one I learned later who had been born deaf and dumb, and I told my helpers to bring her to me.

As she stood before me, I cast the devil out of her, and she spoke and heard. Instantly! The people rejoiced greatly for this miracle from Heaven, and I rejoiced for the word of knowledge that had set this woman free.

Some may think it was strange that she was the only deaf person I prayed for that day. Why her? Why only one? I understood it was because God knew the heart of every man and woman in that room. Only He knew who had faith that was ready to be harvested, who really believed, who could join their faith with mine in that moment, and who I should join myself to.

For me it wasn't about making a show of miracles in abundance, but of being obedient to His revealed word. I did what I did out of obedience to God. She was the only deaf person I felt released to pray for in that service, and so she was the only one I approached. God controlled the situation with a simple word of knowledge, and through that word He changed a precious life, a growing church and a lifeless community forever.

A word of knowledge, pouring forth from an open Heaven, brought a liberty to this woman she had never known, and a freedom she could have missed had not someone in the room been listening for the voice of God. It was me on that particular day, but how often has God tried to speak to us, and we were not aware? I think of this, and I pray I will hear every time. I hope you will, too, because so many people in this world of ours need us to hear; not for ourselves, but for them.

A WORD OF CAUTION

While we all love to hear a word from the Lord in a supernatural way, I must caution you not to use any gift of God to do away with personal study of the Word, godly counsel, prayer or relationships with other people. You cannot substitute your relationship with God's Word with a word of knowledge. You cannot replace the counsel of your pastor or another godly leader with an angelic visitation. You cannot substitute your prayer life with a dream or a vision, nor your relationships with other people with signs and wonders.

We need God's Word to be the anchor in our lives and godly counsel to keep us going in the right direction. We need prayer to keep us grounded and stable, and we need good relationships to sharpen one another and keep it real. I have run into so many Christians over the years who tended to over-spiritualize things, and in so doing they missed the voice of God altogether. For instance, there are single people who over-spiritualize their search for a mate. This is a very common example, and one I have watched folks struggle with time and again.

If you're looking for a mate, let me tell you how to find one: First, you have to spend time with other people. You have to get out of the house! You're not going to find a mate by staying at home every night and fasting for one. As you interact with others, you will find someone like-minded, someone who enjoys the same things you do and who looks at life the same way you do.

This is not the time to buy the ring, but it is the time to develop a good friendship. No one should ever marry someone unless they are first and foremost friends. Everything else in the relationship will change and rearrange, (just look at yourself in the mirror if you don't believe me), so you'd better be friends if you expect your marriage to last.

Once you have built a good friendship, you will begin to discover what your friend's plans and goals are. When you discover your plans and goals and those of your good friend are similar, it may be time to consider if the relationship can move into something more.

On the spiritual side, of course you are fasting, praying and seeking God's direction, expecting to hear Him speak in some way, but while you are doing these things, you are also gathering natural information. You cannot operate in spiritual things alone without ever giving a thought to what it would be like to spend the rest of your days with a certain individual.

God will speak to you as you are becoming friends, making character judgments, making assessments about attitudes and how he or she reacts under pressure. You will need to watch this person in a multitude of settings, and watch how he or she interacts with other people, including his or her own family, before you ever begin to consider becoming more than friends. You can pray and fast all you want, but if you do not use common sense and judge the person's character, you may make a costly mistake.

You also need to judge your friend's lifestyle according to the Word of God. Does he walk a good walk or just talk a good talk? Does she follow through on what she says, or does she make empty promises? And don't neglect the counsel of others. Talk to people who know the person in a variety of settings, and really listen to what they say. You may also want to ask your spiritual elder his or her opinion before you give or receive the ring. You need to grow in your relationship and let the process of time govern it.

Sometimes God is speaking loud and clear through good old fashioned horse sense, as they used to call it, but we are so busy looking for a sign or a wonder, we forget to look at the evidence all around us. It's no different when the gifts of God begin to move in your life. Just because something supernatural happens, don't throw away all of your common sense. Do not make things so spiritual that you neglect the road signs God has placed all around you. Time spent in the Word, prayer, hearing the counsel of others and godly common sense can deliver you and keep you on the right path.

God knows we live in the spiritual world by His Spirit, but He also knows that sometimes we can be a little dense when our hearts are involved, and so He has given us natural signs which accompany spiritual signs so we will have the best chance to hear and obey, protecting ourselves from many, many problems. Never be afraid to obey a "stop sign" along the way, even if the sign is big and red and hanging on a post by the side of a road. God may have placed it there just for you, so don't ignore it, but read it for what it is, and be glad.

BE SOBER

I have a second warning which is found in Romans 12:3: *"For I say, through the grace given unto me, to every man that is among you, not to think of himself more highly than he ought to think; but to think soberly, according as God hath dealt to every man the measure of faith."*

Just because a word of knowledge manifests in your life and you hear from God through that gift, do not allow spiritual pride to become a stumbling block. I hear about this issue repeatedly from husbands and wives.

One spouse hears from God more than the other and gets prideful because of it. The truth is, one has more time to hear than the other, one has different responsibilities than the other, and they both have different personalities, so of course they will hear God in different ways at different times. We may all be believers, but we are not spiritual clones.

We are all equal in God's eyes, this is true, but in each household you will find changing levels of zeal in each person. One will be on fire when another is not. Then later the one on fire may cool down and the other flame up. Why is this? Is one more spiritual than the other? No, but one is graced or gifted in certain areas which allow him or her to press on to certain spiritual levels at different times than another.

In my case, I spend a lot of time in prayer and study, not because I am so super-spiritual, but because it is what I need to do to fulfill my gift. It is the grace of God that motivates me to do what I do. If you removed grace from my life, I'd probably be a TV-watching couch potato like so many others.

God draws and stirs you because He is promoting and directing you, not because you are any more spiritual than anyone else. Some are motivated to study, others are motivated to pray, and still others are moved to do certain things, like serve in the nursery. One gift is not above another, but all flow together, and all are needed for the glory of God. It's not a natural strength which causes us to do what we do, but it is the call of the Spirit which calls us to do things, like pray, that are abnormal for us to desire to do on our own.

When you begin operating in the word of knowledge, don't allow yourself to think you are something you are not. God has allowed you to move in this gift for the well-being of others. It's not to establish your spiritual prominence, but to bless other people.

In every household, there will likely be one who is used more than another to hear the voice of God through the word of knowledge. If it is you, it's not because God wants to puff you up, but just because this is the order He has set for your household. Who do you think is more important, the vessel used to send a message, or the one God thought enough of to send a message to? God will use whatever is necessary to get His message to your family, just as He uses whatever means are necessary to get a message across to a church body.

Remember, the gifts of the Spirit are God's way of telling the world how much He loves them. When love is our motivation, God's love will shine through our words and our actions. You can be sure that a word of knowledge delivered in His love will lead and guide, loose breakthroughs, remove bondages, instill faith and bring forth God's will. Why? Because a word of knowledge is God's love message, showing us He is indeed all powerful and all knowing, all things to all people. I encourage you to let His amazing love shine through all that you say or do.

CHAPTER 17

WISDOM FROM ABOVE

Finally, it was going to happen. I was going to sign the contract that I and the other men in the room had worked so hard to create together. It had been two long months preparing for this meeting, but the end result was going to be worth the effort and the wait. I reached for the pen, placed it on the paper and began to sign.

I had just reached the second letter of my name when the Holy Ghost fell on me and said in a strong inner voice, "Don't sign that!" I replied in my spirit, "I thought you told me to go on the radio." He said, "I did, but not on this station." With that, my day was about to change drastically.

Suddenly, the room temperature seemed to rise several degrees, and drops of sweat began to form at the base of my neck. I squeezed the pen tightly, fully aware that the men looking over my shoulder were wondering why I had stopped so abruptly. The atmosphere was extremely uncomfortable. I laid the pen down and looked up into the eyes of the station manager who had worked so hard to initiate this whole contract idea, and I said, "I have something to tell you."

Thank God, the manager was an understanding guy, and he did not let on that he was hurt by my refusal after so much work. I knew inside he was disappointed because I could see it in the way his eyes fell to the floor. All of the men were disheartened, but I had to obey the word of wisdom from above. I had no choice but to walk away empty-handed, looking for another place to air our radio program.

Today, I truly thank God for this word of wisdom that kept me from doing the wrong thing. Though it caused me a little embarrassment at the time, it was so worth it in the end. I went on to form great relationships with God-appointed radio stations, and we touched thousands of lives as a result. The

Lord knew what He was doing, and thankfully, He was willing to share His insight with me.

THE WORD OF WISDOM

The word of wisdom is not an earthly-born wisdom that is accumulated by experience. It is a supernatural word, a fragment of God's wisdom which empowers an individual to be successful with knowledge and to be victorious in a given situation.

Like the word of knowledge, the word of wisdom is not complete wisdom about a given subject, but just enough to get the job done. If you will do what God says, you will win. If you don't, you will likely have to go around the mountain one more time.

The word of wisdom enables us to execute wisely. It empowers us to use information correctly and infuse God's ways into our situation. This is an invaluable gift that can help us direct our steps, make good decisions, raise godly children and guide our households. Every area of life can be profited by the word of wisdom.

Sometimes we let our desire to solve a problem dictate whether we will wait for God to speak or whether we will act based on what we already know. I would recommend that you always wait for God to speak because His wisdom is far greater than the wisdom of man.

It's easy to get excited about things and move too quickly if we're not careful. The house might look great on the outside when you search for a home on the Internet, but don't act too fast because it may be full of termites beneath the surface. The job may seem Heaven-sent, until you realize the schools in the area are under par, and the nearest Word-based church is 100 miles away.

I always advise taking your time when making big decisions. Be still and hear the voice of God through the operation of the word of wisdom before you act. Not only will God save you from ill-conceived deals, as He did me, but you may be saved from hidden dangers that lie ahead. In every case, the word of wisdom will direct your steps to the path you have been destined by God to take.

GIVEN WHAT TO SAY

When we discussed praying in the Spirit, we referred to Matthew 10:19-20, but in this chapter, I want to look even closer at these verses: *"But when they deliver you up, take no thought how or what ye shall speak: for it shall be given you in that same hour what ye shall speak. For it is not ye that speak, but the Spirit of your Father which speaketh in you."*

Jesus told the disciples they should not try to plan for tribulation or try to figure out what to say or attempt to draw upon their wisdom and experience for answers when trouble came. The words needed for their situation would come from somewhere beyond their own thoughts, memories and past encounters.

Notice Jesus said the words they needed would be given *"in that same hour,"* not a week ahead, or even the night before, but just when they needed them. This is how the word of wisdom works.

Too often when Christians get into trouble they rush to open their mouths to speak instead of opening their hearts to hear. In times of difficulty, you need to close your mouth and open up your heart to receive a word from the Lord that will show you what to say and do. Quoting just any old scripture won't necessarily make things happen. When problems surface, you need a word that is anointed from Heaven, one that is God-sent for you, and one the Holy Spirit reveals and tells you to confess. It will be an empowered word of wisdom for your situation, and it will set you free.

I've seen far too many believers march around quoting scripture after scripture, but still fail in the end. Their failure was not God's fault or the Word's fault. The only problem was their lack of asking God what He would have them to say instead of saying what they thought He wanted them to say.

Our human wisdom will never match the magnitude of God's wisdom, no matter how much we try and fail. A tiny glimpse of His wisdom is all you need to succeed. The key is to ask for this wisdom, and to be wise enough to wait for it before you act.

Imagine once again the scene as Paul stood before King Agrippa. He'd been waiting for this meeting for over two years. I suppose during that time he had planned at least a thousand plausible speeches, but when Paul rose to address the king, the words which flowed naturally out of his mouth probably surprised Agrippa as much as they did Paul. Instead of a disgruntled prisoner with a chip on his shoulder, the king found himself face to face with a man on a mission from God.

Paul talked about his life and his expertise in Jewish customs. He gave a little background on his life as a Pharisee, and then he began to preach the gospel. On and on Paul went, including his ill-fated desire to persecute Christians and his plan to have them arrested. And then Paul did a very strange thing in the king's eyes. Paul told him about his experience on the road to Damascus, and how Jesus visited him at midday.

I'm sure Agrippa's eyes must have grown wider and wider as Paul told him how he saw a light from Heaven that was brighter than the sun, and how he fell to the ground in fear, hearing a voice come from the light, but seeing no man speak. The king probably moved closer to the edge of his seat as Paul described the words of Jesus, and how he had been called to preach to the Gentiles.

I imagine Agrippa was more than a little confused. Where was Paul's anger at being imprisoned? Where was his argument for being set free? Why was this man recounting a story no one could verify, the story of a visitation from a dead man and a bright light shining on a dirt road that led to Damascus? I'm sure all of those thoughts flooded the king's mind as he listened intently, waiting for Paul's legal case to be made.

Finally, Paul showed signs of ending his story, and not a moment too soon. Unable to contain himself anymore, the administrator cried out, "Paul, you are beside yourself! Your education has made you mad!" Paul replied, "I am not mad, most noble Festus, but I speak the words of truth and soberness. The king already knows these things, which is why I have spoken so freely. And besides, I am persuaded that none of these things are hidden from him; for this thing was not done in a corner."

Festus was not impressed with Paul's boldness, but that did not deter him. Paul went on to direct his closing remarks to the king directly, challenging him with the truth of the gospel. At last, the king could not hold back any longer, and he cried out, "Paul, you almost persuade me to be a Christian!" Paul replied, "I would to God, that not only you, but also all that hear me this day, were both almost, and altogether such as I am, except these bonds" (see Acts 26:1-29).

What made Paul so bold in the presence of a king? It was the word of wisdom that gave him what to say in the moment he needed it. As a result, Paul was sent to Rome, as God had designed, and the work of his ministry continued unhindered.

WISDOM FROM ABOVE

A word from a man of the Spirit can loose a demoniac, a blind man or a young man possessed with a deaf and dumb spirit, just as it did for Jesus time and time again. When a man of faith says words which are inspired and empowered by God, nothing can stop the manifestation of God's desire for that situation, because the anointing breaks the yoke, and the word of wisdom is anointed of the Lord.

The word of wisdom will empower you to confound your enemy even while he plans for your destruction. The devil never plans a battle that will be within your own ability to overcome because he intends for you to stay in your trouble, but when God speaks a word of wisdom and reveals what you need to say and do, it doesn't matter what the devil thinks, God's purpose will prevail.

We are told in James 3:16: *"For where envying and strife is, there is confusion and every evil work."* The devil wants you to operate in your own intellect in the midst of hardship. He wants you to function in an earthly-born wisdom because he knows if you do, he will have his desired outcome.

James 3:17 goes on to say: *"But the wisdom that is from above is first pure, then peaceable, gentle, and easy to be entreated, full of mercy and good fruits, without partiality, and without hypocrisy."*

A word of wisdom from above will confound the enemy's attempts to destroy you and your family. It will diffuse confusion and strife, and it will bring peace to your home. I guarantee one word from Heaven is worth a million words which are formed in your mind.

When you encounter confrontations in your family, whether they are the result of the work of the enemy or born of your own human weaknesses, you need to be sure to seek for and receive a word of wisdom from Heaven to resolve your issues. "Well, what about when we're in the middle of a fight?" you may ask. I say stop and go pray. Abort the strife and ask the Lord for a word of wisdom that will not be partial to anyone involved; one that will be peaceable, gentle and unifying so God can uproot any bitterness which is seeking an entrance into your home.

Using earthly wisdom to try to solve family or marriage problems will usually bring hurt, because someone will misinterpret what you mean. But when God gives a word of wisdom, He will speak a clear word that all will understand, one that will be anointed by His Spirit for all to receive. This kind of wisdom will rid your situation of bitterness, strife and envy, and it will bring peace, gentleness, unity, love and joy back to your home.

Many of us have brought hurt to someone in our family because we have tried to use earthly wisdom to diffuse strife, and like it or not, we are not completely impartial in our decisions. Our earthly wisdom will inevitably be partial to someone in the situation, and it will leave another feeling left out. We are not God, who has no respect of persons, so we fall short of that standard no matter how hard we try, and we end up making matters worse by operating in human wisdom.

We cannot afford such an outcome in our homes, so we must begin to depend on the wisdom of the Lord to see us through and solve the issues of life. Whether diffusing strife or solving sticky family issues, the word of wisdom is available, and it is waiting to be withdrawn from Heaven for you.

THE DEPTHS OF THE WORD OF WISDOM

Jesus said: *"For I have not spoken of myself; but the Father which sent me, he gave me a commandment, what I should say, and what I should speak"* (John 12:49).

The Son of God operated in a high level of the word of wisdom. According to this verse, Jesus did not speak anything except that which God told Him to speak. Think of it. What discipline it took to say only what God told Him to say. For most of us, we could only adhere to this command for a very short time before we just had to say something based on our own head knowledge.

The Son of God did not live by His own wisdom, although He was wise enough at the age of twelve to confound the teachers in the synagogue. Jesus knew He would not succeed if He relied on what He knew, so He made sure to rely on the depths of God's wisdom.

Jesus also said, *"...I thank thee, O Father, Lord of heaven and earth, because thou hast hid these things from the wise and prudent, and hast revealed them unto babes"* (Matthew 11:25).

There are great secrets and mysteries in the Bible which have been hidden from the wise in the world's eyes and revealed to those the world calls foolish. We all know that wise in the world's eyes is not necessarily wise in God's sight. The Lord gives words of wisdom to the simple in heart which reveal the mysteries hidden in the scriptures. The Bible is for all, but the depths of God's wisdom are only for those who seek them.

This is why it is essential to study the Word and find what God says about certain things in the Bible. It is even more important to follow up your study with meditation of the Word which will allow God to reveal hidden mysteries. Then, you need to ask Him to give you a specific word of wisdom to rightly divide the word He gives you and use it to its fullest potential in your situation.

The trouble is, all of this takes time, and not many have the desire to spend the hours necessary to receive wisdom such as this. If we did, we would never face a problem alone again, but we would always wait upon the Lord until He renewed our strength, so we could mount up with wings as eagles and soar above our problems on the way to victory! (see Isaiah 40:31).

You cannot live by information alone or by a set of steps someone else derived from their time in the Word. You can only live by faith born of a revelation of God's Word that comes from the word of wisdom.

Let me prove it. In the Old Testament, a man named Naaman was told to go dip in the river Jordan to be cleansed of leprosy, but in the New Testament Jesus told ten lepers to go and show themselves to the high priest (see 2 Kings 5:1-14; Luke 17:12-19). If you were a leper, which do you think you should do to be healed? You can't figure that one out on your own. Only God can give you specific direction which will set you on the path to cleansing and freedom.

If I needed healing, I would first pray based on Colossians 1:9-11: "Father, I ask you to fill me with the knowledge of Your will in all wisdom and spiritual understanding, so I might walk worthy of You, Lord, unto all pleasing, being fruitful in every good work, and increasing in the knowledge of God. I pray I will be strengthened with all might, according to Your glorious power, unto all patience and longsuffering with joyfulness. Reveal to me the wisdom I need to speak a sure word from Your Word, that I may live."

I would pray this way first so God could commission a word for me and show me what I should say about my situation. Only then would I begin a study in the Bible on healing. I wouldn't need a "me word" or a "you word," I would need a "God word"—a word of wisdom that could mix with my inheritance in Christ and bring me deliverance from the hand of my enemy, in this case sickness and disease.

If you ask, God will give you wisdom so you can target the one verse or scripture He has anointed for your situation. Wisdom will rise up from that one phrase or scripture, and it will be the word of wisdom you should speak in the midst of your trouble.

You don't need to throw the whole Bible at your problem. If you do, all you'll have is confusion, but if you allow God to give you what to say, what to believe and what to pray by the word of wisdom, you will not fail. You will conquer tribulation and rise to victory every time.

You have to recognize that when God says a word to you, and then you say it to your storm, it's as if God Himself is speaking it to the storm. The Lord told you He would put His Word in your mouth. Thank God His Word in your mouth does what it would do if He were there in person to say it for you!

When you speak something on your own, your power is all you have to depend on, but when you speak a word sent from the throne of God, it is as if He is standing right there with you dealing with the situation Himself. You need to wait for a word of wisdom revealed from Heaven that will ignite your confession and put faith in motion in this powerful way.

How long will it take? As long as it takes! You can lose quickly or you can take your time and win. I think I'd rather win. Don't let a clock or a calendar direct your steps, but let the Spirit of God do what He needs to do in the time He needs to do it.

I encourage you to step up to the bow of your storm-tossed boat with the Holy Spirit, and let Him speak through you by a word of wisdom. Let it not be you who speaks anymore, but the Spirit of Christ who speaks through you. Then go a step further and be like Jesus, and let it not be you who lives, but the Spirit of Christ who lives through you.

A MIRACLE RELEASED

I remember a time when a woman in our church and her husband called me to their home to pray. The woman had just been diagnosed with an incurable disease, and she believed if I would pray, she would be healed. This is what her mind told her she needed, but as I stood outside their front door, the Spirit of God told me not to pray, but to instruct them instead.

When she came to the door, I knew I was in trouble. She had this expectant look on her face that I knew would disappear in just a few moments, and I knew I would be the reason it left. She and her husband invited me to come in and sit down, and we all managed to make small talk for awhile. She offered me cake, which I refused to eat because I did not have the stomach for it at that moment, knowing what I was about to say. Then she told me her story, in great detail; all the symptoms and all the problems—all leading to the prayer of faith, or so she thought.

Finally, the moment of truth came. They asked me to pray, and I had to answer, "No, I'm not going to pray, but I am going to tell you what God told me to say." I watched their jaws drop in disbelief, but I trudged on. I told them, "As I stood outside your door, God told me not to pray, but to tell you to look up all of the scriptures on healing. Well, I've got to go now."

I wasn't really quite that abrupt, but I'm sure it seemed like it to them. I stood to my feet, made my way to the door and headed to the car as quickly as I could.

Weeks later, this same woman shared her testimony in our church. She started off by saying she had been furious with me that day. Here she was, diagnosed with a life-threatening disease, and I refused to pray. And to make matters worse, I refused to eat the special cake she had bought just for me. (You don't want to mess with a woman with a special cake!)

She said she immediately called her mother to complain about me. Much to her surprise, her mom did not get on the band wagon with her, but instead suggested that maybe she should do what God told me to tell her to do.

So, she did. She and her husband spent the next several days looking up and reading healing scriptures. They read and read, until one day, they both got a revelation. At different times and in different places, God showed them each a verse, and a light went on in their spirits. The husband came home and said, "Look what I found!" At the same time the wife was saying, "Look what I found!" Lo and behold it was the same verse. God gave them revelation and wisdom, and they knew what to do.

They began to speak that verse to her body, and very soon, she went back to the doctor and discovered she no longer had this incurable disease. She was completely whole! Using God's wisdom, this couple worked a miracle.

The wisdom of God is always available for you, just as it was for this woman, if you will simply ask Him for it. James 1:5 says: *"If any of you lack wisdom, let him ask of God, that giveth to all men liberally, and upbraideth not; and it shall be given him."*

Don't ever try to govern your life with your own human wisdom, but let the wisdom of God direct your steps and guide you down the path to victory. Let it be said of you as it was said of Jesus: *"Whence hath this man this wisdom, and these mighty works?"* (Matthew 13:54).

HARVESTING FAITH

Another account where the word of wisdom brought a miracle to someone in need is recorded in Acts 14:7-10: *"And there they preached the gospel. And there sat a certain man at Lystra, impotent in his feet, being a cripple from his mother's womb, who never had walked. The same heard Paul speak: who stedfastly beholding him, and perceiving that he had faith to be healed, said with a loud voice, stand upright on thy feet. And he leaped and walked."*

Here we see how a word of wisdom can successfully harvest the faith of another. Paul relied on a word of wisdom, because only God knew what it would take to get this man to release faith and get back up on his feet. When Paul spoke that word, faith soared and a miracle was manifested.

The word of wisdom is still used today to spark faith and send people in the right direction. This is what often happens in miracle services when you hear someone say, "Now, get up and run!" and then someone pops up out of a wheelchair and runs around the sanctuary. Was that a good guess? No, it was the wisdom of God that revealed what the person in the chair needed to hear to launch their faith and receive their miracle.

Elijah was moved to use this same principle when he encountered the widow woman at Zarephath (see 1 Kings 17:8-16). God gave him a word which was designed to release this woman's faith.

The Lord said to Elijah: *"Arise, get thee to Zarephath, which belongeth to Zidon, and dwell there: behold, I have commanded a widow woman there to sustain thee."* God had commanded this woman to sustain the prophet, but she needed a word of wisdom to release faith in the command.

Elijah gave it to her when he declared: *"Fear not; go and do as thou hast said: but make me thereof a little cake first, and bring it unto me, and after make for thee and for thy son. For thus saith the Lord God of Israel, The barrel of meal shall not waste, neither shall the cruse of oil fail, until the day that the Lord sendeth rain upon the earth."*

This widow woman had nothing more than this simple promise—a single word of wisdom to carry her through to a miracle. She did as the prophet told her, and when she did, her miracle was released, and she, her son and the prophet all ate well during the remainder of the famine.

God gave a word to Elisha for another widow woman in 2 Kings 4:1-7. This woman's sons were about to be sold into slavery to pay off the debt her husband had left behind, but Elisha intervened with a word of wisdom that not only paid those debts, but left her with enough money to run her household, too.

This word of wisdom released her faith in a dimension which could not have been released without it. To borrow pots and pour the little bit of oil she had left from pot to pot until they all overflowed was not a man-made idea; it was a God-sent word of wisdom.

If you read the story, you will notice the woman ran back to the prophet after she poured the oil and asked him what to do next. She realized that she needed the rest of the word to complete the miracle, so she did not dare try to figure it out on her own. Elisha told her what to do; she obeyed, and the miracle not only paid for what she owed, but gave her plenty to live on. One simple word brought this great harvest of faith.

I think we would all agree that salvation is the greatest miracle harvest of all. With this understanding, wouldn't it be a good idea to depend on the word of wisdom when you are witnessing to someone? Let me give you an example.

Let's say you've been trying to reach someone for Jesus, but you can't seem to break through. Why don't you take the time to pray and ask God for a word of wisdom before you see them the next time? Ask Him to show you what they need to hear, and then say it.

Sometimes the blindness in an unbeliever's heart is so dark and deep, it will take more than one or two words of wisdom to break through, but don't give up. Just keep pressing in. Keep saying what God shows you to say. One day, those words of wisdom will break through and the harvest of faith will bring salvation.

A word of wisdom can also be sent from the pulpit to harvest faith on a normal Sunday morning. The next time your pastor stands up and says, "This is what God directed me to preach," remember what he's really saying is that the Lord has given him a message filled with wisdom that will spark faith in you.

Sometimes God will give your pastor a word of wisdom that will shake you up, and on other occasions he will give a word that will set you free, but in each case the word of wisdom is designed by God to help you harvest faith for your own miracle.

WISDOM FOR YOUR CHILDREN

The word of wisdom will work just as effectively in your home if you will allow it to. Wisdom is instruction. It is direction. It is a word that will make your knowledge and your faith work together. A word of wisdom can give you just what your child needs to hear to get over the hump if he's struggling with a certain subject in school. It can also show you how to handle discipline when a child rebels and tries to go the wrong way.

The word of wisdom is especially important when you have been given discerning of spirits concerning your child. God has revealed a problem, but how do you fix it? This is where the word of wisdom takes over.

This gift is extremely necessary when it comes to building faith in your children and then harvesting that faith for breakthroughs in your family. First Corinthians 3:10 tells us : *"According to the grace of God which is given unto me, as a wise masterbuilder, I have laid the foundation, and another buildeth thereon. But let every man take heed how he buildeth thereupon."*

God is the great heart builder. He is the one who places a new heart in your child and removes the heart of stone. Knowing this, you need to be very careful and allow words of wisdom to release the hand of God to build faith in his or her heart. All of your children are different because the Lord has a divine purpose for each one. They will not fit into the same mold, so you will have to adjust how you deal with each personality.

I cannot tell you how to handle your child on a day to day basis because he was not born to me. Your child was born to you, and therefore God has empowered you to meet your responsibility to raise him in the nurture and admonition of the Lord by giving you access to the word of wisdom on a daily basis.

You may want your pastor to be your answer, but he can't be. You have to invest the time necessary to hear from God about your child, using the word of wisdom wisely. You have been empowered, but you have to use what you have been given. No one else can do it for you.

Be wise in the ways of God in order to develop the different personalities which have been divinely selected and positioned in your family for such a time as this. God can show you who they are, but you can only develop, mold, build, construct, create and form them as vessels meet for the Master's use by using the words of the Wise Craftsman.

Remember, there is a price to be paid for the operation of the gifts of the Spirit. The cost is the same no matter what gift you desire. That price is your time invested; time in the Word, time in prayer, time in meditation of the Word and time spent fasting for the release of the gifts.

Children are a divine gift from Heaven—God's precious treasures lent to you for a short time. With His gift, the Lord has given you a divine covenant in the Word and promised to empower you to raise your children. His desire is to help you equip them and release them like arrows from your home, fully prepared to find their mark and reach their destiny in God (see Psalm 127:4).

The thought of destiny is great, but raising children happens one day (one chance to correct and discipline) at a time. Too many parents lack the word of wisdom when it comes to godly correction. More often than not their discipline is accompanied by a word of anger, a word of disappointment, a word of discouragement or a word of irritation, but not a word of wisdom which will reveal how to deal with the rebellion that has been manifested in your child. If you get a word from Heaven about how to correct a child, this rod of correction will reorient the disoriented spirit of that child and will actually be a comfort (see Psalm 23:4).

Does the rod of correction always mean spanking? Not always, but it can definitely include a warm hand on the padded bottom of your child. Spanking is not always the answer to every problem, but when delivered in love and not anger, I am convinced spanking is definitely the answer to many problems (see Proverbs 13:24).

God will give you wisdom to know not only how to correct, but also how to develop the spirit of your child. For instance, if your child resists getting dressed in the morning, you need to know why. Is he rebelling against your authority, or could there be another reason?

If you have a leader on your hands, his resistance may not be against you, but against the fact you do not give him a choice in the matter. For this child, diffusing the morning "get dressed" argument may be as simple as giving him

291

two outfits to choose from. Giving him this choice is not giving in, but is actually helping him develop his leadership skills.

However, for a rebellious child, this will not work at all but will simply feed his rebellion. How will you know the difference? Only by asking God and waiting for the word of wisdom. No two children can be dealt with in exactly the same manner. A word of wisdom for one will not necessarily translate to the next one. You will need to seek God for the heart of every child in every situation.

When God gives you a word of wisdom, your parenting problems will begin to fade, because a word from God is sharper than any two-edged sword (see Hebrews 4:12). It pierces and divides asunder. It slays and sets up rule. It discerns and breaks down the soulish dominion and exalts the spiritual lordship of every man, woman and child.

When you get a word of wisdom from God, He will tell you what to say to your kids. He will show you how to deal with them successfully, and He will teach you how to live together peaceably. Thank God He has given you this great gift.

A WORD OF WISDOM FOR YOUR MARRIAGE

You need a word of wisdom to show you how to love and care for your spouse, too. God can give you a word which will allow you to live well and make your partner happy. He can also show you how to be what your spouse needs you to be in every situation.

Holy matrimony is God-ordained, and you cannot have a good marriage without the Lord's involvement. If you don't believe me, try this: Go buy a new car, the car of your dreams. Then, because you love that car and you want to take care of it, ask the car dealer for a detailed manual to help you do what's right for your shiny new vehicle.

Let's say you bought a Chevy, but the dealer hands you a Ford manual. Will that work? No way! Neither will trying to handle a marriage with the wrong instruction book. When you try to maintain a spiritual union with natural laws, you will fail. Your marriage will only be successful when the wisdom of God rules in your home. You cannot have a divine covenant with your mate unless you live by the divine wisdom of God.

What makes your spouse tick? What makes him or her happy? You may think you know, but God really knows. Why not ask Him to show you what would bless, empower and encourage your mate? Just as every child is different, so is every man and woman. Is your mate a leader or a follower? Trying to treat a follower like a leader will bring unnecessary frustration. Let the leader lead and let the follower follow.

You cannot change your mate's core spiritual make-up, that God-given design which is set for eternity. For example, if God made your wife merciful, you are not going to change her by berating her for her behavior. Let your wife love on people, and don't judge her for feeling their pain. By the same token, if God made your husband a server, don't be upset when he wants to help at every church event. This is what God has given him to do, so encourage him and tell him you're proud of him, but don't chastise him because he spends his Saturday afternoon feeding the hungry instead of cleaning the garage.

Learn to live with the gifts and talents God has given your mate, and stop trying to change them. Allow God's wisdom to teach you to become one with your mate in covenant relationship, and learn how to make the most of the traits and characteristics God has given each of you. A word of wisdom will help you build spiritual maturity and character, doctrine, faith, love and power in your marriage, and it will help you recognize and appreciate the spiritual gifts God has given both of you.

I am so grateful the Lord has given me words of wisdom for my wife over the years. I know I cannot fulfill her triune being on my own, and I know I will never be who God wants me to be in her life without His input. Because I love my wife, and I want to be what she needs me to be, I believe the word of wisdom for me is worth the investment of my time. I believe it is worth the prayer, fasting and waiting it takes for it to be loosed in my life on a regular basis. I believe it is worth a focused, dedicated effort. I hope you do, too.

THE WISDOM OF SOLOMON

Perhaps the most well-known example of the word of wisdom at work is the story of one powerful king and one defenseless bundle of joy.

Two harlots stood before the judgment seat of King Solomon, each claiming to be the mother of a tiny baby boy. The king listened to the real mother tell her story, and she wept as she described how she and her roommate had each delivered baby boys at nearly the same time. She recalled one very dreadful night when the other woman had rolled over onto her baby and killed him. Then, for reasons she did not understand, the woman had come to her bed and taken her son while she slept, and in the morning, claimed he belonged to her.

Solomon thought for a moment, and then he asked for a sword. As the women stood wide-eyed with fear, Solomon gave the command for the baby to be cut in half, with one half of his body to be given to each woman. The lying harlot nodded in approval, but the real mother of the child cried out and pleaded for him to stop and give the baby to the liar, rather than see the child die. Immediately Solomon awarded the boy to the real mother, discerning that her reaction was based on love, not on greed or lies (see 1 Kings 3:16-28).

Where did Solomon get such wisdom? In the verses that come before this story, we find the answer. God had appeared to Solomon in a dream, and He told him he could have anything in the world he wanted; all he had to do was ask. Look at Solomon's response: *"Give therefore thy servant an understanding heart to judge thy people, that I may discern between good and bad: for who is able to judge this thy so great a people?"*

God loved this answer, and He told Solomon He would not only grant his request for wisdom, but would also give him riches and honor because he had chosen so well (see 1 Kings 3:9-13).

You, too, can ask for wisdom from God, and He will give it to you; wisdom for your home, your family, your ministry, your decision making ability, your lifelong outcome and for your eternity. God is more than willing to grant your request and give you a word of wisdom for every situation that you face, preparing a way to victory and blessing you cannot attain on your own. This is what the wisdom of God is all about.

CHAPTER 18

THE SIMPLE GIFT OF PROPHECY

The woman who sat across from my desk was extremely nervous; that was easy to see. She fiddled with a tissue, moving it back and forth from hand to hand as if to try to soothe herself. I waited patiently for her to work up the courage to tell me why she had asked to see me on this day, but I knew it was not going to be easy for her.

Although she could not bring herself to look up, she finally blurted it out. Someone had called her out in a church service and prophesied to her. The gist of the prophecy was that she was going to be a world-wide healing evangelist, touching lives all over the planet. When she finished with her story, she looked up with an expectancy, as if I could tell her what to do to become this great minister.

I felt so sad for this woman, because I knew her, and I knew this prophecy was far from the truth. She was a faithful member of our church, and she and her family had been attending for years. This being true, I cared for her and for them, but I also knew her life far too well to believe this "word of the Lord." And more than this, she was having trouble believing it herself. After all, God had never told her this before, she admitted, and so when the prophecy came, it had been a huge surprise.

That was the special key for me, the surprise element. True prophecy which confirms a call will never surprise you, as we learned in a previous chapter. Sometimes, we have to be honest with ourselves. If an individual gives us a far-fetched prophecy we have never even dreamed of, we need to be sober-minded and give ourselves a big reality check. If you can't see it, it's not you!

We find proof of this truth in several verses, beginning in Romans 8:14-17: *"For as many as are led by the Spirit of God, they are the sons of God. For ye have not received the spirit of bondage again to fear; but ye have received the Spirit of adoption, whereby we cry, Abba, Father. The Spirit itself beareth witness with our spirit, that we are the children of God: And if children, then heirs; heirs of God, and joint-heirs with Christ; if so be that we suffer with him, that we may be also glorified together."*

Then 1 John 2:20 says: *"But ye have an unction from the Holy One, and ye know all things."* And finally 1 John 2:27 adds: *"But the anointing which ye have received of him abideth in you, and ye need not that any man teach you: but as the same anointing teacheth you of all things, and is truth, and is no lie, and even as it hath taught you, ye shall abide in him."*

The Spirit of God inside you is perfectly capable of letting you know what your gifts and calling are without the help of others, so if what someone says does not line up with what you already know through your own personal time with God, toss it aside and don't worry about it. This is what I had to explain to this hopeful, but frightened woman. She was not called to a world-wide ministry, and I knew it. The key was to gently convince her so she did not waste her time trying to be what she was not empowered by God to be.

There is nothing sadder than to see a life wasted as someone tries to apprehend what has not been destined for them to attain. It is far better for us to live in the reality of who we are and who God has anointed and empowered us to be than to dream for things that can never be so.

Remember the parable of the talents? As long as the man with two talents was productive, God considered him successful, and He blessed what he had done. It did not matter that he did not have five talents like the other, but what mattered is what he did with what he had.

The man with the one talent who was afraid and hid it, however, did not make God a happy camper. This man would have been considered just as successful as the other men if he had put his one talent to use, but because he buried it in fear, he was cast into outer darkness and missed his destiny in life and in eternity (see Matthew 25:14-30).

The moral of the story is this: Be who you are in God. If you are the five talent guy, rejoice. If you are the two talent guy, be glad. Even if you are the one talent guy, praise God for what He has given you, put it to work in the

Kingdom, and God will bless you for it; just don't waste your life wishing for what will never be.

THE GIFT OF PROPHECY

As we learned in an earlier chapter, prophecy is one of the more recognized and coveted gifts of the Spirit. This does not make it a more valued gift, but it does make it more important for us to focus on the dos and don'ts found in the Bible. We already made the distinction between the simple gift of prophecy and the five-fold gift of the prophet. You will prophesy if you are a five-fold prophet, but you do not need to be a prophet to operate in the simple gift of prophecy. Let me share the difference from scripture.

First, I want to show you an example of the simple gift of prophecy operating through someone who prophesied, but was not identified as a prophet. We find a great story in Acts 21:8-9: *"And the next day we that were of Paul's company departed, and came unto Caesarea: and we entered into the house of Philip the evangelist, which was one of the seven; and abode with him. And the same man had four daughters, virgins, which did prophesy."* Notice this scripture did not say Philip's daughters were prophets; it simply said they prophesied.

We already looked at a perfect example of a recognized prophet in Agabus, who is mentioned in the very next verse: *"And as we tarried there many days, there came down from Judaea a certain prophet, named Agabus"* (Acts 21:10). He was a recognized five-fold prophet, and there was an anointing which accompanied him that did not reside in Philip's daughters. They prophesied, not being prophets, but Agabus carried the mantle of a prophet in his life.

Let's return to 1 Corinthians 14:3 which shows us the real purpose of prophecy: *"But he that prophesieth speaketh unto men to edification, and exhortation, and comfort."*

Evidently, Philip's house was a place where the apostle Paul knew he could find rest, and could be edified, exhorted and comforted. The prophecies Philip's daughters offered did not give Paul divine direction, but they did give him encouragement on his way to fulfill the destiny God had bound him to by his personal relationship with Christ.

Agabus, on the other hand, had an entirely different role in Paul's life than did the daughters of Philip. While the young women gave comfort and edification, the prophet gave direction and confirmation of Paul's calling and purpose.

Paul's encounter with the daughters of Philip shows us something else significant about the operation of prophecy. It confirms that prophecy is a gift which can manifest in a home as well as in a church. Notice, Paul did not have to seek out a church service to be edified; he only had to visit a home where the gifts of the Spirit flowed.

All of the gifts of the Spirit are given to every man to be profitable in every area. They can operate in your life of witness, in your church life, your home life and even in your business life. The simple gift of prophecy can be a great tool to help you live the way God wants you to live, every day. Allowing prophecy to flow in your household can also make your home a place of refuge for your friends, even as Philip's house was for Paul, making prophecy a valuable gift that you can share.

WHAT IS PROPHECY?

The simple gift of prophecy is a divine utterance given to a believer by God and delivered to a certain person or people for their benefit. To prophesy is to speak under divine inspiration. Prophecy is divine, but it is delivered by human vessels. Since the gifts have been given to all to profit withal, every Spirit-filled Christian is a candidate to operate in the gift of prophecy.

Let's look at 1 Corinthians 14:3 again: *"But he that prophesieth speaketh unto men to edification, and exhortation, and comfort."*

Notice the message is not for you, but for "men," indicating it is for those who hear what God is saying. The Lord will use you to deliver the message, but the one who will benefit is the one who hears, not the deliverer.

Sometimes we try to establish spirituality in our lives by pointing to a message we delivered, when in reality it had nothing to do with us and everything to do with the one God wanted to hear the message. The donkey who spoke in Balaam's encounter with the angel was not the most spiritual vessel, just the one available at the moment (see Numbers 22:21-31). It would do you well to remember the donkey if pride starts to creep in. God will use imperfect human vessels in order to deliver divine utterances for the benefit of those who are facing life's struggles, but let's not elevate the messenger above the message.

The second part of 1 Corinthians 14:3 shows us the divine purpose of prophecy we touched on before. Prophecy edifies, exhorts and comforts the hearer. If you need these in your life and home, then you are a candidate for prophecy.

You can discern the spiritual climate of those you live with more than anyone else they know. Their friends and co-workers only see a glimpse of who your children and spouse really are, but you know the reality of the struggles they go through in daily life.

Sometimes you will be able to sense whether your spouse or children need a touch from God. When you perceive they need edification, exhortation or comfort, it's time to pray and ask God to speak to them through the gift of prophecy.

There have been many times when I have asked my wife to intercede for me and ask God for a word that will see me through whatever I am facing. I know my wife well enough to trust that she will only deliver a true word from the Lord to me and will never dare give me her own opinion. This is so important in our homes. We must be able to not only ask our spouses to intercede for us, but we must be able to trust them to deliver the unfiltered word of the Lord.

Your family is a part of the church, so there is no reason to resist the gift of prophecy in your life, but you should embrace it and look forward to its benefit in your household. We should all be seeking to operate in the level of prophecy those in our lives need, so there will always be an element of edification, exhortation and comfort available for them.

THE RIGHT ATMOSPHERE?

Many people believe the gift of prophecy requires a particular atmosphere, the accompaniment of a song and a certain level of goose bumps before it will flow in a church service, so they believe the same elements would be necessary for it to flow in their personal lives. This is the primary reason they dismiss it as not being practical for everyday life.

Who has the time to prepare a worship service in their home and create just the right atmosphere before a prophecy can come forth? We barely have time to wash our clothes or mow our lawn! The truth of the matter is that the gift of prophecy does not require a specific atmosphere to come forth. This is just a preconceived notion we have developed in our churches over the years.

Should we honor the presence of God? Absolutely. Should we seek Him with all of our heart? Of course, but we do not have to prepare a perfect atmosphere before God can speak to us.

In 1 Corinthians 14:1 we read: *"Follow after charity, and desire spiritual gifts, but rather that ye may prophesy."* If we are all commanded to seek to prophesy, then surely prophecy is available to every one of us, not just the one who manages to keep a certain atmosphere in his home.

When someone in your family needs an encouraging word from the Lord, they need prophecy to operate and flow through you. Your home should also be a supernatural reservoir for others in the Body of Christ. It should not be abnormal for prophecy to come forth through you to help those who visit you in their time of need.

Can you always know ahead of time and plan a worship service when prophecy is needed? No, but you can always be ready to allow this supernatural utterance to flow through you for the benefit of another, no matter how hard your day has been or how unspiritual you may feel at the time. Prophecy flows through imperfect vessels of clay. Not one of us is perfect, not even in a "perfect" worship service in the "perfect" atmosphere.

It's time for us to remove the limitations we have placed on the operation of the gifts of the Spirit and allow God to manifest them through us as He wills, not as we think He wills.

When people visit our homes, and we discern they are concerned about certain issues or are struggling in some area, we should gather to pray and expect that the supernatural gift of prophecy will go into motion to edify, exhort and comfort them. Our words cannot change their situation, but the divine word of the Lord can.

I'm not telling you we should have prophecy parties. Nor am I suggesting we try to mix the manifestation of the office of the prophet with the simple gift of prophecy. That's the kind of thing which happens at planned prophecy events.

In those gatherings, some people will try to prophesy direction to others and will attempt to dabble in areas where only the prophet is anointed to go. They forget that the simple gift of prophecy edifies, exhorts and comforts, period. It does not lead, guide and direct, or foretell extravagant future events.

I'm telling you this as a warning to be careful. Don't allow yourself to be misled by a self-proclaimed prophet in search of a following. If it looks like a fruit, a flake or a nut, it probably is! Stay away from carnal manifestations and allow the genuine gift of prophecy to edify, exhort and comfort the brethren when they visit your house, allowing God to make it a refuge and a safe harbor from the discouraging world in which we live.

There is nothing wrong with receiving an encouraging word from a brother or sister in the Lord, and there is nothing wrong with being a vessel that God can use to deliver the same to someone else through you. If we stay within our gifts and callings, as Philip and his daughters did, we can be used as they were to build someone up on their journey in life. We can all be used, as long as we are willing, Spirit-filled vessels.

ENCOURAGING WORDS

In Luke 1:41-45 we find an encouraging word delivered as a prophecy from Elizabeth to Mary, the mother of Jesus: *"And it came to pass, that, when Elisabeth heard the salutation of Mary, the babe leaped in her womb; and Elisabeth was filled with the Holy Ghost: And she spake out with a loud voice, and said, Blessed art thou among women, and blessed is the fruit of thy womb. And whence is this to me, that the mother of my Lord should come to me? For, lo, as soon as the voice of thy salutation sounded in mine ears, the babe leaped in my womb for joy. And blessed is she that believed: for there shall be a performance of those things which were told her from the Lord."*

Elizabeth is never called a prophet in the Bible, but here we see her being filled with the Spirit and prophesying to Mary. This divine utterance was designed to edify, exhort and comfort Mary. God also used this utterance to confirm the word of the Lord which had been delivered to her by an angel.

Mary must have been under great duress at this time. She had just been told that though she had never known a man, she would conceive and bear a son by the power of the Holy Spirit. Having an encounter with an angel was great, but you know as well as I do that when the light of the angel left the room, Mary's faith was tested.

So off Mary went to see her elder cousin Elizabeth, probably expecting to find comfort there before she had to tell her family. She knew that eventually she would have to go back to face Joseph, her parents and her hometown, and she also knew the chances of anyone believing her were somewhere between slim and none.

I'm sure Mary carried all of these thoughts with her as she made her way to Elizabeth's house. Mary knocked on the door, and lo and behold when she stepped in the room the Holy Spirit fell, and Elizabeth prophesied, confirming everything Mary had come to tell her.

How comforting this must have been for Mary. How much relief she must have felt. In just a moment of time, God encouraged Mary to continue down the path He had prepared for her, and He strengthened her faith to succeed.

God encouraged Mary and Joseph through another prophecy after the birth of Jesus, this time in Luke 2:25-33. Here, a man named Simeon, again just a man, not a prophet, prophesied to Mary and Joseph, and his words comforted them and confirmed that Jesus was the Christ, the Son of God.

Jesus carried the destiny of God on His life, and it was the destiny of all mankind. If He somehow failed in His purpose, all men would be lost. Joseph and Mary were charged with raising the Son of God, which was an awesome responsibility, but God did not leave them to their own devices. He gave them a supernatural word of encouragement through the prophecy delivered by an old man named Simeon, so they could be strengthened to carry out the work set before them.

If you read the whole story, you'll notice that Simeon delivered his prophecy in the form of a prayer. He prayed and thanked God for allowing him to see the Savior, but the word was still prophetic because it edified and comforted Mary and Joseph. What Simeon said was a prophecy, even though he never said, "Thus says the Lord."

Prophecy is always an inspired word, but it does not always come in the form of a direct statement beginning with, "Thus says the Lord God." We say this in church to help bring verification, but in the Old Testament the only people allowed to say, "Thus says the Lord" were those in the office of the prophet.

These words do not necessarily verify a prophecy is real, but the impact of the utterance on lives will verify it. Was anyone edified? Was anyone exhorted? Was anyone comforted? These are the signs we look for to verify prophecy.

EDIFY, EXHORT AND COMFORT

The gift of prophecy can operate in any single dimension of its triune nature. In other words, prophecy can come forth as just a word of comfort, if that is what is needed. It can be just a word of edification or just a word of exhortation. The entirety of the gift edifies, exhorts and comforts, but at any given time, any portion of it can operate independent of the others.

Edification is simply building up or recharging, like when we recharge a battery. Edification does this with any emptiness of your heart and repairs any damage done. It restores zeal and rebuilds unfocused faith. Edification instills joy and reactivates dreams. It also destroys the work of the devil and fear.

Edification through prophecy refortifies and rebuilds the damaged walls in our lives which have allowed zeal, joy and faith to leak out. It literally shoots life back into a vision and a dream, reactivating one's focus on God.

The word "exhort" means to draw near, to rescue, to beseech or call back to the former place of purpose. It reunites the individual with faith and with God. It calls people out of the valley of decision and back to the place where they forsook the gifts and destiny that had been established for their lives.

Far too often, believers stop doing the ministry God has led them to do. They start in the nursery, and they drop out of the nursery. They join the choir, and then they leave the choir. They leave behind their destiny in times of tribulation. But then there are times when God speaks a word of exhortation to someone and the fire reignites. The flame rises back up, and they return to their former place of service for the Kingdom. This is the work of exhortation.

The word "comfort" means to encourage and to create a place of refreshing. To comfort is to give a word in due season. It provides something to speak and confess, and it revives and calls out. It encourages and removes the power of discouragement, because comfort stirs us to action, victory and the receiving of a crown.

You can deliver a prophecy by simply speaking a comforting word to someone in need. God can speak through you to comfort another, without any fanfare or goose bumps at all. None of us is smart enough to deliver a word in due season, but we can all be used in the gift of prophecy if we will open ourselves to its operation.

If someone came to you discouraged and left your conversation feeling better, it is very likely that somewhere in the process, God gave you a word of comfort, a prophecy which encouraged and set that person on sure footing again. If someone who was discouraged left your presence encouraged, you can bank on it, something supernatural happened. It was not you and your brilliant intellect; it was God and His words of comfort.

The gift of prophecy is a powerful gift that can do many amazing things. In reality, it is no longer a mere man speaking, but it is the Spirit of God speaking through that man. When God speaks this way, the word of prophecy feeds weak faith, heals wounded faith and realigns misguided faith. It also strengthens, refocuses, redirects, enlarges, restarts and reaffirms faith.

What's even more amazing is the fact you can allow the gift of prophecy to flow through you at any time, anywhere. The gift will do what God ordained it to do, whether or not the person you spoke to ever understands a gift has come forth. It doesn't matter if you get glory for your delivery, what matters is that God gets glory for His edification, exhortation and comfort.

You may have operated in the gift of prophecy and not even realized it because you did not shake, no one glowed, no one saw an angel, and yet your words edified, exhorted and comforted. Prophecy is not recognizable because of outward signs, but because of an inward touch.

When God fills you with a word of prophecy, you will want to hear it yourself. You'll want to keep talking after the word is finished just to hear some more, because it's not you speaking, but it is the Spirit of God speaking through you. This is why prophecy is a treasure which should be valued and treated with great care.

SUPERNATURAL LIFESTYLE

Prophecy is a supernatural utterance, but we do not need to make it appear so spiritual that its function will seem abnormal to us. You are a supernatural creature, one who has been born again and recreated in the image and likeness of God. As such, the demonstration of the gifts of the Spirit should be natural in your life.

You don't have to change modes or act differently just because a gift is in operation. The Holy Spirit has been in you since you were filled, so you don't have to try to change who you are when a gift flows through you.

Paul tells us: *"Even so ye, forasmuch as ye are zealous of spiritual gifts, seek that ye may excel to the edifying of the church"* (1 Corinthians 14:12).

Your family is a part of the church, and it is the mark of maturity when you begin to function in the gift of prophecy in your household for its edification. You cannot build a supernatural family, but God can. He can establish a family whose success is not based on outward attributes, but on the inward strength the Spirit of God provides.

None of us can impact our family members for eternity on our own, but the gift of prophecy can impact your spouse or your child for all eternity. Just to sit down and edify your son or daughter when they are going through tribulation, or to comfort your spouse in a time of sorrow; these are the things mature believers desire to do every day.

Only a word from God can truly edify and build up, truly exhort and encourage, truly comfort and increase strength. Only prophecy can deliver the heart of God.

Every time you deliver a comforting word that God has sparked in your heart, you have delivered a prophetic utterance that will change a life. Hearing God as He infuses the prophetic into your heart and your mouth is a great and humbling gift, because the gift does not help you, but it does help those around you who need it so much.

This is why Paul could say: *"Wherefore, brethren, covet to prophesy, and forbid not to speak with tongues"* (1 Corinthians 14:39).

We should covet the operation of prophecy in our lives, not for us and our glory, but for those we love and the glory of God. This is the simplicity of prophecy. The simple gift of prophecy exhorts, edifies and comforts. It builds, encourages and infuses strength. It is a divine utterance given through an earthen vessel, making it a wonderful example of the love of God.

Judging Prophecy

Allow me to make a slight turn here and begin to look at how to know for sure that a prophecy is truly a word from the Lord. Prophecy does need to be judged, because it is one of the most easily manipulated and misused gifts. The gift and its giver, which of course is God, are perfect, but the human vessels aren't always so. This does not mean we should fear prophecy, but we should judge it.

When judging a prophecy, always look to the Word. Is what was said scriptural, or did it veer off the norm? A true word from God will always echo scripture and lead the hearer back to the Word for more. It will never direct anyone away from foundational doctrine.

Start with yourself. The best way to judge if a word you deliver is a prophecy or not is to wait for awhile and ask the person you prophesied to an important question. Was what you said a help to them, or did it leave them more confused? If they remember and tell you that what you said really helped them, you're probably on the right track, but if they admit you confused them, you can be sure you probably missed it.

Don't give up or become discouraged, just keep praying and keep trying. You will not be perfect, but if you will stay open, you will find yourself ministering to those around you under a supernatural operation of an utterance given by God.

You must also be careful to judge every word given to you because there will be people who will miss it. Some will make simple mistakes, but others will be puffed up with pride and try to confirm things God never said, or try to establish things God has not ordained for your life.

Don't accept everything you are told just because someone says it is the word of the Lord. Always judge it and compare it with both the written Word and with what you already know in your heart to be true. Judging prophecy is very necessary. Its purpose is not to dishonor or disrespect anyone, but to provide a safeguard God expects you to use to protect yourself and your family.

Because I am a pastor and not a prophet, when I prophesy in my own church I am never offended if someone says, "No, Pastor, that's not me." I can miss it just like everyone else. I am not ashamed to miss it, but I would be ashamed not to try to help someone if I believed God had given me a word for them.

None of us will be perfect, because we are all changing from glory to glory. Each dimension of glory brings us to an area we've never encountered before, so there will be trial and error until we become more familiar with that new area. There will be a time of proving when God moves us into a new dimension of His glory. Mistakes will be made as we grow and exercise ourselves to function under this new covering of glory.

No one is exempt from mistakes. Only a fool will believe everything he says is from God, really is from God, every time without error. I would stay away from fools. I would stay away from people who are dogmatic that what they said to you was from God, even if it did not bear witness with you. It is not up to the one who delivers a word to verify its validity, but it is up to the one who hears to say yea or nay.

Never give in to someone who demands you accept their word as one sent by God. Such an attitude is nothing less than manipulation, a form of rebellion, which is as the sin of witchcraft (see 1 Samuel 15:23). God does not even demand we believe Him. He said in His Word that He set before us life and death, and that it is up to us to choose if we will believe or not. If God does not demand we do things, we should not let others make demands either.

CHECK THE FRUIT

Jesus gave this warning regarding those who say they have a word from God: *"Beware of false prophets, which come to you in sheep's clothing, but inwardly they are ravening wolves. Ye shall know them by their fruits. Do men gather grapes of thorns, or figs of thistles? Even so every good tree bringeth forth good fruit; but a corrupt tree bringeth forth evil fruit. A good tree cannot bring forth evil fruit, neither can a corrupt tree bring forth good fruit. Every tree that bringeth not forth good fruit is hewn down, and cast into the fire. Wherefore by their fruits ye shall know them"* (Matthew 7:15-20).

What fruits did Jesus mean?

First, before we believe anything said to us we must judge if the person who said it is living a good, holy lifestyle. You cannot receive a word of prophecy from someone you do not have confidence in. You must have faith in the messenger, so that the message can have an impact on your life. If someone comes up to me with a "word from God," and I do not have confidence in them because of the lifestyle I know they lead, I am polite, but I tune out what they are saying. If I do not have confidence in that person, I know God is not going to use that individual to give me a message from Heaven.

I have certain criteria about who I will receive a word from, and you should, too. I have certain convictions in my life, and I refuse to receive a word from people who live contrary to what I believe. I won't do it, and neither should you.

Second, you can judge their fruit by finding out if they have been accurate when they prophesied to other people. Have they prophesied a call on someone's life that was not real? If so, it's a red flag that the messenger does not know what he is talking about, and the prophecy is not from God.

Third, you can judge the fruit of a prophecy by asking if it agrees with scripture. Second Peter 1:20-21 says: *"Knowing this first, that no prophecy of the scripture is of any private interpretation. For the prophecy came not in old time by the will of man: but holy men of God spake as they were moved by the Holy Ghost."*

Every prophecy will agree with the written Word of God. It will never veer off course or establish new doctrine. That which is old is new again when prophecy comes forth, but it will never be truly new; it is only what has been established from the beginning and made to seem new by the Spirit of God.

Fourth, ask yourself if the prophecy bears witness with your spirit and with the gifts God has given you. It should never direct or try to re-invent what God has established in your life. Remember, the simple gift of prophecy will not initiate a call. It may confirm it and edify the one who knows that God called him, but it will not be the first sign of a call. God will call you, and you will know it before anyone ever utters a word of prophecy about it.

In 2 Corinthians 11:20 we are told: *"For ye suffer, if a man bring you into bondage, if a man devour you, if a man take of you, if a man exalt himself, if a man smite you on the face."*

Men can bring you into bondage with false prophecies. They can manipulate and devour you, use you and set you up to take advantage of you. This is why it is so important to judge them and know them by their fruit.

You do not want to be caught in a trap by one of these men. They try to control people by using words of "prophecy" to maintain power over them. Normally, this type of person will not be content to stick within the parameters of the simple gift of prophecy, giving out words of edification, exhortation and comfort, but will cross over and attempt to become a prophet, declaring the future, foretelling things to come and depositing gifts into people.

These false prophets are after one thing—a position of power and exaltation in your life. They will try to manipulate you and draw you away from your friends. They will want to be your only source of information, the only person who can find revelation in the scripture. They will try to be the only one with the proper interpretation of the Word, the only judge of right and wrong, the only one who can tell you when to go and when to stay.

These people are not operating in the gift of prophecy because the gifts of the Spirit operate in love, but they are operating in manipulation, rebellion and witchcraft. You need to flee from them.

People like this are quick to pick up on someone who has a great hunger and a need to hear something from God, a person looking for value in his or her life. They will use your insecurities and your low self-esteem to draw you into their web. If you fall into their trap, you will be drawn away from the truth of the Word and will find yourself in the midst of great trouble. If you have fallen into this trap already, run! Get away from them and put up a wall of protection to keep them away from you. This is not something to mess around with. Get away from those who are led by their own lust for power rather than by the Spirit of God.

HIDDEN FOR BATTLE

Let me end this chapter on a positive note by looking at a scripture we read briefly before. The verse is Luke 2:51, and it gives us a great secret for how to handle prophecies that deal with our God-given futures and destinies. The verse says: *"And he went down with them, and came to Nazareth, and was subject unto them: but his mother kept all these sayings in her heart."*

What sayings did Mary keep? She kept the prophecies of Simeon, a man who prophesied, and of Anna, a prophetess who also delivered a word of encouragement (see Luke 2:36-38). Mary held onto those prophecies as precious treasures. Though she received some of the greatest words of the Lord ever recorded, for the most part she kept them to herself. It is important for us to live as Mary did and hide certain things in our hearts, too.

When the gift of prophecy goes into motion, and God speaks to you to confirm certain things about your divine destiny, don't rush to shout it from the housetops. Keep it to yourself as Mary did. Keep it reserved for intercession and judgment, and for future battles.

Paul wrote to Timothy: *"This charge I commit unto thee, son Timothy, according to the prophecies which went before on thee, that thou by them mightest war a good warfare"* (1 Timothy 1:18).

Battles will come after a word of the Lord is delivered which will attempt to separate you from God's desired outcome. When a conflict arises, remind yourself of what the Lord said in the prophecy. You need to fight a good fight with the knowledge of what God said about you, but you do not need to proclaim it to everyone you know.

Sometimes Christians get themselves in frustrating situations that are not necessary because they proclaim their prophecies to all who will hear, sinner and saint alike. The trouble is, everybody will not be interested in hearing what God told you in a prophecy; not even most Christians.

Some of your greatest opposition may come from believers who think they know you, and from your closest family members. While counsel from your pastor and others in authority over you should always be welcomed, the unsolicited opinions of those not affected by the prophecy may try to derail your faith.

When you're not sure whether or not you should tell people about a prophecy, it's best to keep it to yourself. Use the prophecy to encourage yourself, but protect the word like a precious treasure, as Mary did. You will save yourself from many troubles if you do.

Let the true gift of prophecy edify, comfort and exhort you. Don't be afraid of it, but judge and use it as God leads. Prophecy is one of the nine gifts that have been given to profit you, so let edification, exhortation and comfort fill you, and fill others through you.

CHAPTER 19

GIFTS OF HEALING

I remember years ago when a young boy was brought to me for prayer. He was older than he looked because he was only about three feet tall, and his parents had been told he would not grow any taller. A rare disease had stunted his growth, and the doctors had no help to offer.

The young boy's mother brought him to me and asked if there was anything I could do for him. I told her of course there was something that could be done. We could pray, because Jesus had given us power over sickness and disease. We could do something, because God was with us! I never back down from a fight against the devil.

When this lady approached me I was in the middle of a healing line, so I told the boy to grab my belt and follow me. For the next 20 minutes or so, he followed hard on my heels, hanging on for dear life. Wherever I went, he went, and whatever I prayed, he heard me pray. Faith was growing in this boy. At the end of the line, I turned around and told him, "Praise God, you're gonna be okay!"

His mother took him home, and when they returned to the doctor for a scheduled visit, much to the doctor's amazement the little boy had started to grow, and he continued to grow until he reached just the right height for his age. This was years ago, and the last I knew, he was still growing because God is a healing God!

That young boy's dreams would have been crushed had not his mom brought him to a place where healing and miracles happen. Suppose he had dreamed of being a basketball player. How many three foot tall basketball players do you know? His dream could not be sustained without the gifts of healing going into motion on his behalf.

There are far too many children who never reach their potential. Their dreams are broken, and their futures are bleak because they are too sick.

Don't ever let the devil limit what your future is in God, and don't let him restrict what your children are going to do with the dreams that are in their hearts. God gives our children dreams and goals, but the devil tries to snuff them out. We must not let him! Don't allow him to win in your family when the gifts of healing are available to you for the asking. Release the gifts and let God restore the dreams!

THE GIFTS IN OUR LIVES

We've been discovering how God can speak to us through the gifts of the Spirit to help us in our daily lives. It should not be a strange thing for God to speak to us in this manner, but a very common, ordinary part of our way of living. In other words, we can have a family that lives in the supernatural very naturally.

Can you imagine raising John the Baptist without the help of the Spirit of God? Here was a guy who thought eating locusts and dressing in camel's hair was a normal thing. He spent his time far away from society, and he thought he was the voice of one crying in the wilderness for God.

How "normal" do you think he was as a child? Probably not very! I can only imagine how many hardships his parents avoided because they raised him under the guidance of the Holy Spirit instead of raising him based on their own limited intellect. Had they misunderstood who John was, they could have destroyed his gift, missed the direction of God, corrupted the fulfillment of prophecy for his life and left God searching for another man to cry, "Prepare ye the way of the Lord!" (see Isaiah 40:3; John 1:23).

Because John's mom and dad lived by the direction of God's Spirit, they were able to raise him to be all God had called him to be. Today, you and I may not fully understand who we are raising up for God's purpose in our homes, so we need to do our very best to hear from His Spirit and raise our children His way, too.

The operation of the gifts of the Spirit in our homes will help us encourage our children to develop their individual personalities, no matter how quirky they may be. The lives of our loved ones are too precious to leave to the devices of weak humanity, so we all need to be molded by the direction of God's hand for use in His Kingdom.

We need the voice of God in our lives and homes, in our work places and market places. We need His voice to ring out loud and clear so His purpose will be manifested and His desires fulfilled on earth.

One of the more unique ways God can speak to us is through the gifts of healing. The use of the word "gifts" in the plural sense indicates that there are many dimensions to this gift.

Gifts of healing are gifts, not rewards for good behavior or wages earned by effort. They are measures of grace given to men for divine purposes. They are not given because you are special or more spiritual than the next person, and they are not given because you are perfect and have all of your ducks in a row. Our entrance into Heaven does not require our perfection, so why should operating in the gifts of healing be any different? We enter Heaven by grace through faith, and we hear from God through the gifts of healing by grace through faith.

WHAT HEALING SAYS

What is God saying when He speaks through the gifts of healing? When He speaks this way, He reminds us He is a good God, and the God of all comfort and peace. He shows us He is the God who delivers us from all oppression and from every device of the enemy. He tells us He is the Mighty God, the Everlasting Father and the Prince of Peace. He is the Healer, the Provider, the Creator of all things. When God speaks through the gifts of healing, He says in an undeniable voice that He is love, and His mercies are new every morning.

God desires to speak through the gifts of healing in your life on a personal, daily basis in order to promote the well-being of your household, and speak through you as a witness in your community.

The psalmist said: *"Bless the Lord, O my soul: and all that is within me, bless his holy name. Bless the Lord, O my soul, and forget not all his benefits: Who forgiveth all thine iniquities; who healeth all thy diseases"* (Psalm 103:1-3).

Here God said He forgives all of your sins and heals all of your diseases. All means all. There are no trespasses or illnesses left out of this verse. When God speaks through the gifts of healing, He reminds you that healing is a part of your inheritance as a child of God, and the gifts of healing are inheritance benefits which can be bestowed on every willing believer.

As a part of your inheritance, the gifts of healing are just as available to you as is answered prayer. Would you ever expect to go a day without talking to God and receiving an answer? I don't believe so. So why then would you expect to go for days, or even months, without the gifts of healing being manifested in your life? You shouldn't.

The gifts of healing are as much a part of your inheritance as answered prayer is, and they should be as much a part of your daily walk as breathing in and out in prayer. They should not be unexpected events, but prayerfully anticipated interventions in your life.

Since God provided healing in our inheritance, we should be able to access it any time it is needed through the gifts of healing. We should be able to hear the voice of God above the voice of the adversary and become a witness to the world of His goodness.

PROTECTING BLESSING

God also says He cares for our provision when He speaks through gifts of healing. Today, there are thousands of Christians who are losing their retirement savings, their homes, their equity, their pocket money and the funds they have set aside for their children's education, not because it is God's will, but because sickness and disease are in the house.

One of the most rampant reasons for bankruptcies is overwhelming debt brought on by unpaid medical bills and the cost of prescription drugs. No one should have to choose between groceries and medicine. No one should lose a home to pay a hospital bill. No one should have to mortgage their future to pay for their yesterdays.

For those families who do not operate in the gifts of healing, the enemy could bring a devastating financial demise very quickly. Money is a tool, but when it is drained from a family's storehouse by the high cost of treating sickness and disease, the lack of it becomes a burden too great for many to bear.

If you are going to protect the blessing of God, you must allow the gifts of healing to have a place of access in your life. If you don't, and you allow the devil to continually defeat you in this area, every time you gain a little increase the enemy will come and snatch it away through some unexpected sickness. Remember, the thief comes to steal, kill and destroy, and sickness and disease are two of his primary weapons of choice (see John 10:10).

Before my wife Phyllis and I got saved, we figured out our medical bills one year and realized we could have been making a car payment on a new Cadillac instead of always paying for medical treatment. We spent hundreds of dollars a month on allergy shots and medicine for various things, because we were constantly sick. Much of our monthly income was lost trying to beat back one infirmity or another.

Sickness can steal your blessing, but it can also steal your life if you don't have the means to fight. I saw this in Africa many years ago when I met a young man at a clinic who had malaria. The nurse who examined him told me that if he did not receive treatment for his condition within 60 days, he would die. I asked her if she could treat him, and she sadly told me the clinic did not have any medicine for him.

I asked what the cost of the medicine would be, and she told me an incredible figure: $1. One dollar bridged the gap between life and death for this man. I had several dollars in my pocket that I would have willingly offered immediately, but because the medicine was nowhere to be found, this small clinic had no way to save this man.

As I watched him walk away, shoulders slumped in dejection, I realized his life was now valued at a mere 100 pennies. This is all it would take to save him, but lack of proper supplies was going to cost him his life. The disease was not incurable, but because there was no medicine, it was untouchable.

I'm not against doctors or the medical establishment. I thank God for the great health services we have in this country, but I do not believe we should have to depend on them solely for our well-being. Sometimes, as with this man, the medical community does not have the answer, but Jesus always does.

When the gifts of healing are in operation in your home, they protect the blessings of God which bring prosperity and well-being by maintaining your good health (see Proverbs 10:22). They safeguard your bank account and your ability to pay for future needs by shielding you from devastating medical bills. In some cases, they will also protect your life.

HEALING SHOWS LOVE AND BRINGS PRAISE

When the gifts of healing are in operation, they build a foundation of faith in God's love and provision for His people. For example, how can you convince a woman God loves her when you tell her He has all power, but she thinks He never shows up to use it for her benefit?

When the gifts of healing are manifested in a home, the members of that household will always remember, and they will hear God say, "I love you." If they are ever again faced with hopelessness, or with a death sentence from the world, they will know God is their hope, and they will turn to Him in their time of trouble. But when the gifts of healing are not in operation in a home or in a church, the voice of God remains silent. No one hears "I love you!" No one hears, "I am the Healer!" No one hears, "I can deliver you!" No one hears, and no one remembers.

If the gifts of healing are not manifested in your home, you are in effect teaching your children to turn to other sources. No wonder we have Christian children calling the psychic hotline. We've never demonstrated the gift of prophecy, the word of knowledge, or any manifestation of the gifts in our homes, so where do we think our generation will turn if we don't show them?

As Christians, we are made in God's image and have been created to live by the voice of God available in every gift of the Spirit. We have a built-in hunger for the supernatural, and we need to hear a supernatural voice calling from the gifts of the Spirit.

This is why lost humanity reaches out to the unknown regions of darkness. They have a gnawing inside that drives them to search for answers, too, for a supernatural connection and for something greater than themselves. We need to make sure we demonstrate the gifts of healing in our homes and lives so we will shine as a light on a hilltop and show our families, our neighbors and the world that the only way to fill the void is with Jesus.

One of the most important reasons we need to allow the gifts of healing to flow in our lives can be found in Matthew 9:6-8: *"But that ye may know that the Son of man hath power on earth to forgive sins, (then saith he to the sick of the palsy,) Arise, take up thy bed, and go unto thine house. And he arose, and departed to his house. But when the multitudes saw it, they marvelled, and glorified God, which had given such power unto men."*

When you operate in the gifts of healing, you create a place of praise and testimony. People do not sing praises to God when they are smitten with sickness and disease, but they do shout to God when they are delivered.

Jesus said something very powerful, recorded in Luke 13:16: *"And ought not this woman, being a daughter of Abraham, whom Satan hath bound, lo, these eighteen years, be loosed from this bond on the sabbath day?"*

Sickness is bondage. It binds you up and hinders you in every area of life. The bondage of sickness steals your desire to pray, praise and read God's Word, because when you're sick all you want to do is lie around and sleep. Sickness is an instrument from hell which steals the very focus of your life, but the gifts of healing are spiritual tools God has given you to combat the devil's plan and return the song of praise to your home.

The gifts of healing are often the birthplace of praise in our lives, and they are a testimony of God's goodness which cannot be denied. If someone is healed in your house, and they stay healed forever, it will always be a testimony to everyone who visits your home.

Your grandchildren will hear the story of how good God was when He healed Aunt Susie. Everyone who crosses your threshold will know how God visited your house and brought a word of love when He healed her affliction. And later in life when unbelief tries to rear its ugly head, your family will rise up and tell the story of the healing that took place before, and they will stand firm in faith instead of caving in to the pressure to give up.

Your household will always be a place of testimony and praise, and it will become a refuge others seek out in their time of need. When we operate in the gifts of healing and allow God to speak to our families in such a powerful way, we unloose the wellsprings of thanksgiving and praise for generations to come.

Gifts of healing bring a joy unspeakable, filled with God's glory. They restore peace and blessing, and they fortify faith. Once the goodness of God touches your life and you rise up whole, well and sound, I guarantee you are going to make a noise of some kind, a joyful noise unto the Lord!

HEALING IS A TEACHER

The apostle Paul tells us: *"Those things, which ye have both learned, and received, and heard, and seen in me, do: and the God of peace shall be with you"* (Philippians 4:9).

When we operate in the gifts of healing, it gives our family members

317

examples of how to protect themselves, their homes, their children and their own families from the attacks and works of the devil. It teaches them God is their source, and that there is nothing too hard for Him. It prepares them to be a generation of demonstration of His healing power instead of being only dreamers and well-wishers to those who need help.

I remember when my daughter Nicole was about seven years old. It was summertime, and she would ride her bike around the neighborhood visiting people. When she would find a neighbor who was sick, she would immediately ride home, grab the oil bottle, jump back on her bike and go pray for them.

One day I received a call from a woman who told me this story. She said Nicole had come to visit her and had discovered she was not feeling well. The lady said Nicole ran out of the house, and then reappeared a few minutes later with a bottle of oil. The woman reported that Nicole poured some oil on her hand, slapped her on the head and said, "In the name of Jesus, be healed!" Then Nicole looked her dead in the eye and said, "Now get up off this couch and go to work, and believe like God did something."

I remember another time when Nicole came into contact with a man whose hand was crippled from arthritis. His fingers were curled inward, and as he visited with Nicole, he was complaining about the pain. Without so much as a warning, Nicole grabbed his hand, bent his fingers back and shouted, "Be healed!"

The man jumped to his feet and yelled out, "That hurt!" But do you know what? The man's hand was healed from that very moment! Someone with no intention of asking for anything from God was impacted by a young child's faith, all because she was exposed to the gifts of healing in her home.

God is our compassionate deliverer. He cares for us and longs to move on our behalf. It is up to us to live by example, to show the world who God is and to reveal how much He loves them. It is our responsibility to make sure His voice of healing is a prominent voice in our homes, churches, neighborhoods and cities. We need to lead by example, so others will be followers of us as we are followers of Christ (see 1 Corinthians 11:1).

When we encounter sickness, we need to do as Jesus did when He entered Peter's house and found Peter's mother-in-law smitten with a fever. Most Christians would have patted her hand and said, "Well, I hope everything will be alright," but Jesus walked over, confronted the work of the devil, loosed the gifts of healing and rebuked the fever. The fever left her immediately, and she rose up and ministered to them.

We should not be afraid and lurk in dark corners when we enter the home of a loved one afflicted in some way, but we should demonstrate the love of God through the gifts of healing and let the name of Jesus raise them up for a testimony. In Jesus, you are more than the devil can handle. You are more powerful than sickness and disease!

Jesus showed us who we are in Matthew 10:1: *"And when he had called unto him his twelve disciples, he gave them power against unclean spirits, to cast them out, and to heal all manner of sickness and all manner of disease."*

He did not send the disciples out with speculation, but Jesus sent them with a purpose to go and do what He had done. We have this same call according to John 14:12: *"Verily, verily, I say unto you, He that believeth on me, the works that I do shall he do also; and greater works than these shall he do; because I go unto my Father."*

It's not enough to know, but we've got to go and do. Jesus did not expect the disciples to leave anyone sick and diseased when they preached. He expected the disciples, His sent ones, to touch people and leave them healed and delivered when they left town.

If you name the name of Jesus as Lord and Savior, you are a disciple, a sent one, and you have the same call to go and do as the disciples did. You are sent to your home, your neighborhood, your workplace and your city. You are sent to win and bring back the spoils of the enemy. You are sent with the voice of God in your hands.

It's time to shake off fear and feelings of low self-esteem. You may not be anything in and of yourself, but join the crowd; none of us are anything all alone. Only in Christ can we do all things as He strengthens us. Only in Him can we reach out and touch a lost and dying world. Thank God you are no longer alone, but you are fully equipped in Him. It's time to take what you have and give it to those who need it so much.

RELEASING THE GIFTS OF HEALING

Now that we know that we should operate in the gifts of healing, the obvious question is, "How do we release healing into the lives of those we love?"

Some of you may think these gifts only operate in a perfect home, in a perfect environment and in a perfect time. The only trouble with such a theory is that no one would ever be healed if they had to meet those conditions. You do not need to be perfect for God to speak through the gifts of healing, but you do have to be knowledgeable and sincere.

The gifts of the Spirit are released at the discretion of the Holy Spirit, but they are also released by the act of your faith. The Holy Spirit desires to release the gifts into the lives of every Spirit-filled believer who puts his or her faith in motion, but His desire is often hindered by our lack of faith or lack of understanding.

We need to learn how to release what has been given to us, allowing the gifts of healing to operate in and through us for the glory of God. It's pretty simple, really, because the gifts are released by faith, by the words of our mouth and by our unwavering stand on the Word of God.

My wife Phyllis has a tremendous testimony in this area. Years ago she was diagnosed with an incurable disease. When the diagnosis came, though it was unexpected and hard to wrap our minds around, we did not give in to the fear the enemy wanted to sow in our hearts. We talked about what we were going to do, made a decision based on God's Word, and we stuck to it for one very long year.

Sometimes the days were tough, and the pain my wife endured was hard to describe, but we never backed down, because we knew that God was a healing God and His gifts of healing were in operation, even though we could not see the results with our eyes.

We knew that healing was the children's bread and by His stripes we were healed (see Matthew 15:22-28; 1 Peter 2:24). So, we did not shake, quake or faint, and we did not turn to medical science. At that time, the only thing medical science could offer was a round of treatments which would target the symptoms, but would bring no cure. The trouble with this system was that it would introduce five more side effects every time it dealt with one symptom. With this information, we made the decision to stand on the Word and depend on it to be our life-sustaining bread (see Matthew 4:4).

When we refused the treatment option, the doctor told Phyllis she would be confined to a wheelchair within six months, and that she would be in excruciating pain for the rest of her life. He offered her high-powered pain relief, which she refused, but he could offer no way of escape. No matter what they would try, he warned us, it would not work effectively. In essence, they said there was no hope, which left us with only one option, the option of releasing the gifts of healing into our situation. And so, this is exactly what we did.

To loose the gifts of healing, we did several things. We put our faith to work, and we began to fight the fight of faith. It was not a quick fix, but was instead a very long journey we took together, one step, one moment at a time.

Day after long, painful day, my wife stood on the Word, and I stood with her. We spoke the Word over her body, and spoke nothing of the problem to anyone. Only those closest to us whose faith was like-minded were given information for the purpose of prayer. No one else needed to know what was going on.

Every day we released the gifts of healing with the words of our mouths. We did it by speaking the Word, and by prayer. At 5:00 A.M. every day I would wake up and lay my hands on my wife before I left the house.

I would say something like this: "In the name of Jesus, I release the gifts of healing in my wife's body. This disease will not win because it is defeated. I loose the gifts of healing into her body afresh this morning. I loose them to go into every fiber of her body, into every organ, every bone, every cell, and every ounce of her marrow.

"She will live, and she will not die. Devil, you are defeated. The gifts of healing are moving through her body, and they are restoring and bringing long life to her. The blood of the Lamb declares her healed, and it is the witness that she is the redeemed of God; therefore, sickness and disease have no place in her life. She is my wife, and she will see her grandchildren grow up. She will not go to an early grave, but she will live to go up in the rapture. She will not go by the way of the devil; she will go by the way of God!"

Every time she battled the pain during the day, I would lay hands on her again. Phyllis was diligent to speak the Word over herself continually. She kept the Word before her eyes, in her ears and coming out over her lips. Together, we kept loosing the gifts of healing in her body daily. Daily!

Day after day after day, enduring bad report after bad report, until one day she left the house to see the doctor, and came home with news for me.

She said, "Get the kids together. I need to tell you something." Immediately, my brain said, "Uh, oh! You've lost." Phyllis waited until our daughter and son-in-law could get there later in the day, then she sat us down at the breakfast table and said, "I just got back from the doctor, and I have news." She paused for effect, and then went on, "The blood work says there's no more disease in my body. It's over. I'm healed, and now the doctor says I'm healed." We rejoiced with tears of joy— joy that was unspeakable and full of glory. The gifts of healing had manifested, and the victory was ours!

Now, after victory came, I still got up early, and about every third day or so I would lay hands on her and thank God for her healing. I thanked God so she did not get sick again. I was no longer praying for the gifts of healing to be loosed for recovery, but for protection. I was not in a battle anymore to take her health back, but I was proactive and loosing the gifts to guard her health so that it could not be stolen again.

It's important to keep the gifts of healing flowing, even when sickness and disease are not knocking at the door. This is called maintaining divine health, and it is an operation of the Spirit just as much as healing and deliverance are. God wants you to not only get well, but to stay well all the days of your life.

KEEP THE GIFT IN MOTION

If you have sickness and disease in your house, you need to stand on the words of Jesus from Matthew 16:19 just as we did: "*And I will give unto thee the keys of the kingdom of heaven: and whatsoever thou shalt bind on earth shall be bound in heaven: and whatsoever thou shalt loose on earth shall be loosed in heaven.*"

You can loose the gifts of healing into a physical body, knowing that once you loose them, all you have to do is re-verify they are loosed, and that they are operative and moving. You don't have to ask God to redo what the gifts of healing have already done, but you do need to keep the gifts in operation by praying every morning as we did, laying hands on your body and decreeing what the gifts of healing have done for you.

There are many ways to loose the gifts of healing. When my daughter Nicole was young, we did this by playing healing scriptures on tape, instead of just relying on Tylenol™. We would play the tapes by her bedside all night long.

If the Tylenol™ bottle said to give it to her every four hours, we got up every four hours and gave her a dose, but we also gave her a fresh dose of the Word and the laying on of hands, loosing the gifts of healing again and again. We fought the fight of faith for her using our faith mixed with wisdom.

You can do it too! God has given you the gifts of healing to make you profitable against the schemes of the enemy. He didn't give you the gifts of the Spirit to lose in life, but to win and be successful.

When you lay hands on your children, begin to release the gifts of healing, trusting that whatever you loose on earth will be loosed in Heaven, and whatever you bind on earth will be bound in Heaven. God will honor your faith when you place your hands on them. Then you need to remain steadfast and believe that when you prayed and released the gifts on earth, God honored His Word and released them from Heaven. If you do, He will be faithful to you, and will see you through.

Our faith worked, and yours will too if you will do what we did and stand firm. Stand while the gifts of healing manifest fully in your body. Stand until victory overtakes defeat. Your faith won't fail if you refuse to give in. If you crumble, your faith will crumble, but if you stand, your faith will stand.

The gifts of the Spirit can undo anything the devil has ever done in your life. God did not leave you at the mercy of one who does not care, but He filled you with power to make sure you can make it through every trial and situation. The gifts of healing are yours today to use and benefit from. They are yours to treasure and loose in your home.

Your children and grandchildren will thank you because you taught them to do what is right. They'll thank you because they heard the voice of God manifested through the gifts of healing. They will thank you and serve God all of the days of their lives.

AVOID THE EXTREME

I want to insert a brief word of caution. The Bible is very simple and straightforward, but sometimes people take what they have heard others teach and move to the extreme on one side or another. There are some Christians, for instance, who believe the view that God does not heal anymore, and that the gifts of healing passed away with the disciples. This view leaves them totally dependant on medical science for their well-being, which is not a good place to be.

On the other hand, there are people who go to the other extreme and believe supernatural healing is the only answer, and that using the tools of medical science is a sin. Both of these extremes are wrong, and both can lead to tragedy.

I once heard the story of a man, the head of a Christian family, who denied his daughter the medical treatment she needed to treat diabetes. He would not let her take insulin, so unfortunately it wasn't long before this girl died. He thought he was walking in faith, but he was in fact walking in something else altogether.

I do not condone this kind of behavior at all. While we should pray and allow the gifts of healing to have a dominate place of access in our homes, we should never deny a family member medical treatment in a life and death situation.

The fight of faith is a real fight, and it is an exercise of faith. We are all at different levels in our faith walk. Some of us are strong in healing. Others are strong in witnessing. Some are strong in prosperity, while still others are strong in prophecy or other gifts of the Spirit.

When we are faced with a devastating diagnosis, we must be honest about our level of faith concerning healing and never, ever allow a life and death situation to go untreated if our faith is not developed enough to deal with the situation.

Do not make your children walk in your level of faith. You can use your faith for your children right where they are. If they need medicine, you give it in faith. Don't try to leap mountains if your faith or your child's is only strong enough to leap molehills. Use wisdom, and be honest about where you are in life. Having said that, don't use your small faith as an excuse to abandon faith altogether. Get in the Word and build your trust and belief. You can exercise your faith even while you seek medical treatment.

In the case of the little girl whose father denied her medical treatment,

324

the insulin would not have healed her, but it also would not have hindered her faith. What this man needed to do was allow the insulin to deal with the present symptoms so that she could have lived another day to fight the fight of faith. This family was wrong, and I would not have done acted as they did, but they are an example of what can happen if you fail to be wise concerning who you are and where your faith is.

Many times, medicine cannot heal an illness, but it can deal with symptoms which distract our faith, the very faith that can bring healing. I once heard a respected spiritual leader say: "If you're sick, your faith probably hasn't worked. Use every source you can to get out from under Satan's power, and then build your faith so that sickness cannot come again."

We are on a journey, and we are being changed from glory to glory. While we strive for the best, we may need to walk wisely until we reach that state of glory where the gifts of healing are flowing freely in our lives.

KNOW YOUR ENEMY

It is essential to know what you are fighting. Paul made this wise statement in 1 Corinthians 9:26: *"I therefore so run, not as uncertainly; so fight I, not as one that beateth the air."*

Paul always knew who and what he was fighting. He knew when his problem was mere flesh and blood, and he knew when the enemy lurked behind the mask. To be successful in spiritual matters, you must understand what you are fighting, too.

It's no different when it comes to battling sickness and disease. This may surprise you, but when my body doesn't feel quite right, I don't guess and start rebuking devils that may or may not exist, (though I do keep my confession strong and my faith in motion). What I do is what you should do. I go to the doctor to find out what's behind the symptoms.

Once I know what I am fighting, I can speak to the mountain, just as Jesus said I could in Mark 11:23, and it will have to obey me. But if I am ignorant of the mountain's existence, I may die in its shadow.

Let me give you an example. Years ago a man in my congregation came to me and asked me to pray for him. He said he had been having problems with his stomach for quite awhile. Much to his surprise, I refused to pray, and I told him to go to the doctor to find out what was wrong first.

He persisted in asking for prayer, so I asked him what exactly I should pray for. For relief from gas? For healing of an ulcer? He finally got the point, went to the doctor and returned with a surprise diagnosis: colon cancer.

When he returned to tell me what the medical report said, I asked him what he believed now that he knew what he was fighting. He paused for a moment, then said, "I believe if you pray, the operation will go smoothly, the surgeon will be able to get it all, and I will recover quickly." I agreed, and we prayed according to his level of faith.

Sure enough, when time came for the surgery, he came through with flying colors. He recovered in record time, and he has been healed and healthy ever since.

Now, suppose we had just taken a stab at it and prayed for God to heal an ulcer that was not there. Would this man have lived? Probably not, but because he found out what his enemy was, he was able to make a decision based on his level of faith, and we were able to agree in prayer, loose the gifts of healing and watch God do what we had asked Him to do.

Don't ever fight the air. Go to the doctor and find out what's going on before you decide how to react and pray. Once you know your enemy, make a plan of attack and stick to it. Don't let pride make you reach for more than your faith can handle, and on the flip side, don't let fear hold you back from your victory either.

God is ready to meet you right where you are and take you over, through, around or under the mountain to the other side where victory awaits and long life is ready to sustain you. Be wise, and you will be the winner in the end!

CHAPTER 20

MIRACLES TODAY

Construction was under way! The men in camp were working hard, straining to make as much progress as possible every single day. After all, they were building a place to stay, and they were all tired of sleeping under the stars.

Along the way, two of the men went down to the Jordan river to cut some wood there. As one of them was about to strike a tree for the last time, the head of the axe he was using came flying off and dropped straight into the water. He cried aloud, *"Alas, master! For it was borrowed."*

The prophet Elisha was standing nearby and heard the man cry out for help. He asked where it had fallen, and then he did a very strange thing. Elisha cut down a stick and threw it in the river. I'm sure the workmen thought Elisha was a little off at that moment, until the axe head began to swim toward the shore right before their eyes. Yes, you read it right, the iron axe head swam to them. Elisha told the man to grab it from the river, and when he did, he stood silent and amazed at what had happened. "It's a miracle!" is what you would have expected someone to say, but they were all so dumbfounded, they simply returned to work without saying a word (see 2 Kings 6:2-7).

How many times have you heard someone say, "It's a miracle!" when what they were excited about was nothing more than a normal event in a normal day? I've heard it hundreds of times. Too often, our world today equates the word miracle with things like someone getting to work on time, or a man remembering his wife's birthday. Miracles, however, are so much more than conquering life's little challenges.

The word miracle is defined as "an act that turns about the natural course of things." A miracle alters natural events, and it overrides natural and material limitations. A miracle is simply an intervention of God's power which alters something that has already been set in motion, whether spiritual or natural, and turns it around for a victorious outcome on your behalf.

In the second chapter of John, Jesus told the servants at a wedding what to do to receive a miracle. He told them to go fill pots with water, and then to pour the water into wine pitchers and serve it to the wedding guests as wine. Why do you suppose Jesus told them to do such a ridiculous thing? He did it because He had a plan. He had a miracle up His sleeve, but He needed the servants to work with Him to get it done.

Thank goodness they did not know any better than to do what they were told. They did not even seem to mind that the water was still water when they filled the wine pots. Because they did as Jesus told them and followed through with His instructions, the miracle was worked when the water turned into wine as it was obediently poured out of the pots and into the pitchers.

This story shows us that miracles must be worked. First Corinthians 12:10 confirms the point: *"To another the working of miracles..."* Miracles don't just happen. They don't fall out of the sky when we least expect them or come upon us without warning. If a miracle occurs, somebody expected it. Somebody asked for it. Somebody worked it.

You may wonder if miracles can still be manifested today like they were in the Bible. The answer is an emphatic, "Yes!" Miracles are just as available and just as plentiful to those who know how to work them, and God is just as desirous to speak through miracles today as He was in the days of Elisha, whose iron swam, and in the days of Jesus, whose water turned into wine.

WORKING FAITH

There are several keys to working a miracle, and the first is found in Hebrews 4:11 which says: *"Let us labour therefore to enter into that rest, lest any man fall after the same example of unbelief."*

At first glance, this verse sounds like it's talking in circles. How can you labor to rest? How can you labor without getting into works? You do this by laboring the labor of faith. You work faith first to work miracles later. Faith and miracles go hand in hand, and you will never hear God speak through miracles without faith in motion first.

It's important to know you can work the working of miracles using your own fruit of faith, or you may work a miracle by the gift of faith going into operation. We'll look at working a miracle with your own fruit of faith primarily in this chapter, and we will look at using the gift of faith in the next.

The fruit of faith is a power, as if it was a muscle, a spiritual force which must be exercised. In this case you must have the kind of faith that comes by hearing and hearing by the Word (see Romans 10:17).

Another example is found in Galatians 3:5, a verse we will look at closely in this chapter. It says: *"He therefore that ministereth to you the Spirit, and worketh miracles among you, doeth he it by the works of the law, or by the hearing of faith?"* The obvious answer is that you work a miracle by the hearing of faith. In other words, faith must be released in order for a miracle to take place.

The first thing you'll have to concentrate on to make faith work for a miracle is your ear. You need to renew your mind by hearing the Word and filling yourself with faith. When you do this, you will establish a foundation of faith which will show you how to work in the elements that open the door for miracles.

In Proverbs 6:20-22 we read: *"My son, keep thy father's commandment, and forsake not the law of thy mother: Bind them continually upon thine heart, and tie them about thy neck. When thou goest, it shall lead thee; when thou sleepest, it shall keep thee; and when thou awakest, it shall talk with thee."*

Faith comes as you bind the Word to your heart by seeing it, hearing it and meditating on it continually. When you keep the Word bound on your heart it will speak to you and reveal the will of God, and faith will be established as a result.

If you will invest time, your faith will grow stronger, and when it does, it will be very difficult to diminish. It will be as if Hebrews 8:10 has come to pass in your life: *"I will put my laws into their mind, and write them in their hearts: and I will be to them a God, and they shall be to me a people."*

When God's will is written upon your heart, nothing will be impossible to you (see Mark 10:27). What God inscribes will stay there. Storms won't erase it. Deep waters won't wash it away. Fiery trials won't sear it, and darkness won't cover it up. God's Word will always be a lamp unto your feet and a light unto your path (see Psalm 119:105). You will build faith in your heart, and you will see miracles.

When Jesus worked miracles, most of the time He said, "According to your faith…" We think it is according to God's mood, but no, it is according to our faith. Now remember, we are not limited to our fruit of faith, but we can access the gift of faith when circumstances and situations are beyond the scope of our faith's limitations. (We'll discuss this in detail in the next chapter.) But still, miracles are always subject to the activation of some form of faith.

To live the life of the miraculous, it's not about us wishing or hoping, or about the sovereignty of God. It is not about some special favor we have discovered while others have not. In addition, it's not about working ourselves into position where God knows about us and decides to move on our behalf. No, it's about activating faith and standing firm until the miracle manifests. Miracles are waiting to be activated and released by faith, and when faith is in the house, miracles can be produced.

Just look at James 5:14-15 for proof: "*Is any sick among you? Let him call for the elders of the church; and let them pray over him, anointing him with oil in the name of the Lord: And the prayer of faith shall save the sick, and the Lord shall raise him up; and if he have committed sins, they shall be forgiven him.*"

It looks to me like this is a guarantee. What God needs is for our faith to be activated and for us to receive what He has prepared for us. If we will do what He requests, He will do what He promises, and miracles will be the result.

LET PATIENCE WORK

The second thing you will have to work to get a miracle is patience. James 1:2-4 says: "*My brethren, count it all joy when ye fall into divers temptations; knowing this, that the trying of your faith worketh patience. But let patience have her perfect work, that ye may be perfect and entire, wanting nothing.*"

You need to allow patience to have her perfect work in order for faith to come to its intended end. You cannot work a miracle independent of faith, so when you allow patience to work with your faith, you develop yourself in the working of miracles.

Hebrews 6:12 tells us: *"That ye be not slothful, but followers of them who through faith and patience inherit the promises."* Faith and patience work hand in hand, under-girding the working of miracles. Without faith, miracles won't happen, and without patience, faith will never produce God's desire.

So, to be effective as a miracle worker, you must be patient, diligent and steadfast. You cannot waver from one course of action to another and expect a miracle to manifest. If you find yourself wavering and moving from thought to thought, you need to go back to the beginning and re-establish what you found in the Word of God before you continue on in your miracle journey. This takes time, but with God, time is not an issue.

Again, miracles don't just happen. They come because we have faith they will happen, because we are patient and steadfast, standing firm no matter what happens around us, and because we believe when we activated the working of miracles, a miracle took place.

Now, understand, patience is not just sitting around waiting for something to happen. True patience is steadfast confidence, an unwavering state of mind which refuses to back down once faith has been activated. It is a single-minded, assured course of action that trusts that what God said, He will do.

As for God, He always has miracles waiting to be loosed. As we read in Psalm 84:11: *"For the Lord God is a sun and shield: the Lord will give grace and glory: no good thing will he withhold from them that walk uprightly."*

God, who gave His only begotten Son, will not withhold anything from you, but will give you any miracle and any manifestation of His Spirit you need. The only requirement for obtaining good things from God is the activation of your faith and patience, allowing them to work together.

Faith and patience are the foundation of every miracle, so if these two elements are resident, miracles will come. Remember, miracles don't just fall out of the sky, but they are worked.

WHO CAN WORK MIRACLES?

Let's look once again at Galatians 3:5: *"He therefore that ministereth*

331

to you the Spirit, and worketh miracles among you, doeth he it by the works of the law, or by the hearing of faith?" If you can hear by faith, *you* can work a miracle.

The word *worketh* means "to operate, show forth or set in motion." So, we could say that the one who operates, shows forth or sets in motion a miracle does so by the hearing of faith. Let me ask: Who can hear faith? Every believer can. Remember, Romans 10:17 says: *"So then faith cometh by hearing, and hearing by the word of God."*

You need to understand that every time you truly hear the Word, you are laying within yourself the potential of activating miracles in your life. You can work miracles. You can overcome and bring your family into victory right along with you. All it takes is the activation of your faith coupled with God's Word and a healthy dose of patience. Together, they are a miracle waiting to happen.

Hebrews 4:2 tells us: *"For unto us was the gospel preached, as well as unto them: but the word preached did not profit them, not being mixed with faith in them that heard it."* You can work a miracle if you will simply mix faith with the promises of God and remain steadfast and immovable until the miracle takes place and the manifestation is complete. When you do, you allow God to speak to you in an amazing way.

You allow Him to shout from the housetops, "I am here! I am real! I am God!" You allow the world to catch a glimpse of a God who loves you and who loves them, too. You allow Jesus to be revealed in you, because a miracle is a love letter from Heaven.

Miracles are produced in seedbeds of victory prepared for you and your family before you were ever born. God knew you would face needs, so He planned and prepared a way for you to hear His voice and access His power to overcome whatever stands in your way. There are no surprises in Heaven. God knows about every need before it is ever encountered, and He has made more than enough power available to deliver you from every plan of the enemy.

The Word will work miracles for you when you work the Word. I know that thought is not original with me, but it is no less true. The Word of God is an instrument which will produce the miraculous. Open the Word. Read the Word. Believe the Word. Then work the Word for a miracle manifestation in your life.

GOD'S PART AND YOUR PART

I personally believe the new birth is the greatest miracle of all. If I asked you who is responsible for the miracle of salvation you would say, "God is." In truth, God is responsible, but so are you. Don't believe me? Here is what it says in Ephesians 2:8: *"For by grace are ye saved through faith; and that not of yourselves: it is the gift of God."*

Now look at Romans 10:9-10: *"That if thou shalt confess with thy mouth the Lord Jesus, and shalt believe in thine heart that God hath raised him from the dead, thou shalt be saved. For with the heart man believeth unto righteousness; and with the mouth confession is made unto salvation."*

God is responsible for offering grace to every man and woman, grace which is free of charge to everyone who will believe. But, we are responsible to believe. It is *"grace through faith,"* not just grace alone and not just faith alone. The miracle of salvation comes when you work with God. This is how every miracle comes. There is God's part, but there is also your part.

In essence, the new birth is not God's choice, but yours. Salvation is available to all, but only received by *"whosoever will"* (see John 3:15-16). Are all saved? No, only those who believe and exercise their faith. Do all receive miracles? No, only those who believe and exercise their faith. Every believer has the potential to experience miracles, but only those who work the working of miracles by faith will receive them.

Here's an example. The multiplication promise in 2 Corinthians 9:10 says: *"Now he that ministereth seed to the sower both minister bread for your food, and multiply your seed sown, and increase the fruits of your righteousness."* Is the transformation of your finances a miracle? Absolutely. Who is responsible for this miracle? You and God together. God gives seed to the sower, but He can only multiply the seed that is sown. You have to sow before God can grow.

This miracle is not based on whether God wants to (and He does), or whether God can (and He can), but on what you will do in response to His Word. Every promise contains a miracle just waiting to be loosed and worked for your benefit.

God longs to speak to you through the working of miracles because it gives Him a perfect opportunity to say, "I love you!" When God is able to give you what He promised in His Word, it is the ultimate love letter to you, His child.

Don't you as a parent or grandparent love to give good things to your children? Of course you do, especially when it comes to grandbabies. There's nothing in this world like a grandchild. (Grandchildren are God's perfect gift to mankind. We get to love on them, give them everything they could dream of and more, and then we get to send them home when they get cranky!)

Moms and dads melt when a young child's eyes light up at the opening of a special gift. God is touched the same way when He is able to grant you a miracle, because you are His beloved child, the apple of His eye.

When you work the working of miracles and God is able to bless you abundantly, He says to the world, "This is my beloved child in whom I am well pleased." A miracle is a sign to the world that your heavenly Father is real, and that He still cares about them. It tells the world God is more powerful than anything the devil can dish out, and that we are more than conquerors through Him who loves us. It reveals once and for all that God is the same yesterday, today and forever.

Remember, a miracle is that which alters the natural course of things. This is why we can say salvation, healing and financial blessing are all miracles. They are God's love letters to you and me, and to the world watching us every day looking for some proof God does exist. Let's work miracles and show them who our wonderful heavenly Father really is.

FIND GOD'S WILL

There are certain things you must do in order to prepare for your next miracle. First, you need to find God's will for your situation. Notice I didn't say you need find someone else's opinion. I didn't say to ask your pastor or your best friend. I said to find God's will.

Faith will never work unless you discover without question what God's will is for you. The Bible states that Abraham was *"fully persuaded"* (see Romans 4:21). He wasn't half sure, but was fully convinced. Where did this conviction come from? It came from God, not from man. It was what God said to Abram that caused him to be fully persuaded and begin to call himself Abraham. It was a personal revelation that made him stand his ground until Isaac was born.

You have to discover your own personal persuasion and personal revelation. You must find God's will for you, and you find His will in His Word. It is where God will speak to you personally, just as He did to Abraham.

Books are great, but no book, including this one, can impart faith to you. Faith comes by hearing, and hearing by the Word of God. You have to find God's will in His Word for faith to be birthed. When you do, your miracle will be waiting inside the revelation.

If life and death are hanging in the balance, don't you think it's necessary to do whatever it takes to find the will of God for your life? Don't you think it's worth the sacrifice of TV or other pleasures to sit down and read God's Word, study it and wait upon the Lord for revelation? I do. I believe it's not only worth it, but it is your only option.

Personally, I don't like eating leftovers from someone else's plate. I won't take in what another person has spit out. I want fresh meat on a clean plate. This is what your revelation of God's Word is like. It is fresh meat, fresh manna, prepared just for you. No one else has eaten off your plate or spewed it out for you to eat after them. It's just for you, right from the throne of God.

I want the bread of life to be delivered to me directly from the Master's hand. I want it to fall from Heaven, and to gather it myself so I know what I'm receiving. This is why I go to the Word of God for my personal revelation of God's will every day. Books are beneficial, and they can help you get on the right path, but they cannot give you revelation or impart to you like the Word can.

If you depend on someone else's revelation, you will falter and fail. Only your personal revelation will see you through the dark of night and the waiting period that may come as your miracle goes from faith to sight. Remember, some miracles are instantaneous, while others come over time.

Let me give you an example regarding responding to God's will. Let's say you are facing a great financial need, and you only have a small amount of money in your bank account. What do you think God's will is for your situation? God's Word is His will, so you don't have to wonder what the Lord wants; you can read the Bible and discover the answer.

Luke 6:38 shows you exactly what you should do: *"Give, and it shall be given unto you; good measure, pressed down, and shaken together, and running over, shall men give into your bosom. For with the same measure that ye mete withal it shall be measured to you again."*

Here we see that God's will is for you to give so He can multiply your giving and send you a financial miracle. If you give, God will multiply, which is great, but on the flip side, if you don't give, God won't do anything. Again, there is God's part, but there is also your part.

We sometimes get so overbalanced on God's part, on what many call the sovereignty of God, that we fail to move. In reality God is waiting for us to respond to His Word so He can fulfill it and bring it to pass "according to our faith." God is sovereign; I don't dispute that. He has sovereignly promised He will do what He said in His Word He will do. This is true sovereignty—when God is faithful to watch over His Word and perform it for whosoever will (see Jeremiah 1:12).

The Bible tells us how faith and miracles work, but in order to acquire them we must work them as they have been created to work. God is sovereign, but you are responsible to respond to His sovereignty in faith.

Here's another vital point about responding to the will of God. When you find God's will and begin to work a miracle, you have to be prepared to keep at it forever, if that's what it takes. You must be ready for the long haul, and only your revelation of God's Word will make you diligent and steadfast; not my revelation, or Dr. Soandso's, but yours.

God is waiting to speak to you through His Word and tell you what His will is for your life—just as He is ready to speak to you in so many ways, as we have discovered. He can speak to you through a miracle manifestation and say, "I love you, my child, my beloved."

But you must listen and set time aside for intimate fellowship with the Spirit of God. You must press in and hear His voice. Then, you will discover His will, the miracle will come, and the praise of His glory will be heard in all the earth.

FIND GOD'S WISDOM

The second thing you need to do in preparation for a miracle is to find

God's wisdom. Just as it is necessary for the word of wisdom to show you what to do when the discerning of spirits reveals a problem, so it is equally important for you to wait for God's wisdom before you loose a miracle.

Proverbs 2:6-7 tells us: *"For the Lord giveth wisdom: out of his mouth cometh knowledge and understanding. He layeth up sound wisdom for the righteous: he is a buckler to them that walk uprightly."* So many Christians have faith, but they still fail. The reason is because they try to use faith as they see fit, not as God instructs. His wisdom shows you how to use the faith you have from the discovery of His will.

Psalm 37:23 says, *"The steps of a good man are ordered by the Lord: and he delighteth in his way."* Wisdom directs your steps of faith.

For instance, as we just read, the Bible says we can *"Give and it shall be given"* (Luke 6:38). I believe this, but if I am wise, I will ask God where I should give and where my seed should be planted. Wisdom will show me the prepared field which will bear much fruit, but if I don't wait for wisdom, I may sow my seed in unprepared, unfruitful ground, and my harvest will be hindered.

It's like giving your five year old his first bike and then leaving him to his own devices without any instruction. That child will crash his first time out because he thinks he knows what to do, but without proper instruction, he really doesn't.

You may think you know how to use your faith in a given situation, but I guarantee God knows. Wouldn't it be better to wait for the Lord to tell you how to move than to guess for yourself? You can avoid many a crash if you will be still and wait for wisdom to lead you. Discover God's will, then discover His wisdom for you personally.

Imagine the man Jesus spat upon in Mark 7:32-35. Suppose he had backed away and said, "Yuck! I'm not putting up with this!" He would have missed his miracle.

Did Jesus make up that ministry method because He was bored? No, Jesus obeyed what God told Him to do (see John 8:28). This man had faith, but he would have missed his miracle manifestation had he not been willing to submit to the wisdom of God carried out by Jesus. Thank God he endured the spit so he could receive the blessing.

If I was sick, I would go to the Word and find God's will. His will is healing, so after I found all the healing scriptures the Lord revealed to me,

I would ask God for wisdom to use them rightly. I would ask Him to give me wisdom and direct the words of my mouth.

In Matthew 4:4 we read: *"But he answered and said, It is written, Man shall not live by bread alone, but by every word that proceedeth out of the mouth of God."*

Jesus depended upon the written Word of God and the instruction of the Holy Spirit. They were enough for Him to combat the enemy in the wilderness, and they will be enough for you to do the same. You do not need an angelic visitation if the Word spells out what you should do. What you need is a heart of obedience and a voice of thanksgiving for the wisdom given to you in every situation. When the voice of wisdom rises up in your household, the working of miracles will go into motion, and you will receive what you have desired.

TRUE SOVEREIGNTY

Let's look closely at the sovereignty of God, because misunderstanding this concept has created an issue that hinders so many Christians who really need a miracle.

Much of the religious misinformation we have accumulated over the years is based on the teaching that God is sovereign, and that He will do whatever He wants to do, whenever He wants to do it. Most of us have been taught you can never know what God is going to do because there's no way to know what His will is in a given situation. When we are taught this way, we walk in a mindless oblivion not knowing who God is, what's going to happen or when He's going to show up—which is wrong thinking.

God is who the Word says He is, He will do what the Word says He will do, and He will always show up right on time—if you believe. The life of miracles can be your life, if you will learn how to work a miracle. The criteria has already been set in Galatians 3:5. You can allow God to speak to and through you in the working of miracles by the hearing of faith.

In Luke 13:10-13, we find the story of a great miracle: *"And he was teaching in one of the synagogues on the sabbath. And, behold, there was a woman which had a spirit of infirmity eighteen years, and was bowed together, and could in no wise lift up herself. And when Jesus saw her, he called her to him, and said unto her, Woman, thou art loosed from thine infirmity. And he laid his hands on her: and immediately she was made straight, and glorified God."*

If the story stopped there, all the nay-sayers might have a case for the "God is sovereign in all" theory. They could say, "See, Jesus called her out because He wanted to give her a special miracle, but nobody else could get one." Really?

If you go on to finish the story in verses 14-16, you discover this woman did not have to wait for Jesus to come along to receive a miracle at all: *"And the ruler of the synagogue answered with indignation, because that Jesus had healed on the sabbath day, and said unto the people, There are six days in which men ought to work: in them therefore come and be healed, and not on the sabbath day. The Lord then answered him, and said, Thou hypocrite, doth not each one of you on the sabbath loose his ox or his ass from the stall, and lead him away to watering? And ought not this woman, being a daughter of Abraham, whom Satan hath bound, lo, these eighteen years, be loosed from this bond on the sabbath day?"*

According to the ruler of the synagogue, this woman could have come in anytime, six days a week, and received a miracle. Notice Jesus did not dispute his claim, but only rebuked the man for complaining because He had healed on the Sabbath. Evidently, there was healing in God's house all along, but this woman had not availed herself of it until this day.

There was healing in the Old Covenant, if the people would believe, just as there is healing in the New Covenant. Exodus 15:26 says: *"...for I am the Lord that healeth thee."* God was and is a healing God.

This miracle was not subject to His sovereignty, but it was subject to this woman's response. When she came to the synagogue before she had no faith in motion, but when Jesus called her up, her response shows us that her faith was sparked, and then she received her miracle.

Any man or woman who will mix faith with the promises of God can work and receive the supernatural. Sometimes the miracle will manifest instantly, as it did for this woman, but other times it will be received over time as it was for the ten lepers in Luke 17:12-14. No matter the time element, you can rest assured that miracles are God's will for you, and they are waiting to be accessed, waiting to be manifested and waiting to bring breakthroughs to your life. God is sovereignly committed to watch over His Word to perform a miracle for you!

WE HAVE WHAT WE SAY

There is a life-changing miracle principle in Mark 11:12-24, where we find the story of Jesus and the fig tree. Being hungry one day, as He was looking for something to eat, He saw leaves on a distant fig tree. In the world of fig trees the presence of leaves is supposed to indicate the presence of fruit, so Jesus approached the tree with hope. When He saw the tree had no figs, but only leaves, He was not a happy camper, and said: *"No man eat fruit of thee hereafter for ever."*

The disciples were with Him, and I'm sure they were a little surprised at His reaction, but Jesus had a plan. The next day as they passed by the tree again, the disciples were astonished to discover the tree was already drying up from the roots. Just one day later, and the fig tree was withering before their very eyes.

Jesus then revealed His purpose in verses 23-24: *"For verily I say unto you, That whosoever shall say unto this mountain, Be thou removed, and be thou cast into the sea; and shall not doubt in his heart, but shall believe that those things which he saith shall come to pass; he shall have whatsoever he saith. Therefore I say unto you, What things soever ye desire, when ye pray, believe that ye receive them, and ye shall have them."*

Jesus took this opportunity to show the disciples a very important Kingdom principle: *We have what we say in faith.* If we use our faith like God uses His, through the spoken word, we will have whatever we say in faith. The key is to believe when we pray, not when we see. I have a teaching called, *Made in His Image,* where I go into great detail explaining how this law of faith works, but for this example, let me give you the short version.

God created the world using words of faith. In fact, the Bible says: *"Through faith we understand that the worlds were framed by the word of God, so that things which are seen were not made of things which do appear"* (Hebrews 11:3).

We see this principle in Genesis chapter one where we read eight times, *"And God said..."* By these confirming scriptures we know God created the earth with His faith-filled words, but what does this have to do with you

Well, are you not created in God's image and likeness? According to Genesis 1:26 you are: *"And God said, Let us make man in our image, after our likeness: and let them have dominion over the fish of the sea, and over the fowl of the air, and over the cattle, and over all the earth, and over every creeping thing that creepeth upon the earth."*

"That's great," you say, "But what does this have to do with my faith?" Ephesians 5:1 is your answer: *"Be ye therefore followers of God, as dear children."* We are to follow God and act as He acts in every situation.

If God speaks faith-filled words and miracles happen, we can speak faith-filled words and see miracles happen, too. What are these words? The most faith-filled words in the world are the words of the Bible, the Word of God. If you will speak the Word to your mountain, your mountain will move. If you will speak the Word to your fig tree, your unproductive place, it will dry up from the roots and die.

Miracles are in your mouth. You can speak words of faith, even to inanimate objects, and change their influence and activity in your life. You can speak to spiritual things and see them change, too. The only criteria I see in what Jesus said is *"...whosoever shall say..."* The mountain will not move if you don't speak to it. It will stay right where it is, blocking your path and hindering your progress, and God will not make it move. You have the choice in your mouth. You have to work the miracle with wise words of faith.

Of course you realize that the mountain Jesus spoke of was symbolic. I don't recommend you go out tomorrow morning and start demanding that the mole hills in your yard get up and move to your neighbor's yard. We understand Jesus was making a point by using the biggest thing the disciples had ever seen as symbolism.

Jesus pointed to the mountain and told them it would be no match for their words of faith. If they would say something to the mountain, and believe when they said it, they would have whatever they said. They would see a miracle manifestation, a victorious outcome which would remove every obstacle and bring God's blessing.

God will move a mountain for "whosoever"—for whosoever will

believe and say. If you don't believe, or if you don't speak it, the miracle will not come. But if you believe and mix your faith with the spoken word, a miracle will show up right on your doorstep, and God will receive all the glory.

One of the easiest ways to access miracles with the words of your mouth is to be a thankful person. Be grateful for what God is doing and has done in your life. There's nothing more frustrating than an ungrateful child, so don't be one. Be thankful and express your grateful heart to your heavenly Father often.

Here's a simple but great secret that will bring blessing to your home: Shut everything down for one half hour every night and unite your household in thanksgiving for everything you are believing God for. That's right. Click off the TV. Shut down the cell phone. Turn off the internet, and turn your family's attention to the Lord.

If you will come together as one and magnify the intensity of your faith toward the things you've prayed for, your house will become a habitation of praise and thanksgiving, and you will get your family working together toward your miracle. Stop the fussing and arguing. Shut down the outside distractions, and get back into spiritual unity with your family. Unite with those God has given you to live with and be blessed with.

If you will sit down for thirty minutes as a family every day and begin to thank God and proclaim what He has said about you in His Word, you will see things begin to move for you—and see miracle breakthroughs. The working of miracles in your home will become a building block of peace and assurance. Your family will experience His ever-abiding presence and watchful eye over them, verifying Matthew 28:20, where Jesus said: *"I am with you always, even unto the end of the world."*

Trusting God this way will establish the peace of God in the hearts of your family so that no matter what happens in the world around them, they will not be moved. When the working of miracles is demonstrated in your household, no matter how bad things look in the future, your children will not be afraid, but they will turn their faith toward God once again.

Thankful hearts help us work miracles because they cause us to see things the way God sees them. Problems are not an issue with Him, and they should not be issues with us. If we will thank God always, and in all things, we will see miracles come to pass in our lives.

THE WORD IS YOUR EVIDENCE

To work a miracle, you need to be prepared to go the distance, and you must believe the miracle is yours based solely on the Word of God as your evidence.

Remember, the Bible says, *"Give and it shall be given."* If you sought God for wisdom and sowed as He directed, you loosed a miracle harvest, and you now have it, even if you cannot see it yet. Don't look at what you can see, but look at the Word of God, and never let your focus stray from the evidence of that Word.

Paul writes in 2 Corinthians 4:18: *"While we look not at the things which are seen, but at the things which are not seen: for the things which are seen are temporal; but the things which are not seen are eternal."* And we read: *"For we walk by faith, not by sight"* (2 Corinthians 5:7).

In other words, we do not walk by the things which are constantly changing around us, but we walk by the truth of the Word that will never change. It does not matter what your eye can see, what your ear can hear, what your hands can touch or what your body can feel. If you loosed a miracle, you *have* a miracle. Do not be moved by sight or feeling, but stand firm on the Word of God and remain immovable until what is promise becomes visible and tangible.

This is where far too many miracles are lost. Maybe someone prays for a healing miracle, and it manifests as it did for the ten lepers, a little at a time as he goes on his way. It's a progressive miracle, and at first, there is only a slight change to the symptoms. This is not the time to give up and say, "Oh well, God knew what I needed." No, it is the time to let patience have her perfect work and say, "Praise God! I have my miracle! Look what I can do now that I could not do before. I have a miracle, and I will remain steadfast until I see and feel the finished manifestation!"

If you could not see anything before, and now you see a little light, rejoice! Be glad and shout until you see clearly. Jesus once faced a man who after the first prayer went from being blind to seeing men look like trees. Jesus wasn't finished, He stayed there until the man's vision was perfect.

You need to stay in faith until the fullness of your miracle is completed, too. Keep your mind on Jesus and on the Word. Keep your faith directed toward your mountain, your place of hindrance or trouble, and do not back down until what you say from God's Word becomes what you have in life. You will see your miracle in its completed, finished form if you will be diligent and steadfast to remain standing on His promise, no matter what your eyes, ears, hands or body tell you.

Miracles are waiting for you to launch forth and work them. They are waiting to be delivered into your life, your household, and into the lives of those around you. I encourage you to be a miracle worker and let God speak through you to the world. Allow Jesus to be seen in you, and allow God's best to be yours.

CHAPTER 21

PEOPLE OF FAITH

I entered the back of the sanctuary on a balmy summer evening. This was my first visit to this beautiful church, and I was excited about what God had laid on my heart to do. As I walked toward the front of the building, I began to sing along with the praise and worship team. The service was in full swing, and I noticed a strong anointing in the room.

I was casually walking toward the front row when suddenly, everything changed. It was as if a lightning bolt had struck the crowd, and they began to behave in a very unusual way. I vividly remember that I was about halfway down the center aisle when people began jumping across the pews and grabbing me. I looked around for the deacons to come take care of these crazy people, but it continued happening all the way down the aisle as I struggled to reach my seat. People were reaching out, possessed by some strange thing.

I was actually afraid as this experience unfolded all around me. Fear may not be of God, but that night I was shaking in my boots, watching the power of God manifest in a way I had never witnessed before. I had no sense about me at that moment, and I had no idea what was happening among the people. As I continued down the aisle, step after labored step, people strained and leaped over one another to touch me, some of them hitting me so hard I was bouncing around in the midst of them. Just when I thought they were going to overtake me, miracles began to happen. One after another, instantaneous miracles manifested all over the room.

When it was over I asked God what had happened, and He told me it was the gift of faith in motion. My confusion was laid aside as I realized the gift of faith I had just witnessed was not for me, but it was for the people of that church, the people in need. Though I had prayed, "Oh, God, help me!" the Lord had been busy helping them.

Why did God operate this way? He did it because there were people in that church who needed miracles their faith could not obtain for them. Though their personal fruit of faith was not enough, when they cried out for a manifestation of the Spirit, the gift of faith came upon them, and incurable diseases were healed in the blink of an eye. The release of the gift of faith caused them to become possessed of a faith which was not their own, and miracles flowed unhindered.

I will never forget what I learned that day. Through the experience, I realized the gift of faith is God's faith given to men for a moment in time—and will be like none other. When God's faith manifests, men and women are no longer themselves, but they are transformed in the way they think, act and speak.

No longer are they mere Christians. Now, they are men and women of faith, miracles, and of victorious outcomes. Everything they touch in that moment receives the touch of God, and everything they pray receives an answer. When the gift of faith comes, no one has to wonder about it. They know, and they rejoice.

KNOWN BY GOD

We are not always known by men the way we are known by God. In our western culture, for instance, society dubs each generation with a name which reflects what was going on during a particular era. This is why 1701-1723 was called the Awakening Generation, because the world was awakening to a new way of thinking in religious and cultural terms. And a portion of the 1950's became know as the American High because, despite The Great Depression and World War II, America arose to the occasion, and that generation overcame great adversity and established a new kind of prosperity.

Years passed, and then came Generation X, consisting of people born between 1961-1981. This generation grew up in a time of cultural upheaval. The great exploits of WWII were long over and forgotten, and the cold war had everyone on edge believing nuclear annihilation was just over the horizon. Baby Boomers merged into Baby Busters, and finally into Gen X, an era when frustration and lack of core values reigned.

Today, we have reached another turning point, and this current era, beginning with those born in 2001, has been dubbed the New Silent Generation. Others have named it Generation Z, but whatever you call it, this generation is expected to reflect the first Silent Generation of 1925-1945 when great tragedies struck and tremendous change was on the way.

The world does not know what is ahead for this generation, but thanks to the Bible, we do. If your young children are being raised in a Christian home under the guidance of the laws of the Spirit, it does not matter what society says about them, they have a destiny which has been determined by Almighty God. No matter what the world says or does, God will do what He has promised to do. He knows them and loves them in a way the world will never know.

Our current generation may be marked by the silence of the world as they try to sort out how to react in this time of change and upheaval, but as a believer you can rest in the assurance God never changes, and His Word will see you through whatever may come. No matter what the world calls you, God always calls you a man or woman of faith.

You may look at yourself, as I often do, and consider yourself the least likely candidate for the gift of faith. In my eyes, I am the least likely prospect for God to use, because I know all my faults and all my weaknesses. I have so many reservations, tremblings and doubts about things I am doing, what I am going to do and what I need to understand to succeed.

Paul said he was no different than I am in 1 Corinthians 2:3: *"And I was with you in weakness, and in fear, and in much trembling."*

The apostle was not a perfect man, and neither am I. We all have reservations about our qualifications, but just as Paul overcame them and served the Lord in great power, we must overcome our fear and allow God to move through us for the praise of His glory. We must all discover as Paul did that God's grace is sufficient, and it will give us everything we need to overcome every obstacle and fulfill the destiny of God in our lives (see 2 Corinthians 12:9).

The men in the Bible we consider to be the greatest were most often the ones who considered themselves to be the least. Because they recognized their weaknesses and therefore trusted God, He was able to show Himself strong on their behalf and do great exploits through them.

We must realize that though it may seem we are in the darkest hour of humanity since the time of the fall, God is exercising His greatest intensity to overcome it through us. Since we are in a world which is increasing in demonic activity, we as spiritual ambassadors for God must believe that He, who sees us in the image of Jesus, is prepared to do even greater things through those who believe.

We must depend on the supernatural work of the Spirit of God to speak to us, guide and empower us, fulfill divine destiny in us, overcome every obstacle around us and reflect the nature of God to this lost and dying world through us. We must allow ourselves to become known to the world as we are known by God.

SIGNS FOLLOWING

I believe one of the leading gifts of the Spirit in this end time move of God will be the gift of faith. It is a supernatural gift that belongs to the Holy Spirit, is manifested at His discretion and is always subject to Him. The Holy Spirit is the owner and possessor of this gift, yet He is a co-laborer with you and me. He is willing to loose the gift of faith at any time, and He desires this special gift to be used in our lives.

Remember, the gifts of the Spirit are the voice of God confirming the story of redemption we preach (see Hebrews 2:4). The Lord is with us at every turn, attesting to His Word with signs following. Signs and wonders, faith and miracles are God's voice to the world verifying that the story we tell about Jesus is real. Other religions are never accompanied by such a voice. Only Christianity is confirmed by the voice of God that emptied the grave of Jesus with His power by His Spirit.

Buddha left a philosophy behind. He left words of his own interpretation which men follow because they like what they hear, but they have no wonders to back them up. Mohammed left behind a belief system that his followers adhere to even unto death, but they have no signs following them.

Christianity would also be only a philosophy without the confirming voice of God following His Word with signs and wonders in the earth. You can't argue Christian beliefs against other persuasions unless you have something greater than mere words. The signs that follow the preaching of the Word are a voice which cannot be denied.

A few years ago a man who practiced another religion came to me, a doctor from a foreign nation. He told me he had heard about what was going on in our church, and he asked me to define the difference between his religion and mine.

My answer was simple. I told him, "The guy you worship is still in the grave, and the guy I worship is not. The cold hard facts are these: The Man Jesus Christ, the only begotten Son of God, was confirmed to be God's chosen, confirmed to be His truth, His way and His life, and confirmed to be who He said He was by a supernatural resurrection from the dead. If your god is still in the tomb, I'd say you have a problem, but I don't because my God is alive and well."

If a "god" cannot raise himself, how can he help anyone else? The resurrection of Jesus is the first working of miracles which confirmed the Word with signs following and launched the greatest age in the history of mankind, the age of grace. We live as we live because the grace of God was loosed by the sign of the resurrection of the Son of God, Jesus Christ. All other miracles are byproducts which further confirm that Jesus and the Word are real.

When we operate in the gift of faith and manifest miracles in our lives, we show that the gospel we preach is still as relevant and powerful today as it was 2,000 years ago. The world hears God's voice as they witness our testimony in action; they see the goodness of God, and then they believe.

THE FRUIT OF FAITH

The gift of faith is not the fruit of faith. Galatians 5:22-23 says: *"But the fruit of the Spirit is love, joy, peace, longsuffering, gentleness, goodness, faith, meekness, temperance: against such there is no law."*

The fruit of the recreated human spirit includes the fruit of faith. When a man is recreated in the image and likeness of God and born again by grace through faith in Jesus Christ, the fruit of the spirit will begin to manifest in his life, and as a result the law and sin will no longer have rule over him.

So, what is the difference between a fruit and a gift? The fruit of faith is engrafted in your heart in seed form at the new birth, and it must be developed, grown and added to. The gift of faith is the faith of God in its fully developed form, and it is granted to you at the Holy Spirit's discretion for a particular situation.

The fruit of faith is what we discussed in the last chapter, and it is what is described in Romans 10:17: *"So then faith cometh by hearing, and hearing by the word of God."* This kind of faith increases as you fill yourself with the Word. This fruit of faith begins as a seed, and it grows as you discover what

349

God has done for you in Christ Jesus. As these discoveries are made, your faith increases.

First Thessalonians 1:3 tells us: *"We are bound to thank God always for you, brethren, as it is meet, because that your faith groweth exceedingly, and the charity of every one of you all toward each other aboundeth."*

This is the fruit of faith—the measure of faith we were all given at the new birth (see Romans 12:3). We all have this fruit of faith, and we all have the responsibility to make it grow and produce in our lives. We have the command to go from glory to glory and from faith to faith. It is something we must watch over, nurture, and make sure it is ever increasing.

We may also release the gift of faith, a fully developed portion of God's faith given to us for a specific time by the Holy Spirit.

THE GIFT OF FAITH

When God speaks to us through the gift of faith, it is with a specific, ordained purpose in mind. It is not at our discretion, but it is according to our willingness to pursue and loose the gifts in our lives.

The gift of faith is entirely different than the fruit of faith because it is a gift of God's faith. It does not need to grow or to be perfected—and it does not need to be exercised. All it needs is to be used by you.

Just as the word of wisdom is a word of God's wisdom, so the gift of faith is a gift of God's faith. A word of wisdom is not the kind of wisdom man can gain by study or intellectual exercise; neither can any man attain to the gift of faith by study of God's Word, confession of that Word, or by any other exercise of the fruit of faith.

In life, there will be times when your fruit of faith is not enough for a particular situation. Your faith, no matter how developed it is, will not be sufficient to overcome certain circumstances. It is for these times that the gift of faith can be loosed in your life.

There are dimensions God wants you to walk in, plans He desires for you to fulfill, places He wants you to go that your faith will never be able to obtain for you. In these situations, it is impossible for you to succeed without God empowering you with His faith.

Let me give you an example: You will never walk on water unless God gives you the gift of faith. No matter how much you exercise and develop your faith, it will not empower you to supersede natural laws like Jesus did when He walked on the water and invited Peter to come with Him. In layman's terms, you will not be a water-walker unless God is a gift-of-faith-imparter.

I've had people tell me over the years that they were going to walk on water someday. They had no doubt, but I had plenty because I know the limitations of man's faith. Sometimes Christians have silly ideas about what God intends for them to do with their faith.

In Matthew 14:23-33 you can read the story of Jesus walking on the water. What I want you to realize from this story is that even though Jesus was a man whose fruit of faith was highly developed, He did not walk on the water at His discretion. Jesus was only able to do this when the Holy Spirit gave Him the gift of faith to walk there. We know this is true because He did not walk on water all the time.

Jesus preached along the shores of the Sea of Galilee regularly, but He never walked on water before. He even used Peter's boat one time so He could launch out a little way from the crowd. Don't you think if Jesus could walk on water any old time He would have done it then? Wouldn't that have been a great sermon illustrator? I think the altars would have been filled that day if Jesus would have stood on the water and preached, but evidently God did not see it that way.

Jesus' faith alone could not produce the walk described in Matthew 14:23-33. He had the same fruit of faith for normal daily living that you and I have, but He did not supersede the laws of nature except when God allowed Him to through the gift of faith. The gift of faith is a gift of God's faith, a measure or a portion of which is given to accomplish one feat for God's purpose. Once that feat is finished, the gift ceases.

BEYOND YOURSELF

The gift of faith is a gift God is willing to impart into your life to help you accomplish special things for His Kingdom and for your family. When God speaks through this gift, His voice is like no other. He speaks through this gift for a moment in time and for a specific purpose.

Let's look at an example. Second Corinthians 8:1-5 tells us: *"Moreover, brethren, we do you to wit of the grace of God bestowed on the churches of Macedonia; How that in a great trial of affliction the abundance of their joy and their deep poverty abounded unto the riches of their liberality. For to their power, I bear record, yea, and beyond their power they were willing of themselves; praying us with much intreaty that we would receive the gift, and take upon us the fellowship of the ministering to the saints. And this they did, not as we hoped, but first gave their own selves to the Lord, and unto us by the will of God."*

Notice, there was a special faith which arose in the hearts of the people, in fact, in the whole church in this area. This shows us the gift of faith can be imparted to an individual or to a group of people. Any gift of the Spirit can fall on any number of people at one time.

The gift of faith fell on the churches at Macedonia so the people there could get beyond their own power to fulfill the purpose of God. They were not acting in their own faith or strength, but they acted in the power of the gift of faith. This gift on them in the midst of hardship caused them to respond abnormally, beyond their fruit of faith. It allowed them to see beyond the natural and to reach into reservoirs they had not known existed before.

When they did they found a joy which was beyond ordinary, a joy which created a godly liberality in them to meet the needs of others. In the midst of their deep poverty, the gift of faith caused them to become givers. They did not do it because of their fruit of faith, but they went beyond themselves and connected to the gift of faith.

Thank God for this gift that can intervene and take us to a place beyond our human reason and the limitations of our senses; that can take us to a heavenly place, far above principalities, powers, and the rulers of this world system, and empower us to overcome natural laws for supernatural victories. Your level of faith cannot do what the gift of faith can do. The fruit of faith is for a determined, daily purpose, for you to live the abundant life, but then there are special times and special circumstances when your faith is not enough, when only God's own faith will deliver and see you through.

When you connect with the gift of faith, you will go beyond yourself and beyond your own measure of faith. God's gift of faith will cause you to transform your sight, your thinking, your voice, attitude and actions until you become another man or another woman, one possessed of a faith that man cannot stop and the devil cannot hinder.

THE MANTLE OF FAITH

The operation of the gift of faith is as if a mantle of faith falls upon you and takes temporary control of your senses, allowing God to go into motion in an extraordinary way.

I'll never forget the moment well over 20 years ago when I walked into our church with a small but faithful congregation in attendance. At that time our church met in a tiny store-front building, and the entire congregation was less than 25 people. But on this particular day, the gift of faith fell on me, and I began to proclaim what God was going to do for us in the future.

I said, "I'll tell you this, we will be on television, and we will touch the world. We will be a voice in this nation, and God will bring it to pass. No matter what you say or do, you hear me now, this church will be a voice to the world through television out of this town."

My shocked congregation looked at me with eyes as big as houses, and I could tell all they knew was that they were cold and wished I would turn up the heat in my old fuel oil stove. Trouble was, if I did it would have shot black soot into the room, and they would have gone home with "black nose disease" as we called it, which was not a pretty sight.

What they could not see with their fruit of faith I saw clearly with the gift of faith granted to me by God on that day. I saw the future, and for that moment, I was possessed with a mantle of faith to lay hold of what God had for our church. I was another man and not myself when I spoke. I was possessed by the gift of faith, and I could not say anything other than what God had put in my heart. I did not have to think, "Okay, Peter, keep your confession straight." No, I did not have to think at all because it was not me who spoke, but it was the faith of God speaking through me.

I don't believe God said, "Let there be light," and then went around for three weeks confessing, "Light's coming! It's on its way! Just wait until my confession takes hold. Light will be here any day now!" No, when God's faith spoke, light was. In the same way, when the faith of God moves the heart and the mouth of a believer, whatever is spoken in faith is done. It is completed. It is finished right then.

Do you think when I stood in that tiny, unfinished building I could have believed for a television ministry that would touch the world? I couldn't, but the faith of God could. Today, this faith has opened doors for us to minister in over 74 nations by way of our weekly television broadcast. We have touched so many lives because the faith of God poured out of me on a day when what I saw with my eyes did not match what He had placed in my heart. Only God's faith could bring such amazing things to pass. Mine certainly couldn't.

DISCOVERING THE GIFT OF FAITH

Too often Christians are unaware of the gift of faith because so few pay the price to tap into it. This should not be because Jesus said, *"Verily, verily, I say unto you, He that believeth on me, the works that I do shall he do also; and greater works than these shall he do; because I go unto my Father"* (John 14:12).

In order for this verse to be fulfilled in our lives, the gift of faith must be available for every believer in the Body of Christ. We need it to help us do what God has called us to do, and to help us get results our faith has not matured enough to receive. The gift of faith will take us to places we will never be able to access on our own.

Do you think Peter could have walked on the water with his faith alone? Sometimes we forget that Peter did walk for awhile. When Jesus said, "Come," the gift of faith was imparted to Peter to jump out of that boat, separate himself from everything logical and walk a walk no mere man had ever walked before. The gift of faith caused Peter to get beyond himself and become possessed of a faith like no other.

Only when Peter came back to himself did he have problems and begin to sink. He was beyond himself for a moment, for a time of manifestation, but then he looked at the waves and feared. My question is, what did the waves have to do with it? Did Peter think he could walk on smooth water? No, but his mind and logical thinking got in the way of the gift of faith, and the gift ceased to function.

When God tells you to, "Come," nothing will be able to stop you. No need will stop you, no lack will hinder you, and no mountain will be tall enough to keep you from fulfilling the call. When God says, "Come," the gift of faith will cause you to jump out of your boat and walk across the lake to meet Jesus, just as Peter did.

Jesus did not ask Peter to go somewhere alone, but He called him to come to Him, to a prepared place, one where God awaited and victory was assured. The gift of faith always takes you to a prepared place *with* God, not without Him. It takes you to a place where you are no longer dependent on your faith alone, but are now dependent on the very faith of God.

As you move out of your boat of discovery and step out onto the lake of the unknown, God will reach out His hand and guide you step by step, but you must be sure to keep your eyes on Him. Only then will you make it to your destiny.

ACCESSING THE GIFT OF FAITH

God desires to speak to the world through the gift of faith to confirm His Word with signs following, so they may be freed from the spirit of blindness and enter into the Kingdom of His dear Son. To access this dimension of faith is not a free ride. If it was, everybody would be doing it.

Every dimension of spiritual power God has called you to possess and walk in is under guard by principalities and powers, rulers of darkness who do not want you to access this kind of power. I don't say this to scare you, but to make you aware. There is a price to be paid, and when you go there, you will have to deal with certain dimensions of spiritual power in order to inhabit the thrones of authority God has called you to possess.

Jesus referred to this price when He said, *"This kind can come forth by nothing, but by prayer and fasting"* (Mark 9:29).

Jesus was not just talking about greater faith here, He was also speaking of what it takes to loose the gift of faith that can deal with certain spiritual enemies. This kind of faith is not something you can walk in at your discretion, but it is what God will impart to you if you will pray and fast to loose the gift of faith in your life. Remember, we are instructed to covet the gifts, to press in until we reach the inner sanctuary where the gifts flow freely through human vessels. As I said before, you reach this place by much prayer and fasting.

I am at least 28 pounds lighter today than I was when I made a decision to go after the miraculous years ago. I've lost track of how many pant sizes and shirt sizes that is, but I do not miss the old me a bit because I have been able to access, through dedicated prayer and fasting, a dimension of God I will never relinquish. That old man needed to die so a new man could rise up and possess all God had for me.

This new man has not fully arrived yet; I know that, and I am ever pressing forward for more. There are dimensions of power I have yet to tap

355

into that I will possess one day because of the price Christ has paid for me to access them.

But I also know there are enemies in my Canaan just as there were in Israel's Promised Land, and I will have to fight them and dispossess them of that land so I can live where God wants me to live. It's not that the land is not mine already, but there are adversaries there who want to keep me out of the dimensions of power God has laid up for me, and I will have to deal with them one by one.

Every believer who wants to access all God has for him will have to deal with his own enemies in his own land. Your story may be different than mine because your call, your family and your needs are different than mine, but what we have in common is the right of access and the method of access. You can loose the gift of faith in your life by seeking, by prayer and fasting, and by faith in the Holy Spirit who imparts the gift.

The gift of faith has fallen upon so many men, and we have their accounts to encourage us. Men like Smith Wigglesworth of England, who said, "There are two kinds of faith. There is a natural faith, the fruit of faith, but there is a supernatural faith that is the gift of God."

The truth of the matter is, your fruit of faith will never be big enough to fulfill the dreams God has for you. It will never loose you into the supernatural realm where you will fulfill your call and destiny in Him.

Do you think a man who did not graduate from high school could come up with enough faith to build a church of thousands in a town whose population is less than his average attendance on a given Sunday? Do you really think this could be the result of that man's great dedication and study?

I don't because I am that man. I built that church, but my faith was not enough. It took the gift of faith to accomplish what God wanted for my life and for the lives of the people in my congregation. What God has done is far beyond me, and I do not fully comprehend it all.

When God challenges me to go further, I don't even dare think about how it's going to happen because it is too big for me. I tremble when I think I would have to be responsible for doing what God has called me to do. It is too much for my mind to grasp, but it's not too much for the faith of God to handle.

My faith can believe God will be with me and provide for me no matter where I am, but when the Lord asks me to build things that astound the minds of men, He does not do it based on what I can do on my own; He does it based on what His gift of faith can accomplish through me.

In his book, *Ever Increasing Faith,* Smith Wigglesworth wrote, "Your faith comes to an end. How many times I have been to the place where I have had to tell the Lord, 'I have used all the faith I have,' and then He has placed His own faith in me." Thank God we don't have to sit still and do nothing when our faith comes to this end, but we can use our fruit of faith to covet God's gift of faith, and thereby release a faith beyond ourselves.

The gift of faith is so much greater than your faith. When your faith reaches its limit, the gift of faith will cause you to walk a walk where there is nothing under you except the hand of God. You will walk, as it were, on nothing; nothing the eye can see, but on faith only God can see and impart.

The reason most dreams fail is because people don't realize there is a provision greater than they can ever accumulate for themselves by their own personal study and commitment to God. In certain situations, instead of waiting for their faith to grow, they need to press in to access the gift of faith.

We learned in the last chapter that in every miracle there is the element of you going where you can go, but there is always the element of God coming and taking you where you cannot go. This is what the gift of faith provides, the faith of God which takes you far beyond what your mind and your faith alone can ever imagine. Accessing God's faith lifts you into a brand new realm.

MEN AND WOMEN OF FAITH

Today, there are many men who have called Smith Wigglesworth the apostle of faith, but some of these same men will say such things as, "Well, if you pray more than once, it's unbelief." They make such statements because they do not understand how to deal with spiritual powers which are beyond the scope of their own faith. They do not invade spiritual dimensions, nor do they wrestle with the beasts of the spirits of darkness.

Paul said, *"...I have fought with beasts at Ephesus..."* (1 Corinthians 15:32). In the spirit world there are creatures that cannot be comprehended by the mind of man, but they are dealt with through prayer and fasting, consecration, dedication and sanctification. It's not just a simple prayer of faith that is needed when a miracle must be loosed to save a life on the brink of death. The "Seven Steps" to this and that are unable to invade the realm of spiritual warfare when demonic forces are involved and hindering the manifestation of answered prayer.

Remember Mark 9:29: *"And he said unto them, This kind can come forth by nothing, but by prayer and fasting."* Through this verse we understand there are certain dimensions of spiritual activity we will never invade without pressing in and doing everything God needs us to do. It does not matter how much we develop our fruit of faith, it will never be enough to deliver our Gadarenes. It will never be enough to heal the multitudes like Jesus did. It will never be enough to calm every storm or walk upon the sea. We may be men and women of faith, but we need to be men and women of the gift of faith for these last days.

Jesus never sent anyone away saying, "Too bad for you. If you had enough faith, you would have received it." No, Jesus paid the price for the gift of faith to be at the ready for those times when the faith of an individual was not enough. In the same way, we need to be ready to access the gift of faith for others so they may be delivered and set free.

As recorded in Stanley Howard Frodsham's biography, *Smith Wigglesworth, Apostle of Faith,* the evangelist once told the story of a time he was called to the home of a young couple. The wife had given birth seven weeks earlier, and since the time of the birth she had been under some kind of demonic attack. This young woman was bedfast, but she still managed to flop around when they approached her, and she went into a fit when they brought her baby close to her. She was seemingly out of her mind, and no one knew why.

Brother Wigglesworth asked the husband if anyone had tried to help her using their faith. The man was furious that anyone could think he could still operate in faith after seven weeks with no sleep and his wife behaving like a maniac. Brother Wigglesworth was moved with compassion for the woman, and he began to pray.

But he left that place without doing anything. He explained to them that he could do nothing for them with his faith alone, but if they would give him permission to come back at an hour of God's choosing, he promised to help her. The family gave him permission, so he found a place to pray.

He says, "And then with what faith I had, I began to penetrate the heavens. I was soon out on the heights. And I tell you, I have never seen a man get anything from God who prayed on the earth level. If you get anything from God you will have to pray right into Heaven, for all you want is there.

"I saw there, in the presence of that demented girl, limitations to my faith;

but as I prayed there came another faith into my heart that could not be denied, a faith that grasped the promises, a faith that believed God's Word.

"I came from the presence of the glory back to earth. I was not the same man. I confronted the conditions I had seen before, but this time it was in the name of Jesus. With a faith that could shake hell and move anything else, I cried to the demon power that was making this young woman a maniac, 'Come out of her, in the name of Jesus!' She rolled over and fell asleep, and awakened in 14 hours, perfectly sane and perfectly whole."

Brother Wigglesworth was a humble servant who was willing to pay the price necessary to loose the gift of faith which was required to gain the deliverance of another. He laid down his life so God could raise him up to deliver the miraculous to an imprisoned soul.

God desires to speak to the world through all of us with the gift of faith, but He can only do it as we humble ourselves and become willing to pay the price to allow the gift to flow through us. When we do, God will speak through us using this gift, great miracles will manifest, and lives will be changed forever.

DISCONNECT FROM THE WORLD

Let me tell the story of another great man of God, Charles Price, one of the most amazing ministers of his time. Brother Price knew something about faith that most Christians do not know. He understood if he could get enough of the world out of people, he could get them in position to receive from Heaven.

I have been told there were times when Price went to a city to minister that he did not rent a hall for just a night or two, but he would actually put up a slat building and stay there holding meetings for a very long time. Every night he would preach and preach and preach. Night after night after night the meetings would go on until one evening, finally, the atmosphere would begin to change.

The change came when the people began to separate and pull themselves away from their connection with the world. Their inner man began to possess the faith of God, and it wasn't long before miracles began to happen, lives were changed, conversions took place, families were mended and churches were born.

Brother Price tapped into a secret that has been lost on our fast-paced world today. He knew that our connection with the world must be severed before God can be released to do what He desires to do in its fullness. Could he have gotten results in two day crusades? He did time and time again, but the results he saw by staying in a city until the people awoke to the things of God were far greater in measure and well worth the effort.

The truth is, we can't live a half-hearted life and expect to win. There is so much more available to us than what our simple fruit of faith can manage to obtain for us. If we will separate and set ourselves apart unto God, He will do great and mighty things in our midst by His ever-available gift of faith.

There are life-changing miracles waiting to be loosed into your life and the lives of your family members. There are breakthroughs waiting to be released in your ministry, and revivals waiting to be loosed in your church and community. God is waiting to impart the gift of faith into prepared, willing vessels so they may be seen as the light on a hill, and Jesus may be magnified and glorified in all the earth.

Will you be one of these vessels of honor, ready for the Master's use? Will you disconnect from the world system long enough to see a manifestation of God's faith, a mantle of the gift of faith which will bring deliverance, healing and miracles to others? Will you be one who will allow God to speak through you to a lost and dying world, to people struggling and searching for answers? By God's grace I will be. I hope you will be, too.

PART FOUR

LEARNING
AND DISCERNING

CHAPTER 22

KNOW THEM BY THEIR FRUITS

Two brave men stood before the weeping congregation. There was much confusion and fear among the people, and the voice of reason had left them. The mass of humanity murmured against Moses and Aaron. Some cried out, "I wish we had died in the land of Egypt!" Others wept and said, "I wish we had already died in this wilderness!"

The questions had been swirling all night long, some pondering why God had brought them into the wilderness to die, and others wondering if it was time to turn around and go back to the land of Pharaoh, even if it meant living as slaves again. The people felt hopeless, and their despair went beyond anything they had experienced in their long journey together.

By dawn, they had decided it was time for a new leader. They said one to another, "Let us choose a captain, and let us go back to Egypt." Upon hearing this, Moses and Aaron fell on their faces before the assembly of the children of Israel. As they lay face-down on the ground, two men stepped forward to try to calm the situation.

Joshua and Caleb, two of the twelve spies sent to search out the land of Canaan, stood by Moses and Aaron, and they tore their clothes as a sign of grief. They were distressed by the lack of faith in the camp, and grieved that God's people were so quickly turned aside from His will.

Moses, at God's command, had sent the 12 men into Canaan to spy out the land and see what awaited them there. It had been a very long road, this journey to the Promised Land, and they were eager to see what God had prepared for them.

Twelve leading men, one from each of the twelve tribes of Israel, confidently crossed the Jordan river and were awestruck by what they saw on the other side. They came upon grapes the size of which they had never seen before. One cluster was so heavy it had to be slung across a pole to bear the weight. The pomegranates and figs were lush and amazing to behold. Rivers and streams flowed freely, and the fields were ripe for the harvest. The Promised Land was indeed a land of goodness and delight.

The twelve had spent forty days searching the land, and then they returned to give their report. The content of the report was what had struck such fear and grief in the heart of the people. Though all twelve men agreed that the land was abundantly supplied, ten of them were preoccupied with the size and might of the people who lived there. Their uneasiness caused them to give a hearty thumbs-down to the idea of trying to cross over and conquer the inhabitants of the land.

The ten insisted they would fail, saying that the giants who lived there would surely eat the Israelites for lunch! And then they made this statement: "We were in our own sight as grasshoppers, and so we were in their sight." Even though Caleb interjected his faith and assured the people they were well able to go up and possess the land at once, the ten negative men completely overwhelmed and discouraged the people, and they believed the word of man instead of the word of the Lord.

After this gloomy assessment, chaos broke loose in the camp. It was then that Moses and Aaron dropped to the ground, and Joshua and Caleb stepped up to calm the situation. Joshua declared, "The land is an exceedingly good land. If the Lord delights in us, then He will bring us into this land, and will give it to us; for it is a land that flows with milk and honey. Only do not rebel against the Lord, and do not fear the people of the land; for they are bread for us. Their strength is departed from them, and the Lord is with us. Fear them not!" (see Numbers 13:1-33; 14:1-9).

What was the difference here? How could ten of twelve be so discouraged while the other two were encouraged and ready to go in immediately? The difference was in what they perceived to be the truth of the situation.

Joshua and Caleb were led by the voice of God, and so what they perceived did not come by way of the physical eye, but it came by the eye of the Spirit. This spiritual eye empowered them to see something the other ten men could not grasp. Joshua and Caleb saw the same giants, but they perceived that God's chosen people would be more than conquerors against

364

them. Though the ten saw the giants and envisioned themselves as grasshoppers who would be eaten alive, Joshua and Caleb imagined the giants would be bread for them to eat. Someone was going to eat someone; the question was, who to believe.

GOD SPEAKS THROUGH FRUIT

Notice that God did not use words to speak to Joshua and Caleb, but He did speak to them nonetheless. He spoke through the faith which rose up in them when they saw something others could not see. Just like Joshua and Caleb, our spiritual eyes, through the fruit of our faith, will show us who we are in the Word (see James 1:22-25).

As Christians, we are people who bear fruit; the fruit of the spirit, yes, but so much more. We also bear the fruit of sonship, of being sons and daughters of God who are led by His Spirit (see Romans 8:14). We produce fruits of attitude, cultural fruits, moral fruits, educational fruits and the fruits of our upbringing. All of these are important for us to understand.

Speaking through fruit is one of the many ways God uses to lead us (see Acts 8:18-24). It may be through the fruit which is resident in us, or it may be through the fruit we see in others (see John 13:35). Sometimes, God will speak this way, and you will not even realize it, but as you mature in the things of God it will become a very predominate voice.

You may be led by the fruit of the spirit, and that fruit will cause you to see and perceive what God wants you to see and perceive, just like Joshua and Caleb (see Galatians 5:22-23). You may also be led by the fruit of your fellowship with the Holy Spirit, a kind of fruit which causes you to hear and recognize the voice of God inside of you. You may know that you know that you know something, when no one else does. This is being led by fruit, judging all things to see what God wants you to see instead of what the world wants you to see.

It is by this fruit you can see things differently than those around you who have no hope, and it is this same fruit which will reveal if something is of God, or if it is of man. In reality, God speaks through fruit all of the time, through the things which manifest in every life and distinguish that life from all others (see 1 John 3:16-19).

There are many things that make us different from everyone else. Some of these things are a result of the individual gifts and callings that God has placed in us. For instance, if you are a person who is gifted with mercy, a gift found in Romans 12:8, I would expect to see words and acts of mercy evident in your life. Those words and acts would be the fruit of your gift manifesting for the benefit of those around you. If someone had the gift of exhortation, found in the very same verse, I would expect that person to be an encourager, one who speaks words which build others up and help them to find their way in life. This would be the fruit of an exhorter.

There is nothing more frustrating than to make contact with someone who tells you one thing, but lives another. A person's fruit will show you who he really is, rather than who he wants you to believe him to be. Fruit is produced on the inside, and it is revealed through words, actions, attitudes and beliefs. The Spirit of God will make you aware of the fruit that is produced in the life of an individual, and that fruit will tell you what the person is really all about. In showing you the signs of the fruit of every man, the Holy Spirit can speak to you and lead you in the way He needs you to go.

If God needs you to see giants look like loaves of bread, then your fruit of faith will cause you to see them just that way. Perceiving life through fruit will cause you to see things exactly as God intends them to be seen. No more will you be afraid, but you will be courageous and steadfast, even as Joshua and Caleb were in the land of the giants.

THE FRUIT OF THE SPIRIT

There are many different kinds of fruit we all bear in life, but when it comes to hearing the voice of God through fruit, there is none more important than the fruit of the spirit. Let's review what the fruit of the spirit is: *"But the fruit of the Spirit is love, joy, peace, longsuffering* (patience)*, gentleness, goodness, faith, meekness, temperance: against such there is no law"* (Galatians 5:22-23).

Notice verse 22 says, *"the fruit of the Spirit."* It is "fruit" singular, not "fruits" plural. And yet, we see nine different attributes listed. So how can this be?

To understand, think of an orange. An orange is a single piece of fruit, but inside there are many sections, or slices. Imagine if you peeled an orange, and then removed slice number three from it. Would it be whole anymore? No, it would be a partial orange now, not a whole one.

There are nine different "slices," if you will, to the fruit of the spirit, nine different manifestations of the character of God in you. They are all significant, but none of them can function well without the others. We need all parts of the fruit of the spirit, every slice intact, if we are to live successfully.

Try to imagine love without goodness. If you ask any wife if she thinks her husband really loves her even when he is not good to her, the answer will be an emphatic "No!" We express our love through acts of goodness, so we know that those parts of the fruit of the spirit cannot operate without one another.

Joy is not sustainable without peace. Faith is weak without patience, and temperance (also known as self-control) cannot be sustained without faith. You need all parts of the fruit of the spirit to be working together in order to truly hear the voice of God speaking through them.

We also know the fruit of the spirit will be evident in some believers more so than others, because we are all growing at different rates, but we should all have at least some level of fruit in evidence if we are to call ourselves "Christians." We should all be led by the faith-filled, power-packed, glory-exuding Holy Spirit who empowers us to be overcomers in every situation.

THE ISSUES OF LIFE

I want to explain the value of the fruit of the spirit in your life before I show you more about how God speaks through it. We've looked at Proverbs 4:20-23 in a previous chapter, but I want you to read it once more: *"My son, attend to my words; incline thine ear unto my sayings. Let them not depart from thine eyes; keep them in the midst of thine heart. For they are life unto those that find them, and health to all their flesh. Keep thy heart with all diligence; for out of it are the issues of life."*

The fruit of the spirit is a portion of the issues of life. It is a force which enables you to live the life of God that was birthed in you when you were born again. You cannot live in your own power and walk in the Spirit, but you must live in the power of the fruit of the spirit in order to walk in that realm successfully. When you do, you walk in grace through faith, and you are free from the law and Satan's dominion (see Galatians 5:23).

Jesus said in John 8:34: *"Verily, verily, I say unto you, Whosoever committeth sin is the servant of sin."* Sin has the strength to imprison you and separate you from God's voice. It has the ability to bind you up with sickness, lack and every other work of the devil. The good news is that you can overcome the strength of sin by walking in the fruit of the spirit and thereby overcoming the plans of the enemy.

If you will operate within the confines of love, joy, peace, patience, gentleness, goodness, temperance, meekness and faith, the devil will have no place to be strong in your life. He will become weak even as you in your spirit become stronger and stronger. When you walk in the fruit of the spirit, you will resist the devil, and according to the Bible, he will have to flee. He will run from you because you respond to situations by the Spirit, and by the fruit that sustains resistance (see James 4:7).

Sin and the flesh will no longer have dominion over the man or woman who is strong in the fruit of the spirit. For proof, look at these two passages: *"O death, where is thy sting? O grave, where is thy victory? The sting of death is sin; and the strength of sin is the law"* (1 Corinthians 15:55-56). *"But the fruit of the Spirit is love, joy, peace, longsuffering, gentleness, goodness, faith, meekness, temperance: against such there is no law"* (Galatians 5:22-23).

By reading these two scriptures together, we see that the fruit of the spirit is not subject to the law; therefore, sin can be overcome if you operate in the fruit of the spirit, and in the issues of life which were birthed in you by God's love.

FREEDOM!

Jesus said: *"If ye continue in my word, then are ye my disciples indeed; And ye shall know the truth, and the truth shall make you free"* (John 8:31-32).

You can experience freedom through the fruit of the spirit, and you can enjoy reconciliation and redemption. You can walk free, so the things of this world and the evil of the devil's domain have no power over you. You can be free of every bondage, hindrance and imprisonment, because the issues of life, and the fruit of the spirit in particular, have been engrafted into you.

You once faced the devil alone, but when you were born again God implanted His divine ability inside you. Second Corinthians 5:17-18 proves this: *"Therefore if any man be in Christ, he is a new creature: old things are passed away; behold, all things are become new. And all things are of God, who hath reconciled us to himself by Jesus Christ, and hath given to us the ministry of reconciliation."*

Paul adds to this when he writes: *"For we are his workmanship, created in Christ Jesus unto good works, which God hath before ordained that we should walk in them"* (Ephesians 2:10),

And Ephesians 2:6 is the third witness: *"And hath raised us up together, and made us sit together in heavenly places in Christ Jesus."*

When God did this He embedded His divine abilities in you, making you His offspring. Possessing God's character through the fruit of the spirit is subject to your faith, but if you will operate in it, you will be as strong as God is against His foes, and you will freely hear His voice pouring forth from an open Heaven.

Jesus never had a Satan problem, but Satan always had a Jesus problem. You can have the same outcome. You don't have to have devil problems anymore, but the devil can have fruit-of-the-spirit-engrafted Christian problems!

If you want Satan to leave you alone, start walking in the fruit of the spirit. Begin to walk in love instead of bitterness, in joy instead of sorrow, in peace instead of strife, in gentleness instead of an overbearing spirit, in generosity instead of stinginess, in meekness instead of pride, and in temperance instead of lust.

The devil hates it when you live in the fruit of the spirit, because it imprisons him and sets you free. It strengthens you and removes the leverage of sin from him. It opens doors for you and slams them in his face. So let the fruit of the spirit flow from your heart and empower you to live in freedom all the days of your life.

MORTIFIED

Notice what Paul writes in Galatians 5:24: *"And they that are Christ's have crucified the flesh with the affections and lusts."*

In some translations, the word crucified is translated as "mortified," but what does it mean to mortify the flesh? To understand, you have to think of a mortician. I know the thought will make some people uncomfortable, but stay with me so you can understand the point I'm trying to make.

I don't want to paint an ugly picture, so let's just say the job of the mortician is to make sure the body we view in the funeral home does not move in any way. I'm not talking about physically moving, because there is

369

no more life, but of moving because it is unsecured.

Morticians inject certain substances into lifeless bodies, and they also stitch them up in certain places, all so that they will lie perfectly still in the casket. This is all I'm going to say, but I think you get the point.

When you mortify the flesh, you make it immobile and inactive in your life. You inject certain things in it, such as love, joy, peace, patience and goodness, and you stitch it up with other things, like gentleness, meekness, temperance and faith. What is the result of this mortification of the flesh? You make the acts described in Galatians 5:19-21 inactive in your life.

No longer are you subject to adultery, fornication, uncleanness, lasciviousness, idolatry, witchcraft, hatred, variance, emulations, wrath, strife, seditions, heresies, envyings, murders, drunkenness and revellings. Sin is stiff as a board in your life, just like a properly prepared corpse, and you are not subject to its devices anymore. Instead, you are empowered to overcome every wile of the devil and walk in the fullness of who you are in Christ.

WALK IN THE SPIRIT

Once sin is mortified and inactive, you can move on to Galatians 5:25 where it says: *"If we live in the Spirit, let us also walk in the Spirit."* Let me give you some valuable insight here. Because of the way this verse is worded, we can conclude that it is possible to live in one place while we walk in another. You can live in the Spirit, but walk in the flesh if you're not careful. You can live in the Kingdom of God, but fail to succeed there and hear His voice if you don't know how.

Go back to our analogy in an earlier chapter about citizenship. You can live in America, but fail to walk as an American. You can reside here, but never thrive because you lack knowledge of how to live successfully. Suppose you don't know the language of America, which is English. You won't do very well for long. You may make it in your little enclosed community, but when you try to make it in society as a whole, you will fail.

Or suppose you don't know the laws of the land. You may live here, but you won't live freely for long if you don't understand that murder in America is against the law. If you get angry and take matters into your own hands in this country, you are going to jail for the rest of your life. So much for living in the land of the free!

If you are born again, you are living in the Spirit, but let me ask you, are you walking there? Are you living successfully in the Kingdom of God and enjoying the liberty of freedom from sin, or are you merely existing and failing to thrive as a Christian?

In John 17:16, Jesus said to His Father: *"They are not of the world, even as I am not of the world."* You are no longer a citizen of this earthly kingdom, but you are a citizen and a partaker of a heavenly Kingdom, the Kingdom of God where the laws of the Spirit of life in Christ Jesus overrule the laws of sin and death. You have this truth before you, but do you live like it?

This statement from Jesus was a part of a chapter-long prayer. Jesus prayed something very powerful in the verse right before: *"I pray not that thou shouldest take them out of the world, but that thou shouldest keep them from the evil"* (John 17:15).

When people are saved, they are not automatically whisked up into Heaven, but they are empowered, equipped, fortified and energized to live an overcoming life in this world. You can live in the Spirit, walk in the Spirit and hear from the Spirit through the empowering of the fruit of the spirit.

Of course, even when you are a right-possessing citizen of a nation, if you walk contrary to the rules of that nation, you will become vulnerable and liable to its corrections and punishments. You can, through your lack of self-control, put yourself under the power of the lawmaker. In spiritual terms, if you willfully sin, it puts you under the control of the devil because he is the ruler of this world system. You do not want to go there; trust me.

Instead, I encourage you to stay in the Spirit. Walk there and obey the laws of that realm so you can obtain every right and benefit of the Spirit. That's what this teaching on the fruit of the spirit boils down to. There is freedom in the Spirit, but you must allow the fruit thereof to abound in your life. Then you will live successfully and hear the voice of God.

HEARING GOD THROUGH THE FRUIT OF THE SPIRIT

Now that we have established that every believer has been engrafted with certain fruit, including the fruit of the spirit, how can you hear God speak through this fruit? The first way you hear God speak through this gift is by recognizing evidence of the fruit in the lives of others. Jesus said: *"Ye shall know them by their fruits..."* (Matthew 7:16).

If you walked up to a cherry tree in the summertime, you would expect to find cherries on it, right? It's the same in spiritual matters. When you find the fruit of the spirit in abundance in a situation, you will know God is there, too. You can be confident, knowing who you are dealing with by examining the fruit that is evident in them.

For instance, if someone tells you he is a Christian, but you see no fruit to verify what he says, God is in essence telling you the man is not who he says he is. If he tells you he is merciful and yet never exhibits mercy, you have uncovered a fraud. If he says he is a giver but he never lets go of anything for anyone, you have found a liar.

Here's another example. Suppose someone thinks they are called to be a pastor, but they do not bear the fruit of a desire to pray and study God's Word. If I ran into such a man, I would encourage him to look elsewhere for an occupation. God will not send you where your engrafted fruit cannot keep you.

This is where so many people are misled. They think because an individual prophesied and told them they are something particular, then they are, even if they have no desire or fruit to back them up. I can guarantee if God calls you to be something in the Kingdom of God, He will give you every fruit necessary to fulfill the call.

I've had many people come to me over the years to declare the mighty call of God on their lives. The trouble is, they had no fruit to bear them out. When I see no fruit, I hear from God that there is no call.

Where is the goodness? Where is the gentleness? Where is the temperance, the faith, the love and peace? Where is the joy? Where is the patience and meekness? Where is the desire to pray, study and fast for others? Where is the compassion for people of all walks of life? Where is the love of the Father? If I cannot find these things in abundance in a life, I will not find a call there, either.

SEEING YOUR OWN FRUIT

You can know others by their fruit, but you can also judge yourself by the fruit you are producing. Let's say you are engaged in an activity which has not produced any fruit for a long time. If I were in that situation I would ask the Lord for something else to do, because He is not pleased with fruitless vines (see Matthew 3:10).

When you examine your life and find an area where you are unfruitful, it is an unmistakable sign you are not where you are supposed to be. God has said through your lack of fruit, "You're going the wrong way. You have put your hand to the wrong plow."

As an example, let's say you thought God told you to join the choir. So, you sign up for the choir, attend the introductory class that tells you all about the choir, and then you begin to attend the weekly choir rehearsals.

You are having the time of your life for about three weeks, but then something begins to happen. For reasons you don't understand, you begin to dread choir rehearsal. You don't like the choir director, and the man who sits next to you gets on your nerves. You don't like any of the songs the director picks, and you feel your talents are not being highlighted.

Here is the time to judge the fruit of this situation. Is this a normal place of challenge where the fruit of the spirit will empower you to overcome, or have you been led by your own desires instead of by the voice of God?

You can tell the difference by looking for signs of fruit in the situation. Is there any love evident? Is there any peace? Can you maintain joy even when things don't go your way? Are goodness, gentleness and meekness at work? Can you maintain your temperance when you feel neglected, or do you give in and retaliate?

Life is full of challenges, so a perfect choir is not what you should be looking for, but the ability to ride the waves and succeed no matter what comes your way should be in evidence. If you are truly giving your best effort, and you still can't get any peace about a matter, it may be time to step back and ask God if you should let it go.

If you are doing all you know to do, and love is not the motivating factor, you may need to look deep inside and re-evaluate. Did God really call you there, and you just need to use the fruit you have to succeed, or did you call yourself, and the fruit you are missing is telling you it's time to go another direction?

Evident fruit, or the lack of it, can tell you much concerning the situations you are in today. It doesn't mean you bail out every time something becomes difficult, but you do expect the fruit of the spirit to be powerful enough to help you get through the rough spots, and you don't expect every day of your life to be a rough spot.

The apostle Paul met with many hardships in his ministry, but he was able to endure and overcome them all by the power of the Spirit. Had not the fruit of the spirit been evident and active in Paul's life, he would not have been able to finish his course victoriously. A God-led life is not without problems, but it is filled with the fruit of the spirit to help you overcome every one.

HEARING BY ABIDING AND DELIGHTING

Jesus said: *"Abide in me, and I in you. As the branch cannot bear fruit of itself, except it abide in the vine; no more can ye, except ye abide in me. I am the vine, ye are the branches: He that abideth in me, and I in him, the same bringeth forth much fruit: for without me ye can do nothing. If a man abide not in me, he is cast forth as a branch, and is withered; and men gather them, and cast them into the fire, and they are burned. If ye abide in me, and my words abide in you, ye shall ask what ye will, and it shall be done unto you"* (John 15:4-7).

You cannot bear godly fruit without Jesus, but you can labor in the wrong vineyard and be unfruitful all by yourself. Again, check your fruit, and you will hear God speak loud and clear.

The psalmist writes: *"Delight thyself also in the Lord; and he shall give thee the desires of thine hear."* (Psalm 37:4). Delighting in the Lord is another way of describing abiding in Him. When you delight or abide in Him, you stay in His presence, and you are eager to hear His voice and do whatever He asks.

When you delight yourself in the Lord, two things will happen. First, God will instill a specific desire in you. It could be to teach children, or a desire to visit shut-ins, or to give abundantly. God gives you this desire, and then He fulfills it by giving you the fruit to perform it.

Many people fail to recognize the voice of God which is evident in the desires He has given them to do certain things. They make comments such as, "Oh, I've always felt that way." Or, "I've wanted to do that since I was a child." What is that? It's the voice of God manifesting in their desires, but because they have not been taught, they do no recognize Him.

To help you grasp this, let's say you have a desire to help children, and so you ask to join the children's ministry in your church. You delight yourself in the Lord, and He rewards you with a volunteer position in the two year old class. That's great, but did you ever stop to consider why you had the desire to help children in the first place?

Could it be that God spoke to you to go to the children's ministry by giving you this desire, and then He fulfilled it by allowing you to work there?

Of course this is so. God fills us with desire for certain things, and then He gives us what we desire.

The Lord also gives us the fruit we will need to succeed in our desire. To work in the children's ministry, you will need plenty of love and patience, not to mention a great deal of creativity. How amazing you have those very things at work in your life. How amazing you loved art as a child, and now you are teaching young children through art-filled object lessons. How amazing you love to sing, and now you are singing children's songs in class to teach them God's Word.

Sometimes we forget where our fruit came from, and where our talents and gifts originated. If they are useful in the Kingdom, you can be assured they came from you abiding in Him. When these gifts come from God, they come with a message to you and to those you will touch using them. The fruit of your calling says to one and all, "I love you; therefore, I have given you these gifts to use for My glory. Use them and bless others that I may be known."

CHOOSING BASED ON FRUIT

You can also hear God's voice displayed in fruit when you are faced with certain life choices. I often wonder how many sad Christians married the wrong person and discovered it too late, because they were distracted by physical looks and forgot to check the internal fruit. I can tell you that I'd much rather have an ugly woman with godly fruit than a pretty one who was a devil! Thankfully, I did not have to choose between the two. My wife is beautiful, inside and out, a blessing I thank God for every day.

You need to place a priority on finding good fruit before you ever join yourself with anyone in personal matters. I'm not just talking about marriage, but of every friendship and important association in your life.

Business dealings are another place where you need to look for good fruit before you sign the contract. If the person you are about to partner with says they are a Christian, of course you need to look for the fruit of the spirit and allow God to speak to you through its manifestation, or through its absence.

If a potential business partner is not saved, you can still look for fruit that will tell you who he is. Does he have moral character, or does he change his mind with every wind that blows? Does he have a long list of satisfied customers, or has he burned so many bridges you can't tell where he's been before?

Far too many believers have gone down the path to failure, missing God's warning signs completely because they did not understand how to interpret the fruit that they saw in the lives of others. When you see questionable fruit in the life of someone whose lifestyle will affect you personally, ask God to give you discerning of spirits to interpret the meaning of the fruit you see. It will be worth the time and effort to find out if what you see is what you will get. Stop and pray, and allow God to bring fruit to your attention so that He can speak to you through it. Who a man says he is and who he really is may be two entirely different things.

LED BY SIGHT

There may be times you will hear God's voice as you are led by what you see. Here's an example of what I mean. In 1 John 3:17 we read: *"But whoso hath this world's good, and seeth his brother have need, and shutteth up his bowels of compassion from him, how dwelleth the love of God in him?"*

Christians should bear the fruit of a willingness to give to others, without having to be told to give by a sign, a wonder or an audible voice. In other words, God does not need to tell you to feed the hungry brother if you come face to face with him on your way downtown. Why do you suppose you saw the need anyway, when so many others walked right on by and did not seem to notice? Could it be that God put you there, in the right place, at the right time, as a way of speaking to you?

If you see a brother or sister in need, the fruit of your giving spirit should rise up and make you realize God meant for you to see it, and that He also means for you to do everything you can to meet the need. Moving in the fruit of love is a very common way the Lord will speak to you. He does not use words when He speaks this way, but He will use the fruit of His love in you to move you to do what He wants you to do.

When you see something others cannot see, it is the voice of God calling you to respond. I tell people, "If you see a problem, you are probably being called to get involved in and solve that problem." When they say, "Oh, Pastor, the people are hungry on the streets," then I say, "Go home and make sandwiches." I know this sounds harsh, but if you see it and I don't, God's not calling me; He is calling you.

This is a significant point, because when God shows you something, you are then accountable for what He showed you. Jesus verified this principle in Matthew 25:31-46 when He taught about those who clothed the naked, fed the hungry, and visited the sick and imprisoned. He said in verse 40: *"Inasmuch as ye have done it unto one of the least of these my brethren, ye have done it unto me."*

This was a great thing which brought eternal reward, but there were also people at this event who were rebuked because they did not clothe, feed, or visit the sick and imprisoned. Jesus accused them of not taking care of Him in verse 43, and so they asked a valid question in verse 44: *"When saw we thee an hungred, or athirst, or a stranger, or naked, or sick, or in prison, and did not minister unto thee?"*

In other words, "Hey, God! We never saw You naked or sick or imprisoned or hungry and ignored You! How can You make this accusation against us?" But Jesus answered those who were cast into eternal punishment in verse 45: *"Verily I say unto you, Inasmuch as ye did it not to one of the least of these, ye did it not to me."*

Each group of people had observed the same things—hungry people, naked people, sick and imprisoned people—but one group acted while the other did not. What was the difference? One group was moved with compassion because of the fruit of the spirit at work in their lives, while the other group ignored what they saw, not recognizing the voice of God.

We are accountable for what we see and hear. When we see something, even though others don't, we are responsible to recognize the voice of God rising up through the fruit of love, goodness, meekness and gentleness, and act on what we see.

GOD SPEAKS THROUGH YOU

As with every other way that God speaks to you, He will also speak to others through you by the fruit you bear. What do you suppose God is trying to say when you give love to someone who does not deserve it? Could He be saying, "I love you," to that person? Of course, He could. And when He speaks through you in acts of gentleness or goodness, what does this say to people? It says God is a good God, and He truly cares for them.

When you behave meekly and activate temperance in your life, God is revealing His meek and humble nature, and His own self-control. When peace and joy permeate your life, God reveals to the world that He is a God of joy unspeakable and full of glory, and that He is our peace who gave Himself for our recovery.

We should always allow God to speak through fruit, especially through the fruit of the spirit, when we are dealing with sinners. You may be the only Jesus some people will ever see. What they see and hear you do and say, they will believe God also does and says. It is an awesome burden we bear, but we do not bear it alone.

This is why the fruit of the spirit was engrafted in us at the new birth, to make us what God needs us to be in every situation. This fruit keeps us honest and loving toward our brothers and sisters in the Lord, and it keeps our witness to the world pure.

We are God's voice in the world today, and the fruit of the spirit is a vital tool the Lord uses to reach lost humanity. It's essential for you to hear God's voice in the fruit being produced all around you so you can walk in the Spirit for your own freedom and victory, and for the benefit of those God sends you to reach in His name.

Give God your perceptions, and allow them to be led of the Spirit by the fruit of the spirit which indwells you. Some call it letting go and letting God. I call it walking in the Spirit and not in the lust of the flesh, giving God the opportunity to speak to the world through you.

CHAPTER 23

JUDGE WHAT YOU HEAR

Peter, Paul and Barnabas had just finished speaking, each telling of the great things God was doing among the Gentiles, and yet, many in the room were still not convinced. It was a matter of the law, after all, and they believed the Old Covenant law of circumcision should prevail even today among the Gentile believers. It was quite a sticky situation, and one that would not be resolved by the wisdom of men.

James slowly stood to his feet and answered, saying, "Men and brethren, listen to me. Peter has declared how God visited the Gentiles in a miraculous way and prepared to take out of them a people for His name. This is no surprise because the words of the prophets agree, as it is written, 'After this I will return, and will build again the tabernacle of David, which is fallen down; and I will build again the ruins thereof, and I will set it up, that the residue of men might seek after the Lord, and all the Gentiles, upon whom My name is called, says the Lord, who does all these things.'

"Now, we know that God's works have been established from the beginning of the world. So, here is what I say we should do. I say we should not trouble the Gentiles who have turned to God, but that we should write to them and explain to them that they should abstain from pollutions of idols, from fornication, from things strangled and from blood. For the rest, the words of Moses are preached in every city in the synagogue every Sabbath day, and that is enough." James sat down, and the people were quieted by his wisdom (see Acts 15:1-22).

This word of wisdom gave credence to Peter's visitation on the rooftop and his experience in the home of Cornelius, and it also judged as true the signs and wonders Paul and Barnabas had been experiencing every time they preached among the Gentiles.

Notice that James first judged what was said with the written Word. The most important thing to James was what Peter, Paul and Barnabas had said they experienced actually lined up with the written words of the prophets. Then James went on to give counsel which further clarified what Peter had heard, and he gave the church direction when responding to this new way of dealing with the Gentiles. In the last two verses, James told them how to set church order in motion in a practical way.

Even though Peter, Paul and Barnabas were highly esteemed, the early believers still checked what they said against the Word, and then they checked it again with their spiritual leader before they did anything about it. From this counsel, Paul and Barnabas, and many others, returned to preach the gospel to the Gentiles with clearer direction and more unity among the brethren.

JUDGE ALL THINGS

If the early church relied on the Word and counsel to verify visions, signs and wonders, we should do no less. If you have heard from God, now is not the time to act hastily, but it is the time to judge what you heard to determine if what you thought God said really was a word from Heaven.

No one wants bad information. We all spend hours each week trying to find out what's going on in the world to avoid a lack of knowledge. We listen to the radio, watch cable news, check the Internet daily and talk with our friends to make sure we're keeping up with what's happening around us. If we are willing to make such an effort for natural information, it seems to me we should be even more willing to invest our time to make sure our spiritual information is in order.

We need to judge what we think God said to us. This may sound a little high-minded if you don't understand, so let me make it clear. The Bible tells us he that is spiritual judges all things (see 1 Corinthians 2:15). This is a command, not an option, so we must make sure we are doing what the Bible says we should. This does not mean you judge God, but you do judge your perception of what you think He said. In other words, you judge yourself when you judge what you heard, and this is always necessary.

In 1 Corinthians 14:10 we are told: *"There are, it may be, so many kinds of voices in the world, and none of them is without signification."* Voices open doors to our lives, and every voice brings with it a purpose for good or for evil. Because this is true, we need to be very careful to judge what we hear so that we do not fall prey to the purpose of the enemy.

We are warned in 1 John 4:1 *"Beloved, believe not every spirit, but try the spirits whether they are of God: because many false prophets are gone out into the world."* No matter how pretty the package may be, or how refined the delivery is, make sure you know who said what in your life. If Peter, Paul and Barnabas needed to be judged for what they believed God had said to them, we should be quick to judge ourselves and one another without fear.

JUDGE WHAT YOU HEAR BY THE WORD

The Bible has set certain benchmarks by which you can judge what you hear. There are basically five methods you can use. You can judge by the Word, by prayer, by fasting, by the counsel of others and by the passage of time.

When God truly speaks to you, what He says will invoke faith in your life, because faith is the vehicle through which God visits, demonstrates and manifests Himself to man. The world was created by faith, we are born again by faith, we are healed by faith and we live by faith. It is only natural, then, that we hear and experience God by faith.

By now you know where faith comes from. It comes by hearing, and hearing comes by the Word of God (see Romans 10:17). When God speaks, He invokes faith which comes from His Word. This takes us right back to the beginning of this book, where we learned that the primary way God speaks to us is through His Word. This being true, it should be no surprise to discover the primary way we check what we hear is also by the Word of God.

You need to compare what you think you heard with established doctrine, and with "thus says the Lord" in the Bible. Don't ever skip this step. God will not speak something to you which is in opposition to His written Word, so looking to the Bible for answers should be a way of life for you. It should be the foundation upon which everything else is built. It should be the first and last stop on your way to receiving from an open Heaven and hearing the voice of God.

We read this in Acts 17:11: *"These were more noble than those in Thessalonica, in that they received the word with all readiness of mind, and searched the scriptures daily, whether those things were so."*

Here the apostle Paul was busy teaching relatively new believers. He was laying line upon line, precept upon precept, just as the Bible told him to.

Right in the middle of his teaching, these learning Christians had the audacity to read the scripture themselves and check up on what Paul was preaching.

Was Paul offended? No. In fact, he said he was glad they were questioning him, and he was pleased they were searching the scriptures themselves to see if what he said really did come from God. Think of it!

Suppose Christians today would hold their preaching "heroes" accountable to the Word of God. Wouldn't this be amazing? No, but it would be scriptural. We should never support those we have not judged by the Word of God.

The Word alone verifies whether what is spoken by a man comes from Heaven or not. It is not verified by an anointing, because the anointing can be mimicked. It is not verified by a shout, because a shout is a soulish manifestation. It is not verified by a good word, because a word can sound good, but still not be from God. Only the Bible will have the final say.

When you judge what you hear by the Word, you do so for your protection. You need this safeguard, because you can be sure that as much as God is trying to invoke faith in your life, other voices (those of demons, the flesh or self, and even of other people) will attempt to instill something other than faith. If you allow those voices to dictate to you, you will find yourself following an earthly way instead of following Jesus who is *the* way. So be careful. Judge what you hear and filter through the many voices in the world; otherwise, it will be easy for you to be deceived.

This is also why it's necessary for you to allow God to choose how He will speak to you rather than for you to try to dictate how He should speak. God is so much wiser than we are, so He chooses the way He will speak to us and the path we should take based on His infinite wisdom. We must always remember that He is the Creator, and we are merely the created. He is God, and we are His servants.

If you try to force God to speak in a way He has not chosen, you will find yourself hearing and experiencing things which are not from Heaven. You will be deceived and find yourself in a place you did not intend to be. The thing about deception is that once it has come into your heart, you may not be able to hear reproof, chastening or rebuke. Everything produces after its own kind, so once you allow deception in, it will produce more and more deception and cloud your judgment in all things.

To avoid this trap, remember to always, always, judge what you hear according to the Word of God, and keep the foundation of scripture in your life. With a strong foundation of the Word in your spirit, it will be much more difficult for you to be misled.

This is why when I need to hear from God, I always go to the Word first before I ever seek to hear His voice another way. Remember, the Word of God is the primary way God speaks, so chances are if you will give sufficient time to scripture, you will likely find your answer there and will have no need to look in another place.

Jesus tells us: *"Ask, and it shall be given you; seek, and ye shall find; knock, and it shall be opened unto you: For every one that asketh receiveth; and he that seeketh findeth; and to him that knocketh it shall be opened"* (Matthew 7:7-8).

When you search the scriptures, you are unlocking doors and receiving from the open Heaven. If you ask, you will receive an answer. If you knock, the door of revelation will be made available. If you seek, you will find what you are looking for in God's Word.

THE WORD WILL CONFIRM

When we are searching in His Word for proof of what we believe God said, we will come across certain things the Bible tells us to do that should be no-brainers for all of us. For instance, you don't have to ask, "Hey God, should I love my enemies and pray for them?" You might hear, "Duh! I already told you so!" (See Matthew 5:44).

There are other commands in the Bible which are not quite as easy to do without a little more information. So, when you reach one of those confirming verses in the Word that lets you know you are on the right track, but it still leaves you with a question or two, don't panic. It's not unusual. Just trust God to finish what He started, and ask Him to fill in the blanks for you before you act.

Here's an example. Let's say you believe God gave you a dream in which you saw yourself preaching the gospel in an unidentifiable place. You prayed and asked God for the interpretation, and you believe you have it, but you go to the Bible to judge what you think you heard.

So far, so good. You discover the Bible plainly tells all of us that we have the responsibility to share the gospel. Paul said it himself: *"And all things are of God, who hath reconciled us to himself by Jesus Christ, and hath given to us the ministry of reconciliation; to wit, that God was in Christ, reconciling the world unto himself, not imputing their trespasses unto them; and hath committed unto us the word of reconciliation"* (2 Corinthians 5:18-19).

God told you personally, and now you have the Word to back you up, but you still may have to ask, "What do I say," or "How do I do it?" Those are very good questions. Should you go door to door? Should you rent a hall and pass out flyers for your first big crusade? Should you pelt your neighbors with tracts on their cars every day, or should you rain down little Gospel of John booklets from an airplane over the town square?

Probably all of these have been done at least once by someone, but what should you do? If you came to me for counsel, I would tell you to preach the gospel you know to the people you know. Simply tell them your personal testimony. Even here, the Bible will bear me out.

Everywhere the apostle Paul went, he told the story of his experience on the road to Damascus. This was Paul's gospel—what he knew beyond any shadow of a doubt. It didn't matter if Paul was standing before kings or common men, his story was consistent, "Jesus met me on the road to Damascus, and my life has never been the same."

Your testimony will be just as powerful if you will simply obey what God has already said in His Word and tell your story. Share what Jesus has done for you. There's no arguing with a personal testimony, and you don't have to be a Bible scholar to do this. Just tell what Jesus did, and let God do the rest. Let the same faith that touched your life touch another's.

You will undoubtedly have a second question after you talk to me, such as, "Where do I go and who specifically do I tell?" Those are the things you need to return to God and ask Him, because only He knows who is ready and what will work for you. It's not uncommon to have to go back to the Lord for another word, even after you have taken the time to judge the first one.

In your case, you may need an open door during break time at work so you can talk to a co-worker, or you may need an opportunity at the next family reunion, not necessarily to stand up and preach to the whole crowd, but maybe to speak one on one to your cousin or your aunt in a very private way. Who can tell? God can.

Let the Lord lead you, and you will discover many times and places you never thought of before where you can share your story. Maybe the woman in line behind you at the grocery store needs to hear. Ask God. He'll tell you if the door is open or not. Maybe your car mechanic needs to hear. Ask God.

He'll let you know when the soil is ready.

There is a balance in all things. If you go to the Word to judge what you believe God said in your life, and you do what you read in the Bible, don't be afraid to go back to the Lord and ask for more specific direction. God wants you to know more than you do, so give Him an opportunity to answer your questions and set you on the right track.

We read in 1 John 5:6-7: *"This is he that came by water and blood, even Jesus Christ; not by water only, but by water and blood. And it is the Spirit that beareth witness, because the Spirit is truth. For there are three that bear record in heaven, the Father, the Word, and the Holy Ghost: and these three are one."*

When you need that extra step of direction, even it will agree with God's Word. The Holy Ghost will never speak anything to you which is not already established in the scripture, because God, the Word and the Holy Ghost are inseparable; therefore, they will always agree with one another.

Most of the time, Christians who say they do not hear from Heaven have missed God simply because they do not have a good foundation of the Word in them. God is trying to speak to them, but He cannot speak beyond their Word capacity because they will have no place of connection for judgment. The rule of judgment is the Word of God because the Word and the Spirit agree—and God and the Word agree. What you hear from the Lord will be directly linked to His Word, and He will give you the keys to unlock the connection if you will take the time to judge and compare what you hear with what is written. Always let the Word be your first and last judge. If you do, you will not fail.

JUDGE WHAT YOU HEAR BY PRAYER

For me personally, prayer is one of the most essential parts of my life. I pray continually, as the Bible says, but I am especially diligent in my prayer life when I need to know if what I believe about a situation is really what God wants me to do. In these instances, I take the opportunity to judge myself with a time of increased, focused prayer.

Some of the most critical decisions in my church and ministry have to do with the hiring of new staff members when the need arises. I have a great office staff, and I have been blessed and equipped by God with men and women who labor for the Kingdom with passion, and with purity of life and motives. Often, when I first meet someone applying for a position, they will not have a stellar history, but I will judge what I see and hear when I meet them with a time of prayer, rather than just judge what I see on the surface.

My children's pastor is a great example. When I flew Pastor Chuck in from California for his interview, I introduced him to my family and to some of my senior staff, allowing them to spend time with him to form their own opinions. To a person they all returned with the same report, which was basically, "No way! He's not the one. He doesn't have it. He'll never make it!"

To make matters worse, all of his references were negative. I took my time, digested the information, and then I prayed. And then I got quiet and listened for the voice of God. After a time of dedicated prayer and listening, I knew what I had to do. On Saturday night after the final interview, I was at home with my wife when I told her that God had spoken to me to hire Pastor Chuck as our children's pastor. Phyllis agreed that if God had spoken to me, then we had to do what He wanted us to do, no matter what others thought.

So, we hired Pastor Chuck, and the rest of the story is one of sweet, sweet success. There is absolutely no other individual I would rather have as my children's pastor. He has turned our children's church completely around. It has grown by leaps and bounds, and he has designed a fantastic new children's facility, one I know will bless the generations to come. God knew what He was doing, and I am so glad I took time to pray and listen before I moved. I believe my family and staff are glad, too.

Suppose I had acted based on the opinions of others, assuming they carried the voice of God for me. I would have missed a great opportunity for our children had I not taken the time through focused prayer to judge how I should respond. Prayer was the key that unlocked a hidden treasure for our church.

Prayer is fellowship with the Father. This is why every time you believe God has spoken to you, you need to devote time to focused prayer in order to judge what you believe God said. Again, you're not judging God when you do this, but you are allowing Him to help you judge yourself. Do what I did. Pray, and then be still and listen. Give God time to respond and either confirm what He said, or correct you if you made a mistake.

Prayer is so much more than just talking to God. While this is an important part of it, prayer is also listening carefully to hear the voice of God. Give the Lord your time when you pray, and do not be given to a quick, "Oh, well!" if you don't hear Him speak right away. Sometimes God answers immediately, but at other times He may wait. Don't give up, but be still and know that He is God.

When judging yourself, prayer should be a time of intense listening. Ask, and then listen. Speak, and then be still. Knock, but wait until the door is opened before you move on to the next issue on your list. If you only talk and never listen when you pray, you will only have half a prayer life. You will say everything you want to say, but God will have much more to say than you will ever know.

Let the God who spoke the universe into being have time enough each day to say what you need to hear about every situation. You will be astounded how much you've been missing!

JUDGE WHAT YOU HEAR BY FASTING

There is a revelation of God which can only be found in the stillness of man. Often, this stillness is only reached through times of fasting—which provides another way to judge what you hear from God. When you take what you hear to prayer and fasting, you separate yourself for a time so the many voices of the world are cut off and the only voice remaining is God's.

In Exodus 19:3 we read: *"And Moses went up unto God, and the Lord called unto him out of the mountain, saying, Thus shalt thou say to the house of Jacob, and tell the children of Israel."*

Moses pulled himself away from the people and all the noise in the camp, and he went up to the mountain to meet with God alone. He removed himself from the distractions and hindrances which were evident all around him, and he set himself to hear from the Lord. Because he did, God's voice became crystal clear to him, and Moses received a divine message for Israel.

We see a similar outcome in Acts 13:1-3: *"Now there were in the church that was at Antioch certain prophets and teachers; as Barnabas, and Simeon that was called Niger, and Lucius of Cyrene, and Manaen, which had been brought up with Herod the tetrarch, and Saul. As they ministered to the Lord, and fasted, the Holy Ghost said, Separate me Barnabas and Saul for the work whereunto I have called them. And when they had fasted and prayed, and laid their hands on them, they sent them away."*

These men separated themselves for a time of prayer and fasting so they could judge a word from the Lord. The Holy Ghost said he had already called

Paul and Barnabas, but this fast brought forth a confirmation and a specific time for them to begin their ministry. God spoke clearly and made one of the most crucial declarations for the New Testament church.

You can hear your own personal instruction confirmed if you will be diligent to seek your own answer through prayer and fasting, as these men did (see Isaiah 58:8; 1 Corinthians 14:13).

Most of us are so connected to the world by the daily cares of life, we need to disconnect for a day or two and decompress before God can be heard. The influences of television, newspapers and the Internet alone can clog our brains with information until the Word of God is choked out, and we are left on the outside looking in when God wants to speak.

Even good input needs to be shut down for a season now and then. I know some Christians who have not had a truly quiet moment since they discovered Christian radio and CDs. Thank God for Christian music, but how about shutting down all the noise for one day and allowing your mind to settle down so that you can hear God clearly? How about removing the influence of the world that clouds your judgment so you can discern the voice of the Lord? How about being still for just one day so that you can know He is God? (See Psalm 46:10).

One of my favorite fasts is when I set myself apart for 24 hours, and I fast five things. I fast food, talking, hearing, reading and pleasure. When I do this, I fast all food, and I don't drink anything but water. I fast all talking, even to my wife. During this particular fast I don't even pray. I just shut my mouth altogether for 24 hours.

I don't listen to anything but the Word. I don't read anything but the Word, and I don't allow any earthly pleasure at all. When I do all this, I sanctify my members to hear from the Lord, and I allow myself time to hear from God and to verify what I have heard before.

Fasting should have a prominent place in your life, a place of priority which allows God an entrance to speak to you and impart His wisdom, revelation and blessing. Fasting may not be your favorite thing, but if you will set yourself to do it, I guarantee you will enjoy the benefits afterward.

God often told the children of Israel to call a fast and sanctify themselves, to put away the unclean things of the world and prepare themselves, because He wanted to speak to them. He knew they would not be able to hear unless they prepared themselves to hear.

This is what a time of fasting is; it's a time of preparation, a time to set your heart to hear from God without distraction. Whether you are trying to hear God for the first time on a matter, or trying to judge what you think you heard, a time of prayer and fasting will be a key component to your success.

Now, a word of warning about fasting: You will be more open to hearing the voice of God, but you will also be open to hearing the voice of the enemy, so be careful. Be discerning, and most of all, be sure to include the next step before you do anything with what you hear.

JUDGE WHAT YOU HEAR BY COUNSEL

Proverbs 11:14 tells us: *"Where no counsel is, the people fall: but in the multitude of counsellors there is safety."*

And in Ecclesiastes 4:9-12 we read: *"Two are better than one; because they have a good reward for their labour. For if they fall, the one will lift up his fellow: but woe to him that is alone when he falleth; for he hath not another to help him up. Again, if two lie together, then they have heat: but how can one be warm alone? And if one prevail against him, two shall withstand him; and a threefold cord is not quickly broken."*

The devil loves people who try to live as islands unto themselves. No one can go through life alone, but we all need others to help us, lead us, teach us and watch over us. The truth of the matter is, only immature children hate to be guided. Only immature children rebel when they are told what to do.

"Johnny, go to the bathroom before we leave on this trip," says a well-meaning mother. What does Johnny do? He ignores her and keeps on playing until the last minute. When it's time to hit the road Johnny runs for the car, and not two minutes later he yells out this revelation, "I have to go potty!"

Johnny's mama told him what to do to make his trip a happy experience, but Johnny wanted to do things his way. Now Johnny's uncomfortable and unhappy because papa isn't going to pull over until he's been on the road for at least 30 minutes. We all know how that works!

Christians should not be Johnnies. We should have enough sense to listen when our pastor or other spiritual leader tells us what to do in a certain situation. We should not be as little children, hearing only what we want to hear because we think we have a better plan.

The Bible says: *"The way of a fool is right in his own eyes: but he that hearkeneth unto counsel is wise"* (Proverbs 12:15). A fool thinks he doesn't need anyone to help him. He thinks he's got it all under control himself. The trouble is, the devil loves fools!

We should never launch out with a word from the Lord without comparing it to the written Word first. After we do this, we should spend time praying and fasting, and then we should ask those who lead us spiritually to judge and see if what we heard was really from God. It is much wiser to slow down a little bit and make sure you heard from Heaven than to have to clean up a mess if you get in a hurry and miss it.

Counsel will help you judge and weigh things out before you do them. Don't ever be afraid to allow yourself to be placed under the light of the Word and the judgment of counsel. If what you have is from God, it will withstand the scrutiny, but if not, you are far better off knowing before you do anything about it.

I've been rebuked by some great men of God. I count it an honor that they took time out of their busy schedules to chasten me, because it did me good. I need these men, and I love them. They have been set in my life for a purpose, and I know that if what I say stands their scrutiny, it's probably the Lord. They know more than I do, so I submit to their counsel and do what they tell me.

Submission to counsel after you believe you hear from God is never easy, but it will keep you from making mistakes, and it will help you grow in your own personal discernment. Once you've been rebuked a few times in an area, you will begin to get the picture that maybe the way you have tried is not the best way to get something done.

Wise counsel is invaluable. It is more precious than any treasure, because it is freely given by men and women who love you and watch for your soul. Your spiritual leaders have worked long and hard to get to where they are, so for them to freely give you advice which will save you years of heartache is quite a gift. Appreciate it; cherish it; love it; but never fear it.

Speaking the truth in love is one of the most wonderful things someone could ever do for you. If they tell you you've heard from God, shout the victory and go on, but if they tell you you've missed it, get back up and go again. Mistakes are simply a part of the process.

You must go through the learning experience to reach your purpose in life. Shortcuts shortchange, so I do not recommend you travel that road. Stay the course, and you will learn, grow and become more confident in your ability to hear God speak.

JUDGE WHAT YOU HEAR BY THE PASSAGE OF TIME

One final thing you need to do when proving whether something is from God or not is to allow the passage of time to bring its own judgment. For most, this is the hardest one of all. Galatians 1:15 says: *"But when it pleased God, who separated me from my mother's womb, and called me by his grace."* This speaks of a time that pleased God, not when it pleased man.

Time is a very valuable commodity. It cannot be re-lived, so we want to get it right from the beginning. Often, time passed translates into seasons endured.

We all know you cannot tell if a fruit tree is healthy in the winter; you have to wait until summertime to see what you really have. It's the same in the spiritual world. You have to wait sometimes to see if what you think you heard God say bears any fruit. If it does, you know you're on the right track, but if not, it's time to re-evaluate.

Imagine a man in a big hurry, buying plants at a road-side stand. He grabs the first thing that looks like a tomato plant, but he doesn't take the time to read the marker to check what he's buying. He runs home, plunks his purchase in the ground and goes away rejoicing. How sad when harvest time comes and he realizes he planted stinkweed instead of tomato plants! That man will look pretty silly to his neighbors.

This is what the hasty Christian looks like when he thinks he's heard from God and launches out into some new venture without any judgment. He'll look rather foolish when the passage of time proves he did not hear from God at all.

Like the unprepared gardener, he would have been better off to wait until fruit began to appear before he proudly proclaimed what his coming harvest was going to be. Better to have a few fruit-bearing plants in your spiritual garden than to have a lot of nothing-bearing plants. You can't make stinkweed bear tomatoes no matter how much you prophesy!

If I wanted a particular harvest from my garden, I would be willing to wait for it. Likewise, if I want a specific harvest from my spiritual plantings, I will be willing to wait on the Lord and let the process of time unveil a fruit which was hidden from me.

Remember, the Kingdom of God is as if a man would plant a seed in the ground (see Mark 4:26). The whole Kingdom of God is a connection of time periods and processes going on behind the scenes. It's all about seasons passing before harvest comes. If you violate the process, you will abort your harvest, but if you live within the principles of the process, you will reap great victory.

When you study Galatians 1:15 further, you discover Paul waited three years after his call before he went up to Jerusalem to meet with church leaders, and it was another 15 years or so before he truly took his place in the Kingdom. Paul allowed season upon season to pass before he walked in the fullness of what he had discovered on the road to Damascus. He allowed himself and his teaching to be proved by the Word, by much personal prayer and fasting, by the spiritual leaders of his day and by the passage of time.

To allow time to pass is necessary for you, too. God is unchangeable, and what He says is already established in Heaven, so His words cannot be altered. If He calls you one day, and a month of waiting follows, or even a year, or many years, the passage of time will not unravel your call.

If you're called to be something in the Kingdom, only time will truly tell. There's no need to hurry. Just wait and allow God's voice to be confirmed in the fruit of your life. Allow His will and call for you to be judged by the passage of time. God expects you to judge the call, so there is no rush.

Time is your friend. It gives the opportunity to judge, examine, scrutinize, look closely at, put under the lamp and put to the test what you believe you heard. When you act hastily and remove the element of time you are actually putting judgment away, and that's not good. Most hurried acts are prompted by one of two things, the flesh or the devil—and neither is desirable.

Unspiritual people circumvent God's way and ignore judgment when they hurry, and they override the blessing of the passage of time. Spiritual people wait until the time of the harvest is at hand, and then they wait until God gives them the release to move forward. While they wait, they keep the call in their hearts. They nurture it, pray and fast over it, and they accept counsel for it. They study to show themselves approved in it. Then they wait some more until God's speaks to them a second time and sends them out.

This Bible pattern is repeated over and over again. Abraham waited until he was 100 years old before he reached the destiny God had spoken over him. Joseph waited thirteen years to reign as he had been told he would in a dream.

Moses waited forty years on the back side of the desert, then another forty in the wilderness before he saw the Promised Land. Paul waited until the end of his life before he could say with confidence that he had completed the course and won the race. Waiting is a life long process. I encourage you to embrace it and allow it to complete you and bring you to victory, too.

You can judge God's voice by His Word, by prayer, by fasting, by counsel and by the passage of time. When you do, God will be pleased with you for being obedient to His command to judge all things. His voice will always be a breath of fresh air, and you will be drawn by His Spirit to continue to ask, seek and knock to find hidden treasure.

CHAPTER 24

THE LEARNING CURVE

Samuel lay quietly, listening for a response, but none came. He was a very young boy, and as he lay, hearing his heart pound in his chest, he wondered who had spoken to him in the dark of the night. Afraid he was needed for something important, Samuel ran to the priest Eli and said, "Here I am. You called me?" Eli was a little miffed at being awakened from a deep sleep, and he answered sternly, "I did not call you. Go lie down." Puzzled, Samuel went back to his chamber and crawled into bed.

The voice was louder the second time, saying, "Samuel!" He jumped to his feet and ran to the priest's bedside again, saying "Here I am!" Once more, Eli sent him back to bed, assuring him he was not needed at this ridiculous hour. Dejected and confused, Samuel went back to bed and crawled under the covers one more time.

A third time, the voice called out, "Samuel!" Once more he obediently jumped to his feet and ran to Eli saying, "Here I am. You surely called me." By now Eli was fully awake, and it dawned on him what was happening. He told Samuel, "Go lie down, and if the voice calls for you again, say, 'Speak, Lord; for your servant hears.'"

Excited and nervous, Samuel crept back into his bed chamber, and he slid under the covers as quietly as he could, trying not to disturb anyone. Very soon, the Lord came and stood by his side. One last time He said, "Samuel. Samuel!" Full of wonder Samuel replied, "Speak, Lord; for your servant hears."

God did speak, saying, "Behold, I will do a thing in Israel, at which both the ears of every one who hears shall tingle. In that day I will perform against Eli all of the things I have spoken concerning his house. When I begin, I will also make an end. For I have told him I will judge his house forever for the iniquity which he knows; because his sons made themselves vile, and he restrained them not. And therefore I have sworn to the house of Eli, that the iniquity of his house shall not be purged with sacrifice nor offering forever."

That was it. Samuel's first prophetic word of the Lord had come, and now it was over. Poor Samuel lay awake until the morning, pondering what he had to do. As the day dawned he opened the doors of the house of the Lord, as was his duty every day, but Samuel was afraid to tell Eli what he had heard.

Eli immediately called Samuel to his side and asked him, "Samuel, my son, what did the Lord say to you? Please do not hide it from me." Samuel hesitated, but Eli was so vexed by what he feared God had said, he swore a curse upon Samuel if he did not tell. Samuel chose wisely and told Eli everything, holding back nothing, letting him have the unvarnished truth. Eli quickly saw that his sin was exposed, and he said, "It is the Lord. Let Him do what seems good to Him." Not many days later, Eli and his sons were dead (see 1 Samuel 3:1-18).

This story is near and dear to my heart, because it is the very story God used to lead me to my own conversation with Him, the first of many. Imagine how apprehensive this young boy must have been. Having left his family to enter the ministry as a toddler, he had lived with Eli the priest and knew no other life. Even with his unique upbringing, living and working for the Lord, Samuel had never heard of God speaking to anyone face to face, because the word of the Lord was very rare and precious at that time.

Do you think young Samuel had any reservations about his ability to hear the voice of God? Do you suppose he trembled at the words the Lord had spoken, words that were the voice of doom for his spiritual authority? I think he had plenty to be afraid of, and I believe he feared greatly as he stood before a towering Eli and told him his days on earth were numbered.

I suppose we can all relate to Samuel in one way or another. In fact, I've heard this question hundreds of times: "What if I miss it, Pastor?" Every time this question has been raised, it has been by a sincere Christian, by someone who truly loves God and desires to hear His voice, but who is also afraid of making a mistake.

My response is always the same: "Don't be afraid to try." This was my answer when my daughter first learned to ride a bike. She didn't want to fall off, ever, but I had to explain that if she never tried, she would never learn. Fear is the enemy when you desire to hear the voice of God. It will stop you from trying. It will keep you on the sidewalk watching everyone else enjoy themselves while you are worried about skinned knees.

As you begin to enter into spiritual things, growing and stepping out by faith into new areas of the supernatural, you will make mistakes because life is not error-free. Often, we learn by the process of elimination rather than by hitting the mark on the first try. That's okay, because mistakes are just a part of learning. You may think you heard the voice of God, then later discover you were mistaken, but don't give up. This is part of the process of learning and growing in the things of God.

Do you remember your school days and how often you found red marks on your homework papers? Red marks were not any fun, but they did tell you what would not work. They told you what mistakes to avoid the next time around. Sometimes, we have to learn things by discovering what does not work, so that when we do hit the mark there will be no question we finally got it right.

Reproof and instruction are necessary parts of the learning process. You will never grow unless you allow others who are more experienced and more educated than you to instruct and correct you. Mrs. Jones might have ruffled your feathers when she marked red lines through your answers in third grade, but she helped you to perform better in fourth grade, because she took the time to correct your thinking. In reality, she did this because she cared about you. She could have let you go through life believing 2 x 2 = 5, but you would have been a sorry case in line at the grocery store twenty years later arguing about the amount of change you were due. Mrs. Jones saved you that embarrassment by correcting you as a child.

God does the same for us. He has given us pastors and other spiritual leaders to correct us when we have the wrong answers on our spiritual papers. If the Lord let us continue on with wrong spiritual information, it would be a sign He did not love us. We know this is not true, so we also know that when a spiritual authority points out a mistake, we ought to take it in stride, just as we did in third grade, and learn from our mistakes.

Personally, I have probably failed five times more than I have succeeded, but in my failures I have discovered how to do certain things, and how not to do others. I have learned how to recognize God's voice, His hand, His leading, and His abiding presence, but it has not come without the cost of frequent mistakes and errors.

When you miss the mark, you need to keep moving ahead and refuse to dwell on your shortcomings. You will never be alone in your failure, because we have *all* failed at one time or another. It's a part of life we may not like, but we need to endure until our perfected selves see Jesus face to face.

THE PROVING PROCESS

When I first began to seek to hear the voice of God, I was just like you. I was afraid of making a mistake. I wanted to hear perfectly every time, but it didn't happen. I would launch out in faith, stay in tune for awhile, and then I would miss it somehow and feel like a failure. Over the years, I discovered a secret that kept me going. Proverbs 24:16 says: *"For a just man falleth seven times, and riseth up again..."* No matter how often I failed, I had to get up and try again.

I also learned my mistakes would never be bigger than my opportunities to go beyond them. I may be rebuked twenty times trying to go in a certain direction, but the bottom line is, I'm going to get there. I've decided I'll take the rebuke like a man and get over all the hurt, because I am determined to pursue and be all God wants me to be.

I have resolved in my spirit that there is enough love in me by the Holy Ghost and His empowerment in me to overcome the setbacks and take me where I need to go. Faith will always resurrect me, because faith works by love. Faith will help me forgive others and continue on in God's predetermined purpose for me. Reproofs are a way of life, so I will not let them deter me.

Behind who I am today lie at least a thousand failures. That's okay, because now I am more sure about hearing God than I was so long ago when I was first saved. Having been through the process of time I am more confident about God's direction, His dealings with me, and how He prepares and sets me in certain places. I am more aware of His seasonal dealings with me, and I am more confident about what God is doing in my life by experience and by proving His voice.

The process of proving is not a quick one. You have to begin at the beginning because there are no shortcuts in the Kingdom. Hebrews 5:8 says: *"Though he were a Son, yet learned he obedience by the things which he suffered."* Even Jesus, the Son of God, had to learn certain things by experience. Hearing the voice of God is one of those things.

Knowledge is good, but until knowledge becomes experience, it will bear no fruit. You may have to swallow your pride more than once when you tell your story to your pastor or another mature believer and hear them say, "Well, I'm not so sure that was God." That's okay. It's not time to panic and give up, but it is time to listen and learn.

The apostle Paul told Timothy to entrust the leaders of his church with responsibility only after they had been instructed, admonished and rebuked. We all have to be willing to go through the stages of learning and correction if we want to receive the rewards of the Kingdom.

You'll quickly discover what you're made of the first time you face correction for missing it. Don't be downtrodden about the matter, but pick yourself up, thank the person who corrected you, and go on to hear the voice of God again. The mark of a mature believer is clearly evident when he or she can accept correction and move on to learn from it without offense.

God is never disappointed when we misinterpret or misunderstand the process. He knows we are learning a new language and a new set of interpreting skills. He is pleased we are launching out into new territory, seeking to hear His voice for the benefit of others. He realizes we will have to go through a season of learning and correction before we can be trusted to hear, interpret and deliver His message, and so He is patient with us, ever moving to help us learn and grow.

DELIGHT IN THE PROCESS

We read Psalm 37:4 in an earlier chapter, but I want to return there once again. It says: *"Delight thyself also in the Lord; and he shall give thee the desires of thine heart."*

God gives us desires, and He expects us to judge those desires as we do everything else in the Kingdom. We always want to check carefully before we take any action. As the carpenter says, "Measure twice and cut once." Seek your confirmation in the Word, but also seek it in wise counsel, in prayer and fasting and by judging the fruit of your actions and motives. Take your time and be honest with yourself.

Here's why. Sometimes we need the benefits born out of the seeking process to strengthen us when we go and do. We need the benefit of the long fast, the benefit of extended times in the Word, and the benefit of times of face-to-face worship to sustain us when we hit the road to destiny.

As an example, suppose you wanted your ten year old son to become a successful baseball player because this was his greatest dream in life. Wouldn't you do everything in your power to help him prepare before his first big game? Sure you would.

You'd buy him the best ball glove you could afford. You'd play catch every night after supper. You'd toss him fly balls and teach him how to get down with two hands to stop the bouncing infield hits. You would take him to practice early and stay late to talk to the coach, and you'd take him for long walks to build up his stamina.

Why would you invest so much time and energy to do all of this? You would do it so your son would be trained and ready for that very first pitch in his first real game. God is no less concerned with your success than you are with your son's.

God wants to make sure you are trained, strengthened and equipped for your destiny, so He will give you opportunities for strength training, opportunities which include seeking God, fasting and prayer, worship, time in the Word and wise counsel. Don't ever despise the process, but instead, rejoice in it as you delight in the Lord. The proving process is simply a time where you focus on spiritual strength-building activities which will prepare you for the hardships that lie ahead.

God is a very good Father. He knows just what it will take for you to grow into your gifts and calling. He knows how to extract the very best from you, and He is willing to invest a lifetime to help you reach your goals in Him.

Let the process bring you to the Father's desired outcome. Let it build you up on your most holy faith. Let the times of closeness with your heavenly Father linger on so when you begin to move in your destiny, His leading voice will still be echoing in your mind. Be prepared to invest as much time as it takes to delight in the process so God's plans and purposes can be brought to pass in your life.

GOD SPEAKS IN SEASONS

I want to switch gears for just a moment and talk about changing seasons. Many of us are creatures of habit, and we like things to stay the same. God, however, may choose to deal with you in different ways at different times just to keep you seeking for Him, instead of seeking for an experience. Familiarity can sometimes weaken faith or make it half-hearted.

God may speak to you in a certain way for a certain season, and then one day, He will change and speak to you another way. He does this to help you avoid the trap of familiarity. The reason is because if you always hear from God in only one way, it would be very easy for you to begin to allow your own thoughts to mimic the voice of God without even knowing it. The old saying "familiarity breeds contempt" is very true. What you know from repeated use you tend to take for granted, and this is never good when it comes to the things of the Spirit.

God is so kind to us in this matter. Instead of risking our failure, He will dry up one well of contact and send us seeking for another one. Elijah the prophet learned this very lesson one day while he waited in the wilderness for the voice of the Lord.

Elijah had prophesied to King Ahab that a drought was coming upon the land. He told him three years would pass without a single drop of rain. After Elijah spoke to Ahab, God told him to go hide himself beside a brook by the name of Cherith. It was a tributary for the Jordan river, and God had arranged for Elijah to live there safely while the drought brought unrest to the land.

God told Elijah, "And it shall be, that you shall drink of the brook; and I have commanded the ravens to feed you there." Elijah thought this sounded like a pretty good deal, so off he went for a little rest and relaxation. Every morning, the ravens brought him bread and meat to eat, and they returned with another portion every evening. Even though no rain fell anywhere, the brook kept flowing, and Elijah had plenty of water to drink.

It was all going well, until one day Elijah went down to the edge of the brook for a cup of water, and he suddenly realized it had dried up. The drought was finally upon him, and Elijah did not know what to do. Pondering his situation, Elijah sought the voice of the Lord. After awhile he heard God say, "Arise and go to Zarephath in Zidon, and dwell there. Behold, I have commanded a widow woman there to sustain you."

Elijah got up from his comfortable place and traveled down to Zarephath. Of course you know the rest of the story. Elijah met the widow woman, and because she believed the word of the prophet more than she believed her circumstance, she, her son and the prophet were sustained supernaturally throughout the remainder of the drought. God sent a miracle multiplication to her barrel of meal and her pot of oil, and they were sustained for many days, for just as long as it was necessary until the rains fell once again (see 1 Kings 17:1-16).

Elijah learned an important lesson here. When God sends us one place, and then that place begins to lose its sustaining power, it's not the time to give up, but rather the time to seek the Lord for a word which will move us to a new place. What if the brook had kept flowing for Elijah, and the birds had kept coming with room service every day; would Elijah have sought God for an answer? No, he would not have sought unless he first had a question.

God sent Elijah to the brook, but when the Lord needed him to go to Zarephath to save the widow woman and her son, God let the brook dry up so the prophet would be compelled to seek Him again. Thankfully, Elijah didn't just curl up in a ball and die; he knew enough to wait for the voice of the Lord to show him what to do next.

We have to be careful in these times of changing seasons, because sometimes when we get hungry and thirsty for certain things, and we begin to feel the discomfort of that hunger and thirst, we may decide to circumvent the process in order to get to the prize. This is not God's way. Everything in the Kingdom of God operates off of the seed principle. We plant, we water, we watch over—and then we wait.

Hang in there! The promise of Jesus is about to come to pass: *"Blessed are they which do hunger and thirst after righteousness: for they shall be filled"* (Matthew 5:6). Don't let outward circumstances drive you away from God, but be sharp enough to realize that sometimes God will use those circumstances to draw you to Him so He can lead you to the next step in your lifelong journey.

It's the same with hearing the voice of God. If you are too familiar with one way of hearing God speak, He may have to "dry it up" so He can move you in a new direction. Let's say you have heard from God through prophecy on many occasions. You like it this way, but God sees you are becoming more dependent on the prophetic than you are on Him. What do you suppose He will do?

The next time God needs to tell you something, He will probably choose another method so you will have to return to your dependency on Him. He will do this to help, not hurt you. God is always trying to help you grow and mature, but sometimes His assistance may not please you. At first, you may wonder what you did wrong. You may think you have lost your ability to hear God's voice, but hopefully you'll soon get the picture that God is about to do something new, and you'll begin to dig new trenches where He can flow forth in a new way.

Psalm 29:3 says: *"The voice of the Lord is upon the waters: the God of glory thundereth: the Lord is upon many waters."* The more trenches and wells you have dug in your life, the more places God will be able to fill with His thundering, yet flowing word of revelation when you need it.

Don't be surprised if God keeps you on your toes over the course of your life as He speaks to you in different ways at different times. He does not want you to become complacent or lazy about hearing His voice, but He wants His voice to be as fresh manna every day; always the same because it is based on His Word, but always different because He makes it new for you through revelation.

Be alert, and when dryness comes to one area, begin to seek God for the flow in another area. There is always a brook flowing somewhere in the Spirit. It's up to you to be still and listen until God speaks and tells you where it is to be found.

GO ONLY WHERE SENT

Let me give you a principle which must be adhered to for success. We find it in Deuteronomy 4:2: *"Ye shall not add unto the word which I command you, neither shall ye diminish ought from it, that ye may keep the commandments of the Lord your God which I command you."*

When you hear from God, you should be resolved to progress no further than you were instructed to go, but you should also strive to go no less. When you arrive there, it is equally important to wait until He speaks again. We have a perfect example in Acts chapter eight where Philip was in the city of Samaria, and great things were happening there. In the midst of Philip's success, the Holy Ghost sent him out into the wilderness. We mentioned this story before, but this time I want to concentrate on Philip's response to God's voice.

At God's call, Philip left his comfort zone in Samaria and headed for the unknown in the desert. He went out in obedience, but at first there appeared to be nothing there for him to do. Philip had to wait for the Ethiopian eunuch to come by before he was given his next move.

Most Christians would not do what Philip did. First, they would not want to leave their place of comfort and success, the Samaria of their lives. Then, if they did give in and go out in the desert, they would expect some great crowd to follow them. If that did not happen, they would likely turn around and high tail it back into town where they perceived success to be. Thank God Philip waited until the eunuch came by, because he was able to plant a seed in this seeking man's heart which brought a harvest for the Kingdom of God.

Think of that. God moved Philip away from the crowds for one man in the desert. But also realize if Philip had not obeyed, he would have missed one of the greatest miracles of his life because, remember, when all was said and done, God translated Philip to another city to preach. Philip would have missed the best ride of his life had he not obeyed (see Acts 8:5-40).

Obedience in the Kingdom puts God in motion. It brings a constant revelation of what living in the Spirit is all about. There is the voice of God coming to pass, and there is the process of you going as far as you can go, doing what you can do, then waiting by faith and trusting in God until He does what only He can do.

We've read Isaiah 28:10 numerous times in this book, where we learned how God speaks in fragments, here a little and there a little. When we encounter the voice of God in bits and pieces, we need to do what He tells us, and then stand, trust and wait for Him to speak again and add to what He has already given us.

Sometimes, God will tell me nothing more than, "Be quiet." I know when He tells me this, I better shut up and wait because when I do, God will tell me what to say next. If I get ahead of Him, I will miss it and say the wrong thing. I do not want to ever mislead someone by my mistake, but even then, God will not leave me to my own devices. If I do make a mistake along the way, I may need to apologize, but I do not need to give up. As long as we learn from our errors, the Lord will allow us to continue to grow.

If we will obey God and go and do as He directs, we can be sure He will speak again and again, and the flow of His Spirit in our lives will grow into a mighty river that waters the world around us.

DRAWN BY GOD

I want to touch on some things God may use to help you while you are learning to hear His voice. One of those is an inner drawing, a pulling and a leading that gets you to the right place at the right time.

Acts 17:16 is a great example. It says: *"Now while Paul waited for them at Athens, his spirit was stirred in him, when he saw the city wholly given to idolatry."* Paul was stirred up by the Spirit of God, and this stirring invoked him to preach in that city. God can stir you in the same way so you will be in position to fulfill His call and do what He has called you to do.

You may wake up one morning and have a strong desire to go and see a particular person. You could ignore this feeling and go on about your daily routine, or you could stop, pray and ask God what He wants you to do. It could be God needs you to go and minister to that person. Or it could be He has a specific message to send to them. Don't jump the gun and go over half empty. Stop and ask God for direction, and then proceed, doing as He says.

There will also be times when God will speak to you through an inward knowing, a supernatural ability to understand what to do and when to do it, where to go, or what is happening around you. In these cases, God gives you light.

In Proverbs 20:27 we read: *"The spirit of man is the candle of the Lord, searching all the inward parts of the belly."* God lights our candle with His voice. This light is not seen by the human eye, nor heard by the human ear. It is not comprehended by the human mind, but it is a supernatural illuminating, an observation, an ability to see, to hear and to know what God wants you to do in a certain situation. It's not so much about hearing words, but about hearing the heart of God.

You are connected to your heavenly Father in a very unique way. He is a Spirit, and you are a born again spirit. There is a spiritual umbilical cord, if you will, which connects you to God in your innermost being. Sometimes, the Lord will pull on that cord, or nudge you with a slight tap in the spirit. This gentle touch will get your attention focused in the right direction, and it will lead you to move where God needs you to go.

It's the same thing parents do when they lead their children through heavy pedestrian traffic. Have you ever taken your family to an amusement park, or a street fair, or even the local mall? Where did you keep your hand? Likely on the shoulder of the child walking right in front of you. Your child could not see you, and she had no idea where you intended for her to go, but all you had to do was put a little pressure on her shoulder, and you could guide her safely to your destination.

There may be times when you may feel an unusual urge to go somewhere or do something. You won't be able to put your finger on why, but you will

405

go anyway, and when you get there you will discover God had a plan and a destiny for you that you did not hear with your ear, but you felt as you experienced His guiding nudge in the spirit. This is what happens many times when you are being led by the Spirit of God.

Paul tells us: *"For as many as are led by the Spirit of God, they are the sons of God"* (Romans 8:14). The Father's desire to lead and teach you will permeate everything He uses to reach you while you are learning to hear. God will not leave you without His voice while you are growing in the process, but He will use whatever He can to help you hear and to lead you to your destiny in Him.

HIDDEN PROVISION

Were you aware that God knows where every hidden thing in the world is located? I wasn't, until He moved me with His gentle urging to a place where a miracle lay in wait.

It was a wonderful day when I made my discovery. I was a young Christian, only saved for a short time, and I had a need. It was a big mountain in my eyes, but not so much in God's eyes. Phyllis and I were broke; flat broke— spelled with capital letters and bold print. Try as we might, we had no means of raising the cash we needed to get us out of the problem we were facing.

My wife and I were tithers and givers, even at this young age in Christ, and so we had our faith extended toward God; we just had no clue what He planned to do about our situation. At this time we were not mature enough to understand that believing God is more than a growth process within a situation; it is a spiritual process that continues for a lifetime.

John wrote something in his third letter we can all hold onto in times of trouble. Inspired of the Holy Ghost he said: *"Beloved, I wish above all things that thou mayest prosper and be in health, even as thy soul prospereth"* (3 John 2).

Our souls were just beginning to prosper. We were developing, being changed, transformed and built up in the faith by our discovery of the things God desired for us to have as joint heirs in Christ Jesus. What we did not fully understand is that there are sometimes struggles on the journey to victory. There are battles until we reach the place where we are confident God will provide, and where our faith can give Him access to provide.

So, here we were, on the way to being fully matured and dependent on the Lord, and yet we were still fully broke. Thankfully, this did not deter God. As I was driving to a nearby lake on this appointed day, I was praying and discussing the situation with my heavenly Father. I said, "God, here I am a believer. I am the head of my household, the father of a young child, and I have a wife to care for, and yet I cannot even meet the simple needs of my family today."

I wasn't asking for diamonds and Rolexes, all I wanted was to be able to buy a loaf of bread for dinner and surprise my wife with a bottle of pop, which she was craving so much. As little as I needed, I could not supply it by myself. For me, all I wanted was an ice cream cone. With that, the world would have been at peace in my mind.

So I continued my discussion with God, wondering all the while how this was going to end. I reminded Him that I truly believed in Him, and that I loved Him with all of my heart. I told God I was willing to stand in faith, but I also had many questions in my young Christian mind. I ended by saying I knew that some way, somehow, He would work things out. I was a simple man with simple needs, so I asked for help with the simple faith of a little child.

When I finished my business on the far side of the lake, I got back in the car and started home. It was a crisp fall afternoon as I began to drive back around the lake, and I noticed the state park was already closed for the season. As I looked at the "Closed" sign hanging on a wire at the roadside rest area I was passing, I felt a sudden urge to stop my car and pull alongside. I knew it was a leading of the Lord, and so I stopped right beside the wire that was across the drive to keep people like me out of the parking lot.

As I sat there, I reminded God that the park was closed and I really should not be there. Still, the feeling I needed to be there for some reason persisted, and so I got out of the car and walked into the park. This state park was very primitive, and I headed for a restroom which did not even have an exterior door. As I exited the building I felt the wind pick up, and the cold air began to cut through me. I was not dressed for a fall hike, and I was not sure where I was going anyway, so I hoped this adventure would be over soon.

I decided to head back to the car to get out of the cold, and then I felt the urge to look down at the ground. What do you think I saw? I saw a one dollar bill just lying there on the sidewalk, held there by nothing as the wind whipped across the path. I snapped it up like a frog on a fly. And then I saw another one, and another one. It seemed like every step I took was laced with dollar bills.

I am not exaggerating. Every 30 to 36 inches, there was a dollar bill lining the sidewalk, all the way back to my car door. It was as if someone had followed me and dropped dollars like popcorn to show me the way back home. I quickly looked up, half expecting to see someone standing there and laughing for the practical joke they were playing on me, but no one was there.

I figured that if I did not pick up all of the bills the wind would take them away, and since I saw no need for such waste, I began to scoop them up, one by one. As I gathered them up, my heart swelled, realizing that God had somehow, some way provided those dollar bills just for me.

I gathered my treasure, and then I hesitated for a moment, wondering if I had missed them on my way into the building. I quickly reminded myself that I was born blonde, but I was not so blonde that I could miss dollar bills lining a wide open path with nothing to block my view! There was nothing on the sidewalk when I went into the restroom building, but there were perfect dollar bills all lined in a row when I came out.

I could not explain it, but I could rejoice. I could rejoice for a tri-fold miracle. Number one, as hard as the wind was blowing, it was a miracle the bills had not blown away. Second, it was a miracle they landed on a flat sidewalk with nothing to hold them down. And third, it was a miracle of God's divine provision.

I jumped back in the car and drove straight to the grocery store with a fist full of dollar bills. I didn't even straighten them out; I just stuffed them in my pocket and headed to the bread aisle. I bought two loaves of Wonder Bread, and I picked up a bottle of pop for my wife. And then I did the most important thing of all; I stopped and bought myself a big ice cream cone. I celebrated all the way home for the wonderful way God had provided for me and my family.

The next day as I was driving to work, the Lord reminded me that He had been faithful to provide for our need. My response to God, which was not a very honorable one, was: "Well, it didn't take very much to make me happy." Thankfully, I have grown well past that negative, dishonoring response, and now I am so grateful for every blessing God sends my way. No matter how big or how small, they all are love letters to me and my family He sends just when we need them.

The point I want to make is that no matter how windy the conditions may seem in your life, and regardless of how many seasons have passed since the storm began; no matter how many times it seems your prayers have gone unanswered, know this: God knows where you are, and He is working diligently to lead you to the place where your hidden provision will be revealed. Always stay close to God, because He and His answer are always very close to you.

VESSELS OF CLAY

I want to conclude this book with one last, but very important point. Failure may happen when you first launch out to hear God's voice precisely because He has chosen to use you, a mere human vessel, to carry His message to the world around you. This is a pretty tall order, and it takes a lot of faith on God's part.

God is the potter, and we are the clay. Clay can be fragile sometimes, and hard as a rock at other times, depending on how it has been shaped, molded and fired. We can thank God that His hands are always upon us in some form or fashion, re-shaping, re-molding and smoothing us out for His use and glory. On the way to our destiny, there may be pitfalls and stumblings, but there will never be utter failure as long as we are in His hands.

When God speaks to you and through you, His message will always start out perfect, but by the time it has passed through your vessel of clay, it may come out as less than perfect because you handled it. Don't get upset, because this is God's chosen method, and He is fully aware you will have to be re-shaped, re-molded and re-fired again and again before His message will make it through you unscathed.

Even when you miss it and water down the message God gave you by making mistakes or misinterpreting what He said, you can be assured the Lord still loves you and wants to use you. He is not worried about the learning process. He has no stop watch, so don't give in to the temptation to try to hurry the process along for Him. God knows that with time and practice, you will come closer to hearing His voice and delivering His message the right way. Until then, He is pleased with your attempts to hear. He is fully aware of your weaknesses, and yet He chooses to use you anyway.

I had more chips and dings in my vessel when I was a young Christian than I care to remember. I rented places to preach, thinking for sure God had told me to, and then only one person showed up. Do you know how hard it is to preach a revival to one person?

I've had my share of mistaken ideas, because I was learning and growing in grace, but I really do not regret them. Through these times of learning, I discovered many things about myself and about God. I discovered that as long as we learn from our mistakes, and as long as we are striving to be what God needs us to be, we will continue to grow, and He will continue to use us.

I remember when I first received my call to ministry, for weeks and weeks I stayed in the house praying, "Oh God! Just tell me where to go!" I begged for a sign, but a sign never came. One day I heard God say, "I'd rather have you go out there and miss Me a thousand times by faith than sit in here whining and doing nothing. At least you might get somebody saved by accident if you'd get out of this prayer room!"

So, I got out of the room. I would go into my town and preach on street corners because no one would let me in their church, but at least I was doing something. It was then and there I realized that the Christian life is 90 percent activity and 10 percent prayer. It is more about doing than preparing. It is more about moving in faith than standing still in fear.

Fear causes us to become idle, useless vessels, going nowhere and doing nothing for Jesus. We can't let fear dominate us and relegate us to the sidelines. We may be imperfect human vessels, but as long as we are perfectly joined to Jesus and totally willing, He will make up for our weaknesses and lend us His strength.

We must remember that because of our relationship with the Father, we have the power and right to hear and know His voice. Here's what Jesus said: *"To him the porter openeth; and the sheep hear his voice: and he calleth his own sheep by name, and leadeth them out. And when he putteth forth his own sheep, he goeth before them, and the sheep follow him: for they know his voice"* (John 10:3-4).

We have the right to hear God's voice, but we have to develop ourselves and grow into that right. Remember, the Bible is written to us as if we are children. When a child is born, the baby does not automatically recognize the voice of the one caring for him. He does not know his mother's voice or the touch of her hand until he has experienced them for awhile. Voice recognition is a process for infants, and it is a process for believers.

John 10:25-27 goes on to say: *"Jesus answered them, I told you, and ye believed not: the works that I do in my Father's name, they bear witness of me. But ye believe not, because ye are not of my sheep, as I said unto you. My sheep hear my voice, and I know them, and they follow me."*

There is a supernatural, inward mechanism inside you called the human spirit, and it is created in the image of Christ. It is the spirit of adoption whereby you cry, "Abba Father." This born again spirit enables you to know, distinguish and recognize God's voice, but again, it takes time to develop your recognition skills.

God's voice is what we call rhema, the spoken word which is breathed from God's mouth into your spirit. It is this rhema word we so desperately need to hear, recognize and follow. Without it we are mere mortals, but with the spoken word of God we are more than conquerors, above and not beneath, blessed in all ways and all places, children of God and heirs according to promise.

Learning to hear and recognize this voice will be a life-long process. Our listening skills will be refined over time, and we will become more and more acquainted with how God speaks, but we will never tire of hearing. We will never grow weary of learning and being led by that still, small voice which abides in our hearts; the voice of God that declares He loves us and desires to meet our every need.

We will grow and mature, but we will never outgrow God's tender care, or the gentle leading of His hand. We will become better acquainted with how He speaks, but we will never lose our sense of wonder. We will know as we are known, yet we will never cease to be amazed at His love. We are His dear children, and we will always crave His personal touch.

In Psalm 28:1 we read: *"Unto thee will I cry, O Lord my rock; be not silent to me: lest, if thou be silent to me, I become like them that go down into the pit."* Here David basically is saying, "God, if you do not speak to me, my end will be the end of those who do not know You." What a terrible end that would be! To live without the voice of God would be to merely exist and not really live at all.

God's voice is my strength, my hope and my motivation. His voice is my direction, my fortress, my sustaining power and my breath of life. I could not live without God's voice. I could not move forward or maintain my walk

411

without it. I could not live in a godly manner or fulfill my call without hearing His voice every day in some form or fashion.

We all need the voice of God in our lives, both His scriptural voice and how He speaks to us with wisdom, direction, counsel and insight. In the process, He infuses His abundant life into our vessels of clay.

The voice of God in your life will cause you to live very differently than the ungodly, the unrighteous, the faithless and the unbelieving. You are not of those who have no hope, but you are one who lives in fellowship with a God who loves you, provides for you, and wants to be in close communion with you every day of your life.

Having read this book and discovered the wonderful voice of God in so many ways, I challenge you to do three things: First, let the voice of God be heard in you. Then, let His voice be heard through you. Finally, let His voice resound in everything you say and do. Remember, in Him we live and move and have our being (see Acts 17:28).

I'll answer these burning questions once again: Is Heaven open for you? Of course it is! Is God speaking to you? Yes, He really is! Can you hear Him personally? Absolutely!

At this very moment He is saying, "Let's talk!"

NOTES

FOR A COMPLETE LIST OF MEDIA RESOURCES
OR TO CONTACT THE AUTHOR:

PETER DOESCK
ONLY BELIEVE MINISTRIES CHRISTIAN CENTER
13815 BOTKINS RD.
BOTKINS, OH 45306

PHONE: 937-693-3554
EMAIL: obmcc@obmcc.org
INTERNET: www.obmcc.org